HALSBURY'S
Laws of England

FOURTH EDITION
2009

Additional Materials:
Trade, Industry and Industrial Relations

Fifth Edition volumes:

1 (2008), 2 (2008), 7 (2008), 11 (2009), 12 (2009), 13 (2009), 18 (2009), 39 (2009), 40 (2009), 41 (2009), 48 (2008), 49 (2008), 50 (2008), 54 (2008), 65 (2008), 66 (2009), 67 (2008), 68 (2008), 69 (2009), 72 (2009), 73 (2009), 79 (2008), 93 (2008), 94 (2008), 100 (2009), 101 (2009)

Fourth Edition volumes (bold figures represent reissues):

1(1) (2001 Reissue), **1(2)** (2007 Reissue), **2(2)**, **2(3)**, **3(1)** (2005 Reissue), **3(2)** (2002 Reissue), **4(1)** (2002 Reissue), **4(2)** (2002 Reissue), **4(3)**, **5(1)** (2004 Reissue), **5(2)** (2001 Reissue), **5(3)** (2008 Reissue), **5(4)** (2008 Reissue), **7(1)** (2004 Reissue), **7(2)** (2004 Reissue), **7(3)** (2004 Reissue), **7(4)** (2004 Reissue), **8(1)** (2003 Reissue), **8(2)**, **8(3)**, **9(1)**, **9(2)** (2006 Reissue), **10**, **11(1)** (2006 Reissue), **11(2)** (2006 Reissue), **11(3)** (2006 Reissue), **11(4)** (2006 Reissue), **12(1)**, **12(2)** (2007 Reissue), **12(3)** (2007 Reissue), **13** (2007 Reissue), **14**, **15(1)** (2006 Reissue), **15(2)** (2006 Reissue), **15(3)** (2007 Reissue), **15(4)** (2007 Reissue), **16(2)**, **17(2)**, **18(2)**, **19(1)** (2007 Reissue), **19(2)** (2007 Reissue), **19(3)** (2007 Reissue), **20(1)**, **20(2)**, **21** (2004 Reissue), **22** (2006 Reissue), **23(1)**, **23(2)**, **24**, **25** (2003 Reissue), **26** (2004 Reissue), **27(1)** (2006 Reissue), **27(2)** (2006 Reissue), **27(3)** (2006 Reissue), **28**, **29(2)**, **30(1)**, **30(2)**, **31** (2003 Reissue), **32** (2005 Reissue), **33**, **34**, **35**, **36(1)** (2007 Reissue), **36(2)**, **38** (2006 Reissue), **39(1A)**, **39(1B)**, **39(2)**, **40(1)** (2007 Reissue), **40(2)** (2007 Reissue), **40(3)** (2007 Reissue), **41** (2005 Reissue), **42**, **44(1)**, **44(2)**, **45(1)** (2005 Reissue), **45(2)**, **46(1)**, **46(2)**, **46(3)**, **48** (2007 Reissue), **49(1)** (2005 Reissue), **50** (2005 Reissue), **51**, **52**

Additional Materials: *Shipping and Water (Pollution)* containing vol **43(2)** (Reissue) paras 1135–1369 and vol **49(3)** (2004 Reissue) paras 658–746; *Local Government Finance* containing vol **29(1)** (Reissue) paras 514–618, 624–634; *Trade, Industry and Industrial Relations* containing vol **47** (2001 Reissue) paras 1–4, 601–1000

Fourth and Fifth Edition volumes:

2008 Consolidated Index (A–E), 2008 Consolidated Index (F–O), 2008 Consolidated Index (P–Z), 2009 Consolidated Table of Statutes, 2009 Consolidated Table of Statutory Instruments, etc, 2009 Consolidated Table of Cases (A–L), 2009 Consolidated Table of Cases (M–Z, ECJ Cases)

August 2009

HALSBURY'S
Laws of England

FOURTH EDITION

LORD MACKAY OF CLASHFERN
Lord High Chancellor of Great Britain
1987–97

Additional Materials:
Trade, Industry and Industrial Relations

2009

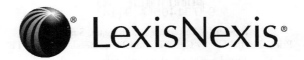

Members of the LexisNexis Group worldwide

United Kingdom	LexisNexis, a Division of Reed Elsevier (UK) Ltd, Halsbury House, 35 Chancery Lane, LONDON, WC2A 1EL, and London House, 20–22 East London Street, EDINBURGH, EH7 4BQ
Australia	LexisNexis Butterworths, Chatswood, New South Wales
Austria	LexisNexis Verlag ARD Orac GmbH & Co KG, Vienna
Benelux	LexisNexis Benelux, Amsterdam
Canada	LexisNexis Canada, Markham, Ontario
China	LexisNexis China, Beijing and Shanghai
France	LexisNexis SA, Paris
Germany	LexisNexis Deutschland GmbH Munster
Hong Kong	LexisNexis Hong Kong, Hong Kong
India	LexisNexis India, New Delhi
Italy	Giuffrè Editore, Milan
Japan	LexisNexis Japan, Tokyo
Malaysia	Malayan Law Journal Sdn Bhd, Kuala Lumpur
New Zealand	LexisNexis NZ Ltd, Wellington
Poland	Wydawnictwo Prawnicze LexisNexis Sp, Warsaw
Singapore	LexisNexis Singapore, Singapore
South Africa	LexisNexis Butterworths, Durban
USA	LexisNexis, Dayton, Ohio

FIRST EDITION	*Published in 31 volumes between 1907 and 1917*
SECOND EDITION	*Published in 37 volumes between 1931 and 1942*
THIRD EDITION	*Published in 43 volumes between 1952 and 1964*
FOURTH EDITION	*Published in 56 volumes between 1973 and 1987, with reissues between 1988 and 2008*
FIFTH EDITION	*Commenced in 2008*

A CIP Catalogue record for this book is available from the British Library.

ISBN 13 (complete set, standard binding): 9780406047762

ISBN 13: 9781405749114

ISBN 978-1-4057-4911-4

9 781405 749114

Typeset by Letterpart Ltd, Reigate, Surrey
Printed in the UK by CPI William Clowes Beccles NR34 7TL
Visit LexisNexis at www.lexisnexis.co.uk

Editor in Chief

THE RIGHT HONOURABLE

LORD MACKAY OF CLASHFERN

LORD HIGH CHANCELLOR OF GREAT BRITAIN

1987–97

This booklet is reproduced from:

TRADE, INDUSTRY AND INDUSTRIAL RELATIONS

Parts 6, 9, 10
Contributed by
RICHARD WHISH, BA, BCL,
a Solicitor of the Supreme Court;
Professor of Law, King's College, University of London

Parts 7, 8
Contributed by
The Publisher's Editorial Staff

The law stated in this volume is in general that in force on 1 November 2001, although subsequent changes have been included wherever possible.

Any subsequent and future updating material will be found in the Current Service and annual Cumulative Supplement to Halsbury's Laws of England.

TABLE OF CONTENTS

NOTE 1. A general list of the abbreviations of law reports and other sources used in this work can be found at the beginning of the Consolidated Table of Cases.

NOTE 2. Where references are made to other publications, the volume number precedes and the page number follows the name of the publication; eg the reference '12 Forms & Precedents (5th Edn) 44' refers to volume 12 of the Encyclopaedia of Forms and Precedents, page 44.

NOTE 3. An English statute is cited by short title or, where there is no short title, by regnal year and chapter number together with the name by which it is commonly known or a description of its subject matter and date. In the case of a foreign statute, the mode of citation generally follows the style of citation in use in the country concerned with the addition, where necessary, of the name of the country in parentheses.

NOTE 4. A statutory instrument is cited by short title, if any, followed by the year and number, or, if unnumbered, the date.

TRADE, INDUSTRY AND INDUSTRIAL RELATIONS

REPRODUCED FROM VOLUME 47

TABLE OF
STATUTORY INSTRUMENTS

TABLE OF EUROPEAN
COMMUNITY LEGISLATION

1. ADMINISTRATION

(1) THE DEPARTMENT OF TRADE AND INDUSTRY AND OTHER CENTRAL DEPARTMENTS

1.   Government responsibility in general. Government responsibility in relation to matters of trade and industry is vested in the Department of Trade and Industry[1]. Certain functions, in so far as they are exercisable in relation to Wales, have been transferred to, or are now exercisable concurrently with, the National Assembly for Wales[2].

1   As to this department see para 2 post; and CONSTITUTIONAL LAW AND HUMAN RIGHTS vol 8(2) (Reissue) paras 505–508.

2   See the National Assembly for Wales (Transfer of Functions) Order 1999, SI 1999/672, which provides for such transfer or concurrent exercise, with or without modifications in each case. Few functions relevant to this title have actually been so transferred; those that have, or are now exercisable concurrently, relate to:
  (1)   industrial designs: see the Industrial Organisation and Development Act 1947 s 11; and para 820 post;
  (2)   the development of tourism: see the Development of Tourism Act 1969 ss 1(3), (6), 2(8), 4(1), (4), 6(1)–(4), 17(4); the Tourism (Overseas Promotion) (Wales) Act 1992; the Tourism (Sleeping Accommodation Price Display) Order 1977, SI 1977/1877; and generally para 813 et seq post;
  (3)   the Welsh Development Agency: see the Welsh Development Agency Act 1975, and the Industry Act 1980 s 2 (as amended); and generally para 856 et seq post;
  (4)   industrial development generally: see the Industrial Development Act 1982; and generally para 821 et seq post.
    As to the National Assembly for Wales generally see CONSTITUTIONAL LAW AND HUMAN RIGHTS.
    The National Assembly for Wales exercises functions under the Regulatory Reform Act 2001: see para 16 post.

2.   Government departments and the Secretary of State. Matters relating to trade were originally within the general jurisdiction of the Board of Trade[1]. Subsequently specialised ministries were established such as those relating to technology, power, science[2] and aviation. In 1970 certain powers previously exercised by such ministries were transferred to the Secretary of State[3], which in practice meant the Secretary of State for Trade and Industry[4], who was also empowered to exercise concurrently the powers of the Board of Trade[5]. This device of assigning powers simply to 'the Secretary of State' was used again in 1974 when the Department of Trade and Industry was divided and its functions transferred en bloc to the Secretary of State[6] and distributed by administrative arrangements[7] among the four successor Departments of Trade, Industry, Energy[8] and Prices and Consumer Protection[9].

In 1983 the Departments of Trade and of Industry were once again amalgamated to form a single department, known as the Department of Trade and Industry, and the functions of the Secretary of State for Trade and the Secretary of State for Industry were transferred en bloc to the Secretary of State for Trade and Industry[10], who may use the title 'President of the Board of Trade'[11].

Certain functions of the Board of Trade relating to employment were transferred to the Minister of Labour in 1916[12] and from him to the Secretary of State for Employment and Productivity on the dissolution of the Ministry of Labour in 1968[13]. The title of that Secretary of State was changed in 1970 to Secretary of State for Employment, but a number of employment functions are now exercisable once again by the Secretary of State for Trade and Industry[14]. Functions relating to tourism were transferred from the Secretary of State for Trade and Industry to the Secretary of State for Employment in 1985[15] but subsequently transferred to the Secretary of State for National Heritage[16]; and functions relating to small businesses also transferred to him in 1985 were subsequently transferred to the Secretary of State for Trade and Industry[17]. The functions of the Secretary of State for Employment relating to general indices of retail prices and the family expenditure survey were transferred to the Chancellor of the Exchequer in 1989[18].

1   As to the Board of Trade see CONSTITUTIONAL LAW AND HUMAN RIGHTS vol 8(2) (Reissue) para 505. The Board of Trade is still mentioned in many statutes and still theoretically exists. However, in time its functions came to be exercised mainly by its President. The office of President of the Board of Trade is now held by the Secretary of State for Trade and Industry, who exercises the President's functions concurrently and may use the title (see text and note 11 infra): Secretary of State for Trade and Industry Order 1970, SI 1970/1537, art 2(1)(b). Certain functions of the Board of Trade and Secretary of State are now exercisable concurrently with the Chancellor of the Exchequer: Transfer of Functions (Economic Statistics) Order 1989, SI 1989/992, art 2. Others are exercisable concurrently with or transferred to the Treasury: Transfer of Functions (Financial Services) Order 1992, SI 1992/1315.

2   Certain functions of this minister were transferred to the Secretary of State for Education and Science by virtue of the Secretary of State for Education and Science Order 1964, SI 1964/490, and subsequently to the former Minister of Technology by virtue of the Minister of Technology Order 1964. SI 1964/2048. Other functions were transferred to the Secretary of State for Education and Science in 1964 and retained by him until 1992, when his title was changed to Secretary of State for Education: see the Transfer of Functions (Science) Order 1992, SI 1992/1296. The Secretary of State for Trade and Industry now exercises functions under the Science and Technology Act 1965 (see LIBRARIES AND OTHER SCIENTIFIC AND CULTURAL INSTITUTIONS): Transfer of Functions (Science) Order 1995, SI 1995/2985; and see the Transfer of Functions (Scientific Research) Order 1999, SI 1999/2785.

3   See the Secretary of State for Trade and Industry Order 1970, SI 1970/1537 (amended by SI 1971/716; and by the Supply Powers Act 1975 s 8(1), Sch 2 Pt II).

4   See the Secretary of State for Trade and Industry Order 1970, SI 1970/1537, art 2(1)(a). The Secretaryship of State is theoretically one office and a reference simply to the Secretary of State means one of Her Majesty's Principal Secretaries of State, without being specific: see the Interpretation Act 1978 s 5, Sch 1; and CONSTITUTIONAL LAW AND HUMAN RIGHTS vol 8(2) (Reissue) para 355 et seq.

5   See the Secretary of State for Trade and Industry Order 1970, SI 1970/1537, art 2(1)(a).

6   See the Secretary of State (New Departments) Order 1974, SI 1974/692 (amended by SI 1976/1775).

7   See 871 HC Official Report (5th series) written answers col 178.

8   In 1992 the former functions of the Department of Energy were transferred to the Secretary of State for Trade and Industry, except for energy efficiency functions which were transferred to the Secretary of State for the Environment: see the Transfer of Functions (Energy) Order 1992, SI 1992/1314.

9   In 1979 the remaining functions of the Secretary of State for Prices and Consumer Protection were transferred to the Secretary of State for Trade: see the Secretary of State for Trade Order 1979, SI 1979/578.

10 See the Transfer of Functions (Trade and Industry) Order 1983, SI 1983/1127, art 2(1). The civil aviation and shipping functions of the Secretary of State for Trade were transferred to the Secretary of State for Transport: art 2(3).

11 See e g Department of Trade and Industry Press Notice P/92/241, dated 15 April 1992.

12 See the New Ministries and Secretaries Act 1916 s 1 (repealed).

13 See the Secretary of State for Employment and Productivity Order 1968, SI 1968/729.

14 See the Secretary of State for Trade and Industry Order 1970, SI 1970/1537; and the Transfer of Functions (Education and Employment) Order 1995, SI 1995/2986. The

7. LEGISLATIVE CONTROLS

(1) GENERAL CONTROLS

(i) Supply

601. Powers of the Secretary of State. The Secretary of State[1] has power to acquire, produce or process articles required for the public service[2] or articles to be exchanged for such articles; to sell, exchange or otherwise dispose of any such articles or any government surplus materials[3]; to store and transport any such articles and materials; and to do all such things in the exercise of these powers (including the erection of buildings and the execution of works) as appear to him necessary or expedient for the exercise of these powers[4]. He may also make payments by way of grant or loan, in accordance with arrangements approved by the Treasury, to any person producing, dealing in or having control of any article required for the public service and to any person carrying on the business of storing goods, for the purpose of inducing the augmentation of stocks of that article or of any other article which can conveniently be used for or in connection with its production, or the improvement of facilities available for the storage of any such stocks or any articles required for the public service[5].

The Secretary of State may also by notice in writing require any person producing, dealing in or having control of any article required for the public service to make periodical and other returns, at such times, and containing such particulars as may be specified in the notice, as to (1) the stocks of that article for the time being held by him and the quantities of any such article which by virtue of any contract are to be delivered by or to him and the date of such delivery; and (2) the facilities available for producing that article or storing stocks of it[6]. He may by the like notice require any person carrying out works required for the public service[7], or carrying on a business which in the opinion of the Secretary of State is suitable for or can be adapted to carrying out such works, or who has under his control accommodation suitable for the storage of any articles required for that service, to make periodical and other returns, at times specified in the notice and containing particulars so specified, as to (a) the facilities for carrying out such works[8]; or (b) the nature and extent of the accommodation, the period for which any part of it is already required and its purpose, and the facilities available for making use of it[9].

Her Majesty may by Order in Council apply in relation to the Secretary of State[10] any of the provisions of certain specified enactments[11] for the purpose of conferring on him any powers, rights and privileges in relation to the acquisition and holding of land for the purpose of discharging any of his functions, and in relation to the management, use and disposal in any manner of land acquired for that purpose, which under those enactments are vested in the Secretary of State for Defence for any purpose[12]. No recommendation may, however, be made to make such an order unless a draft of the order has been laid before Parliament and has been approved by a resolution of each House of Parliament[13]; and any such order may be varied or revoked by a subsequent order[14].

1　As to the Secretary of State see para 2 ante. As to the transfer of certain functions of the Secretary of State, so far as exercisable in relation to Wales, to the National Assembly for Wales see para 1 note 2 ante.

2 For the meaning of 'articles required for the public service' see para 602 post.

3 'Government surplus materials' means surplus articles of any government department and surplus articles of the government of any country outside the United Kingdom to be disposed of by Her Majesty's government in the United Kingdom in pursuance of an agreement between those governments: Supply Powers Act 1975 s 7. 'Government department' includes a Northern Ireland department: s 7. For the meaning of 'United Kingdom' see para 37 note 1 ante.

4 Ibid s 1(1). Without prejudice to his powers of inspection under s 1(1), the Secretary of State may, at the request of the parties concerned, carry out or supervise the carrying out of any inspection for the purposes of or in connection with the production of any articles where the inspection can conveniently be carried out or supervised by him in connection with the exercise of his functions: s 1(2).

5 Ibid s 3. As to untrue statements etc for the purpose of obtaining such a payment see para 603 post. As to the Treasury see CONSTITUTIONAL LAW AND HUMAN RIGHTS vol 8(2) (Reissue) paras 512–517.

6 Ibid s 4(1). Where a government department or any body or person has, by virtue of any Act, power to obtain for any purpose information as to matters with respect to which the Secretary of State is empowered by s 4(1)–(3) to require returns to be made: (1) that department or body must, if so required by him, exercise that power for the purpose of assisting him in obtaining any such information (s 4(4)(a)); and (2) any such information obtained by that department or body may, whether upon a requisition of the Secretary of State or otherwise, notwithstanding anything in any enactment, be furnished to him (s 4(4)(b)). As to unauthorised disclosure of information see para 603 post.

7 For the meaning of 'works required for the public service' see para 602 post.

8 Supply Powers Act 1975 s 4(2). See also note 6 supra.

9 Ibid s 4(3). See also note 6 supra.

10 References in ibid s 2 to the Secretary of State do not include the Secretary of State for Defence: s 2(6). As to the Secretary of State for Defence see CONSTITUTIONAL LAW AND HUMAN RIGHTS vol 8(2) (Reissue) para 438 et seq.

11 Ie the enactments specified in ibid s 2(1), Sch 1 Pt I. The specified enactments are the Defence Acts 1842–1873; the Ordnance Board Transfer Act 1855; the Lands Clauses Consolidation Acts Amendment Act 1860 s 7; the Militia (Lands and Buildings) Act 1873 s 7 (as amended); the Municipal Corporations Act 1882 s 254; and the Military Lands Act 1892 Pt II (ss 14–18) (as amended): Supply Powers Act 1975 Sch 1 Pt I. Any of the provisions of the Harbours, Docks and Piers Clauses Act 1847 s 28 (as amended), with any necessary modifications or adaptations, may also be applied by Order in Council in relation to the Secretary of State acting in the discharge of any of his functions under the Supply Powers Act 1975 or to property for the time being vested in or under his control for the purpose of discharging any of those functions: s 2(2), Sch 1 Pt II (amended by the Transport and Works Act 1992 s 68(1), Sch 4 Pt I).

12 Supply Powers Act 1975 s 2(1).

13 Ibid s 2(4). If, at any time when Parliament is dissolved or prorogued or when both Houses of Parliament are adjourned for more than 14 days, it is shown to the satisfaction of the Secretary of State that the making of an Order in Council under s 2 is urgently necessary, a draft of the order need not be laid before Parliament, but the order ceases to have effect, except as respects things previously done or omitted to be done, at the expiration of the period of 28 days beginning with the date on which the House of Commons first sits after the making of the order unless within that period resolutions approving the order are passed by both Houses of Parliament: s 2(5).

14 Ibid s 2(3).

602. Articles and works required for the public service. 'Articles required for the public service' means:

(1) articles[1] required for the discharge of its functions by any government department[2], the United Kingdom Atomic Energy Authority[3], the Civil Aviation Authority[4] or any research council[5];

(2) articles required for the defence of any part of the Commonwealth[6], including any territory under Her Majesty's protection or in which she has jurisdiction, or for the maintenance

or restoration of peace and security in any part of the world or for any measures arising out of a breach or apprehended breach of peace in any part of the world[7];

(3) articles required by any international organisation of which the United Kingdom[8] is a member or (where the relevant international agreement so provides) by any other member of such an organisation[9];

(4) articles which in the opinion of the Secretary of State[10] would be essential for the needs of the community in the event of war[11];

(5) articles for supply to a person carrying on an undertaking which includes the production of articles of that or any other description where that person requests the Secretary of State to supply those articles, and the Secretary of State is satisfied that the supply will serve the interests of the community[12]; and

(6) anything which, in the opinion of the Secretary of State, is or is likely to be necessary for or in connection with the production of any such articles as are mentioned in heads (1) to (5) above[13].

'Works required for the public service' is to be construed accordingly[14].

1 'Articles' includes substances: Supply Powers Act 1975 s 7.
2 For the meaning of 'government department' see para 601 note 3 ante.
3 As to the United Kingdom Atomic Energy Authority see FUEL AND ENERGY vol 19(2) (Reissue) para 1152 et seq.
4 As to the Civil Aviation Authority see AVIATION vol 2 (Reissue) para 1044 et seq.
5 Supply Powers Act 1975 s 7(a). The provision refers to any research council within the meaning of the Science and Technology Act 1965: see s 1 (as amended); and LIBRARIES AND OTHER SCIENTIFIC AND CULTURAL INSTITUTIONS vol 28 (Reissue) para 468 et seq.
6 As to the Commonwealth see generally COMMONWEALTH AND DEPENDENCIES.
7 Supply Powers Act 1975 s 7(b).
8 For the meaning of 'United Kingdom' see para 37 note 1 ante.
9 Supply Powers Act 1975 s 7(c).
10 As to the Secretary of State see para 2 ante. As to the transfer of certain functions of the Secretary of State, so far as exercisable in relation to Wales, to the National Assembly for Wales see para 1 note 2 ante.
11 Supply Powers Act 1975 s 7(d).
12 Ibid s 7(e).
13 Ibid s 7(f).
14 Ibid s 7.

603. Disclosure of information, offences and penalties. No information with respect to an individual business which has been obtained under or by virtue of the Supply Powers Act 1975 may be disclosed without the consent of the person carrying on that business[1], but this does not apply to the disclosure of any information to a government department[2], or any person authorised by a government department, requiring that information for the purpose of the discharge of that department's functions, or any disclosure for the purposes of any prosecution for an offence under that Act[3].

If any person knowingly or recklessly makes any untrue statement or untrue representation for the purpose of obtaining a payment, either for himself or for another person, for the creation of a reserve[4], or discloses any information in contravention of the above provisions, he is guilty of an offence[5].

If any person fails to make any return which he is required[6] to make, or knowingly or recklessly makes any untrue statement in any such return, he is guilty of an offence[7].

Where any of the above offences committed by a body corporate is proved to have been committed with the consent or connivance of any director, manager, secretary or other officer of that body, he, as well as the body corporate, is guilty of the offence and is liable to be proceeded against and punished accordingly[8].

1   Supply Powers Act 1975 s 5(1).
2   For the meaning of 'government department' see para 601 note 3 ante.
3   Supply Powers Act 1975 s 5(2).
4   Ie a payment under ibid s 3: see para 601 ante.
5   Ibid s 6(1). A person guilty of such an offence is liable on summary conviction to imprisonment for a term not exceeding three months or to a fine not exceeding the prescribed sum, or to both, or on conviction on indictment to imprisonment for term not exceeding two years or a fine, or to both: s 6(1)(a), (b) (amended by virtue of the Criminal Law Act 1977 s 32(1); and the Magistrates' Courts Act 1980 s 32(2)). As to the prescribed sum see para 122 note 18 ante.
6   Ie under the Supply Powers Act 1975 s 4: see para 601 ante.
7   Ibid s 6(2). A person guilty of such an offence is liable on summary conviction to a fine not exceeding level 3 on the standard scale: s 6(2) (amended by virtue of the Criminal Justice Act 1982 ss 38, 46). Where the failure continues after conviction, he is guilty of a further offence and liable on summary conviction to a fine not exceeding £50 for each day on which the failure continues: Supply Powers Act 1975 s 6(2). As to the standard scale see para 16 note 21 ante.
8   Ibid s 6(3).

(ii) Imports and Exports

604. General legislative powers of control. The import and export of goods is subject to general control under legislation now largely consolidated in the Customs and Excise Acts 1979[1]. The import of certain goods is specifically prohibited under the Customs Consolidation Act 1876 and other enactments[2]. However, in addition, under the Import, Export and Customs Powers (Defence) Act 1939 the Secretary of State[3] may by order[4] regulate or prohibit the import into or export from the United Kingdom[5], or any specified part of it, of any goods[6]. This power was originally conferred on the basis that it would expire at the end of the wartime emergency which necessitated it[7] but it was never withdrawn and is now exercisable on a permanent basis[8].

1   The Acts which may be cited together as the Customs and Excise Acts 1979 are the Customs and Excise Duties (General Reliefs) Act 1979, the Alcoholic Liquor Duties Act 1979, the Hydrocarbon Oil Duties Act 1979, the Tobacco Products Duty Act 1979, and the Customs and Excise Management Act 1979: s 178(2) (amended by the Finance (No 2) Act 1992 s 82, Sch 18 Pt II). As to customs duties generally see CUSTOMS AND EXCISE vol 12(2) (Reissue) para 1 et seq; and as to free movement of goods within the European Union see EUROPEAN COMMUNITIES.
2   See the Customs Consolidation Act 1876 s 42 (amended by the Statute Law Revision Act 1883; the Revenue Act 1883 s 19, Schedule; the Finance Act 1896 s 5; the Copyright Act 1911 s 36, Sch 2; the Finance Act 1917 s 6; the Finance Act 1929 ss 5, 6, Schedule; the Finance Act 1946 ss 2(1), 67(10), Sch 12 Pt I; the Isle of Man (Customs) Act 1946 s 1(1); the Customs and Excise Act 1952 s 320, Sch 12 Pt I; the Hallmarking Act 1973 s 23, Sch 7 Pt I; the Diseases of Animals Act 1975 s 4(3), Sch 2; the Forgery and Counterfeiting Act 1981, Schedule Pt II; and the Statute Law (Repeals) Act 1993). As to restrictions on the import and export of animals see ANIMALS vol 2 (Reissue) paras 241–247; as to restrictions on the import and export of certain plants see AGRICULTURE vol 1(2) (Reissue) paras 866–867; and as to restrictions on the import of controlled drugs see MEDICINE, PHARMACY, DRUGS AND MEDICINAL PRODUCTS vol 30 (Reissue) para 1010. As to drug trafficking offences see CRIMINAL LAW, EVIDENCE AND PROCEDURE vol 11(1) (Reissue) para 397 et seq.

3   Powers under the Import, Export and Customs Powers (Defence) Act 1939 were originally vested in the Board of Trade, but are now exercisable by the Secretary of State for Trade and Industry (who is President of the Board of Trade at the date at which this volume states the law): see para 2 ante.

4   See the Import of Goods (Control) Order 1954, SI 1954/23 (amended by SI 1954/627; SI 1975/2117; and SI 1978/806); the Export of Goods (Control) Order 1994, SI 1994/1191 (as amended); and para 609 et seq post. Orders may also be made in respect of individual countries or territories: see eg the Export of Goods (Federal Republic of Yugoslavia) (Control) Order 1998, SI 1998/1530.

5   For the purposes of the Import, Export and Customs Powers (Defence) Act 1939, the Isle of Man forms part of the United Kingdom: s 8(1)(a). For the meaning of 'United Kingdom' generally see para 37 note 1 ante.

6   See ibid s 1(1); and CUSTOMS AND EXCISE vol 12(2) (Reissue) paras 990, 1021. 'Goods' includes stores and baggage; 'stores' means goods for use in a ship or aircraft and includes fuel and spare parts and other articles of equipment, whether or not for immediate fitting; and 'ship' includes any boat or other vessel whatsoever and any hovercraft: Customs and Excise Management Act 1979 s 1(1), (2), (4) (as amended); applied by the Import, Export and Customs Powers (Defence) Act 1939 s 9(2) (amended by the Customs and Excise Management Act 1979 s 177(1), Sch 4 para 12, Table Pt I). An order under the Import, Export and Customs Powers (Defence) Act 1939 s 1 (as amended) may suspend wholly or in part the operation of any enactment, proclamation, Order in Council or order prohibiting or regulating the import or export of any goods and may contain such provisions (including penal provisions) as appear to the Secretary of State necessary for securing the operation and enforcement of the order: see s 1(3). The order may be varied or revoked by a subsequent order: s 1(2). Without prejudice to the provisions of enactments for the time being in force relating to customs or excise with respect to ships and aircraft, the taking into or out of the United Kingdom of ships or aircraft may be prohibited or regulated by an order under s 1 (as amended) as an import or export of goods, notwithstanding that the ships or aircraft are conveying goods or passengers, and whether or not they are moving under their own power: s 1(4) (amended by the Customs and Excise Management Act 1979 Sch 4 para 12, Table Pt I). Notwithstanding anything in the Customs and Excise Management Act 1979 s 145 (as amended) (see CUSTOMS AND EXCISE vol 12(2) (Reissue) para 1188), a prosecution for an offence under such an order may be instituted by or under the authority of the Secretary of State: Import, Export and Customs Powers (Defence) Act 1939 s 1(5) (amended by the Customs and Excise Management Act 1979 Sch 4 para 12, Table Pt I).

     Nothing in any order made under the Import, Export and Customs Powers (Defence) Act 1939 s 1 (as amended) applies to the importation into the United Kingdom of any cocoa beans and such products as are for the time being defined as cocoa products for the purposes of the International Cocoa Agreement (New York, 15 November 1972): International Cocoa Agreement Act 1973 s 1(1), (6), (7). Such goods may only be imported under a licence granted by the Secretary of State under that Act which may be revoked or varied at any time, and may be granted subject to a condition requiring the production of evidence that any contribution chargeable under the International Cocoa Agreement has been paid or secured: see the International Cocoa Agreement Act 1973 s 1(2)–(4). Any person who, for the purpose of obtaining such a licence, makes a statement or furnishes any document or information which to his knowledge is false in a material particular or recklessly makes a statement which is false in a material particular is liable on summary conviction to a fine not exceeding level 5 on the standard scale: s 1(5) (amended by virtue of the Criminal Justice Act 1982 ss 38, 46). As to the standard scale see para 16 note 21 ante.

7   See the Import, Export and Customs Powers (Defence) Act 1939 s 9(3) (repealed) whereby the Act was to continue in force until such date as Her Majesty might by Order in Council declare to be the date on which the emergency that was the occasion of the passing of the Act came to an end, and was then to expire. No such order had been made at the date at which that provision was repealed: see note 8 infra.

8   See the Import and Export Control Act 1990 s 1 (repealing the Import, Export and Customs Powers (Defence) Act 1939 s 9(3) (cited in note 7 supra) with effect from 6 December 1990).

605.   Power to impose charges.

In connection with any scheme of control contained in an order made by the Secretary of State[1], the Treasury may by order provide for imposing and recovering such charges as may be specified in the first mentioned order². Any charges so recovered must be paid either into the Exchequer or into such public fund or account as may be specified in the Treasury order³.

1   Ie an order made under the Import, Export and Customs Powers (Defence) Act 1939 s 1 (as amended): see para 604 ante. As to the Secretary of State see para 2 ante. As to the transfer of certain functions of the Secretary of State, so far as exercisable in relation to Wales, to the National Assembly for Wales see para 1 note 2 ante. See also para 604 note 3 ante.

2   Ibid s 2(1). Any such order must be laid before the House of Commons: see s 2(3) (amended by the Statute Law (Repeals) Act 1986); the Statutory Instruments Act 1946 s 4 (as amended); and STATUTES vol 44(1) (Reissue) para 1515. If an order imposes or increases a charge, it ceases to have effect on the expiration of 28 days (not counting any time when Parliament is dissolved or prorogued, or during which the House of Commons is adjourned for more than four days) from the date of the making of the order unless at some time before the expiration of that period it has been approved by a resolution of the House of Commons, without prejudice, however, to the validity of anything previously done under the order or to the making of a new order: see the Import, Export and Customs Powers (Defence) Act 1939 s 2(4); and cf the Statutory Instruments Act 1946 s 4(3); and STATUTES vol 44(1) (Reissue) para 1515. At the date at which this volume states the law, no such order had been made.

3   Import, Export and Customs Powers (Defence) Act 1939 s 2(2).

606.   Offences.   If any goods¹ are imported, exported or brought to any quay or other place² or waterborne for the purpose of being exported in contravention either of an order made under the Import, Export and Customs Powers (Defence) Act 1939³, or of the law relating to trading with the enemy⁴, those goods are to be deemed prohibited goods and forfeited⁵. The exporter⁶ of the goods or his agent, or the shipper of the goods, is or are liable, in addition to any other penalty under the enactments for the time being in force relating to customs and excise⁷, to a customs penalty⁸.

1   For the meaning of 'goods' see para 604 note 6 ante.

2   The words 'or other place' are not to be construed ejusdem generis with 'quay': *Emerson v Woods* [1942] NI 118; *A-G for Palestine v Fakhry Ayyas* [1947] AC 332, PC; *Roe v Hemmings* [1951] 1 KB 676, [1951] 1 All ER 389, DC.

3   Ie an order made under the Import, Export and Customs Powers (Defence) Act 1939 s 1 (as amended): see para 604 ante.

4   See in particular the Trading with the Enemy Act 1939; and WAR AND ARMED CONFLICT vol 49(1) (Reissue) para 634 et seq. 'Enemy' means (1) any state, or sovereign of a state, at war with Her Majesty; (2) any individual resident in enemy territory; (3) any body of persons (whether corporate or unincorporate) carrying on business in any place, if and so long as the body is controlled by a person who, under this provision, is an enemy; (4) any body of persons constituted or incorporated in, or under the laws of, a state at war with Her Majesty; or (5) any other person who for the purposes of any Act relating to trading with the enemy is to be deemed to be an enemy; but does not include any person by reason only that he is an enemy subject: Import, Export and Customs Powers (Defence) Act 1939 s 8(1)(b). 'Enemy territory' means any area which is under the sovereignty of, or in the occupation of, a power with whom Her Majesty is at war, not being an area in the occupation of Her Majesty or of a power allied with Her Majesty: s 8(1)(d). 'Enemy subject' means (a) an individual who, not being either a British subject or a British protected person, possesses the nationality of a state at war with Her Majesty; or (b) a body of persons constituted or incorporated in, or under the laws of, any such state: s 8(1)(c). For the meanings of 'British subject' and 'British protected person' for these purposes see BRITISH NATIONALITY AND IMMIGRATION vol 4(2) (Reissue) paras 52, 58.

      A certificate of a Secretary of State that any area is or was under the sovereignty of, or in the occupation of, any power, or as to the time at which any area became or ceased to be under such sovereignty or in such occupation is for these purposes conclusive evidence of the facts stated in the certificate: s 8(2). As to the Secretary of State see para 2 ante. As to the transfer of certain functions of the Secretary of State, so far as exercisable in relation to Wales, to the National Assembly for Wales see para 1 note 2 ante. See also para 604 note 3 ante.

5   Ibid s 3(1). An order may also contain provisions relating to the carriage of goods coastwise or the shipment of goods or ships' stores (see para 613 post), in which case identical provisions apply: see s 3(1). If an order prohibits the export of any goods unless consigned to a particular place or person and those goods are delivered otherwise than to that place or person, as the case may be, the vessel in which they were exported is deemed to have been used in the conveyance of prohibited goods: s 3(2). In an action for the forfeiture of goods imported contrary to a control order, it is for the Crown to prove that the goods were imported (or exported, as the case may be) and for the defendants to prove lawful authority: *Customs and Excise Comrs v Hebson Ltd, Customs and Excise Comrs v DS Blaiber & Co Ltd* [1953] 2 Lloyd's Rep 382.

6   'Exporter', in relation to goods for exportation or for use as stores, includes the shipper of the goods and any person performing in relation to an aircraft functions corresponding with those of a shipper: Customs and Excise Management Act 1979 s 1(1); applied by the Import, Export and Customs Powers (Defence) Act 1939 s 9(2) (amended by the Customs and Excise Management Act 1979 s 177(1), Sch 4 para 12, Table Pt I).

7   As to offences in relation to customs and excise see CUSTOMS AND EXCISE.

8   Import, Export and Customs Powers (Defence) Act 1939 s 3(1) (amended by the Customs and Excise Management Act 1979 Sch 4 para 12, Table Pt I). The penalty must not exceed level 5 on the standard scale: Import, Export and Customs Powers (Defence) Act 1939 s 3(1) (amended by virtue of the Criminal Justice Act 1982 ss 38, 46). As to the standard scale see para 16 note 21 ante. As to the institution by the Secretary of State of a prosecution for an offence under an order see para 604 note 6 ante. If any goods are imported, exported, carried coastwise or shipped as ships' stores, or are brought to any quay or other place, or waterborne, for the purpose of being exported or of being so carried or shipped, an officer of customs and excise may require any person possessing or having control of the goods to furnish proof that the act is not unlawful by virtue either of an order or of the law relating to trading with the enemy (see note 4 supra) and if such proof is not furnished to the satisfaction of the Commissioners of Customs and Excise, then, unless the contrary is proved, the goods are deemed to be prohibited goods and are to be forfeited: Import, Export and Customs Powers (Defence) Act 1939 s 3(3) (amended by the Customs and Excise Act 1952 s 320, Sch 12 Pt I; and the Emergency Laws (Miscellaneous Provisions) Act 1953 s 1, Sch 1 para 5). As to proceedings under the customs and excise enactments see the Customs and Excise Management Act 1979 ss 145–156 (as amended), s 171 (as amended); and CUSTOMS AND EXCISE vol 12(2) (Reissue) para 1188 et seq. As to the Commissioners of Customs and Excise see CUSTOMS AND EXCISE vol 12(2) (Reissue) para 905 et seq.

607. Suspected false declarations. Where a person about to export goods[1] from the United Kingdom[2] in the course of making entry of those goods before shipment makes a declaration as to their ultimate destination[3] and the Commissioners of Customs and Excise have reason to suspect that the declaration is untrue in any material particular, the goods may be detained until the commissioners are satisfied as to the truth of the declaration; and if the commissioners are not so satisfied the goods must be forfeited[4].

1   For the meaning of 'goods' see para 604 note 6 ante.

2   As to the meaning of 'United Kingdom' for these purposes see para 604 note 5 ante. For the meaning of 'United Kingdom' generally see para 37 note 1 ante.

3   The country of ultimate destination means the country to which the goods are really going: see *The Kim* [1915] P 215 at 277 (revsd on fresh evidence (1921) 90 LJP 188, PC); *The Louisiana* [1918] AC 461, PC; *Hodson v Superheater Co Ltd* [1968] 3 All ER 144, Crown Ct.

4   Import, Export and Customs Powers (Defence) Act 1939 s 7(1). As to additional information that may be required in relation to goods imported and exported see the Customs and Excise Management Act 1979 s 77 (as amended), s 77A (as added and amended); and CUSTOMS AND EXCISE vol 12(2) (Reissue) paras 1040–1041. As to the Commissioners of Customs and Excise see CUSTOMS AND EXCISE vol 12(2) (Reissue) para 905 et seq.

608. Proof that exported goods have not reached an enemy. The Commissioners of Customs and Excise may require any exporter[1] or shipper of goods[2] which have been exported from the United Kingdom[3] to satisfy them that those goods have not reached any enemy or any enemy territory[4]. If he fails so to do, unless he proves that he did not consent to or connive at the goods reaching an enemy or enemy territory and that he took all reasonable steps to secure that the ultimate destination was that specified in the documents shown or furnished to the officers of customs and excise in connection with the exportation of the goods, he incurs a customs penalty[5].

1 For the meaning of 'exporter' see para 606 note 6 ante. As to the Commissioners of Customs and Excise see CUSTOMS AND EXCISE vol 12(2) (Reissue) para 905 et seq.

2 For the meaning of 'goods' see para 604 note 6 ante.

3 As to the meaning of 'United Kingdom' for these purposes see para 604 note 5 ante. For the meaning of 'United Kingdom' generally see para 37 note 1 ante.

4 Import, Export and Customs Powers (Defence) Act 1939 s 7(2). For the meanings of 'enemy' and 'enemy territory' see para 606 note 4 ante.

5 The customs penalty is treble the value of the goods or a penalty not exceeding level 3 on the standard scale at the election of the commissioners: ibid s 7(2) (amended by virtue of the Criminal Justice Act 1982 ss 38, 46). As to the standard scale see para 16 note 21 ante. As to additional information that may be requested by the Commissioners of Customs and Excise see the Customs and Excise Management Act 1979 s 77 (as amended), s 77A (as added and amended); and CUSTOMS AND EXCISE vol 12(2) (Reissue) paras 1040–1041. As to proceedings under the customs and excise enactments see ss 145–156 (as amended), s 171 (as amended); and CUSTOMS AND EXCISE vol 12(2) (Reissue) para 1188 et seq.

(iii) Particular Controls

A. IMPORT OF GOODS

609.   Import licences. All goods[1], other than goods which are proved to the satisfaction of the Commissioners of Customs and Excise to have been consigned from the Channel Islands[2], are prohibited to be imported into the United Kingdom[3] except under the authority of a licence[4] granted by the Secretary of State[5] and in accordance with any condition[6] attached to the licence[7]. The Secretary of State may modify or revoke the licence at any time[8]. Any licence which may have been granted in connection with an application for which any person makes any statement or furnishes any document or information which to his knowledge is false in a material particular, or recklessly makes any statement which is false in a material particular, is void as from the time the licence was granted[9].

1 Unless otherwise specified, 'goods' means both used and unused goods: Import of Goods (Control) Order 1954, SI 1954/23, art 6(1). The order was made in the exercise of powers under the Import, Export and Customs Powers (Defence) Act 1939 s 1 (as amended) (see para 604 ante) and came into operation on 21 January 1954 (see the Import of Goods (Control) Order 1954, SI 1954/23, art 8). For the meaning of 'goods' for the purposes of the Import, Export and Customs Powers (Defence) Act 1939 see para 604 note 6 ante.

2 See ibid art 3. This exception does not, however, extend to (1) the following dyes, dyestuffs and intermediates: (a) synthetic organic dyestuffs, including pigment dyestuffs, whether soluble or insoluble; (b) compounds, preparations and articles manufactured from any such dyestuffs, except any such compounds, preparations and articles as are not suitable for use in dyeing; (c) organic intermediate products used in the manufacture of any such dyestuffs; (2) the following arms and ammunition: (a) lethal firearms, including any lethal barrelled weapon of any description from which any shot, bullet or other missile can be discharged and other weapons of whatever description designed or adapted for the discharge of any noxious liquid, gas or other thing; (b) component parts of any such firearm or such other weapon, any accessory to any such firearm or other weapon designed or adapted to diminish the noise or flash caused by firing the weapon; (c) ammunition, including grenades, bombs and other like missiles, and any ammunition containing or designed or adapted to contain any noxious liquid, gas or other thing, and

component parts of any such ammunition; and (3) plumage, other than plumage of birds imported alive and other than plumage of birds ordinarily used in the United Kingdom as articles of diet: art 3(a)–(c). As to the Commissioners of Customs and Excise see CUSTOMS AND EXCISE vol 12(2) (Reissue) para 905 et seq.

3   Ibid art 1. For the meaning of 'United Kingdom' see para 37 note 1 ante; but c f para 604 note 5 ante.

4   Licences may be individual (i e enabling specified individuals or classes to import specified goods) or general (i e enabling persons generally to import certain goods from certain countries without the need to apply for an individual licence). Such licences are not printed in the form of statutory instruments, but are announced by the Department of Trade and Industry and may be obtained from The Stationery Office.

5   Import of Goods (Control) Order 1954, SI 1954/23, art 2. As to the Secretary of State see paras 2, 604 note 3 ante.

6   A licence granted under ibid art 2 permitting goods to be imported for transit or transhipment may be granted subject to either or both of the following conditions: (1) that the goods be exported to a specified destination; (2) that they be exported within a specified time: art 2A(1)(a), (b) (art 2A added by SI 1978/806). If goods are imported under the authority of such a licence and any such condition imposed by the licence is contravened or not complied with, the goods are liable to forfeiture: Import of Goods (Control) Order 1954, SI 1954/23, art 2A(2) (as so added).

7   Ibid art 2. As to the compatibility of import licences with Community law see CUSTOMS AND EXCISE vol 12(2) (Reissue) para 20.

8   Ibid art 5(1).

9   Ibid art 4. In addition, that person commits an offence for which he is liable on summary conviction to a fine not exceeding £500 or to imprisonment for a term not exceeding six months, or to both: art 4.

B. EXPORT OF GOODS

610.   Export licences. In exercise of his power to regulate the export of goods[1], the Secretary of State[2] has provided that all goods of a specified description[3] are prohibited to be exported to any destination[4]. Nothing in these provisions[5], however, prohibits the export of any goods under the authority of a licence in writing granted by the Secretary of State, provided that all conditions attaching to that licence are complied with[6].

A licence so granted or having effect as if so granted may be either general, or special, may be limited so as to expire on a specified date unless renewed and may be varied or revoked by the Secretary of State at any time[7]. A licence may be subject to or without conditions, and any such condition may require any act or omission before or after the export of goods under the licence[8]. A person who has exported any goods under the authority of any general licence so granted that does not provide otherwise must, before or within 30 days after the first such export, give written notice to the Secretary of State of the specified particulars[9] and must give written notice to the Secretary of State of any change in those particulars within the same period[10]. Any person who has exported goods under the authority of a general licence must keep records, subject to the provisions of the particular general licence under which he has exported the goods, of every such export[11]. Where any such records are kept in a form which is not legible the exporter must, at the request of the person authorised by the Secretary of State[12], produce such records in a legible form[13].

1   Ie under the Import, Export and Customs Powers (Defence) Act 1939 s 1 (as amended) (see para 604 ante). As to the compatibility of export restrictions with Community law see CUSTOMS AND EXCISE vol 12(2) (Reissue) para 20.

2   As to the Secretary of State see para 2 ante. As to the transfer of certain functions of the Secretary of State, so far as exercisable in relation to Wales, to the National Assembly for Wales see para 1 note 2 ante. See also para 604 note 3 ante.

3   Ie goods of a description specified in the Export of Goods (Control) Order 1992, SI 1992/3092, art 2, Sch 1 Pt I Group 2 (antiques); and the Export of Goods (Control) Order 1994, SI 1994/1191, art 2, Sch 1 (as amended) (see para 611 post). 'Goods', unless otherwise specified, means both used and unused goods: art 1(2). See also para 604 note 6 ante. The Export of Goods (Control) Order 1992, SI 1992/3092 is revoked, except in so far as it applies to the export of antiques, by the Export of Goods (Control) Order 1994, SI 1994/1191, art 9, Sch 2 Pt 1.

4   See the Export of Goods (Control) Order 1992 SI 1992/3092, art 2; and the Export of Goods (Control) Order 1994, SI 1994/1191, art 2 (amended by SI 2000/2618; SI 2001/729; and SI 2001/3166). A prohibition on export is a prohibition on export from the United Kingdom, including a prohibition on shipment as ships' stores: Export of Goods (Control) Order 1992, SI 1992/3092, art 1(3)(a); Export of Goods (Control) Order 1994, SI 1994/1191, art 1(3)(a) (amended by SI 1996/2663). As to ships' stores, however, see para 613 post. For the meaning of 'United Kingdom' see para 37 note 1 ante; but cf para 604 note 5 ante.

    The Export of Goods (Control) Order 1994, SI 1994/1191 (as amended) does not apply in respect of the export of dual-use items or certain other specified items, other than the export of goods which are items in transit, in which case it is modified: see the Dual-Use Items (Export Control) Regulations 2000, SI 2000/2620, reg 13. As to the export of dual-use items see paras 616–620 post.

5   Ie nothing in the Export of Goods (Control) Order 1992, SI 1992/3092 (as amended) or the Export of Goods (Control) Order 1994, SI 1994/1191 (as amended): see note 3 supra.

6   Export of Goods (Control) Order 1992, SI 1992/3092, art 3(a); Export of Goods (Control) Order 1994, SI 1994/1191, art 3(1)(a) (amended by SI 1999/63; and SI 1999/1777).

    For the purposes of the Export of Goods (Control) Order 1994, SI 1994/1191, art 3(1)(a) (as amended) but subject to art 3(3) (as added) (see infra), the exportation of goods to a destination outside the customs territory of the European Community is to be regarded as being under the authority of a licence granted by the Secretary of State to or for the benefit of a particular person only if: (1) he is the person on whose behalf the export declaration is made; and (2) he is established within the European Community and either (a) he is the owner of the goods or has a similar right of disposal over them, or (b) if no person who is owner of the goods or has a similar right of disposal over them is established within the European Community, he is party to one or more contracts under which ownership of the goods or a similar right of disposal over them has passed to a person not established within the European Community and pursuant to which the goods are to be, are being or have been exported from the customs territory of the European Community: art 3(2) (added by SI 1999/63). The Export of Goods (Control) Order 1994, SI 1994/1191, art 3(2) (as added) does not apply if no person falls within head (2) supra or if the export is of goods imported into the United Kingdom for transit or transhipment in respect of which the conditions in art 3B(2) (as added and amended) (see para 611 note 12 post) are met: art 3(3) (added by SI 1999/63). As to the customs territory of the European Community see CUSTOMS AND EXCISE vol 12(2) (Reissue) para 22.

7   Export of Goods (Control) Order 1992, SI 1992/3092, art 7(1); Export of Goods (Control) Order 1994, SI 1994/1191, art 7(1).

8   Export of Goods (Control) Order 1992, SI 1992/3092, art 7(2); Export of Goods (Control) Order 1994, SI 1994/1191, art 7(2).

9   Export of Goods (Control) Order 1992, SI 1992/3092, art 8(1); Export of Goods (Control) Order 1994, SI 1994/1191, art 8(1). The specified particulars are: (1) the name of the person; and (2) the address at which copies of the records referred to in the text and notes 12–13 infra may be inspected by any person authorised by the Secretary of State: Export of Goods (Control) Order 1992, SI 1992/3092, art 8(1)(i), (ii); Export of Goods (Control) Order 1994, SI 1994/1191, art 8(1)(i), (ii). Any notice to be given by a person under the Export of Goods (Control) Order 1992, SI 1992/3092, art 8(1) or (2) or the Export of Goods (Control) Order 1994, SI 1994/1191, art 8(1) or (2) (see the text and note 10 infra) may be given by the agent of that person and must be sent by post or delivered to the Secretary of State at the Applicant Services and Compliance Unit, Department of Trade and Industry, 4 Abbey Orchard Street, London SW1P 2HT: Export of Goods (Control) Order 1992, SI 1992/3092, art 8(5); Export of Goods (Control) Order 1994, SI 1994/1191, art 8(5) (amended by SI 2000/2264).

10 Export of Goods (Control) Order 1992, SI 1992/3092, art 8(2); Export of Goods (Control) Order 1994, SI 1994/1191, art 8(2). See also note 9 supra.

11 Export of Goods (Control) Order 1992, SI 1992/3092, art 8(3); Export of Goods (Control) Order 1994, SI 1994/1191, art 8(3). The records must include the following information: (1) in so far as it is known to him, the name and address of any consignee of the goods, and any person to whom the goods are to be, or have been, delivered; (2) his address; (3) the date of export; (4) a description of the goods including the quantity of goods exported; and (5) any further information required by the licence to be kept: Export of Goods (Control) Order 1992, SI 1992/3092, art 8(3)(a)–(e); Export of Goods (Control) Order 1994, SI 1994/1191, art 8(3)(a)–(e). Any such records must be kept for at least 4 years from the date of the relevant export: Export of Goods (Control) Order 1992, SI 1992/3092, art 8(3); Export of Goods (Control) Order 1994, SI 1994/1191, art 8(3).

12 The exporter must permit any such records to be inspected, and copied, by any person authorised by the Secretary of State; and for these purposes any such person has the right at all reasonable hours to enter the premises the address of which has been most recently notified to the Secretary of State (see note 11 supra), on producing some duly authenticated document showing his authority if required to do so: Export of Goods (Control) Order 1992, SI 1992/3092, art 8(3); Export of Goods (Control) Order 1994, SI 1994/1191, art 8(3).

13 Export of Goods (Control) Order 1992, SI 1992/3092, art 8(4); Export of Goods (Control) Order 1994, SI 1994/1191, art 8(4).

611. Prohibited goods and exceptions. The goods[1] which may not be exported without a licence[2] are specified as follows[3]:

(1) Part I: explosive-related goods[4], antiques[5]; and certain vehicles prohibited to be exported to certain countries only[6]; and

(2) Part III: military, security and paramilitary goods and arms, ammunition and related material[7].

There are exceptions relating to exports to the Channel Islands[8], the export of aircraft[9] and vessels[10] and certain firearms and ammunition[11].

The export of any goods which have been imported into the United Kingdom for transit or transhipment is not prohibited provided certain conditions are met[12].

1 For the meaning of 'goods' see para 610 note 3 ante. The Export of Goods (Control) Order 1994, SI 1994/1191 (as amended) does not apply in respect of the export of dual-use items or certain other specified items, other than the export of goods which are items in transit, in which case it is modified: see the Dual-Use Items (Export Control) Regulations 2000, SI 2000/2620, reg 13; and para 616 et seq post.

2 See para 610 ante.

3 See the Export of Goods (Control) Order 1994, SI 1994/1191, art 2, Sch 1 (amended by SI 1994/1632; SI 1995/271; SI 1996/2663; SI 1997/2758; SI 1999/63; SI 1999/1777; SI 1999/3411; SI 2000/1239; SI 2000/2264; and SI 2001/729); Export of Goods (Control) Order 1992, SI 1992/3092, art 2, Sch 1. The Export of Goods (Control) Order 1992, SI 1992/3092 is revoked, except in so far as it applies to the export of antiques, by the Export of Goods (Control) Order 1994, SI 1994/1191, art 9, Sch 2 Pt 1.

4 Export of Goods (Control) Order 1994, SI 1994/1191, Sch 1 Pt I Group 2 (amended by SI 1997/2758; SI 1999/63; and SI 2001/729).

5 Export of Goods (Control) Order 1992, SI 1992/3092, Sch 1 Pt I Group 2.

6 Ie certain all wheel drive utility vehicles, heavy duty recovery vehicles and drop sided trucks which may not be exported to any destination in the Federal Republic of Yugoslavia: see the Export of Goods (Control) Order 1994, SI 1994/1191, Sch 1 Pt I Group 3 (amended by SI 1997/2758; and SI 1999/3411).

7 Export of Goods (Control) Order 1994, SI 1994/1191, Sch 1 Pt III (amended by SI 1994/1632; SI 1996/2263; SI 1996/2663; SI 1997/2758; SI 1999/63; SI 1999/1777; SI 2000/1239; SI 2000/2264; and SI 2001/729). Subject to the provisions of Export of Goods (Control) Order 1994, SI 1994/1191, Sch 1 (as amended), or any contrary provisions in a licence, a licence granted in relation to any goods specified in Sch 1 Pt III (as amended) must also authorise the export of the minimum technology required for the installation, operation, maintenance and repair of the goods, to the same destination as the goods: art 7(4). As to export licences see para 610 ante.

In a criminal trial for conspiracy knowingly to be concerned in the exportation of goods with intent to evade the prohibition under Sch 1 Pt III, confusion between two descriptions of prohibited exports for military use is a material misdirection: *R v Daghir, R v Speckman* [1994] Crim LR 945, CA.

8   The Export of Goods (Control) Order 1992, SI 1992/3092 (as amended) continues to prohibit the exportation of antiques (see the text and notes 3, 5 supra) to any destination in the Channel Islands: art 3(b).

9   The Export of Goods (Control) Order 1994, SI 1994/1191 (as amended) does not prohibit the exportation of any aircraft which is being exported (except to a destination in Iran, Iraq or Libya or in a country or destination specified in Sch 3 (as amended) (see infra)) after temporary importation into the United Kingdom provided that there has been no change of ownership or registration since such importation and that no goods of a description specified in Sch 1 Pt III (as amended) (see head (2) in the text) have been incorporated into the aircraft since such importation other than by way of replacement for a component essential for the departure of the aircraft, or any aircraft the immediately preceding importation of which was on a scheduled journey and which is intended for further scheduled journeys: art 3(1)(c) (amended by SI 1995/271; SI 1997/323; SI 1997/2758; SI 1999/63; SI 1999/1777; and SI 2000/1239). 'Aircraft' means a fixed wing, swivel wing, rotary wing, tilt rotor or tilt wing airborne vehicle or helicopter; 'importation' and 'exportation' in relation to a vessel, submersible vehicle or aircraft includes the taking of it into or out of the United Kingdom notwithstanding that it is conveying goods or passengers, and whether or not it is moving under its own power, and cognate expressions are to be construed accordingly: Export of Goods (Control) Order 1994, SI 1994/1191, art 1(2). For the meaning of 'vessel' see para 617 note 22 post.

    The countries and destinations specified in Sch 3 (as amended) are: Afghanistan, Angola, Argentina, Armenia, Azerbaijan, Bosnia and Herzegovina, Burma (Myanmar), Burundi, People's Republic of China excluding Special Administrative Regions, Croatia, Democratic Republic of the Congo, Eritrea, Ethiopia, Liberia, Macao Special Administrative Region, Rwanda, Sierra Leone, Somalia, Sudan, Tanzania, Uganda, Federal Republic of Yugoslavia and Zimbabwe: Sch 3 (amended by SI 1994/2711; SI 1997/323; SI 1997/2464; SI 1997/2758; SI 1999/335; SI 1999/2609; SI 2000/109; SI 2000/1239; and SI 2000/1396).

10 The Export of Goods (Control) Order 1994, SI 1994/1191 (as amended) does not prohibit the exportation of any vessel: (1) registered or constructed outside the United Kingdom which is being exported (except to a destination in Iran, Iraq or Libya or in a country or destination specified in Sch 3 (as amended) (see note 9 supra) after temporary importation into the United Kingdom provided that no goods of a description specified in Sch 1 Pt III (as amended) (see head (2) in the text) have been incorporated into the vessel since such importation other than by way of replacement for a component essential for the departure of the vessel; or (2) departing temporarily from the United Kingdom on trials: art 3(1)(d) (amended by SI 1995/271; SI 1997/323; SI 1997/2758; and SI 2001/1239). 'Vessel' includes any ship, surface effect vehicle, vessel of small waterplane area or hydrofoil, and the hull or part of the hull of a vessel; 'surface effect vehicle' means any air cushion vehicle, whether side wall or skirted, and any vehicle using the wing-in-ground effect for positive lift: Export of Goods (Control) Order 1994, SI 1994/1191, art 1(2) (amended by SI 1996/2663). See also note 9 supra.

11 The Export of Goods (Control) Order 1994, SI 1994/1191 (as amended) does not prohibit the exportation of any firearm which falls within EEC Council Directive 91/477 on control of the acquisition and possession of weapons (OJ L256, 13.9.91, p 51) Annex 1, category B, C or D, or of any related ammunition and telescopic sight for use therewith to any destination in a member state of the European Communities if (1) the firearm and ammunition form part of the personal effects of a person who is in possession of a European firearms pass which has been issued to him under the Firearms Act 1968 s 32A (as added and amended) (see CRIMINAL LAW, EVIDENCE AND PROCEDURE) or a document which has been issued to him under the provisions of a law of a member state corresponding to that provision and which, in either case, relates to the firearm in question; and (2) either that pass or document issued to him contains authorisation for the possession of that firearm from the member state of destination and any other member state through which the holder intends that the firearm will pass on its way to that destination, or the holder of the firearm can on request satisfy the proper officer of the customs and excise at the place of export (a) that the export of the firearm is necessary to enable the holder to participate in one of the activities specified in EEC Council Directive 91/477 art 12.2 (ie hunting and marksmanship); (b) that the firearm falls within the

category appropriate to that activity in accordance with art 12.2; and (c) that the export or passage of the firearm is not to or, as the case may be, through a member state which prohibits or requires an authorisation for the acquisition or possession of that firearm: Export of Goods (Control) Order 1994, SI 1994/1191, art 3(1)(e)(i) (amended by SI 1994/2711; and SI 1999/63). Nor does the order prohibit the exportation of any firearm which is authorised to be possessed or, as the case may be, purchased or acquired, by a valid firearm certificate or shot gun certificate granted under the Firearms Act 1968 (see CRIMINAL LAW, EVIDENCE AND PROCEDURE vol 11(1) (Reissue) paras 200–201) or by a visitor's firearm or shot gun permit granted under the Firearms Amendment Act 1988 s 17 (as amended) (see CRIMINAL LAW, EVIDENCE AND PROCEDURE vol 11(1) (Reissue) para 216) or by a valid firearm certificate granted under the Firearms (Northern Ireland) Order 1981, SI 1981/155 (as amended) or granted in the Isle of Man under the Firearms Act 1947 (as amended) (an Act of Tynwald), and related ammunition and telescopic sight for use therewith (i) to any destination in a member state by any person or body specified in EEC Council Directive 91/477 art 2.2 or by the holder of a firearm certificate granted under that Act of Tynwald; or (ii) to any other destination, other than a destination in Iran, Iraq or Libya or in a country or destination specified in the Export of Goods (Control) Order 1994, SI 1994/1191, Sch 3 (as amended) (see note 9 supra) provided that the firearm, ammunition and telescopic sight form part of the personal effects of the holder of the certificate, and, in a case to which head (ii) supra applies, the certificate is produced by the holder, or his duly authorised agent, with the firearm and ammunition to the proper officer of customs and excise at the place of export: art 3(1)(e)(ii) (amended by SI 1994/1632; SI 1994/2711; 1997/2758; SI 1999/63; and SI 2000/1239).

12   Export of Goods (Control) Order 1994, SI 1994/1191, art 3B(1) (art 3B added by SI 1994/2711; art 3B(1) (as added) substituted by SI 2001/729). Nothing in the Export of Goods (Control) Order 1994, SI 1994/1191 (as amended) is to be taken to prohibit the exportation of any goods which have been imported into the United Kingdom for transit or transhipment, provided that they are not goods to which art 2(2) (as amended) (see para 610 ante) applies and that the conditions in art 3B(2) (as added) (see infra) are met: art 3B(1) (as so added and substituted). The provisions of art 3B(1) (as added and substituted) do not apply to: (1) anti-personnel landmines; (2) certain restraints designed for restraining human beings or devices designed to administer electric shocks (ie any goods falling within Sch 1 Pt III entry PL5001 para c or g (as substituted and amended)); (3) components specially designed for goods falling within head (1) supra; (4) equipment, technology or software falling within Sch 1 Pt III entry ML18, ML21 or ML22 (as substituted and amended) specifically related to goods falling within head (1) or head (2) supra; (5) any goods being exported to a destination in Iran, Iraq, Libya or North Korea; or (6) any military, security and para-military goods of a description specified in Sch 1 Pt III (as substituted and amended) being exported to a destination in any country specified in Sch 3 (see note 9 supra): art 3B(1A) (added by SI 1997/2758; and amended by SI 1999/63).

The conditions are that: (a) the goods remain on board a ship or aircraft for the period that they remain in the United Kingdom or are goods on a through bill of lading or through air waybill and in any event are exported within 30 days of their importation; (b) the destination for those goods following exportation from the United Kingdom has been determined in the country from which they were originally exported prior to their original exportation in connection with the transaction which has given rise to transit or transhipment and has not been changed prior to their exportation from the United Kingdom, or the goods are being returned to that country; and (c) the goods in question were exported from that country in accordance with any laws or regulations relating to the export of goods applying therein at the time of exportation therefrom of those goods: Export of Goods (Control) Order 1994, SI 1994/1191, art 3B(2) (added by SI 1994/2711; and amended by SI 1997/2758). References to goods specified, or of a description specified, in the Export of Goods (Control) Order 1994, SI 1994/1191, Sch 1 Pt III (as substituted and amended), do not include goods brought within the effect of the Export of Goods (Control) Order 1994, SI 1994/1191 (as amended) by the Dual-Use Items (Export Control) Regulations 2000, SI 2000/2620, reg 13) (see note 1 supra; and para 610 note 4 ante): Export of Goods (Control) Order 1994, SI 1994/1191, art 1(3)(c) (added by SI 1996/2663; and amended by SI 2000/2618); Interpretation Act 1978 s 17(2).

612. Proof of destination. Any exporter or shipper of goods[1] exported[2] from the United Kingdom[3] must, if so required by the Commissioners of Customs and Excise, furnish within such time as they may allow proof to their satisfaction that the goods have reached either a destination to which they were authorised to be exported by an export licence[4], or a destination to which their exportation was not prohibited[5]. If he fails to do so he is liable to a customs penalty[6] unless he proves that he did not consent to or connive at the goods reaching any destination other than such a destination[7].

1   For the meaning of 'goods' see para 610 note 3 ante.
2   For the meaning of 'exportation' and cognate expressions in relation to vessels, submersible vehicles and aircraft see para 611 note 9 ante.
3   For the meaning of 'United Kingdom' see para 37 note 1 ante; but cf para 604 note 5 ante.
4   Ie a licence granted for the purposes of the Export of Goods (Control) Order 1994, SI 1994/1191 (as amended): see para 610 ante. As to the Commissioners of Customs and Excise see CUSTOMS AND EXCISE vol 12(2) (Reissue) para 905 et seq.
5   Ibid art 4(a), (b). As to prohibitions on export to certain destinations see para 610 ante. The Export of Goods (Control) Order 1994, SI 1994/1191 (as amended) does not apply in respect of the export of dual-use items or certain other specified items, other than the export of goods which are items in transit, in which case it is modified: see the Dual-Use Items (Export Control) Regulations 2000, SI 2000/2620, reg 13; and para 616 et seq post.
6   The customs penalty must not exceed £2,000: Export of Goods (Control) Order 1994, SI 1994/1191, art 4. As to customs penalties see CUSTOMS AND EXCISE vol 12(2) (Reissue) para 1021 et seq.
7   Ibid art 4.

613.   Ships' stores.   Nothing in the general prohibition of exports of specified goods[1] prohibits the shipment of any goods[2] as ships' stores[3] with the permission of the proper officer of customs and excise at the port of departure for use on board the ship provided that all conditions attaching to the permission are complied with[4].

1   Ie the Export of Goods (Control) Order 1994, SI 1994/1191 (as amended): see paras 610–612 ante.
2   For the meaning of 'goods' see para 610 note 3 ante.
3   A prohibition on exportation includes a prohibition on shipment as ships' stores: see the Export of Goods (Control) Order 1994, SI 1994/1191, art 1(3)(a); and para 610 note 4 ante. 'Stores' does not include any goods to which the Dual-Use Items (Export Control) Regulations 2000, SI 2000/2620 (as amended) apply (see para 616 et seq post): Export of Goods (Control) Order 1994, SI 1994/1191, art 1(2) (definition added by SI 1995/271); Interpretation Act 1978 s 17(2).
4   Export of Goods (Control) Order 1994, SI 1994/1191, art 3A (added by SI 1994/2711). Any permission so granted may be modified or revoked by such officer at any time: Export of Goods (Control) Order 1994, SI 1994/1191, art 7(3). As to offences in connection with obtaining such permission see para 614 post.
    The Export of Goods (Control) Order 1994, SI 1994/1191 (as amended) does not apply in respect of the export of dual-use items or certain other specified items, other than the export of goods which are items in transit, in which case it is modified: see the Dual-Use Items (Export Control) Regulations 2000, SI 2000/2620, reg 13; and para 616 et seq post.

614.   Offences in connection with export licences or permissions for shipment.   A person is guilty of an offence if (1) he makes any statement or furnishes any document or information which to his knowledge is false in a material particular; or (2) he recklessly makes any statement or furnishes any document or information which is false in a material particular, for the purpose of obtaining any export licence[1] or permission for the exportation[2] or shipment as ships' stores[3] of any goods[4]. A person guilty of such an offence is liable on summary conviction to a fine not exceeding the statutory maximum, and on conviction on indictment to a fine or imprisonment for a term not exceeding two years, or to both[5], and any such licence or permission which may have been granted in connection with the application for which the false statement was made or the false document or information was furnished is void as from the time it was granted[6].

A person is also guilty of an offence, and liable to the like penalties, if he has exported goods from the United Kingdom[7] under the authority of a licence granted by the Secretary of State[8] and he fails to comply with any condition attaching to that licence, or with the requirements[9] as to notice, information and records[10]. He is not, however, guilty of such an offence where the licence had been previously modified by the Secretary of State without that person's consent, the alleged failure to comply would not have been a failure had the licence not been so modified, and that person proves that the export from the United Kingdom had taken place before the modification had been made[11].

1 Ie a licence under the Export of Goods (Control) Order 1994, SI 1994/1191 (as amended): see para 610 ante.
2 For the meaning of 'exportation' and cognate expressions in relation to vessels, submersible vehicles and aircraft see para 611 note 9 ante.
3 As to such permissions see para 613 ante.
4 Export of Goods (Control) Order 1994, SI 1994/1191, art 5(1). For the meaning of 'goods' see para 610 note 3 ante. The Export of Goods (Control) Order 1994, SI 1994/1191 (as amended) does not apply in respect of the export of dual-use items or certain other specified items, other than the export of goods which are items in transit, in which case it is modified: see the Dual-Use Items (Export Control) Regulations 2000, SI 2000/2620, reg 13; and para 616 et seq post.
5 Export of Goods (Control) Order 1994, SI 1994/1191, art 5(2). For the meaning of 'the statutory maximum' see para 16 note 21 ante.
6 Ibid art 5(1).
7 For the meaning of 'United Kingdom' see para 37 note 1 ante; but c f para 604 note 5 ante.
8 Ie a licence granted in pursuance of the Export of Goods (Control) Order 1994, SI 1994/1191, art 3(1)(a) (as amended): see para 610 ante. As to the Secretary of State see para 2 ante. As to the transfer of certain functions of the Secretary of State, so far as exercisable in relation to Wales, to the National Assembly for Wales see para 1 note 2 ante. See also para 604 note 3 ante.
9 Ie the requirements of ibid art 8 (as amended): see para 610 ante.
10 Ibid art 5(3).
11 Ibid art 5(3) proviso (substituted by SI 1999/1777).

615. Declarations by, and search of, persons leaving the United Kingdom. If required to do so by an officer of customs and excise, any person who is about to leave the United Kingdom[1] on any occasion must declare whether or not he has with him any goods[2] the export of which from the United Kingdom is subject to any prohibition or restriction[3] and produce any such goods which he has with him[4]. The officer and any person acting under his directions may search the person for the purpose of ascertaining whether he has with him any such goods[5]. Any person who without reasonable excuse refuses to make a declaration, fails to produce any goods or refuses to allow himself to be searched in accordance with these provisions is guilty of an offence and liable to a customs penalty[6]. Any person who makes a declaration which to his knowledge is false in a material particular or recklessly makes any declaration which is false in a material particular is also guilty of an offence[7].

1 For the meaning of 'United Kingdom' see para 37 note 1 ante; but c f para 604 note 5 ante.
2 For the meaning of 'goods' see para 610 note 3 ante.
3 Ie any prohibition or restriction under the Export of Goods (Control) Order 1994, SI 1994/1191 (as amended): see paras 610–611 ante.

4   Ibid art 6(1)(a), (b). The Export of Goods (Control) Order 1994, SI 1994/1191 (as amended) does not apply in respect of the export of dual-use items or certain other specified items, other than the export of goods which are items in transit, in which case it is modified: see the Dual-Use Items (Export Control) Regulations 2000, SI 2000/2620, reg 13; and para 616 et seq post.
5   Export of Goods (Control) Order 1994, SI 1994/1191, art 6(1). No person, however, may be searched except by a person of the same sex: art 6(1) proviso.
6   Ibid art 6(2). The customs penalty must not exceed £1,000: art 6(2). As to customs penalties see CUSTOMS AND EXCISE vol 12(2) (Reissue) para 1021 et seq.
7   Ibid art 6(3). A person guilty of such an offence is liable on summary conviction to a customs penalty not exceeding £2,000, and on conviction on indictment to a customs penalty of any amount or imprisonment for a term not exceeding two years, or to both: art 6(3).

C. EXPORT OF DUAL-USE ITEMS

616.   Licences to export dual-use items.   Dual-use items, that is to say items which are designed for civil use but which can be used for military purposes such as telecommunication equipment and radar, may only be exported under licence. 'Export', unless the context otherwise requires, means export from the United Kingdom[1], including: (1) export to a destination within the customs territory of the European Community; and (2) the transmission of software or technology by fax, telephone[2] or other electronic media[3].

The Secretary of State[4] may grant licences[5] and Community Licences[6] which may be: (a) either general or individual[7]; (b) limited so as to expire on a specified date unless renewed[8]; (c) subject to or without conditions, and any such condition may require or prohibit any act before or after the export of items under that licence or Community Licence[9]; and (d) varied or revoked by the Secretary of State[10].

1   For the meaning of 'United Kingdom' see para 37 note 1 ante.
2   Oral transmission of technology by telephone is included only where the technology is contained in a document the relevant part of which is read out over the telephone, or is described over the telephone in such a way as to achieve substantially the same result as if it had been so read: Dual-Use Items (Export Control) Regulations 2000, SI 2000/2620, reg 2(1).
3   Ibid reg 2(1). 'Exporter' and other cognate expressions are to be construed accordingly (except that where the export is to a destination outside the customs territory of the European Community, 'exporter' has the same meaning as in the definition in EC Council Regulation 1334/2000 setting up a Community regime for the control of exports of dual-use items and technology (OJ L159, 30.6.2000. p 1) art 2(c), to the extent that that definition applies): Dual-Use Items (Export Control) Regulations 2000, SI 2000/2620, reg 2(1). As to the customs territory of the European Community see CUSTOMS AND EXCISE vol 12(2) (Reissue) para 22.
4   As to the Secretary of State see para 2 ante. As to the transfer of certain functions of the Secretary of State, so far as exercisable in relation to Wales, to the National Assembly for Wales see para 1 note 2 ante.
5   A licence granted by the Secretary of State is the authorisation required by EC Council Regulation 1334/2000 (OJ L159, 30.6.2000, p 1) art 21(1) for the export to another member state of items listed in EC Council Regulation 1334/2000 (OJ L159, 30.6.2000, p 1) Annex IV: Dual-Use Items (Export Control) Regulations 2000, SI 2000/2620, reg 4(2).
6   Ibid reg 3(1). A Community Licence is the authorisation required by: (1) EC Council Regulation 1334/2000 (OJ L159, 30.6.2000, p 1) art 3(1) for the export from the European Community of any item listed in Annex I; and (2) art 4(1), (2), (3) for the export from the European Community of dual-use items not listed in Annex I: Dual-Use Items (Export Control) Regulations 2000, SI 2000/2620, reg 4(1). 'Community Licence' means an authorisation granted under EC Council Regulation 1334/2000 (OJ L159, 30.6.2000, p 1) or EC Council Regulation 3381/94 setting up a Community regime for the control of

exports of dual-use goods (OJ L 367, 31.12.94, p 1) by a competent authority for the export of dual-use items from the European Community: Dual-Use Items (Export Control) Regulations 2000, SI 2000/2620, reg 2(1).
7   Ibid reg 3(2)(a).
8   Ibid reg 3(2)(b).
9   Ibid reg 3(2)(c).
10 Ibid reg 3(2)(d).

617.   Prohibited items and exceptions.   The export[1] of the following items[2] is prohibited to certain destinations[3] unless the items are in transit[4]:

(1)   materials, chemicals, microorganisms and toxins[5];

(2)   telecommunications and information security equipment[6];

(3)   equipment, assemblies and components for marine use[7]; and

(4)   aircraft, space vehicles, propulsion systems and related equipment[8].

No person is permitted to make to any destination any export consisting of the transmission by fax, telephone or other electronic media of dual-use items in the form of software or technology which are items in transit[9] and which[10]:

(a)   that person (or, if that person is not within the United Kingdom, any agent of that person within the United Kingdom concerned in the export or intended export) has been informed by a competent authority[11] are or may be intended, in their entirety or in part, for use in connection with the development, production, handling, operation, maintenance, storage, detection, identification or dissemination of chemical, biological or nuclear weapons or other nuclear explosive devices, or the development, production, maintenance or storage of missiles capable of delivering such weapons[12]; or

(b)   that person is aware are intended, in their entirety or in part, for any of the uses referred to in head (a) above[13]; or

(c)   that person has grounds for suspecting are or may be intended, in their entirety or in part, for any of the uses referred to in head (a) above, unless that person has made all reasonable enquiries as to their proposed use and is satisfied that they will not be so used[14].

No person is permitted to export to any destination not in a member state any dual-use items which that person has grounds for suspecting are or may be intended, in their entirety or in part, for any of the uses referred to in head (a) above, unless that person has made all reasonable enquiries as to their proposed use and is satisfied that they will not be so used[15].

No person may export to a destination in a member state certain specified dual-use items[16] if that person knows at the time of export that the final destination of those items is outside the European Community and no processing or working is to be performed on those items in any member state to which they are to be exported[17]. This provision does not apply to items in transit[18].

None of the above provisions prohibits the export of any items in relation to which a licence in writing has been granted by the Secretary of State, provided that all conditions attaching to the licence are complied with[19].

No person is permitted to make any export consisting of the transmission by fax, telephone or other electronic media of dual-use items in the form of software or technology to certain destinations[20].

Nothing in the regulations controlling the export of dual-use items[21] prohibits the export[22] of:

(i)   any aircraft on a scheduled journey[23];

(ii)   any aircraft the immediately preceding import of which was on a scheduled journey and which is intended for further scheduled journeys[24];

(iii)   any vessel which is departing temporarily from the United Kingdom on trials[25]; and

(iv)   any vessel proceeding on a normal commercial journey[26].

1   For the meaning of 'export' see para 616 ante.
2   'Items' means both used and unused items: Dual-Use Items (Export Control) Regulations 2000, SI 2000/2620, reg 2(1).
3   See ibid reg 4(3)(a), Sch 2 (amended by SI 2000/3304; and SI 2001/1344): Dual-Use Items (Export Control) Regulations 2000, SI 2000/2620, reg 4(3)(a). Any person who contravenes reg 4(3) is guilty of an offence and may be arrested, and for these purposes the Customs and Excise Management Act 1979 s 68(2) (as amended) (see CUSTOMS AND EXCISE vol 12(2) (Reissue) para 1023) does not apply: Dual-Use Items (Export Control) Regulations 2000, SI 2000/2620, reg 11(1)(a). A person guilty of such an offence is liable on conviction on indictment to a fine or imprisonment for a term not exceeding two years or to both, or on summary conviction to a fine not exceeding the statutory maximum: reg 11(2). The offence under reg 11(1) is an arrestable offence within the meaning of the Police and Criminal Evidence Act 1984 s 24(2) (as amended) (see CRIMINAL LAW, EVIDENCE AND PROCEDURE vol 11(1) (Reissue) para 703): see the Dual-Use Items (Export Control) Regulations 2000, SI 2000/2620, reg 11(5). As to the statutory maximum see para 16 note 21 ante. As to the application of the Customs and Excise Management Act 1979 to offences under the Dual-Use Items (Export Control) Regulations 2000, SI 2000/2620 (as amended) see reg 12.
4   See ibid reg 5(2).
5   See ibid Sch 2, Category 1 (amended by SI 2000/3304). The export of some of these items (such as vaccines for protection against bacillus anthrax) is prohibited to any destination but some (eg certain chemical mixtures) may be exported to member states: see the Dual-Use Items (Export Control) Regulations 2000, SI 2000/2620, Sch 2, Category 1 (as so amended).
6   See ibid Sch 2, Category 5. Items under this heading may not be exported to any destination in Iran or Iraq: see Sch 2, Category 5.
7   See ibid Sch 2, Category 8 (amended by SI 2001/1344). Items under this heading may not be exported to any destination in Iran or Iraq: see the Dual-Use Items (Export Control) Regulations 2000, SI 2000/2620, Sch 2, Category 8 (as so amended).
8   See ibid Sch 2, Category 9 (amended by SI 2001/1344). Items under this heading may not be exported to any destination in Iran or Iraq: see the Dual-Use Items (Export Control) Regulations 2000, SI 2000/2620, Sch 2, Category 9 (as so amended).
9   'Items in transit' means: (1) items which only pass through the territory of the Community, that is those which are not assigned a customs-approved treatment or use other than the external transit procedure or which are merely placed in a free zone or free warehouse and where no record of them has to be kept in an approved stock record; and (2) items being exported to another member state which are not being transferred from the United Kingdom to that other member state within the meaning of EC Council Regulation 1334/2000 setting up a Community regime for the control of exports of dual-use items and technology (OJ L159, 30.6.2000, p 1) art 21: Dual-Use Items (Export Control) Regulations 2000, SI 2000/2620, reg 2(1); EC Council Regulation 1334/2000 (OJ L159, 30.6.2000, p 1) art 3(4). For the meaning of 'United Kingdom' see para 37 note 1 ante.
10 Dual-Use Items (Export Control) Regulations 2000, SI 2000/2620, reg 4(3)(b). As to the penalty for failure to comply with this provision see note 3 supra.
11 'Competent authority' means the Secretary of State or any authority empowered by another member state to grant export authorisations for dual-use items under EC Council Regulation 1334/2000 (OJ L159, 30.6.2000, p 1): Dual-Use Items (Export Control) Regulations 2000, SI 2000/2620, reg 2(1). As to the Secretary of State see para 2 ante. As to the transfer of certain functions of the Secretary of State, so far as exercisable in relation to Wales, to the National Assembly for Wales see para 1 note 2 ante.
12 Ibid reg 4(3)(b)(i).
13 Ibid reg 4(3)(b)(ii).
14 Ibid reg 4(3)(b)(iii).

15 Ibid reg 4(3)(c). As to the penalty for failure to comply with this provision see note 3 supra.

16 The items are: (1) any items listed in EC Council Regulation 1334/2000 (OJ L159, 30.6.2000, p 1) Annex I but not in Annex IV; (2) any items specified in the Dual-Use Items (Export Control) Regulations 2000, SI 2000/2620, Sch 2 (as amended) (see heads (1)–(4) in the text); or (3) any dual-use items not listed in EC Council Regulation 1334/2000 (OJ L159, 30.6.2000, p 1) Annex I and not specified in the Dual-Use Items (Export Control) Regulations 2000, SI 2000/2620, Sch 2 (as amended) but for the export of which from the European Community an authorisation is required in accordance with EC Council Regulation 1334/2000 (OJ L159, 30.6.2000, p 1) art 4(1), (2) or (3) or under art 4(4): Dual-Use Items (Export Control) Regulations 2000, SI 2000/2620, reg 4(3)(d)(i)–(iii).

17 Ibid reg 4(3)(d). As to the penalty for failure to comply with this provision see note 3 supra.

18 Ibid reg 5(2).

19 Ibid reg 4(4). As to licences to export dual-use items see para 616 ante.

20 Ibid reg 4(5). Such export is not permitted: (1) to any destination not in a member state, if the export is contrary to the restriction imposed by EC Council Regulation 1334/2000 (OJ L159, 30.6.2000, p 1) art 3(1); and (2) to any destination in a member state, if the export is contrary to the restriction imposed by art 21(1): Dual-Use Items (Export Control) Regulations 2000, SI 2000/2620, reg 4(5)(a), (b). Any person who contravenes reg 4(5)(a) with intent to evade the restriction imposed by EC Council Regulation 1334/2000 (OJ L159, 30.6.2000, p 1) art 3(1) or who contravenes the Dual-Use Items (Export Control) Regulations 2000, SI 2000/2620, reg 4(5)(b) with intent to evade the restriction imposed by EC Council Regulation 1334/2000 (OJ L159, 30.6.2000, p 1) art 21(1) is guilty of an offence and may be arrested, and for these purposes the Customs and Excise Management Act 1979 s 68(2) (as amended) (see CUSTOMS AND EXCISE vol 12(2) (Reissue) para 1023) does not apply: Dual-Use Items (Export Control) Regulations 2000, SI 2000/2620 reg 11(1)(a). A person guilty of such an offence is liable on conviction on indictment to a fine or imprisonment for a term not exceeding two years or to both, or on summary conviction to a fine not exceeding the statutory maximum: reg 11(2). Any person who contravenes reg 4(5) is guilty of an offence and is liable on summary conviction to a fine not exceeding level 3 on the standard scale: reg 11(4). See also note 3 supra. As to the standard scale see para 16 note 21 ante.

    Subject to the provisions of the Dual-Use Items (Export Control) Regulations 2000, SI 2000/2620 (as amended): (a) reg 4(5)(a) does not prohibit the export of any items under the authority of the Community General Export Authorisation, or in relation to which a licence in writing has been granted by the Secretary of State or a Community Licence has been granted by any competent authority, provided that all conditions applying to that Authorisation or attaching to the licence or Community Licence are complied with; and (b) reg 4(5)(b) does not prohibit the export of any items in relation to which a licence in writing has been granted by the Secretary of State provided that all conditions attaching to the licence are complied with: reg 4(6). 'The Community General Export Authorisation' means the export authorisation constituted by EC Council Regulation 1334/2000 (OJ L159, 30.6.2000, p 1) art 6(1), Annex II: Dual-Use Items (Export Control) Regulations 2000, SI 2000/2620, reg 2(1). For the meaning of 'Community Licence' see para 616 note 6 ante.

21 Ie the Dual-Use Items (Export Control) Regulations 2000, SI 2000/2620 (as amended).

22 'Import' and 'export' in relation to a vessel, submersible vehicle or aircraft includes the taking into or out of the United Kingdom of the vessel, submersible vehicle or aircraft notwithstanding that it is conveying goods or passengers, and whether or not it is moving under its own power; and cognate expressions are to be construed accordingly: ibid reg 2(1).'Vessel' includes any ship, surface effect vehicle, vessel of small waterplane area or hydrofoil, and the hull or part of the hull of a vessel: reg 2(1). 'Surface effect vehicle' means any air cushion vehicle (whether side wall or skirted) and any vehicle using the wing-in-ground effect for positive lift: reg 2(1).

23 Ibid reg 5(1)(a). 'Scheduled journey' means one of a series of journeys which are undertaken between the same two places and which together amount to a systematic service operated in such manner that its benefits are available to members of the public from time to time seeking to take advantage of it: reg 2(1).

24 Ibid reg 5(1)(b).

25 Ibid reg 5(1)(c).

26 Ibid reg 5(1)(d). 'Normal commercial journey' means a journey providing transport
    services in the ordinary course of business: reg 2(1).

618. Provision of information and record keeping. Not later than 30
days after any person first makes an export[1] from the United Kingdom[2] or
from the European Community under the authority of any licence[3] or
Community Licence[4], as the case may be, granted by the Secretary of State[5]
that does not provide otherwise[6], or any person established in the United
Kingdom first makes an export from the United Kingdom under the
authority of the Community General Export Authorisation[7], that person is
required to give to the Secretary of State written notice of certain
particulars[8] and of any changes to those particulars[9].

Any person established in the United Kingdom who exports any items
from the European Community under the authority of a Community
Licence, and any such person who exports any items from the United
Kingdom under the authority of the Community General Export
Authorisation, is required to maintain in relation to each such export
records that contain the following information[10]:

(1)   a description of the items[11];

(2)   the quantity of the items[12];

(3)   the person's name and address[13];

(4)   the name and address of any consignee of the items[14];

(5)   in so far as it is known to that person, the end-use of the items and
      the name and address of the end-user[15]; and

(6)   in the case of an export under the authority of a Community
      Licence, any further information required by the Community
      Licence to be kept[16].

These records must be kept for at least three years from the end of the
calendar year in which the export took place, and the person concerned
must permit any such records to be inspected and copied by any person
authorised by the Secretary of State or the Commissioners of Customs and
Excise[17].

Any person who has been granted a Community Licence[18] in relation to
the export from the European Community of any items must, upon request
in writing by the Secretary of State or the commissioners, produce any
documents or other records he may hold that relate to the application for
that Community Licence; and any such documents or records must be kept
for at least three years from the end of the calendar year in which such
application was made, and that person must permit any such documents or
records to be inspected and copied by any person authorised by the
Secretary of State or the commissioners[19].

Where any such documents or records are kept in a form which is not
legible the exporter must at the request of the person authorised by the
Secretary of State or the commissioners, as the case may be, reproduce such
documents or records in a legible form[20].

The information referred to in heads (1) to (5) above must also be kept in
relation to intra-Community transfers of dual-use items[21].

1   For the meaning of 'export' see para 616 ante.
2   For the meaning of 'United Kingdom' see para 37 note 1 ante.
3   As to licences see para 616 ante.
4   For the meaning of 'Community Licence' see para 616 note 6 ante.

5 As to the Secretary of State see para 2 ante. As to the transfer of certain functions of the Secretary of State, so far as exercisable in relation to Wales, to the National Assembly for Wales see para 1 note 2 ante.
6 Dual-Use Items (Export Control) Regulations 2000, SI 2000/2620, reg 9(1)(a).
7 Ibid reg 9(1)(b). For the meaning of 'the Community General Export Authorisation' see para 617 note 20 ante.
8 Ibid reg 9(1). The particulars are: (1) the name of the person; and (2) the address at which copies of the records referred to in reg 10 (see the text and notes 10–21 infra) may be inspected by any person authorised by the Secretary of State or the Commissioners of Customs and Excise under reg 10: reg 9(1)(i), (ii). Certain additional particulars must be given in the case of the export of any item listed in EC Council Regulation 1334/2000 setting up a Community regime for the control of exports of dual-use items and technology (OJ L159, 30.6.2000, p 1) Annex I, Category 5 Pt 2 but not specified in the Dual-Use Items (Export Control) Regulations 2000, SI 2000/2620, reg 9(3), Sch 3 Pt I: see reg 9(3), (4). For the meaning of 'items' see para 617 note 2 ante. As to the Commissioners of Customs and Excise see CUSTOMS AND EXCISE vol 12(2) (Reissue) para 905 et seq.
   Any person who fails to comply with reg 9 or reg 10 (see the text and notes 10–21 infra) is guilty of an offence and is liable on conviction on indictment to a fine or imprisonment for a term not exceeding two years, or to both, or on summary conviction to a fine not exceeding the statutory maximum: reg 11(3). As to the statutory maximum see para 16 note 21 ante.
9 See ibid reg 9(2). Any notice to be given by a person under this provision may be given by the agent of that person; and must be sent by post or delivered to the Secretary of State at the Applicant Services and Compliance Unit, Department of Trade and Industry, 4 Abbey Orchard Street, London SW1P 2HT: reg 9(5). As to the penalty for failure to comply with reg 9 see note 8 supra.
10 Ibid reg 10(1). As to the penalty for failure to comply with reg 10 see note 8 supra.
11 Ibid reg 10(1)(a).
12 Ibid reg 10(1)(b).
13 Ibid reg 10(1)(c).
14 Ibid reg 10(1)(d).
15 Ibid reg 10(1)(e).
16 Ibid reg 10(1)(f).
17 Ibid reg 10(2). Any person authorised by the Secretary of State or the commissioners may, on producing if required to do so a duly authenticated document showing his authority, at any reasonable hour enter the premises of which the address has most recently been notified to the Secretary of State under reg 9 (see the text and notes 6–9 supra): reg 10(4)(a). As to the penalty for failure to comply with reg 10 see note 8 supra.
18 Ie granted such a licence under the Dual-Use Items (Export Control) Regulations 2000, SI 2000/2620: see para 616 ante.
19 Ibid reg 10(3). Any person authorised by the Secretary of State or the commissioners may, on producing if required to do so a duly authenticated document showing his authority, at any reasonable hour enter any premises of which the address has been notified for this purpose by the exporter to a competent authority when applying for a licence: reg 10(4)(b). As to the penalty for failure to comply with reg 10 see note 8 supra.
20 Ibid reg 10(5). As to the penalty for failure to comply with reg 10 see note 8 supra.
21 See ibid reg 10(6), (7); EC Council Regulation 1334/2000 (OJ L159, 30.6.2000, p 1) art 21(5). The Dual-Use Items (Export Control) Regulations 2000, SI 2000/2620, reg 10(4), (5) (see the text and notes 17–20 supra) also apply to such transfers: see reg 10(6). As to the penalty for failure to comply with reg 10 see note 8 supra.

619. Customs and Excise powers. Certain dual-use items[1] may be detained by the proper officer of Customs and Excise as if they were liable to forfeiture if and so long as that officer has reason to believe that a competent authority[2] (after, if necessary, having had the impending export brought to its attention) might inform the exporter that the items in question may be intended for use in connection with chemical, biological or nuclear weapons, or be intended for a military end-use[3].

Where: (1) a Community Licence has been granted by a competent authority in another member state for the export of any items to any destination outside the European Community[4]; (2) the export of any items is authorised by the Community General Export Authorisation[5]; or (3) items, of which the exporter[6] is established in a member state other than the United Kingdom but not in the United Kingdom, are or have been detained[7], the Secretary of State[8] may give notice to the proper officer of Customs and Excise that he considers that export of the items would be contrary to the essential foreign policy or security interests, or to the fulfilment of the international obligations or commitments, of the United Kingdom; and in such a case the export is prohibited notwithstanding, in a case within head (1) above the grant of the Community Licence, or in a case within head (2) above the Community General Export Authorisation[9].

In the case of an export which includes the transmission of software or technology by fax, telephone or other electronic media, the Secretary of State must send a copy of any such notice given to the exporter (or, if the exporter is not within the United Kingdom, any agent of the exporter within the United Kingdom concerned in the export or intended export)[10].

Certain items[11] in relation to which a Community Licence has been granted which are brought to any place in the United Kingdom for the purpose of being exported to a destination outside the European Community may be detained by the proper officer of Customs and Excise for a period of ten working days as if they were liable to forfeiture where that officer or the Secretary of State has grounds for suspicion that relevant information was not taken into account when the Community Licence was granted, or circumstances have materially changed since the issue of the Community Licence[12].

Any exporter must, if so required by the Commissioners of Customs and Excise, furnish within such time as they may allow proof to their satisfaction that the items exported have reached either: (a) a destination to which they were authorised to be exported by the Community General Export Authorisation or by a Community Licence or by a licence granted for the purposes of the regulations controlling the export of dual-use items[13]; or (b) a destination to which their export was not prohibited by those regulations, and an exporter who fails to do so is guilty of an offence[14] unless he proves that he did not consent to or connive at the items reaching any destination other than such a destination[15].

1   Ie dual-use items not listed in EC Council Regulation 1334/2000 setting up a Community regime for the control of exports of dual-use items and technology (OJ L159, 30.6.2000, p 1) Annex I, in relation to which a Community Licence has not been granted and which are brought to any place in the United Kingdom for the purpose of being exported to a destination outside the European Community, not being items which only pass through the territory of the Community, that is those which are not assigned a customs-approved treatment or use other than the external transit procedure or which are merely placed in a free zone or free warehouse and where no record of them has to be kept in an approved stock record: art 3(4); Dual-Use Items (Export Control) Regulations 2000, SI 2000/2620, reg 6(1). For the meaning of 'Community Licence' see para 616 note 6 ante; for the meaning of 'items' see para 617 note 2 ante; and for the meaning of 'United Kingdom' see para 37 note 1 ante.

2   For the meaning of 'competent authority' see para 617 note 11 ante.

3   Dual-Use Items (Export Control) Regulations 2000, SI 2000/2620, reg 6(1); EC Council Regulation 1334/2000 (OJ L159, 30.6.2000, p 1) art 4(1), (2), (3).

4   Dual-Use Items (Export Control) Regulations 2000, SI 2000/2620, reg 6(2)(a).

5   Ibid reg 6(2)(b). For the meaning of 'the Community General Export Authorisation' see para 617 note 20 ante.

6   For the meaning of 'exporter' see para 616 ante.

7   Dual-Use Items (Export Control) Regulations 2000, SI 2000/2620, reg 6(2)(c).

8   As to the Secretary of State see para 2 ante. As to the transfer of certain functions of the Secretary of State, so far as exercisable in relation to Wales, to the National Assembly for Wales see para 1 note 2 ante.

9   Dual-Use Items (Export Control) Regulations 2000, SI 2000/2620, reg 6(2). Any person who contravenes reg 6(2) is guilty of an offence and may be arrested, and for these purposes the Customs and Excise Management Act 1979 s 68(2) (as amended) (see CUSTOMS AND EXCISE vol 12(2) (Reissue) para 1023) does not apply: Dual-Use Items (Export Control) Regulations 2000, SI 2000/2620 reg 11(1)(a). A person guilty of such an offence is liable on conviction on indictment to a fine or imprisonment for a term not exceeding two years or to both, or on summary conviction to a fine not exceeding the statutory maximum: reg 11(2). As to the statutory maximum see para 16 note 21 ante. The offence under reg 11(1) is an arrestable offence within the meaning of the Police and Criminal Evidence Act 1984 s 24(2) (as amended) (see CRIMINAL LAW, EVIDENCE AND PROCEDURE vol 11(1) (Reissue) para 703): see the Dual-Use Items (Export Control) Regulations 2000, SI 2000/2620, reg 11(5). As to the application of the Customs and Excise Management Act 1979 to offences under the Dual-Use Items (Export Control) Regulations 2000, SI 2000/2620 (as amended) see reg 12.

10 Ibid reg 6(3). Such notice must be given at the address stated in the particulars given under reg 9(1) or (2) (see para 618 ante), or if no such particulars have been given: (1) if the exporter or agent is a body corporate, at the address of its registered or principal office in the United Kingdom; or (2) in any other case, at the usual or last known address in the United Kingdom of the exporter or agent (whether of the exporter's or agent's residence or a place where the exporter or agent carries on business): reg 6(3)(a), (b).

11 Ie items listed in EC Council Regulation 1334/2000 (OJ L159, 30.6.2000, p 1) Annex I.

12 Dual-Use Items (Export Control) Regulations 2000, SI 2000/2620, reg 6(4). The period must be extended to 30 working days where the Secretary of State certifies that a request for such an extension in accordance with EC Council Regulation 1334/2000 (OJ L159, 30.6.2000, p 1) art 12.4 has been received from the member state which granted the licence: Dual-Use Items (Export Control) Regulations 2000, SI 2000/2620, reg 6(4) proviso.

13 Ie the Dual-Use Items (Export Control) Regulations 2000, SI 2000/2620 (as amended). As to the Commissioners of Customs and Excise see CUSTOMS AND EXCISE vol 12(2) (Reissue) para 905 et seq.

14 A person guilty of such an offence is liable on summary conviction to a fine not exceeding level 4 on the standard scale: ibid reg 6(5). As to the standard scale see para 16 note 21 ante.

15 Ibid reg 6(5).

620. Misleading applications and failure to comply with licence conditions. For the purposes of obtaining any licence from the Secretary of State[1] or any Community Licence[2] from any competent authority[3] no person is to make any statement or furnish any document or information which to that person's knowledge is false in a material particular[4], or recklessly make any statement or furnish any document or information which is false in a material particular[5]. Any licence or Community Licence which may have been granted by the Secretary of State in connection with an application for which a false statement was made or a false document or information was furnished is void as from the time it was granted[6].

Any person is guilty of an offence[7] who:

(1)   has exported items[8] from (a) the United Kingdom[9] under the authority of a licence granted by the Secretary of State or of the Community General Export Authorisation[10]; (b) the European Community under the authority of a Community Licence granted by the Secretary of State[11]; or (c) the European Community under the authority of a Community Licence sought by or on behalf of a person in, or established in, the United Kingdom[12]; and

(2)   fails to comply with any condition attaching to that licence or Community Licence or applying on use of the Community General Export Authorisation, as the case may be[13].

No person is guilty of such an offence where:

(i)   as the case may be (A) in the case of a licence the condition in question had been previously modified without that person's consent by the Secretary of State; (B) in the case of a Community Licence the condition in question had been previously modified without that person's consent by the Secretary of State or other competent authority which granted that Community Licence; or (C) in the case of the Community General Export Authorisation the condition in question had been previously modified[14];

(ii)   the alleged failure to comply would not have been a failure had the licence, Community Licence or Community General Export Authorisation not been so modified[15]; and

(iii) that person proves that the items in relation to which he has failed to comply with the condition had, at the time the condition was modified, been exported from the United Kingdom in the case of a licence or from the European Community in the case of a Community Licence or the Community General Export Authorisation[16].

1   As to the Secretary of State see para 2 ante. As to the transfer of certain functions of the Secretary of State, so far as exercisable in relation to Wales, to the National Assembly for Wales see para 1 note 2 ante. As to licences see para 616 ante.

2   For the meaning of 'Community Licence' see para 616 note 6 ante.

3   For the meaning of 'competent authority' see para 616 note 11 ante.

4   Dual-Use Items (Export Control) Regulations 2000, SI 2000/2620, reg 7(a).

5   Ibid reg 7(b).

6   Ibid reg 7. Any person who fails to comply with reg 7 is guilty of an offence and is liable on conviction on indictment to a fine or imprisonment for a term not exceeding two years, or to both, or on summary conviction to a fine not exceeding the statutory maximum: reg 11(3). As to the statutory maximum see para 16 note 21 ante.

7   A person guilty of such an offence is liable on summary conviction to a fine not exceeding the statutory maximum, and on conviction on indictment to a fine or imprisonment for a term not exceeding two years, or to both: ibid reg 8(2).

8   For the meaning of 'export' see para 616 ante; and For the meaning of 'items' see para 617 note 2 ante..

9   For the meaning of 'United Kingdom' see para 37 note 1 ante.

10   Dual-Use Items (Export Control) Regulations 2000, SI 2000/2620, reg 8(1)(a)(i). For the meaning of 'the Community General Export Authorisation' see para 617 note 20 ante.

11   Ibid reg 8(1)(a)(ii).

12   Ibid reg 8(1)(a)(iii).

13   Ibid reg 8(1)(b).

14   Ibid reg 8(3)(a).

15   Ibid reg 8(3)(b).

16   Ibid reg 8(3)(c).

D. PARTICULAR GOODS

621. Control under particular enactments. In addition to general controls on imports and exports, many enactments place particular restrictions on the importation or exportation of particular goods. Most of these restrictions, which are dealt with specifically elsewhere in this work, are on importation, often with a view to the prevention of the spread of disease or the control of dangerous things[1]. Such restrictions may, however, be modified so as to allow the importation of goods from other EC member states[2]. The export of dangerous chemicals is controlled under Community law[3].

Restrictions may also be imposed by Order in Council under the United Nations Act 1946[4] in order to give effect to sanctions imposed by the United Nations Security Council[5]; and the Secretary of State[6] has power to require persons carrying on business in the United Kingdom[7] to give him notice of any requirement or prohibition imposed or threatened to be imposed on those persons by measures by or under the law of any overseas country for regulating or controlling international trade which may be damaging to the trading interests of the United Kingdom, and to prohibit compliance with any such measures[8].

1   See eg the Anthrax Prevention Order 1971, SI 1971/1234 (as amended); and PROTECTION OF ENVIRONMENT AND PUBLIC HEALTH vol 38 (Reissue) para 446.

2   See eg ibid arts 4, 5 (amended by SI 1993/745). As to the free movement of goods within the European Union see EUROPEAN COMMUNITIES.

3   See the Export of Dangerous Chemicals Regulations 1992, SI 1992/2415, made by the Secretary of State in exercise of powers conferred by the European Communities Act 1972 s 2(2) in order to give effect to EEC Council Regulation 2455/92 concerning the export and import of certain dangerous chemicals (OJ L251, 29.8.92, p 13) which aims to establish a common system of notification and information for imports from and exports to countries which are not member states. The Health and Safety Commission is the designated authority competent for these notification and information procedures: Export of Dangerous Chemicals Regulations 1992, SI 1992/2415, reg 2. As to the Health and Safety Commission see HEALTH AND SAFETY AT WORK vol 20 (Reissue) para 457 et seq. An exporter must not provide information pursuant to the Community law requirements knowing it to be false or misleading in a material particular or being reckless as to whether it is false or misleading in a material particular (reg 3); and the enforcement and offences provisions of the Health and Safety at Work etc Act 1974 apply to any requirement or prohibition imposed upon an exporter by EEC Council Regulation 2455/92 (OJ L251, 29.8.92, p 13) or by the Export of Dangerous Chemicals Regulations 1992, SI 1992/2415 as if the requirement or prohibition concerned had been imposed by regulations made under the Health and Safety at Work etc Act 1974 s 15 (as amended) (see HEALTH AND SAFETY AT WORK vol 20 (Reissue) paras 559–560): Export of Dangerous Chemicals Regulations 1992, SI 1992/2415, reg 4(1). The Health and Safety (Enforcing Authority) Regulations 1989, SI 1989/1903 (see now the Health and Safety (Enforcing Authority) Regulations 1998, SI 1998/494 (as amended); and HEALTH AND SAFETY AT WORK vol 20 (Reissue) paras 469–470), do not, however, apply to any such requirement or prohibition: Export of Dangerous Chemicals Regulations 1992, SI 1992/2415, reg 4(2).

4   Ie under the United Nations Act 1946 s 1 (as amended): see FOREIGN RELATIONS LAW vol 18(2) (Reissue) para 1006.

5   See eg the Libya (United Nations Sanctions) Order 1993, SI 1993/2807; and CONSTITUTIONAL LAW AND HUMAN RIGHTS vol 8(2) (Reissue) para 808.

6   As to the Secretary of State see para 2 ante. As to the transfer of certain functions of the Secretary of State, so far as exercisable in relation to Wales, to the National Assembly for Wales see para 1 note 2 ante.

7   For the meaning of 'United Kingdom' see para 37 note 1 ante.

8   See the Protection of Trading Interests Act 1980 s 1; and FOREIGN RELATIONS LAW vol 18(2) (Reissue) para 813.

(2) EXCISE RESTRICTIONS

622. Excise licences. An excise licence[1] must be in such form and contain such particulars as the Commissioners of Customs and Excise[2] direct and, subject to any enactment relating to the licence or trade in question, may be granted by the proper officer[3] on payment of any appropriate duty[4]. If any person who is the holder of an excise licence to carry on any trade or to manufacture or sell any goods fails to produce his licence for examination within one month after being so requested by an officer, his failure attracts a penalty[5].

1 As to excise licences generally see CUSTOMS AND EXCISE vol 12(2) (Reissue) para 678 et seq; INTOXICATING LIQUOR vol 26 (Reissue) para 15.

2 As to the Commissioners of Customs and Excise see CUSTOMS AND EXCISE vol 12(2) (Reissue) para 905 et seq.

3 Subject to the Customs and Excise Management Act 1979 s 8(2), which enables any person to be engaged in customs and excise duties (see CUSTOMS AND EXCISE vol 12(2) (Reissue) para 906), 'officer' means a person commissioned by the Commissioners of Customs and Excise; and 'proper', in relation to the person by, with or to whom, or the place at which, anything is to be done, means the person or place appointed or authorised in that behalf by the commissioners: s 1(1).

4 Ibid s 101(1) (amended by the Finance Act 1986 s 8(6), Sch 5 para 1). An excise licence for the carrying on of a trade is to be granted in respect of one set of premises only, but a licence for the same trade may be granted to the same person in respect of each of two or more sets of premises: Customs and Excise Management Act 1979 s 101(2). Where an excise licence trade is carried on at any set of premises by two or more persons in partnership, then, subject to any special provisions relating to the licence trade in question, not more than one licence is required to be held by those persons in respect of those premises at any one time: s 101(3) (amended by the Finance Act 1986 Sch 5 para 1).

5 Customs and Excise Management Act 1979 s 101(4) (amended by the Finance Act 1994 s 9(9), Sch 4 para 5). The penalty is under the Finance Act 1994 s 9 (as amended) (civil penalties): see CUSTOMS AND EXCISE vol 12(2) (Reissue) para 1218.

623. Hydrocarbon oils. With a view to the protection of the revenue[1] the Commissioners of Customs and Excise[2] may make regulations: (1) prohibiting the production of hydrocarbon oil[3] except by a person holding a licence; (2) specifying the circumstances in which any such licence may be surrendered or revoked; (3) regulating the production, storage and warehousing[4] of hydrocarbon oil and the removal of any such oil to or from premises used in its production; (4) prohibiting the refining of hydrocarbon oil elsewhere than in a refinery[5]; (5) prohibiting the incorporation of gas in hydrocarbon oil elsewhere than in a refinery; and (6) regulating the use and storage of hydrocarbon oil in a refinery[6]. They may also protect the revenue by (a) regulating or prohibiting the removal to a refinery of hydrocarbon oil in respect of which any rebate[7] has been allowed; (b) regulating the removal of imported hydrocarbon oil to a refinery without payment of the excise duty on such oil; (c) making provision for securing payment of the excise duty on any imported hydrocarbon oil received into a refinery; (d) relieving from the excise duty chargeable on hydrocarbon oil produced in the United Kingdom[8] any such oil intended for exportation or shipment[9] as stores[10]; (e) conferring power to require information relating to the supply or use of aviation gasoline[11] to be given by producers, dealers and users; and (f) requiring producers and users of and dealers in aviation gasoline to keep and produce records relating to aviation gasoline[12].

Where any person contravenes or fails to comply with such a regulation his contravention or failure to comply attracts a penalty[13] and any goods[14] in respect of which any person contravenes or fails to comply with any such regulation are liable to forfeiture[15].

In addition to the above provisions, the Secretary of State[16] is empowered to make regulations for the implementation of EC Treaty[17] obligations in relation to the conditions for granting and using authorisations for the prospection, exploration and production of hydrocarbons[18].

1 As to revenue and excise duties on hydrocarbon oil see CUSTOMS AND EXCISE vol 12(2) (Reissue) para 530 et seq (excise duties).

2 As to the Commissioners of Customs and Excise see CUSTOMS AND EXCISE vol 12(2) (Reissue) para 905 et seq.

3   'Hydrocarbon oil' means petroleum oil, coal tar and oil produced from coal, shale, peat or any other bituminous substance, and all liquid hydrocarbons, but does not include such hydrocarbons or bituminous or asphaltic substances as are (1) solid or semi-solid at a temperature of 15° C; or (2) gaseous at a temperature of 15° C and under a pressure of 1013.25 millibars: Hydrocarbon Oil Duties Act 1979 ss 1(2), 27(1).

4   'Warehouse', except in the expressions 'Queen's warehouse' and 'distiller's warehouse', means a place of security approved by the Commissioners of Customs and Excise under the Customs and Excise Management Act 1979 s 92(1) (excise warehouse) or s 92(2) (customs warehouse) or both s 92(1) and s 92(2) and, except in s 92, also includes a distiller's warehouse; and 'warehoused' and cognate expressions are, subject to s 92(4) and any regulations made by virtue of s 93(2)(da)(i) or (e) or (4), construed accordingly: s 1(1) (amended by the Finance (No 2) Act 1992 s 3, Sch 2 para 1); definition applied by the Hydrocarbon Oil Duties Act 1979 s 27(3).

5   'Refinery' means any premises which: (1) are approved by the Commissioners of Customs and Excise for the treatment of hydrocarbon oil; or (2) are approved by them for the production of energy for use in the treatment of hydrocarbon oil at such approved premises or in the production of hydrocarbon oil at other premises used for the production of such oil; and the commissioners may approve any such premises if it appears to them that more than one-third of the energy will be produced for such use: ibid s 27(1) (definition substituted by the Finance Act 1981 s 5(3)). If in the case of any premises which the commissioners can approve it appears to them appropriate to do so, they may direct that the provisions of the Hydrocarbon Oil Duties Act 1979 (other than the definition of 'refinery') applies to them as if, instead of being a refinery, they were other premises used for the production of hydrocarbon oil: s 27(1A) (added by the Finance Act 1981 s 5(4)).

6   Hydrocarbon Oil Duties Act 1979 s 21(1)(a), Sch 3 Pt I paras 1–6 (amended by the Finance Act 1986 s 8(6), Sch 5 para 4). In the case of regulations made for the purposes of the Hydrocarbon Oil Duties Act 1979 Sch 3 Pt I (paras 1–11), different regulations may be made for different classes of hydrocarbon oil; and the power to make such regulations must include power to make regulations: (1) regulating the allowance and payment of drawback under or by virtue of the Hydrocarbon Oil Duties Act 1979 s 15 (drawback of duty on exportation etc of certain goods) (see CUSTOMS AND EXCISE vol 12(2) (Reissue) para 565); and (2) for making the allowance and payment of drawback by virtue of an order under s 15(2) subject to such conditions as the commissioners see fit to impose for the protection of the revenue: s 21(2)(a), (b). Any power to make regulations under the Hydrocarbon Oil Duties Act 1979 is exercisable by statutory instrument, subject to annulment in pursuance of a resolution of either House of Parliament: s 25. See the Hydrocarbon Oil Regulations 1973, SI 1973/1311 (amended by SI 1976/443; SI 1977/1868; SI 1981/1134; SI 1985/1033; SI 1985/1450; SI 1992/3149; SI 1993/2267;SI 1994/694; and SI 1996/2537), which were originally made under the Hydrocarbon Oil (Customs and Excise) Act 1971 (repealed) but now have effect under the Hydrocarbon Oil Duties Act 1979 ss 21, 24, Sch 3 Pts I, II, Sch 4 by virtue of s 28(6) and the Interpretation Act 1978 s 17(2)(b). By virtue of the Hydrocarbon Oil Duties Act 1979 s 20AA (as added), s 24 (as amended), the regulations also cover the granting of reliefs, the mixing of oil, the marking of oil, the control of storage and supply of oil, the keeping of records and the entry of premises: CUSTOMS AND EXCISE vol 12(2) (Reissue) para 566. The sampling of oil is governed by the Hydrocarbon Oil Duties Act 1979 s 24(5), Sch 5: see CUSTOMS AND EXCISE vol 12(2) (Reissue) para 596.

7   'Rebate' means rebate of duty under ibid ss 11, 13A, 14 or 20B (as added and amended) (see CUSTOMS AND EXCISE vol 12(2) (Reissue) para 552 et seq) and 'rebated' has a corresponding meaning: Hydrocarbon Oil Duties Act 1979 s 27(1) (definition amended by the Finance Act 1987 s 1(3), (4); and the Finance Act 2001 s 3(3)).

8   For the meaning of 'United Kingdom' see para 37 note 1 ante.

9   'Shipment' includes loading into an aircraft, and 'shipped' and cognate expressions must be construed accordingly: Customs and Excise Management Act 1979 s 1(1); definitions applied by the Hydrocarbon Oil Duties Act 1979 s 27(3).

10   For the meaning of 'stores' see the Customs and Excise Management Act 1979 s 1(1); and para 604 note 6 ante; definition applied by the Hydrocarbon Oil Duties Act 1979 s 27(3).

11   'Aviation gasoline' means light oil which is specially produced as fuel for aircraft, is not normally used in road vehicles, and is delivered for use solely as fuel for aircraft: ibid s 27(1) (definition added by the Finance Act 1982 s 4(1)). 'Light oil' means hydrocarbon oil of which at least 90% by volume distils at a temperature not exceeding 210° C, or which gives off an inflammable vapour at a temperature of less than 23° C when tested in the manner prescribed by the Acts relating to petroleum: Hydrocarbon Oil Duties

Act 1979 ss 1(3), 27(1). 'Road vehicle' means a vehicle constructed or adapted for use on roads but does not include any vehicle which is an excepted vehicle within the meaning given by Sch 1: s 27(1) (definition amended by the Finance Act 1995 s 8(1), (3)).

12　Hydrocarbon Oil Duties Act 1979 Sch 3 Pt I paras 7–10C (para 10A added by the Finance Act 1982 s 4(5); and substituted by the Finance Act 1990 s 3(5); and the Hydrocarbon Oil Duties Act 1979 Sch 3 paras 10B, 10C added by the Finance Act 1982 s 4(5)). Power is also conferred for securing and collecting the excise duty chargeable on hydrocarbon oil: Hydrocarbon Oil Duties Act 1979 Sch 3 Pt I para 11 (amended by the Finance Act 1985 Sch 4 para 4, Sch 27 Pt I). See CUSTOMS AND EXCISE vol 12(2) (Reissue) para 590.

13　Ie a penalty under the Finance Act 1994 s 9 (as amended) (civil penalties): see CUSTOMS AND EXCISE vol 12(2) (Reissue) para 1218.

14　For the meaning of 'goods' see the Customs and Excise Management Act 1979 s 1(1); and para 604 note 6 ante; definition applied by the Hydrocarbon Oil Duties Act 1979 s 27(3).

15　Ibid s 21(3) (amended by the Finance Act 1994 s 9(9), Sch 4 para 55).

16　As to the Secretary of State see para 2 ante. As to the transfer of certain functions of the Secretary of State, so far as exercisable in relation to Wales, to the National Assembly for Wales see para 1 note 2 ante.

17　Ie the Treaty Establishing the European Community (Rome, 25 March 1957; TS 1 (1973); Cmnd 5179).

18　See the European Communities (Designation) (No 2) Order 1994, SI 1994/1327, made under the European Communities Act 1972 s 2(2).

624.　Licence to methylate or deal wholesale in methylated spirits.

Any distiller, rectifier or compounder[1] may be authorised by the Commissioners of Customs and Excise[2] to methylate spirits[3], and any person not so authorised may only methylate spirits or deal wholesale[4] in methylated spirits if he holds an excise licence as a methylator[5] or in the case of dealing wholesale is exempted by regulations from holding such a licence[6]. The commissioners may at any time revoke or suspend any such authorisation or licence[7].

1　'Distiller' means a person holding a distiller's licence under the Alcoholic Liquor Duties Act 1979 s 12 (see CUSTOMS AND EXCISE vol 12(2) (Reissue) paras 428–429); 'rectifier' means a person holding a licence as a rectifier under s 18 (see CUSTOMS AND EXCISE vol 12(2) (Reissue) para 440); and 'compounder' means a person holding a licence as a compounder under s 18 (see CUSTOMS AND EXCISE vol 12(2) (Reissue) para 440): s 4(1).

2　As to the Commissioners of Customs and Excise see CUSTOMS AND EXCISE vol 12(2) (Reissue) para 905 et seq.

3　Alcoholic Liquor Duties Act 1979 s 75(1) (prospectively amended by the Finance Act 1995 s 5(5)–(7), Sch 2 para 5 as from a day to be appointed). Any person so authorised is referred to as an 'authorised methylator': Alcoholic Liquor Duties Act 1979 s 4(1) (prospectively amended by the Finance Act 1995 Sch 2 para 1 as from a day to be appointed). 'Spirits' means, subject to the Alcoholic Liquor Duties Act 1979 s 1(7)–(9) (as amended) (see CUSTOMS AND EXCISE vol 12(2) (Reissue) para 411): (1) spirits of any description which are of a strength exceeding 1.2%; (2) any such mixture, compound or preparation made with spirits as is of a strength exceeding 1.2%; or (3) liquors contained, with any spirits, in any mixture which is of a strength exceeding 1.2%, but does not include methylated spirits: s 1(2) (amended by the Excise Duty (Amendment of the Alcoholic Liquor Duties Act 1979; and the Hydrocarbon Oil Duties Act 1979) Regulations 1992, SI 1992/3158; and prospectively amended by the Finance Act 1995 s 162, Sch 29 Pt 1 as from a day to be appointed). 'Methylated spirits' means spirits mixed in the United Kingdom with some other substance in accordance with regulations made under the Alcoholic Liquor Duties Act 1979 s 77 (as amended) (see CUSTOMS AND EXCISE vol 12(2) (Reissue) para 526) or spirits mixed outside the United Kingdom with some other substance, if the spirits and other substance, and the proportions in which they are mixed, are such as prescribed by those regulations for the production of methylated spirits in the United Kingdom: s 4(1) (amended by the Finance Act 1990 s 8(1); and prospectively repealed by the Finance Act 1995 s 162, Sch 29 Pt I as from a day to be appointed). References in these provisions to methylated spirits are to be construed as including references to denatured alcohol of any description from time to time specified in regulations made for the purpose of the Finance Act 1993 s 8(1): s 8(2)(a) (s 8 prospectively repealed by the Finance Act 1995 Sch 29 Pt I as from a day to be appointed).

At the date at which this volume states the law, no such regulations had been made. For the meaning of 'United Kingdom' see para 37 note 1 ante.

4   'Dealing wholesale' means the sale at any one time to any one person of a quantity of methylated spirits of not less than 20 litres or such smaller quantity as the commissioners may by regulations specify: Alcoholic Liquor Duties Act 1979 s 75(7) (amended by the Alcoholic Liquors (Amendment of Enactments Relating to Strength and to Units of Measurement) Order 1979, SI 1979/241, art 33; and prospectively amended by the Finance Act 1995 s 5(5)–(7), Sch 2 para 5 as from a day to be appointed). At the date at which this volume states the law, no such regulations had been made.

5   Alcoholic Liquor Duties Act 1979 s 75(2) (prospectively amended by the Finance Act 1995 Sch 2 para 5 as from a day to be appointed). Where any person not being an authorised methylator (see note 3 supra), methylates spirits otherwise than under and in accordance with a licence under the Alcoholic Liquor Duties Act 1979 s 75 (as amended) (see CUSTOMS AND EXCISE vol 12(2) (Reissue) para 526) his doing so will attract a penalty under the Finance Act 1994 s 9 (as amended) (civil penalties) (see CUSTOMS AND EXCISE vol 12(2) (Reissue) para 1218): Alcoholic Liquor Duties Act 1979 s 75(5) (amended by the Finance Act 1994 s 9, Sch 4 para 45; and prospectively amended by the Finance Act 1995 Sch 2 para 5 as from a day to be appointed). As to excise licences generally see para 622 ante.

6   See the Alcoholic Liquor Duties Act 1979 s 77(1)(d) (amended by the Finance Act 1981 s 11(1), Sch 8 para 23(a); and prospectively amended by the Finance Act 1995 Sch 2 para 5 as from a day to be appointed). As to the penalties for failing to comply with regulations made under the Alcoholic Liquor Duties Act 1979 s 77 (as amended) see para 625 post.

7   Ibid s 75(6).

625.   Manufacture, storage and transfer of methylated spirits.   With a view to the protection of the revenue the Commissioners of Customs and Excise[1] may make regulations[2]:

(1)   regulating the methylation of spirits[3] and the supply, storage, removal, sale, delivery, receipt, use and exportation or shipment[4] as stores[5] of methylated spirits[6].

(2)   prescribing the spirits which may be used, and the substances which may be mixed with them, for methylation[7];

(3)   permitting spirits to be methylated in warehouse[8];

(4)   permitting dealing wholesale[9] without a licence in specified methylated spirits[10];

(5)   regulating the importation, receipt, removal, storage and use of spirits for methylation[11];

(6)   regulating the storage and removal of substances to be used in methylating spirits[12];

(7)   prescribing the manner in which account is to be kept of stocks of methylated spirits in the possession of authorised or licensed methylators[13] and of retailers[14] of methylated spirits[15];

(8)   for securing any duty[16] chargeable in respect of methylated spirits of any class[17].

If any person contravenes or fails to comply with any such regulation, or with any condition, restriction or requirement imposed under such a regulation, his contravention or failure to comply attracts a penalty[18]. If, save as permitted by any regulation, any person deals wholesale in methylated spirits otherwise than under and in accordance with a licence[19], his doing so attracts a penalty[20], and any spirits or methylated spirits in respect of which there is such a contravention or failure to comply or any such dealing is liable to forfeiture[21]. If any person authorised by the regulations to supply any kind of methylated spirits knowingly supplies such spirits to any person not authorised to receive them, then, without prejudice to any penalty he may have incurred, he must pay the duty payable on the spirits[22]. If any person other than an authorised or licensed methylator has in his possession any methylated spirits obtained otherwise than from a person authorised by regulations to supply those spirits, his having them in his possession attracts a penalty[23] and the methylated spirits are liable to forfeiture[24].

1   As to the Commissioners of Customs and Excise see CUSTOMS AND EXCISE vol 12(2) (Reissue) para 905 et seq.

2   The power to make regulations is exercisable by statutory instrument (Alcoholic Liquor Duties Act 1979 s 90(1)), and any such statutory instrument is subject to annulment in pursuance of a resolution of either House of Parliament (s 90(2)). Different regulations may be made under s 77 (as amended) with respect to different classes of methylated spirits or different kinds of methylated spirits of any class: s 77(2) (prospectively amended by the Finance Act 1995 s 5(5)–(7), Sch 2 para 5 as from a day to be appointed). Without prejudice to the generality of the Alcoholic Liquor Duties Act 1979 s 77(1) (as amended), regulations may: (1) provide for the imposition of conditions and restrictions relating to the matters there mentioned; and (2) frame any provision of the regulations with respect to the supply, receipt or use of denatured alcohol by reference to matters to be contained from time to time in a notice published in accordance with the regulations by the commissioners and having effect until withdrawn in accordance with the regulations; and (3) impose or provide for the imposition of requirements on authorised or licensed methylators and on retailers of methylated spirits to keep and preserve records relating to their businesses as such and to produce them to an officer when required to do so for the purposes of allowing him to inspect them, copy or take extracts from them or remove them at a reasonable time and for a reasonable period: s 77(2)(a), (aa), (b) (amended by the Finance Act 1981 s 11(1), Sch 8 para 23(b); prospectively amended by the Finance Act 1995 s 5(5)–(7), Sch 2 para 5 as from a day to be appointed; and the Alcoholic Liquor Duties Act 1979 s 77(2)(aa) prospectively added by the Finance Act 1995 Sch 2 para 6 as from a day to be appointed). Where documents removed under this power are lost or damaged, the commissioners are liable to compensate their owner for any expenses reasonably incurred by him in replacing or repairing them: Alcoholic Liquor Duties Act 1979 s 77(2A) (added by the Finance Act 1981 Sch 8 para 23(b)).

See the Methylated Spirits Regulations 1987, SI 1987/2009, which make provision as to premises and plant (regs 3–7), the control of goods (regs 8–13), denaturants, markers, dyes and classes of methylated spirits (regs 14, 15), the operations of methylators (regs 16–19), the movement and distribution of goods (regs 20–26), and records and returns (regs 27–30).

3   For the meaning of 'spirits' see para 624 note 3 ante.

4   For the meanings of 'shipment' and 'shipped' see para 623 note 9 ante; definitions applied by the Alcoholic Liquor Duties Act 1979 s 4(3).

5   For the meaning of 'stores' see para 604 note 6 ante; definition applied by ibid s 4(3).

6   Ibid s 77(1)(a) (s 77(1)(a), (c), (d), (e)–(h) prospectively amended by the Finance Act 1995 Sch 2 para 5 as from a day to be appointed). For the meaning of 'methylated spirits' see para 624 note 3 ante. References in these provisions to methylated spirits, and the reference in head (5) in the text to spirits for methylation, are to be construed as including references to denatured alcohol of any description from time to time specified in regulations made for the purpose of the Finance Act 1993 s 8(1): s 8(2)(a) (s 8 prospectively repealed by the Finance Act 1995 s 162, Sch 29 Pt I as from a day to be appointed). At the date at which this volume states the law, no such regulations had been made.

7   Alcoholic Liquor Duties Act 1979 s 77(1)(b) (prospectively repealed by the Finance Act 1995 s 162, Sch 29 Pt I as from a day to be appointed).

8   Alcoholic Liquor Duties Act 1979 s 77(1)(c) (as prospectively amended: see note 6 supra). For the meaning of 'warehouse' see para 623 note 4 ante; definition applied by s 4(3).

9   Ie within the meaning of ibid s 75 (as amended): see para 624 ante.

10 Ibid s 77(1)(d) (amended by the Finance Act 1981 Sch 8 para 23(a); and as prospectively amended: see note 6 supra).

11 Alcoholic Liquor Duties Act 1979 s 77(1)(e) (as prospectively amended: see note 6 supra).

12 Ibid s 77(1)(f) (as prospectively amended: see note 6 supra).

13 'Authorised methylator' means a person authorised to methylate spirits under ibid s 75(1), and 'licensed methylator' means a person holding a licence under s 75(2): s 4(1) (both definitions prospectively substituted by the Finance Act 1995 Sch 2 para 1 as from a day to be appointed). See para 624 ante.

14 'Retailer' means, in relation to dutiable alcoholic liquor, a person who sells such liquor by retail: Alcoholic Liquor Duties Act 1979 s 4(1) (definition amended by the Finance Act 1981 s 139(6), Sch 13 Pt III). 'Dutiable alcoholic liquor' means any of the liquors mentioned in the Alcoholic Liquor Duties Act 1979 s 1(1) (see CUSTOMS AND EXCISE vol 12(2) (Reissue) para 410): see ss 1(1), 4(1).

15 Ibid s 77(1)(g) (as prospectively amended: see note 6 supra).

16 'Duty' means excise duty: ibid ss 1(1), 4(1).

17 Ibid s 77(1)(h) (as prospectively amended: see note 6 supra).

18 Ibid s 77(3) (amended by the Finance Act 1981 Sch 8 para 23(c); and the Finance Act 1994 s 9, Sch 4 para 46(1)). The penalty is under the Finance Act 1994 s 9 (as amended) (civil penalties): see CUSTOMS AND EXCISE vol 12(2) (Reissue) para 1218.

19 Ie a licence under the Alcoholic Liquor Duties Act 1979 s 75 (as amended): see s 77(4); and para 625 ante.

20 Alcoholic Liquor Duties Act 1979 s 77(4) (amended by the Finance Act 1981 Sch 8 para 23(d), Sch 19 Pt III; and prospectively amended by the Finance Act 1995 Sch 2 para 5 as from a day to be appointed). The penalty is under the Finance Act 1994 s 9 (as amended) (civil penalties): see CUSTOMS AND EXCISE vol 12(2) (Reissue) para 1218.

21 Alcoholic Liquor Duties Act 1979 s 77(5) (amended by the Finance Act 1994 Sch 4 para 46(3); and prospectively amended by the Finance Act 1995 Sch 2 para 5 as from a day to be appointed).

22 Alcoholic Liquor Duties Act 1979 s 78(3) (prospectively substituted by the Finance Act 1995 Sch 2 para 5 as from a day to be appointed). As to the duty payable on spirits see CUSTOMS AND EXCISE vol 12(2) (Reissue) para 420 et seq.

23 Ie under the Finance Act 1994 s 9 (as amended) (civil penalties): see CUSTOMS AND EXCISE vol 12(2) (Reissue) para 1218.

24 Alcoholic Liquor Duties Act 1979 s 78(4) (amended by the Finance Act 1994 Sch 4 para 47; and prospectively substituted by the Finance Act 1995 Sch 2 para 7 as from a day to be appointed). As to the effect of a conviction for any offence in relation to methylated spirits on a licence to keep or use a still see CUSTOMS AND EXCISE vol 12(2) (Reissue) para 526.

626. Liability for deficiency on account of methylated spirits. If, at any time when an account is taken and a balance struck of the quantity of any kind of methylated spirits[1] in the possession of an authorised or licensed methylator[2], there is a difference between the quantity of alcohol[3] in the methylated spirits in his possession and the quantity of alcohol which ought to be in those methylated spirits, such quantity of spirits[4] as contains an amount of alcohol equal to the excess, or such part of it as the Commissioners of Customs and Excise[5] may determine, is liable to forfeiture[6]. If there is a deficiency in the quantity of alcohol which ought to be in the methylated spirits in his possession, the methylator must, on demand by the commissioners, pay on the deficiency, or on such part of it as the commissioners may specify, the duty[7] payable on spirits[8]. These provisions do not apply if the excess is not more than 1 per cent or the deficiency is not more than 2 per cent of the aggregate of (1) the quantity of alcohol in the balance of spirits struck when an account was last taken; and (2) the quantity of alcohol contained in any spirits which have since been lawfully added to the methylator's stock[9].

1 For the meaning of 'methylated spirits' see para 624 note 3 ante. References in these provisions to methylated spirits or spirits (except in the text to note 8 infra), are to be construed as including references to denatured alcohol of any description from time to time specified in regulations made for the purposes of the Finance Act 1993 s 8(1): s 8(2)(a) (s 8 prospectively repealed by the Finance Act 1995 s 162, Sch 29 Pt I as from a day to be appointed by order under s 5(6)). At the date at which this volume states the law, no such regulations had been made.

2   For the meanings of 'authorised methylator' and 'licensed methylator' see para 625 note 13 ante.
3   'Alcohol' means ethyl alcohol: Alcoholic Liquor Duties Act 1979 ss 2(2), 4(1).
4   For the meaning of 'spirits' see para 624 note 3 ante.
5   As to the Commissioners of Customs and Excise see CUSTOMS AND EXCISE vol 12(2) (Reissue) para 905 et seq.
6   Alcoholic Liquor Duties Act 1979 s 78(1)(a) (s 78(1), (2) substituted by the Alcoholic Liquors (Amendment of Enactments Relating to Strength and to Units of Measurement) Order 1979, SI 1979/241; and prospectively substituted by the Finance Act 1995 s 5(5)–(7), Sch 2 para 7 as from a day to be appointed).
7   For the meaning of 'duty' see para 625 note 16 ante. As to the duty on spirits cf CUSTOMS AND EXCISE vol 12(2) (Reissue) para 420.
8   Alcoholic Liquor Duties Act 1979 s 78(1)(b) (as substituted and prospectively substituted: see note 6 supra).
9   Ibid s 78(2)(a), (b) (as substituted and prospectively substituted: see note 6 supra).

627.   Inspection and examination of methylated spirits. An officer of Customs and Excise[1] may, in the daytime, enter and inspect the premises of any person authorised[2] to received methylated spirits[3]. He may inspect and examine any methylated spirits on the premises and take samples of any methylated spirits, or of any goods[4] containing methylated spirits, paying a reasonable price for each sample[5].

1   For the meaning of 'officer' see para 622 note 3 ante; definition applied by the Alcoholic Liquor Duties Act 1979 s 4(3). For the general powers of search of such officers see CUSTOMS AND EXCISE vol 12(2) (Reissue) para 1137 et seq.
2   Ie under the Alcoholic Liquor Duties Act 1979 s 77 (as amended): see para 625 ante.
3   Ibid s 79 (prospectively amended by the Finance Act 1995 s 5(5)–(7), Sch 2 para 5 as from a day to be appointed). For the meaning of 'methylated spirits' see para 624 note 3 ante. References in these provisions to methylated spirits or spirits are to be construed as including references to denatured alcohol of any description from time to time specified in regulations made for the purposes of the Finance Act 1993 s 8(1): s 8(2)(a) (s 8 prospectively repealed by the Finance Act 1995 s 162, Sch 29 Pt I as from a day to be appointed by order under s 5(6)). At the date at which this volume states the law, no such regulations had been made.
4   For the meaning of 'goods' see para 604 note 6 ante; definition applied by the Alcoholic Liquor Duties Act 1979 s 4(3).
5   Ibid s 79 (as prospectively amended: see note 3 supra). The powers conferred by s 79 (as prospectively amended) are without prejudice to any other power conferred by the Customs and Excise Acts 1979 (as to which see para 604 note 1 ante): Alcoholic Liquor Duties Act 1979 s 79. For the general power to take samples see CUSTOMS AND EXCISE vol 12(2) (Reissue) para 1138.

628.   Prohibition of methylated spirits as a beverage. With certain exceptions[1] it is prohibited:

(1)   to prepare, or attempt to prepare, any methylated spirits[2], methyl alcohol or any mixture containing either of these liquors as a beverage or as a mixture with a beverage[3];

(2)   to sell any such liquor, whether so prepared or not, as a beverage or mixed with a beverage[4];

(3)   to use any such liquor or any derivative of it in the preparation of any article capable of being used wholly or partially as a beverage or internally as a medicine[5];

(4)   to sell or possess any such articles[6] in the preparation of which any such liquor or any derivative of it has been used[7]; or

(5)   except as permitted by the Commissioners of Customs and Excise and in accordance with any conditions imposed by them, to purify or attempt to purify any such liquor or, after any such liquor has

once been used, to recover or attempt to recover the spirit or alcohol contained in it by distillation or condensation or in any other manner[8].

Any person committing such acts contrary to the above provisions is liable on summary conviction to a penalty, and the liquor in respect of which the offence was committed is liable to forfeiture[9].

1   Nothing in these prohibitions affects the use of any methylated spirits, methyl alcohol or their derivatives or mixtures: (1) in the preparation for use as a medicine of sulphuric ether, chloroform or any other article which the Commissioners of Customs and Excise may by order specify; or (2) in the making for external use only of any article sold or supplied in accordance with regulations made by the commissioners under the Alcoholic Liquor Duties Act 1979 s 77 (as amended) (see para 625 ante); or (3) in any art or manufacture: s 80(2)(a)–(c), (3) (s 80(3) prospectively amended by the Finance Act 1995 s 5(5)–(7), Sch 2 para 5 as from a day to be appointed). The prohibition does not affect the sale or possession of any article permitted to be prepared or made as stated in heads (1) or (2) supra where the article is sold or possessed for use as mentioned in those heads: Alcoholic Liquor Duties Act 1979 s 80(2). As to the Commissioners of Customs and Excise see CUSTOMS AND EXCISE vol 12(2) (Reissue) para 905 et seq.

2   For the meanings of 'methylated spirits' and 'spirits' see para 624 note 3 ante. References in these provisions to methylated spirits or spirits are to be construed as including references to denatured alcohol of any description from time to time specified in regulations made for the purposes of the Finance Act 1993 s 8(1): s 8(2)(a) (s 8 prospectively repealed by the Finance Act 1995 s 162, Sch 29 Pt I as from a day to be appointed by order under s 5(6)). At the date at which this volume states the law, no such regulations had been made.

3   Alcoholic Liquor Duties Act 1979 s 80(1)(a), (3) (as prospectively amended: see note 1 supra).

4   Ibid s 80(1)(b).

5   Ibid s 80(1)(c).

6   Ie any article capable of being used wholly or partially as a beverage or internally as a medicine: ibid s 80(1)(c), (d).

7   Ibid s 80(1)(d).

8   Ibid s 80(1)(e).

9   Ibid s 80(1). The penalty must not exceed level 3 on the standard scale: s 80(1) (amended by virtue of the Criminal Justice Act 1982 ss 38, 46). As to the standard scale see para 16 note 21 ante.

629.   Petrol substitutes.   Where any person:

(1)   puts to a chargeable use[1] any liquid[2] which is not hydrocarbon oil; and

(2)   knows or has reasonable cause to believe that there is duty charged[3] on that liquid which has not been paid and is not lawfully deferred,

his putting the liquid to that use attracts a penalty[4], and any goods in respect of which any person contravenes this provision are liable to forfeiture[5].

1   Ie within the meaning of the Hydrocarbon Oil Duties Act 1979 s 6A (as added): see CUSTOMS AND EXCISE vol 12(2) (Reissue) para 537.

2   For these purposes, 'liquid' does not include any substance which is gaseous at a temperature of 15° C and under a pressure of 1013.25 millibars: ibid s 22(2).

3   Ie under ibid s 6A (as added): see CUSTOMS AND EXCISE vol 12(2) (Reissue) para 537.

4   Ie under the Finance Act 1994 s 9 (as amended) (civil penalties): see CUSTOMS AND EXCISE vol 12(2) (Reissue) para 1218.

5   Hydrocarbon Oil Duties Act 1979 s 22(1) (amended by the Finance Act 1993 s 11(3); and the Finance Act 1994 s 9, Sch 4 para 56(1)). The Finance Act 1994 s 10 (exception for cases of reasonable excuse) (see CUSTOMS AND EXCISE vol 12(2) (Reissue) para 1218) does not apply in relation to conduct attracting a penalty by virtue of the Hydrocarbon Oil Duties Act 1979 s 22(1): s 22(1A) (added by the Finance Act 1994 s 9, Sch 4 para 56(2)).

(3) PARTICULAR TRADES

(i) In general

630. Miscellaneous restrictions. Particular statutory restrictions, which are considered subsequently in this title, exist in respect of:

(1)   shipbuilding and aircraft manufacture[1];

(2)   dealing in scrap metal[2];

(3)   employment agencies[3]; and

(4)   hairdressers and barbers[4].

Particular restrictions (not considered in this title) also exist in relation to pyramid selling schemes[5], acupuncturists and tattooists[6], trading stamps[7] and certain offensive and dangerous trades[8].

There are a variety of restrictions, which are not considered in this title, governing the use of premises for certain trades and industries. In particular, such restrictions exist in relation to:

(a)   pet shops[9];

(b)   bookmakers[10];

(c)   dairies[11];

(d)   slaughterhouses[12];

(e)   inns and hotels[13];

(f)   massage parlours and establishments for special treatment[14];

(g)   pharmaceutical chemists[15];

(h)   food premises[16];

(i)   mines and quarries[17]; and

(j)   cinemas, sex cinemas and sex shops[18].

Examples of commercial activities which, though not considered in this title, are subject to control by licence include: (i) the manufacture of explosives[19]; (ii) the manufacture, assembly, sale, supply, import or export of medicinal products[20]; and (iii) street trading[21].

1   See paras 637 et seq, 656 post.
2   See para 657 et seq post.
3   See para 674 et seq post.
4   See para 666 et seq post.
5   See SALE OF GOODS AND SUPPLY OF SERVICES vol 41 (Reissue) para 875 et seq.
6   See PROTECTION OF ENVIRONMENT AND PUBLIC HEALTH vol 38 (Reissue) para 493 et seq.
7   See SALE OF GOODS AND SUPPLY OF SERVICES vol 41 (Reissue) para 726 et seq.
8   See e g FUEL AND ENERGY vol 19(2) (Reissue) para 1623 (petroleum and other inflammable substances), and BUILDING (celluloid and cinematograph film).
9   See ANIMALS vol 2 (Reissue) para 465 et seq.
10   See BETTING, GAMING AND LOTTERIES vol 4(1) (Reissue) para 44 et seq.
11   See FOOD vol 18(2) (Reissue) para 345 et seq.
12   See FOOD vol 18(2) (Reissue) para 470 et seq.
13   See INNS AND INNKEEPERS vol 24 (Reissue) paras 1103–1104.
14   See MEDICINE, PHARMACY, DRUGS AND MEDICINAL PRODUCTS vol 30 (Reissue) para 1130 et seq.
15   See MEDICINE, PHARMACY, DRUGS AND MEDICINAL PRODUCTS vol 30 (Reissue) para 702 et seq.
16   See generally FOOD.
17   See MINES, MINERALS AND QUARRIES.
18   See THEATRES AND OTHER FORMS OF ENTERTAINMENT vol 45(2) (Reissue) para 136 et seq.
19   See EXPLOSIVES vol 17(2) (Reissue) para 924 et seq.
20   See MEDICINE, PHARMACY, DRUGS AND MEDICINAL PRODUCTS vol 30 (Reissue) para 853 et seq.
21   See MARKETS AND FAIRS.

(ii) The Iron and Steel Industry

631. Privatisation of the iron and steel industry: creation of British Steel plc. After its initial nationalisation in 1949 and denationalisation in 1953[1], the iron and steel industry was largely renationalised in 1967 under the control of the British Steel Corporation[2]. However, as from 5 September 1988[3] all the property, rights and liabilities of the corporation became vested in British Steel plc[4], the successor company nominated by the Secretary of State[5] under the British Steel Act 1988[6].

The company was wholly owned by the Crown on the appointed day, but provision was made for the issue and allotting of shares in it, with a view to it ceasing to be wholly owned by the Crown[7]. The Secretary of State was thereupon required to fix a target investment limit for government shareholding in the company; a new such limit may by order be fixed from time to time, provided that each new limit is lower than the one it replaces, and that no order may be revoked except by an order fixing a new limit[8].

The British Steel Corporation continues to exist in order to carry out transitional functions[9]. When the Secretary of State is satisfied that nothing further remains to be done by the corporation under the transitional provisions he may, after consulting the corporation and British Steel plc, by order dissolve the corporation as from a day specified in the order[10].

No information, and nothing contained in a forecast, obtained under the Iron and Steel Act 1982[11] or any of its predecessors[12] may be disclosed except by consent, or in summary form relating to a number of businesses, or for the institution or other purposes of criminal proceedings under the Act or its predecessors[13]. Disclosure in contravention of this prohibition is an offence punishable on summary conviction by imprisonment for up to three months or a fine not exceeding the statutory maximum, or both, and on conviction on indictment to imprisonment for up to two years or a fine, or both[14]. Where such an offence committed by a body corporate is proved to have been committed with the consent or connivance of, or to be attributable to any neglect on the part of, any director[15], manager, secretary or other similar officer of the body corporate, or any person purporting to act in any such capacity, he as well as the body corporate is guilty of the offence and liable to be proceeded against and punished accordingly[16].

1   See the Iron and Steel Acts 1949 and 1953 (both repealed).
2   See the Iron and Steel Act 1967 (repealed). The former legislation was consolidated in the Iron and Steel Act 1982, which has been largely repealed by the British Steel Act 1988. See the text and notes 3–10 infra.
3   See the British Steel Act 1988 (Appointed Day) Order 1988, SI 1988/1375, made under the British Steel Act 1988 s 1(1). On the date mentioned in the text the repeal of most of the Iron and Steel Act 1982 came into force: British Steel Act 1988 s 16(3), Sch 2 Pt I. The full repeal of the Iron and Steel Act 1982 s 1 and Sch 1 will take effect as from the date of dissolution of the corporation (see the text and note 9 infra): British Steel Act 1988 Sch 2 Pt II. After that date, the only provisions of the Iron and Steel Act 1982 remaining in force will be s 33 and s 34 (both amended by the British Steel Act 1988 Sch 2 Pt I) (disclosure of information, and offences relating thereto: see the text and notes 11–16 infra).
4   See the British Steel Act 1988 (Nominated Company) Order 1988, SI 1988/1376, made under the British Steel Act 1988 s 1(2). For provisions relating to the financial structure of the company see s 7. The Secretary of State was empowered, before the company ceased to be wholly owned by the Crown, to make loans to the company: see s 8; see also s 9 (temporary restrictions on borrowings). On 6 October 1999, British Steel plc merged with the Dutch company Koninklijke Hoogovens to become the Corus Group.
5   Ie the Secretary of State for Trade and Industry. The expenses of the Secretary of State under the British Steel Act 1988 are payable out of money provided by Parliament: s 14. As to the Secretary of State see para 2 ante.

6 Ibid s 1, and see Sch 1 for supplementary provisions relating to the vesting. Provision was made for the reduction and extinguishment of liabilities of the British Steel Corporation prior to the appointed day: see s 2. Provision may be made for such amendment of enactments as may be necessary or expedient in connection with references to the corporation: s 16(2). Any order under the British Steel Act 1988 must be made by statutory instrument: s 13(1). Orders under s 6 or s 16(2) are subject to annulment in pursuance of a resolution of either House of Parliament: s 13(2).

7 See ibid ss 3, 4, 15(2). Powers of the Secretary of State or the Treasury are exercisable by duly appointed nominees: s 5.

8 See ibid s 6(3), (4). The target investment limit was fixed by the British Steel Act 1988 (Government Shareholding) Order 1989, SI 1989/824, at 0.0472% of the voting rights exercisable in all circumstances at general meetings of British Steel plc: see art 2. It is the duty of the Treasury and the Secretary of State to ensure that the government shareholding does not exceed that limit, but subject to this, the Treasury and Secretary of State may exercise their powers to take up rights available to them, or to direct their nominees to do so: British Steel Act 1988 s 6(5), (6). The temporary suspension of voting rights is disregarded: s 6(7). As to orders under s 6 see note 5 supra.

   Provision is made in relation to the liability of British Steel plc to corporation tax (see INCOME TAXATION), and for the application of the Trustee Investments Act 1961 Sch 1 Pt IV para 3(b) (see TRUSTS vol 48 (Reissue) para 874): see the British Steel Act 1988 ss 11 (as amended), 12.

9 Ibid s 10(1). As to the transitional functions see s 16(4), Sch 3 paras 2–12. The period from the appointed day (ie 5 September 1988: see the text and notes 3–5 supra) and the day specified as the day of dissolution is the transitional period: s 10(1).

10 Ibid s 10(2). As to the constitution and composition of the corporation, and other provisions relating to the performance of its functions see the Iron and Steel Act 1982 s 1, Sch 1 (as prospectively repealed (see note 3 supra); both amended, in relation to the transitional period, by the British Steel Act 1988 Sch 3 para 1).

11 See notes 2–3 supra.

12 The predecessors of the Iron and Steel Act 1982 are the Iron and Steel Act 1949, the Iron and Steel Act 1953, the Iron and Steel Act 1967 and the Iron and Steel Act 1975: Iron and Steel Act 1982 s 33(4). See notes 1–2 supra.

13 Ibid s 33(1), (2) (amended by the British Steel Act 1988 Sch 2 Pt I).

14 Iron and Steel Act 1982 s 33(3). For the meaning of 'the statutory maximum' see para 16 note 21 ante.

15 In relation to the British Steel Corporation, or a body corporate established to carry on a nationalised industry and managed by its members, 'director' means a member of the corporation or body in question: ibid s 34(2).

16 Ibid s 34(1) (amended by the British Steel Act 1988 Sch 2 Pt I).

(iii) The Sugar Industry

632.   Deregulation of the sugar industry. The sugar industry was formerly subject to considerable regulation by the Sugar Act 1956, which gave the Sugar Board[1] powers to buy sugar from abroad (pursuant to the Commonwealth Sugar Agreement[2]), and the British Sugar Corporation Ltd[3] powers to buy domestically grown sugar beet. However, this statutory system of regulation was substantially repealed by the European Communities Act 1972 and the Agriculture (Miscellaneous Provisions) Act 1976[4]. The Sugar Board was dissolved on 15 February 1977[5], and the corporation no longer exercises major statutory powers. There remain, as exceptions, two areas of statutory control, namely:

(1)   the provisions relating to research and education in sugar beet growing[6]; and

(2)   a ministerial reserve power to arrange the setting of the price in any year of home-grown beet[7] in default of agreement between growers and processors[8].

1   The Sugar Board was established by the Sugar Act 1956 s 1(1) (repealed).

2   The Commonwealth Sugar Agreement dated 21 December 1951 was made between the Minister of Food on behalf of the United Kingdom government and representatives of the sugar industries and exporters in Australia, the British West Indies, Fiji, Mauritius and the Union of South Africa: see the Sugar Act 1956 s 1(9), Sch 1 (repealed).

3   The British Sugar Corporation was originally formed under the Sugar Industry (Reorganisation) Act 1936 s 3 (repealed).

4   The major repeals were effected by the European Communities Act 1972 s 4(1), (2), Sch 3 Pt II, by a series of orders fixing appointed days for the repeals to come into effect, namely the Sugar Act 1956 (Repeals) (Appointed Day) Order (No 1), SI 1973/135; the Sugar Act 1956 (Repeals) (Appointed Day) Order (No 2), SI 1973/1019; the Sugar Act 1956 (Repeals) (Appointed Day) Order (No 3), SI 1975/1164; the Sugar Act 1956 (Repeals) (Appointed Day) Order (No 4), SI 1976/548; the Sugar Act 1956 (Repeals) (Appointed Day) Order (No 5), SI 1976/2016; and the Sugar Act 1956 (Repeals) (Appointed Day) Order (No 6), SI 1981/1192. The repeals contained in the Agriculture (Miscellaneous Provisions) Act 1976 Sch 4 Pt I were principally to dissolve the Sugar Board, and under s 27(4) came into effect with the coming into force on 15 February 1977 of the Sugar Board (Dissolution) Order 1977, SI 1977/224.

5   See the Agriculture (Miscellaneous Provisions) Act 1976 s 1(4); and the Sugar Board (Dissolution) Order 1977, SI 1977/224, arts 1, 2. On 1 December 1976 the property, rights and liabilities of the Sugar Board became vested in the Minister of Agriculture, Fisheries and Food: Sugar Board (Transfer of Property etc) (Appointed Day) Order 1976, SI 1976/1963, art 2 (revoked).

6   See para 633 post.

7   For the meaning of 'home-grown beet' see para 633 note 2 post.

8   See para 629 post.

633.   Research and education in sugar beet growing. The appropriate minister[1], after consulting with the processors of home-grown beet[2] and any body which in his opinion is substantially representative of growers of home-grown beet, must prepare for each year[3] a programme of research and education in matters affecting the growing of sugar beet and may by order[4] provide for carrying any such programme into effect[5]. The programme for any year must contain an estimate of the amount of expenditure to be incurred in carrying it out, and any order for carrying it out must, in particular, provide for assessing the contributions[6] to be made by the processors and by every grower of home-grown beet who delivers beet to the processors in that year[7], and for the collection of the contributions and the recovery of unpaid contributions by the appropriate minister[8].

Although the above statutory requirements are still in force, the Government has terminated the system of funding for sugar beet research and education by means of a statutory levy and intends to pass responsibility for the future funding of this work to the sugar beet industry[9].

1   'The appropriate minister', in relation to a programme or order extending to the whole of Great Britain, means the Secretary of State for the Environment, Food and Rural Affairs, the Secretary of State for Scotland and the Secretary of State for Wales, acting jointly; in relation to a programme or order extending only to England and Wales, it means the Secretary of State for the Environment, Food and Rural Affairs and the Secretary of State for Wales, acting jointly: Food Act 1984 s 68(6). For the meaning of 'Great Britain' see para 31 note 2 ante. As to the Secretary of State for the Environment, Food and Rural Affairs see para 123 note 11 ante.

2   'Home-grown beet' means sugar beet grown in Great Britain: ibid s 68(6) (definition added by the Food Safety Act 1990 s 52(b), Sch 2 paras 12, 13).

3   'Year' means a period of 12 months beginning with 1 April: Food Act 1984 s 68(6) (definition added by the Food Safety Act 1990 Sch 2 paras 12, 13).

4   Such an order must be made by statutory instrument, subject to annulment in pursuance of a resolution of either House of Parliament: Food Act 1984 s 68(5A) (added by the Food Safety Act 1990 Sch 2 paras 12, 13).

5 Food Act 1984 s 68(1) (amended by the Food Safety Act 1990 Sch 2 paras 12, 13). The last order made was the Sugar Beet (Research and Education) Order 1999, SI 1999/415, which came into operation on 1 April 1999 and became spent on 1 April 2000. See further the text and note 9 infra.

6 All contributions must be paid into a research and education fund under the control of the appropriate minister, out of which he may defray expenditure certified by him as having been properly incurred in carrying out the programme, including expenditure incurred by him or on his behalf: Food Act 1984 s 68(3), (4), (5). An annual account of the revenue and expenditure of the fund must be transmitted (not later than 30 November in the following year) by the minister to the Comptroller and Auditor General, who must examine and certify it and lay a copy of it and his report on it before Parliament: s 68(5). As to the Comptroller and Auditor General see CONSTITUTIONAL LAW AND HUMAN RIGHTS vol 8(2) (Reissue) paras 724–726.

7 Ibid s 68(2)(a) (amended by the Food Safety Act 1990 Sch 2 para 12, 13).

8 Food Act 1984 s 68(2)(b).

9 See MAFF News Release 492/98 (18 December 1998); and MAFF News Release 136/99 (12 April 1999).

634. Determination of price of home-grown beet. If in any year it is made to appear to the ministers[1] by the processors of home-grown beet[2] or by a body which is in their opinion substantially representative of the growers of home-grown beet, that the processors and that body are unable to agree on the prices and other terms and conditions for the purchase of that home-grown beet by the processors, the ministers may determine (or designate a person to determine) those prices, terms and conditions[3]. Any purchase by processors for which prices, terms and conditions have been so determined, or a contract for such a purchase, takes effect as a purchase or contract at those prices and on those terms and conditions[4].

For the purpose of facilitating:

(1) the making of such a determination as is described above; or

(2) the preparation or conduct of discussions concerning Community arrangements for or relating to the regulation of the market for sugar[5],

the appropriate minister[6] may serve on any processor of home-grown beet a notice requiring him to furnish specified information in writing within a specified period[7]. Information so obtained may not be disclosed except with the previous written consent of the person who furnished it, and a person who contravenes this prohibition is liable on conviction on indictment to a fine or imprisonment for up to two years or both, or on summary conviction to a fine not exceeding the statutory maximum[8] or imprisonment for up to three months or both[9]. However, this does not restrict:

(a) the disclosure of information to any of the ministers[10]; or

(b) the disclosure of information obtained under head (1) above to a person designated to make a determination as described above or to a body which substantially represents the growers of home-grown beet[11]; or

(c) the disclosure of information obtained under head (2) above to the Community institution concerned[12].

1 'The ministers' means the Secretary of State for the Environment, Food and Rural Affairs, the Secretary of State for Scotland and the Secretary of State for Wales, acting jointly: Food Act 1984 s 69(3) (amended by the Food Safety Act 1990 s 52(b), Sch 2 paras 12, 14). As to the Secretary of State for the Environment, Food and Rural Affairs see para 123 note 11 ante.

2 For the meaning of 'home-gown beet' see para 633 note 2 ante.

3 Food Act 1984 s 69(1).

4 Ibid s 69(2).

5   As to the common organisation of the market in sugar see AGRICULTURE vol 1(2) (Reissue) para 1113.

6   'Appropriate minister' means, in relation to England the Secretary of State for the Environment, Food and Rural Affairs (see note 1 supra), and in relation to Scotland or Wales, the Secretary of State: Food Act 1984 s 69A(4) (s 69A added by the Food Safety Act 1990 Sch 2 paras 12, 15).

7   Food Act 1984 s 69A(1) (as added: see note 6 supra).

8   For the meaning of 'the statutory maximum' see para 16 note 21 ante.

9   Food Act 1984 s 69A(2) (as added: see note 6 supra).

10   Ibid s 69A(3) (as added: see note 6 supra).

11   Ibid s 69A(3)(a) (as added: see note 6 supra).

12   Ibid s 69A(3)(b) (as added: see note 6 supra).

(iv) The Cinematograph Industry

635. Deregulation of the cinematograph industry. There was formerly in existence a system under which a statutory body, the British Film Fund Agency[1], was empowered to impose a levy on film exhibitors and to make payments out of the proceeds of the levy to another statutory body, the National Film Finance Corporation[2], and others, to provide finance for the production and distribution of films[3]. That system was discontinued by the Films Act 1985 and regulations made thereunder[4], and the two statutory bodies were abolished[5]. The remaining statutory provisions relating to the cinematograph industry empower the Secretary of State to give financial assistance for the production of films[6] and to make grants to the British Film Institute[7].

1   The British Film Fund Agency was established by the Cinematograph Films Act 1957 s 1 (repealed) and continued by the Film Levy Finance Act 1981 s 1(1) (repealed).

2   The National Film Finance Corporation was established by the Cinematograph Film Production (Special Loans) Act 1949 (repealed) and continued by the National Film Finance Corporation Act 1981 s 1(1) (repealed).

3   This system was operated under the Film Levy Finance Act 1981 and the National Film Finance Corporation Act 1981 (both repealed). As to the licensing etc of cinemas and the showing of films see THEATRES AND OTHER FORMS OF ENTERTAINMENT vol 45(2) (Reissue) para 58 et seq.

4   See the Films Act 1985 s 2(4) (repealed); and the Films (Ending of Final Levy and Final Distribution Periods) Order 1985, SI 1985/811 (spent).

5   See the British Film Fund Agency (Dissolution) Order 1988, SI 1988/37; and the National Film Finance Corporation (Dissolution) Order 1985, SI 1985/1943.

6   See THEATRES AND OTHER FORMS OF ENTERTAINMENT vol 45(2) (Reissue) para 78.

7   See para 636 post.

636. Grants to the British Film Institute. The Treasury[1] may from time to time make grants to the British Film Institute[2] of such amounts as it thinks fit out of money provided by Parliament[3].

1   This function of the Treasury is now exercisable by the Secretary of State for Culture, Media and Sport: see the Transfer of Functions (National Heritage) Order 1992, SI 1992/1311 (amended by SI 1997/1744).

2   The British Film Institute is a company incorporated for the purpose of encouraging the use and development of the cinematograph as a means of entertainment and instruction: see the Report of the Committee on the British Film Institute (1948) (Cmd 7361) para 3, App III.

3   British Film Institute Act 1949 s 1 (amended by the Sunday Cinema Act 1972 s 4, Schedule; and the Transfer of Functions (National Heritage) Order 1992, SI 1992/1311, art 3(1), Sch 1 Pt I). As to cinemas generally see THEATRES AND OTHER FORMS OF ENTERTAINMENT vol 45(2) (Reissue) para 58 et seq.

(v) Shipbuilding

A. BRITISH SHIPBUILDERS

637. Constitution of British Shipbuilders. In 1977, the greater part of the British shipbuilding industry was taken into public ownership, with the assets of the companies involved being vested in British Shipbuilders, a corporation established for that purpose[1]. The corporation consists of a chairman and not less than 2 nor more than 20 members appointed by the Secretary of State[2] after consultation with the chairman[3]. Subject to the power of the Secretary of State to make regulations governing procedure[4], the corporation may determine the arrangements relating to its meetings, and the validity of any of its proceedings is not affected by any vacancy among its members or in the office of chairman or by any defect in the appointment of a member[5]. The corporation is not the servant or agent of the Crown and does not enjoy any status, privilege or immunity of the Crown, nor is its property to be regarded as property of or held on behalf of the Crown[6]. The corporation must pay to its members such remuneration, allowances, pensions and compensation for loss of office as the Secretary of State may with the consent of the Treasury determine[7].

The Secretary of State must maintain a register of members' financial interests and must ensure that all members enter in it the same information as they would be required to enter in the register of interests of members of the House of Commons if they were members of that House[8].

Most of the assets of British Shipbuilders have now been privatised but it remains a public corporation responsible for commitments and liabilities arising from its former manufacture of ships and marine engines.

1   Aircraft and Shipbuilding Industries Act 1977 s 1(1). As to the vesting of assets see paras 645–646 post. The Act also took into public ownership the companies engaged in the manufacture of aircraft, whose assets were vested in the other corporation established by the Act, British Aerospace: see s 1(1)(a) (repealed). This policy was, however, reversed in relation to aircraft by the British Aerospace Act 1980, which dissolved British Aerospace as from 31 December 1981: s 10(9); British Aerospace (Dissolution) Order 1981, SI 1981/1793, art 2. All references to the aircraft industry and British Aerospace in the Aircraft and Shipbuilding Industries Act 1977 are therefore repealed: British Aerospace Act 1980 ss 10(1), 15(2), Sch 3. See further para 652 post.
    The Secretary of State may by order made by statutory instrument specify a different name for British Shipbuilders, in which case any reference to British Shipbuilders in any enactment, instrument or document must be construed accordingly: Aircraft and Shipbuilding Industries Act 1977 s 1(7) (amended by the British Aerospace Act 1980 Sch 3). This includes power to vary or revoke any such order previously made: Aircraft and Shipbuilding Industries Act 1977 s 1(8). Any such order is subject to annulment in pursuance of a resolution of either House of Parliament: s 1(8).
2   The Secretary of State is in practice the Secretary of State for Trade and Industry: see para 2 ante.
3   Aircraft and Shipbuilding Industries Act 1977 s 1(2) (amended by the British Shipbuilders Regulations 1991, SI 1991/1560, reg 2). See also note 4 infra.
4   The Secretary of State may by regulations made by statutory instrument (1) substitute different minimum or maximum numbers of members; (2) establish offices other than that of chairman; (3) make provisions governing appointment and the tenure of and vacation of office by members; (4) make provision with respect to the disclosure of interests by members; (5) make provision concerning the quorum, proceedings and meetings of the corporation and the execution and proof of documents; and (6) make supplementary or incidental provisions: Aircraft and Shipbuilding Industries Act 1977 s 1(3)(a)–(f). Any such statutory instrument is subject to annulment in pursuance of a resolution of either House of Parliament: s 1(8). As to such regulations see the British Shipbuilders Regulations 1977, SI 1977/626 (amended by SI 1991/1560). The quorum of the corporation is set at the

majority of members: reg 5(1) (as so amended). Members of the corporation are disqualified for membership of the House of Commons: see the House of Commons Disqualification Act 1975 s 1(1)(f), Sch 1 Pt II (amended by, inter alia, the Aircraft and Shipbuilding Industries Act 1977 s 1(10)); and PARLIAMENT vol 34 (Reissue) para 607 et seq.
5 Aircraft and Shipbuilding Industries Act 1977 s 1(4).
6 Ibid s 1(6).
7 See ibid s 1(5); Transfer of Functions (Minister for the Civil Service and Treasury) Order 1981, SI 1981/1670, art 2(2). For the meaning of 'pension' for the purposes of the Aircraft and Shipbuilding Industries Act 1977 see para 651 note 3 post.
8 Ibid s 1(9) (spent in respect of British Shipbuilders by virtue of the Industry Act 1980 s 20). As to the register of interests of members of the House of Commons see PARLIAMENT vol 34 (Reissue) para 1001.

638.   Activities of British Shipbuilders. It is the duty of British Shipbuilders (referred to as 'the corporation') so to exercise its powers as to secure that the carrying on of the activities that have fallen to be carried on under its ultimate control is organised, so far as regards their direction, in the most efficient manner[1]. The corporation must not make, or permit to be made, any substantial change in the manner in which the carrying on of the activities that have fallen to be carried on under its ultimate control is organised, so far as regards their direction, except with the consent of the Secretary of State[2].

After consultation with the corporation, the Secretary of State may by order[3] give it directions:

(1)   to discontinue or restrict any of its activities or to dispose of any of its property, rights and liabilities[4]; or

(2)   to secure the discontinuance or restriction of any of the activities of a wholly owned subsidiary[5] of the corporation or the disposal of all or any of its property, rights and liabilities or the winding up of any such subsidiary[6].

However, he must not give any such direction unless he is satisfied that the giving of it will further the national interest[7].

Any such direction to dispose or secure the disposal of property, rights or liabilities may in particular include a direction:

(a)   to form a company for the purpose of acquiring the property or rights and assuming the liabilities to be transferred in pursuance of the direction[8];

(b)   prohibiting, except with the consent of the Secretary of State, the disposal to, or acquisition from any person by, any company which will acquire property or rights in pursuance of the direction of assets used or capable of use in the carrying on of activities of a description, or of activities other than activities of a description, specified in the direction[9].

The exercise of these powers to direct the formation of a company and to restrict the disposal or acquisition of assets is restricted to the extent that (i) no company may be directed to be formed otherwise than as a wholly owned subsidiary of the corporation[10]; and (ii) no such restriction is to be imposed except on a company which is, or when formed will be, a wholly owned subsidiary of the corporation, or is to be binding after it ceases to be such a subsidiary[11]. So long as the restriction on the disposal or acquisition of assets is binding on the corporation or any of its wholly owned subsidiaries the statutory provisions relating to the capacity of the corporation or of the subsidiary have effect subject to the restriction[12].

Except in so far as it is satisfied that adequate machinery already exists, the corporation must consult any relevant trade union[13] with a view to concluding agreements for the establishment and maintenance of machinery for certain purposes[14], namely:

(A)   the settlement by negotiation of terms and conditions of employment of persons employed by the corporation and its wholly owned subsidiaries[15];

(B)   the resolution of trade disputes[16];

(C)   the promotion and encouragement of measures affecting efficiency, in any respect, in the carrying on of their activities by the corporation and its wholly owned subsidiaries[17]; and

(D)   the discussion of other matters of mutual interest[18].

In each year[19], after consulting any relevant trade union, the corporation must formulate a corporate plan relating to the conduct, during such period beginning in that year as it considers appropriate, of the operations of the corporation and its wholly owned subsidiaries[20]. In formulating the plan and determining the period to which it is to relate, and in the general conduct of the operations of the corporation and its wholly owned subsidiaries in each year, the corporation must act on lines settled from time to time with the approval of the Secretary of State[21].

In such manner and at such times as the Secretary of State may specify, the corporation must furnish him with such information as he may specify in writing, and as it can reasonably be expected to obtain, with respect to such matters relating to the corporation and its wholly owned subsidiaries, or the activities (past, present or future), plans or property of any of them as he may specify[22]. The Secretary of State may give directions[23] to the corporation requiring it to publish in the specified manner specified information relating to its operations and those of its wholly owned subsidiaries, and to its policy and plans for the general conduct of its undertaking and the business of all or any of its wholly owned subsidiaries[24].

1   Aircraft and Shipbuilding Industries Act 1977 s 4A(1) (ss 4A, 4B added by the British Shipbuilders Act 1983 s 2(1)).

2   Aircraft and Shipbuilding Industries Act 1977 s 4A(2) (as added: see note 1 supra). As to the Secretary of State see para 2 ante.

3   Any power to make orders under these provisions is exercisable by statutory instrument subject to annulment in pursuance of a resolution of either House of Parliament: ibid s 4B(7) (as added: see note 1 supra).

4   Ibid s 4B(1)(a) (as added: see note 1 supra).

5   'Wholly owned subsidiary' and 'subsidiary' have the same meanings as they have for the purposes of the Companies Act 1985 s 736 (as substituted) (see COMPANIES vol 7(2) (1996 Reissue) para 827): Aircraft and Shipbuilding Industries Act 1977 s 56(1) (definitions amended by the Companies Consolidation (Consequential Provisions) Act 1985 s 30, Sch 2; definition of 'wholly owned subsidiary' further amended by SI 1986/1035, art 23, Sch 1 Pt II; definition of 'subsidiary' further amended by the Companies Act 1989 s 144(4), Sch 18 para 16).

6   Aircraft and Shipbuilding Industries Act 1977 s 4B(1)(b) (as added: see note 1 supra).

7   Ibid s 4B(2) (as added: see note 1 supra). This specific power of the Secretary of State is without prejudice to his power under s 4(2) (see para 639 post) to give directions of a general character to the corporation as to the exercise of its functions in relation to matters affecting the national interest: s 4B(1) (as so added).

Where he gives a direction under s 4B(1) (as added) which requires the disposal to an outside person of an interest in a company which is a wholly owned subsidiary of the corporation, or gives his consent to such a disposal under s 3(3) (see para 639 post), or s 9(3) (see para 640 post), then, after consultation with the corporation, the Secretary of State may by order give it directions to secure that: (1) the company's articles of association are altered in a specified manner; (2) the company's share capital is increased by a specified sum and in a specified manner and that any shares representing the whole or any part of that sum are issued to the Secretary of State or to his nominee; and (3) an employees' share scheme is established in respect of the company in specified terms and making specified provision: s 4B(6) (as so added). 'Outside person' means a person who is not a member of the group; 'the group' means British Shipbuilders and all its wholly owned subsidiaries taken together; and 'employees' share scheme' means a scheme for encouraging or facilitating the holding of shares or debentures in a company by or for the benefit of (a) the bona fide employees or former employees of the company or of a subsidiary of the company, or (b) the wives, husbands, widows, widowers or children or stepchildren under 18 of such employees or former employees: s 4B(8) (as so added).

8   Ibid s 4B(3)(a) (as added: see note 1 supra).
9   Ibid s 4B(3)(b) (as added: see note 1 supra).
10   Ibid s 4B(4)(a) (as added: see note 1 supra).
11   Ibid s 4B(4)(b) (as added: see note 1 supra).
12   Ibid s 4B(5) (as added: see note 1 supra).
13   'Relevant trade union' means any independent trade union within the meaning of the Trade Union and Labour Relations (Consolidation) Act 1992 (see para 1014 post), which the corporation or any of its wholly owned subsidiaries recognises for the purposes of collective bargaining within the meaning of that Act (see para 1301 post): Aircraft and Shipbuilding Industries Act 1977 s 56(1) (definition amended by the Trade Union and Labour Relations (Consolidation) Act 1992 s 300(2), Sch 2 para 8(1), (3)).
14   Aircraft and Shipbuilding Industries Act 1977 s 6(1). This does not prohibit the corporation or its wholly owned subsidiaries from taking part together with other employers or organisations of employers in the establishment and maintenance of such machinery for any of the purposes listed: s 6(3).
15   Ibid s 6(2)(a).
16   Ibid s 6(2)(b) (amended by the Trade Union and Labour Relations (Consolidation) Act 1992 Sch 2 para 8(1), (2)), which refers to trade disputes within the meaning of the Trade Union and Labour Relations (Consolidation) Act Pt IV (ss 178–218) (as amended): see para 1435 post.
17   Aircraft and Shipbuilding Industries Act 1977 s 6(2)(c).
18   Ibid s 6(2)(d).
19   'Year' means the period of 12 months beginning on 1 January: ibid s 7(4).
20   Ibid s 7(1). The plan must deal with (1) capital investment; (2) research and development; (3) employment of persons; (4) forecasts of income and expenditure on profit and loss account and of payments and receipts of the corporation and its wholly owned subsidiaries; (5) such other matters as the corporation considers appropriate; and (6) such other matters as the Secretary of State may specify in writing to the corporation: s 7(1)(a)–(f). However, if the Secretary of State so directs, the plan for any year need not deal with such of the matters in heads (1)–(4) supra as are specified in the direction: s 7(2).
21   Ibid s 7(1).
22   Ibid s 8(1).
23   Before giving any such directions the Secretary of State must consult the corporation: ibid s 8(3).
24   Ibid s 8(2).

639. Powers of British Shipbuilders. British Shipbuilders[1] has power to carry on the following activities:

(1)   the design, development, production, sale, repair and maintenance of ships and slow speed diesel marine engines[2];

(2)   research into related matters[3];

(3)   any activities which were carried on immediately before the date of transfer[4] by a company which, by virtue of the Aircraft and Shipbuilding Industries Act 1977, became a wholly owned subsidiary[5] of the corporation[6], and

(4)   with the consent of the Secretary of State[7], or in accordance with any general authority given by him, any other activities to which the consent or authority relates[8].

The corporation may also promote the carrying on of any of these activities to such extent as it thinks fit by other persons none of whom need be its wholly owned subsidiary[9].

Except with the consent of the Secretary of State or in accordance with the terms of any general authority given by him[10], the corporation may not: (a) acquire by agreement and hold interests in other bodies corporate[11]; (b) form or take part in forming bodies corporate[12]; (c) enter into partnerships[13]; or (d) dispose of an interest in any of its wholly owned subsidiaries[14]. The corporation has power to exercise all rights conferred by the holding of interests in bodies corporate[15].

The corporation has power, with the consent of the Secretary of State, to enter into and carry out agreements with the minister responsible for overseas development[16], under which the corporation acts at the expense of that minister as the instrument by means of which technical assistance is furnished by the minister under certain statutory provisions[17]. The corporation also has power, with the consent of the Secretary of State and the minister responsible for overseas development, to enter into agreements under which, for the purposes of the same statutory provisions, the corporation furnishes technical assistance in a country or territory outside the United Kingdom against reimbursement to the corporation of the cost of furnishing that assistance[18].

The corporation may, with the consent of the Secretary of State, promote or, without such consent, oppose Bills in Parliament[19]. The corporation has a general power to do anything or enter into any transaction (whether or not involving the expenditure, borrowing or lending of money, or the acquisition or disposal of any property or rights) which in its opinion is calculated to facilitate the exercise or performance of any of its statutory functions or which is in its opinion incidental or conducive to such exercise or performance[20].

The above provisions[21] relate only to the capacity of the corporation as a statutory corporation, and do not authorise the disregard by the corporation of any enactment or rule of law[22].

In addition to his power to add to or alter the functions of the corporation or lay down objectives and conditions[23], the Secretary of State has power to give directions of a general character as to the exercise and performance by the corporation of its functions (including the exercise of rights conferred by the holding of interests in bodies corporate, whether or not incorporated in the United Kingdom) in relation to matters appearing to him to affect the national interest[24]. The corporation must give effect to any such direction, and so far as appropriate must secure that each of its wholly owned subsidiaries also does so[25].

1   As to British Shipbuilders see para 637 ante.
2   Aircraft and Shipbuilding Industries Act 1977 s 3(1)(a) (s 3(1) substituted by the British Shipbuilders Act 1983 s 1(3)).
3   Aircraft and Shipbuilding Industries Act 1977 s 3(1)(b) (as substituted: see note 2 supra).
4   Ie 1 July 1977: see para 643 post.
5   For the meaning of 'wholly owned subsidiary' see para 638 note 5 ante.
6   Aircraft and Shipbuilding Industries Act 1977 s 3(1)(c) (as substituted: see note 2 supra).
7   As to the Secretary of State see para 2 ante.
8   Aircraft and Shipbuilding Industries Act 1977 s 3(1)(d) (as substituted: see note 2 supra).
9   Ibid s 3(1) (as substituted: see note 2 supra).
10 See ibid s 3(3)(a).

11 Ibid s 3(2)(a), (3)(a). This power, and those referred to in the text to notes 12, 15 infra, is exercisable in relation to bodies corporate whether or not they are or will be incorporated in the United Kingdom: s 3(4). For the meaning of 'United Kingdom' see para 37 note 1 ante.

12 Ibid s 3(2)(b), (3)(a). See also note 11 supra.

13 Ibid s 3(2)(c), (3)(a). This power is exercisable in relation to a partnership whether or not the partnership will be governed by the law of any part of the United Kingdom: s 3(4). As to the law of partnership generally see PARTNERSHIP.

14 Ibid s 3(3)(b). However, disposal to another wholly owned subsidiary requires neither consent nor authorisation: s 3(3)(b).

15 Ibid s 3(2)(d). See also note 11 supra.

16 'The minister responsible for overseas development' means the Secretary of State for the time being discharging the functions conferred by the Overseas Development and Co-operation Act 1980 s 1 (as amended) (provision of assistance to or for the benefit of overseas countries): s 2(6).

17 Ibid s 2(1)(a), (3)(b), Sch 1 Pt III. The statutory provisions referred to are those contained in s 1(1) (power to furnish assistance to overseas countries).

18 Ibid s 2(1)(b), (3)(c), Sch 1 Pt III.

19 Aircraft and Shipbuilding Industries Act 1977 s 3(7).

20 Ibid s 3(8).

21 Ibid s 3(9) refers only to the preceding provisions of s 3 (as amended), not to the Overseas Development and Co-operation Act 1980. However, it is suggested that since the provisions of the Overseas Development and Co-operation Act 1980 cited in notes 16–18 supra were enacted partly in direct replacement of the Aircraft and Shipbuilding Industries Act 1977 s 3(6) (repealed), s 3(9) may be considered to apply to those provisions of the Overseas Development and Co-operation Act 1980 in so far as they relate to British Shipbuilders.

22 Aircraft and Shipbuilding Industries Act 1977 s 3(9).

23 See para 638 ante.

24 Aircraft and Shipbuilding Industries Act 1977 s 4(2). Before giving such directions he must:
   (1) consider all factors relating to the corporation that appear to him to be relevant (s 4(3)(a));
   (2) consult the corporation (s 4(3)(b)); and
   (3) have full regard to the need
      (a) to co-ordinate the corporation's operations with those of the British shipping industry (s 4(4)(a));
      (b) to take account of any shipbuilding policy for the time being adopted by any international organisation of which the United Kingdom is a member (s 4(4)(b));
      (c) to ensure that the corporation is able to compete in world markets on equal terms with its competitors in other countries (s 4(4)(c)); and
      (d) to take account of any special considerations relating to parts of the United Kingdom, and in particular to those relating to employment (s 4(4)(d)).
   When he gives a direction the Secretary of State must lay a copy before each House of Parliament within 28 days, unless he has notified the corporation that in his opinion this would be contrary to the national interest or he accepts the corporation's contention that it would be against the corporation's commercial interests: s 4(5). Such a notice may be revoked by notice to the corporation: see s 18(3); and para 644 text and note 12 post.

25 Ibid s 4(1).

640. Control by British Shipbuilders of its wholly owned subsidiaries. British Shipbuilders[1] must secure that, notwithstanding anything in the memorandum or articles of association of any of its wholly owned subsidiaries[2], none of those subsidiaries:

   (1) carries on any activity which the corporation itself has no power to carry on or has power to carry on only with the consent of the Secretary of State[3];
   (2) acquires any interest in a body corporate or forms or takes part in forming a body corporate[4]; or

(3) enters into a partnership with any other person except with the consent of, or in accordance with the terms of any general authority given by, the Secretary of State[5].

The corporation must secure that, except with the consent of, or in accordance with the terms of any general authority given by, the Secretary of State, none of its wholly owned subsidiaries disposes of an interest in any other of its wholly owned subsidiaries, unless the disposal is to the corporation itself or to another of its wholly owned subsidiaries[6].

It is the duty of the corporation to secure that none of its wholly owned subsidiaries borrows otherwise than from the corporation or from another such subsidiary except with the consent of the Secretary of State and the approval of the Treasury[7].

1 As to British Shipbuilders see para 637 ante.
2 For the meaning of 'wholly owned subsidiary' see para 638 note 5 ante.
3 Aircraft and Shipbuilding Industries Act 1977 s 9(1)(a). As to the activities and powers of the corporation see paras 638–639 ante. As to the Secretary of State see para 2 ante.
4 Ibid s 9(1)(b). This applies whether or not the body corporate is or will be incorporated in the United Kingdom: s 9(2). For the meaning of 'United Kingdom' see para 37 note 1 ante.
5 Ibid s 9(1)(c). This applies whether or not the partnership will be governed by the law of any part of the United Kingdom: s 9(2).
6 Ibid s 9(3).
7 Ibid s 11(5). As to borrowings generally see para 642 post.

641. Financial duties. The financial duties of British Shipbuilders[1] are determined from time to time by the Secretary of State[2] with the approval of the Treasury and after consultation with the corporation[3]. Such a determination may relate to a period beginning before the date on which it was made and may contain incidental or supplemental provisions[4]. The Secretary of State and the Treasury must be satisfied that the duties laid upon the corporation by the determination are likely, taken together, to result in an adequate return on the capital employed by the corporation and its subsidiaries[5]. Each report[6] of the corporation for any accounting year[7] must set out any such determination, other than one which was wholly superseded before the beginning of the accounting year to which the report relates[8].

1 As to British Shipbuilders see para 637 ante.
2 As to the Secretary of State see para 2 ante.
3 Aircraft and Shipbuilding Industries Act 1977 s 10(1). The Secretary of State must give notice of any such determination to the corporation as soon as possible after it is made (s 10(3)), and must as soon as possible lay a copy of it before each House of Parliament (s 10(7)).
4 Ibid s 10(6).
5 Ibid s 10(5). For the meaning of 'subsidiary' see para 638 note 5 ante.
6 As to the annual report for the accounting year of the corporation see ibid s 18; and para 644 post.
7 As to the accounting year of the corporation see ibid ss 17(5), (6), 56(1); and para 644 post.
8 Ibid s 10(4).

642. Borrowings by, and loans to, British Shipbuilders. British Shipbuilders[1] may borrow money in accordance with the following provisions[2]. The corporation may borrow temporarily, by way of overdraft or otherwise:

(1) from the Secretary of State in sterling; or

(2) with his consent and the approval of the Treasury, or in accordance

with a general authority given by the Secretary of State with the approval of the Treasury, in sterling or some other currency from some other person,

such sums as may be required for meeting the obligations and discharging the functions of the corporation or its wholly owned subsidiaries[3].

The corporation may borrow, otherwise than by way of temporary loan:

(a)   from the Secretary of State in sterling; or

(b)   with his consent and the approval of the Treasury, in sterling from the Commission of the European Communities[4] or the European Investment Bank[5] or in any other currency from a person other than the Secretary of State,

such sums as may be required by the corporation or any of its wholly owned subsidiaries for capital purposes or for fulfilling any guarantee entered into by it[6].

The corporation may borrow from any of its wholly owned subsidiaries without any consent, approval or other authority[7].

The aggregate of (i) the amounts outstanding otherwise than by way of interest, in respect of money borrowed by the corporation and its wholly owned subsidiaries (other than money borrowed on excluded loans[8]); and (ii) the public dividend capital received by the corporation, must not exceed £1,700m[9], but the Secretary of State may, with the consent of the Treasury, by order[10] increase or further increase that limit, but not beyond £1,800m[11].

The Secretary of State may[12], with the approval of the Treasury, lend to the corporation any sums which it has power to borrow from him under the provisions described above[13], and the Treasury may issue to him out of the National Loans Fund[14] any sums necessary to enable him to make such loans[15]. Any such loans must be repaid to the Secretary of State at such times and by such methods, and interest paid at such times and rates, as he may, with the approval of the Treasury, from time to time direct[16]. The Secretary of State must prepare in respect of each financial year an account[17] of the sums issued to him by the Treasury to enable him to make loans and his disposal of those sums, and of the public dividend capital[18] received and the public dividend[19] paid by the corporation[20]. The Secretary of State must send the account to the Comptroller and Auditor General before the end of November next following the end of the financial year to which it relates; the Comptroller and Auditor General must examine, certify and report on each of the accounts and lay copies of it and his report before each House of Parliament[21].

The Treasury may guarantee, in such manner and on such conditions as it thinks fit, the repayment of the principal of, the payment of interest on, and the discharge of any other financial obligation in connection with, any sums borrowed by the corporation from any person other than the Secretary of State[22]. Immediately after such a guarantee is given, the Treasury must lay a statement of it before each House of Parliament[23]. Any sum required by the Treasury for fulfilling the guarantee is charged on and issued out of the Consolidated Fund[24]. Where any sum is issued, the Treasury must lay a statement relating to that sum before each House of Parliament, as soon as possible after the end of each financial year beginning with the year in which the sum is issued and ending with the year in which all liability in respect of the principal sum and the interest on it is discharged[25]. If any sums are issued by the Treasury in fulfilment of a guarantee, the corporation must make to the Treasury, at such times and in such manner as the Treasury may

from time to time direct, payments of such amounts as the Treasury directs
in or towards repayment of the sums issued, and of interest at such rate as
the Treasury directs on what is for the time being outstanding in respect of
the sums issued[26].

1   As to British Shipbuilders see para 637 ante.
2   Aircraft and Shipbuilding Industries Act 1977 s 11(1).
3   Ibid s 11(2). For the meaning of 'wholly owned subsidiary' see para 638 note 5 ante. As to
    the Secretary of State see para 2 ante.
4   As to the European Commission see EUROPEAN COMMUNITIES.
5   As to the European Investment Bank see EUROPEAN COMMUNITIES.
6   Aircraft and Shipbuilding Industries Act 1977 s 11(3).
7   Ibid s 11(4).
8   A loan is an excluded loan for this purpose if:
    (1)   it consists of money borrowed by the corporation from one of its wholly owned
          subsidiaries, or by one such subsidiary from another (Aircraft and Shipbuilding
          Industries Act 1977 s 11(9)(a));
    (2)   it is a loan under what is now the Industrial Development Act 1982 s 7 or s 8
          (assistance for industry) (see paras 828–831 post) (Aircraft and Shipbuilding
          Industries Act 1977 s 11(9)(b) (amended by the British Aerospace Act 1980
          s 15(2), Sch 3));
    (3)   it is a loan guaranteed under the Industry Act 1972 s 10 (as amended)
          (construction credits for ships) (see para 655 post) (Aircraft and Shipbuilding
          Industries Act 1977 s 11(9)(c));
    (4)   the purpose of the loan is to pay off the whole or part of the commencing debt of
          the corporation (see s 15; and para 643 post) (s 11(9)(d)); or
    (5)   the purpose of the loan is to pay off a previous loan which was an excluded loan
          by virtue of head (4) supra (s 11(9)(e)).
9   The limit was increased from £1,550m by the British Shipbuilders Borrowing Powers
    (Increase of Limit) Order 1988, SI 1988/1401, art 2.
10 The power to make such an order includes power to vary or revoke any previous such
    order; a draft of any order must be laid before and approved by the House of Commons:
    Aircraft and Shipbuilding Industries Act 1977 s 11(10) (amended by the British Aerospace
    Act 1980 Sch 3). Such an order may increase or further increase the limit by any sum not
    exceeding £150m: Aircraft and Shipbuilding Industries Act 1977 s 11(10) (as so amended).
11 Ibid s 11(7) (amended by the British Shipbuilders (Borrowing Powers) Act 1983 s 1(1); the
    British Shipbuilders (Borrowing Powers) Act 1987 s 1(1); and the British Shipbuilders
    Borrowing Powers (Increase at Limit) Order 1988, SI 1988/1401 (see note 9 supra)). No
    part of the commencing capital of the corporation is taken into account under this
    provision: Aircraft and Shipbuilding Industries Act 1977 s 11(8) (amended by the British
    Aerospace Act 1980 Sch 3). As to the commencing capital of the corporation see para 643
    post.
12 This is without prejudice to his powers under any other enactment: Aircraft and
    Shipbuilding Industries Act 1977 s 12(1).
13 Ie under ibid s 11 (as amended: see the text and notes 1–11 supra).
14 As to the National Loans Fund see CONSTITUTIONAL LAW AND HUMAN RIGHTS vol 8(2)
    (Reissue) para 727 et seq.
15 Aircraft and Shipbuilding Industries Act 1977 s 12(1).
16 Ibid s 12(2). Any such sums received by the Secretary of State must be paid into the
    National Loans Fund: s 12(3).
17 The form of the accounts and the manner of preparing them must be such as the Treasury
    may direct: ibid s 12(6).
18 For the meaning of 'public dividend capital' see para 643 post.
19 For the meaning of 'public dividend' see para 643 post.
20 Aircraft and Shipbuilding Industries Act 1977 s 12(4).
21 Ibid s 12(5). As to the Comptroller and Auditor General see CONSTITUTIONAL LAW AND
    HUMAN RIGHTS vol 8(2) (Reissue) paras 724–726.
22 Ibid s 13(1) (amended by the Miscellaneous Financial Provisions Act 1983 s 4, Sch 2).
23 Aircraft and Shipbuilding Industries Act 1977 s 13(2).
24 Ibid s 13(3). As to the Consolidated Fund see CONSTITUTIONAL LAW AND HUMAN RIGHTS
    vol 8(2) (Reissue) para 711 et seq; PARLIAMENT vol 34 (Reissue) paras 952 et seq.
25 Ibid s 13(2).

26 Ibid s 13(4). Any such sums received by the Treasury must be paid into the Consolidated Fund: s 13(5).

643.   Rights and obligations transferred to British Shipbuilders.   On 1 July 1977[1] the rights and obligations of the Secretary of State with respect to certain government loans[2] to companies which came into public ownership on that date[3] were transferred to British Shipbuilders[4]. The Secretary of State, with the approval of the Treasury, was required to prescribe a commencing capital for the corporation, and the division of the commencing capital between commencing debt and public dividend capital[5].

The Secretary of State may[6], with the approval of the Treasury, pay to the corporation such sums, known as public dividend capital, as he thinks fit[7]. In consideration of receiving such sums the corporation must make payments, known as public dividends, to the Secretary of State[8]. In each accounting year[9] the corporation must decide whether or not to propose to the Secretary of State to pay any public dividend, and if so, the amount it proposes to pay[10]. If it makes such a proposal which is agreed by the Secretary of State with the consent of the Treasury, the corporation must pay the public dividend proposed for that year[11]. If no proposal is made or agreed the corporation must pay a public dividend of such amount as the Secretary of State may determine, with the consent of the Treasury and after consultation with the corporation[12].

1   Ie the shipbuilding industry vesting date: see the Aircraft and Shipbuilding Industries Act 1977 ss 19(2), 56(1); the Aircraft and Shipbuilding Industries (Shipbuilding Industry Vesting Date) Order 1977, SI 1977/540, art 1; and para 645 post.
2   As to the loans in question see the Aircraft and Shipbuilding Industries Act 1977 s 14(3) (amended by the British Aerospace Act 1980 s 15(2), Sch 3).
3   As to these companies see para 645 note 3 post.
4   Aircraft and Shipbuilding Industries Act 1977 s 14(2). As to British Shipbuilders see para 637 ante.
5   Ibid s 15(1)–(3) (s 15(2) amended by the British Aerospace Act 1980 Sch 3). The Secretary of State was empowered from time to time to determine the terms for paying off the commencing debt of the corporation, and obliged to pay sums received by way of repayment or interest into the National Loans Fund (see CONSTITUTIONAL LAW AND HUMAN RIGHTS vol 8(2) (Reissue) para 727 et seq): Aircraft and Shipbuilding Industries Act 1977 s 15(4), (5). As to the Secretary of State see para 2 ante.
6   This is subject to the provisions of ibid s 11 (as amended): see para 642 ante.
7   Ibid s 16(1). Sums required by the Secretary at State for payments of public dividend capital are defrayed out of moneys provided by Parliament: s 16(6).
8   Ibid s 16(2).
9   As to the accounting year of the corporation see ibid ss 17(5), (6), 56(1); and para 644 post.
10 Ibid s 16(3). Any public dividends received by the Secretary of State must be paid into the Consolidated Fund: s 16(6). As to the Consolidated Fund see CONSTITUTIONAL LAW AND HUMAN RIGHTS vol 8(2) (Reissue) para 711 et seq; PARLIAMENT vol 34 (Reissue) para 952 et seq.
11 Aircraft and Shipbuilding Industries Act 1977 s 16(4).
12 Ibid s 16(5).

644.   Accounts, audits and reports.   British Shipbuilders[1] must:

(1)   keep proper accounts and proper records in relation to them[2];

(2)   prepare in respect of each accounting year[3] a statement of accounts[4] giving a true and fair view of the state of affairs and profit or loss of the corporation[5]; and

(3)   prepare in respect of each accounting year such a statement or statements of consolidated accounts dealing with, and giving a true

and fair view of the state of affairs and profit or loss of, the corporation and all of its subsidiary undertakings[6] ('the group'), or some (but not all) members of the group as the corporation may determine and the Secretary of State and the Treasury may for the time being approve[7].

The accounts kept, and all statements prepared by, the corporation, must be audited by auditors appointed for each accounting year by the Secretary of State[8]. As soon as they have been audited the corporation must send to the Secretary of State:

(a) a copy of the statements;

(b) copies of the statements of accounts for such of its subsidiary undertakings as the corporation may determine with the approval of the Secretary of State and the consent of the Treasury; and

(c) if the Secretary of State, with the consent of the Treasury, so requires by notice in writing, copies of the statements of accounts for each subsidiary undertaking which is specified in the notice,

together with a copy of any report made by the auditors on the statements or on the accounts of the corporation; and the Secretary of State must lay a copy of every statement and report of which a copy is received by him before each House of Parliament[9].

The corporation must make to the Secretary of State, as soon as possible after the end of each accounting year, a report on the corporation's operations and those of its wholly owned subsidiaries[10] during that year[11]. The report must set out any direction given to the corporation during that year by the Secretary of State, unless the Secretary of State has given (and not revoked) a notice that laying it before Parliament would be against the national interest[12]. The report must also set out any consent given to it for the change of its activities[13], and include a general account of the changes in organisation made during the year in consequence of a consent given in that or any other accounting year[14]. A copy of the register of members' financial interests must be annexed to the report[15]. The Secretary of State must lay a copy of every report made to him under the provisions described above before each House of Parliament[16].

1 As to British Shipbuilders see para 637 ante.

2 Aircraft and Shipbuilding Industries Act 1977 s 17(1)(a).

3 The Secretary of State was required to direct a period as the first accounting year of the corporation; subsequent accounting years are successive periods of 12 months, following the first period: ibid s 17(5). The Secretary of State may direct an alternative finishing date for any accounting year: s 17(6). As to the Secretary of State see para 2 ante.

4 Every statement of accounts required to be prepared by the corporation must comply with any requirement notified to the corporation in writing by the Secretary of State, with the consent of the Treasury, in relation to (1) the information to be contained in the statement; (2) the manner in which the information is to be presented; and (3) the methods and principles according to which it must be prepared: ibid s 17(3). Subject to any such requirement, in preparing any such statement the corporation must follow, with respect to any matter specified in heads (1) to (3) supra, such course as may for the time being be approved by the Secretary of State with the consent of the Treasury: s 17(4).

5 Ibid s 17(1)(b).

6 'Subsidiary undertaking' has the same meaning as in the Companies Act 1985 Pt VII (ss 221–262A) (as amended) (see COMPANIES vol 7(2) (1996 Reissue) para 828): Aircraft and Shipbuilding Industries Act 1977 s 17(10) (added by the Companies Act 1989 Sch 10 para 28(1), (4)).

7 Aircraft and Shipbuilding Industries Act 1977 s 17(1)(c) (amended by the Companies Act 1989 s 23, Sch 10 para 28(1), (2)). If the Secretary of State, with the consent of the Treasury, so requires by notice in writing, the corporation must, in respect of any

accounting year to which the notice relates, comply with this obligation by preparing a statement of consolidated accounts dealing with the specified members of the group and giving a true and fair view of their state of affairs and profit or loss: Aircraft and Shipbuilding Industries Act 1977 s 17(2).

8   Ibid s 17(7). A person must not be appointed unless he is eligible for appointment as a company auditor under the Companies Act 1989 s 25 (see COMPANIES vol 7(2) (1996 Reissue) para 956): Aircraft and Shipbuilding Industries Act 1977 s 17(8) (substituted by the Companies Act 1989 (Eligibility for Appointment as Company Auditor) (Consequential Amendments) Regulations 1991, SI 1991/1997).

9   Aircraft and Shipbuilding Industries Act 1977 s 17(9) (amended by the Companies Act 1989 Sch 10 para 28(1), (3)).

10   For the meaning of 'wholly owned subsidiary' see para 638 note 5 ante.

11   Aircraft and Shipbuilding Industries Act 1977 s 18(1).

12   Ibid s 18(2). As to the notices referred to see s 4(5); and para 639 note 24 ante. Such notices may be revoked by notice to the corporation: s 18(3).

13   As to such consent see ibid s 4A(2) (as added); and para 638 text and note 2 ante.

14   Ibid s 18(3A) (added by the British Shipbuilders Act 1983 s 2(3)).

15   Aircraft and Shipbuilding Industries Act 1977 s 18(5) (spent in respect of British Shipbuilders by virtue of the Industry Act 1980 s 20). As to that register see the Aircraft and Shipbuilding Industries Act 1977 s 1(9); and para 637 text and note 8 ante.

16   Ibid s 18(6).

B. VESTING OF ASSETS

645. Acquisition of securities and assets. On 1 July 1977[1] the securities[2] of specified companies in the shipbuilding industry[3] (other than excepted companies[4]) vested in British Shipbuilders[5], and the corporation succeeded at once, without the normal formalities of transfer, to all the rights and liabilities attached to those securities[6].

Provision consequent upon that vesting was made for:

(1)   the transfer of rights and liabilities where a company acquired by the corporation was the wholly owned subsidiary[7] of another company which was not so acquired, and for the transfer of rights and liabilities under agreements for the rendering of personal services[8];

(2)   inter-company debts owed by an acquired company to an associated person[9] to be treated as securities[10];

(3)   the cancellation of any rights of third persons to acquire securities in, or to appoint or be appointed as director of, a company which came into public ownership[11];

(4)   the limitation of payments of interest and of dividends during a specified period ending with the vesting date, and the repayment of amounts paid in excess of the limits specified[12];

(5)   the addition of further companies to those taken into public ownership, and the removal of any company from those which were to be acquired[13];

(6)   the prevention of transfer, before the vesting date, of rights in relation to any works[14], the recovery of assets transferred by an acquired company before the vesting date to a body which was not to be taken into public ownership[15], and measures to be taken where assets of a company to be acquired were dissipated by the company before the vesting date[16];

(7)   the measures to be taken by the corporation in respect of unreasonable or onerous transactions entered into by a company before the vesting date[17];

(8)   approvals which the Secretary of State might give to certain transactions otherwise prohibited[18]; and

(9)   the furnishing of specified information to persons authorised by the Secretary of State, and the restriction of disclosure of information so furnished[19].

1   Ie the shipbuilding industry vesting date: see para 643 note 1 ante.

2   'Securities' in relation to a company means any shares, debentures, debenture stock, loan stock, income notes, income stock, funding certificates and securities of a like nature: Aircraft and Shipbuilding Industries Act 1977 s 56(1). However, under s 19(5) (see note 4 infra) certain securities forming part of the loan capital of the company were excepted.

3   The companies taken into public ownership are listed in ibid Sch 2 Pt I, under the headings 'shipbuilding companies', 'companies manufacturing slow speed diesel marine engines' and 'training companies'. The Secretary of State was empowered to add or remove companies from the list at the time of vesting in certain circumstances, and there were provisions safeguarding the assets of companies to be acquired: see ss 26–34; and the text and notes 12–17 infra. As to the Secretary of State see para 2 ante.

4   Excepted companies were any company: (1) which before 21 November 1975 a court had ordered to be wound up; (2) which before that date had passed a resolution for voluntary winding up; or (3) of whose property a receiver had been appointed before that date: ibid s 19(5).

5   Ibid s 19(2), Sch 2. As to British Shipbuilders see para 637 ante.

6   Ibid s 19(3).

7   For the meaning of 'wholly owned subsidiary' see para 638 note 5 ante.

8   Aircraft and Shipbuilding Industries Act 1977 s 20, Sch 3. For a case on the liability of a parent company whose subsidiary had been acquired by British Shipbuilders see *Anglomar Shipping Co Ltd v Swan Hunter Shipbuilders Ltd and Swan Hunter Group Ltd, The London Lion* [1980] 2 Lloyd's Rep 456, CA.

9   'Associated person', in relation to a company or its wholly owned subsidiary, means (1) a person who controls the company; or (2) a body corporate controlled by a person who also controls the company: Aircraft and Shipbuilding Industries Act 1977 s 56(1).

10   See ibid s 21. If not resolved by agreement, disputes under s 21 could be submitted to the Aircraft and Shipbuilding Industries Arbitration Tribunal: see para 647 post.

11   See ibid s 22(1), (2). Provision was also made for the payment of compensation for loss arising under this provision (s 22(3)), and for the submission of the claim to arbitration in default of agreement (see note 10 supra) (s 22(4)).

12   See ibid ss 23–25 (s 23 amended by the Companies Consolidation (Consequential Provisions) Act 1985 s 30, Sch 2).

13   See the Aircraft and Shipbuilding Industries Act 1977 ss 26, 27.

14   See ibid s 28. For the meaning of 'works' see s 56(1), (6) (definition in s 56(1) amended by the Civil Aviation Act 1982 s 109, Sch 15 para 18).

15   See the Aircraft and Shipbuilding Industries Act 1977 s 29, Sch 4.

16   See ibid s 30.

17   See ibid ss 31–33.

18   See ibid s 34.

19   See ibid ss 51, 52 (as amended).

646.   Compensation.   Compensation for the securities[1] of companies vested in British Shipbuilders[2] was to be paid by the issue of government stock, referred to as 'compensation stock'[3]. The amount of compensation was generally equal to the base value of the securities[4] and was not payable before a date (called 'the conversion date') specified in an order made by the Secretary of State[5]. In certain circumstances a deduction could be made from the amount of compensation which would otherwise be payable[6]. Provision was made for the appointment of a stockholders' representative to act on behalf of holders of securities in each company which came into public ownership[7].

Provision was made regarding the payment of compensation for loss by employees of employment, emoluments or pension rights[8].

1   For the meaning of 'securities' see para 645 note 2 ante.

2   As to British Shipbuilders see para 637 ante.

3   Aircraft and Shipbuilding Industries Act 1977 s 35(1), (9), Sch 5. The rate of interest of compensation stock and conditions as to repayment, redemption and other matters were determined by the Treasury: see s 40. The procedure for the issue of stock was governed by the Aircraft and Shipbuilding Industries (Issue of Compensation Stock) Regulations 1977, SI 1977/754.

4   See the Aircraft and Shipbuilding Industries Act 1977 s 35(3). The base value of quoted securities was determined according to s 37 and that of unquoted securities according to s 38.

5   Ibid s 36(1). Provision governing the determination of the conversion date is contained in s 36(2)–(8). Orders made under s 36(1) are not statutory instruments and are not dealt with in this work. As to the Secretary of State see para 2 ante.

6   See ibid s 39. The circumstances were, broadly speaking, that payments of dividend or interest had been made by directors before the vesting date, or transactions designed to dissipate the assets of the company, or onerous transactions, had been entered into: see s 39(1), (2). As to such payments and transactions see para 645 text and notes 12, 16–17 ante.

7   See ibid s 41, Sch 6. Disputes unresolved by agreement were to be submitted to the arbitration tribunal: see para 647 post.

8   See ibid s 50; and para 652 post.

C. ARBITRATION

647. The Aircraft and Shipbuilding Industries Arbitration Tribunal. A tribunal, known as the Aircraft and Shipbuilding Industries Arbitration Tribunal, was established to determine any question or dispute expressly required by the Aircraft and Shipbuilding Industries Act 1977 to be determined by or referred to arbitration under the Act, or any matter in respect of which the Act gave jurisdiction to the tribunal[1]. The Lord Chancellor may direct that the tribunal sit as a single tribunal or in two or more divisions[2]. It consists of a president[3] and two other members[4], all of whom are disqualified for membership of the House of Commons[5]. The arbitration tribunal is under the direct supervision of the Council on Tribunals[6].

The members of the tribunal hold office for the period determined at the time of their appointment[7]. However, notwithstanding that that period has not expired:

(1)   a member may resign on at least one month's notice given to his appointor[8];

(2)   a member's appointor may declare the member's office vacant on the ground that he is unfit to continue in office[9]; and

(3)   if any member becomes bankrupt or makes a composition with his creditor, his office becomes vacant[10].

If any member of the tribunal becomes temporarily incapable of performing his duties by reason of illness or other infirmity his appointor must appoint some other fit person to discharge those duties for up to six months at a time, and the person so appointed has the same powers as the person whose place he takes[11].

The members of the tribunal must be paid such sums (whether by way of salary or fees) and such allowances as the Secretary of State may determine with the approval of the Treasury[12].

The tribunal may appoint such staff as it considers necessary to assist it in the proper execution of its duties[13].

1   Aircraft and Shipbuilding Industries Act 1977 s 42(1). The tribunal is a court of record with an official seal which must be officially noticed: s 42(2).

2   Ibid s 42(3). As to the Lord Chancellor see CONSTITUTIONAL LAW AND HUMAN RIGHTS vol 8(2) (Reissue) para 477 et seq.

3   The president must be a person appointed by the Lord Chancellor who has a seven year general qualification within the meaning of the Courts and Legal Services Act 1990 s 71 (see COURTS), or a member of the Bar of Northern Ireland or a Solicitor of the Supreme Court of Northern Ireland of at least seven years' standing: Aircraft and Shipbuilding Industries Act 1977 s 42(3)(a) (amended by the Courts and Legal Services Act 1990 s 71(2), Sch 10 para 40). See further note 7 infra as to prospective provisions regarding the person to be appointed president of the tribunal.

4   These two members are appointed by the Secretary of State after consultation with all the stockholders' representatives; one must be a person of experience in business, and the other a person of experience in finance: Aircraft and Shipbuilding Industries Act 1977 s 42(3)(b). As to stockholders' representatives see para 646 text and note 7 ante. As to the Secretary of State see para 2 ante.

5   House of Commons Disqualification Act 1975 s 1(1)(f), Sch 1 Pt II (amended by the Aircraft and Shipbuilding Industries Act 1977 s 42(9)). See PARLIAMENT vol 34 (Reissue) para 607 et seq.

6   Tribunals and Inquiries Act 1992 s 1(1), Sch 1 para 2. As to the Council on Tribunals see ADMINISTRATIVE LAW vol 1(1) (2001 Reissue) para 55 et seq.

7   Aircraft and Shipbuilding Industries Act 1977 s 42(5) (amended by the Judicial Pensions and Retirement Act 1993 s 26(10), Sch 6 para 47). As from a day to be appointed, no appointment of a person to be president of the tribunal may be such as to extend beyond the day he reaches 70, subject to certain transitional provisions: Aircraft and Shipbuilding Industries Act 1977 s 42(5A) (added by the Judicial Pensions and Retirement Act 1993 Sch 6 para 47, and expressed to be subject to s 26(4)–(6) (power to authorise continuance in office up to 75)). The transitional provisions referred to are those set out by s 26(11), Sch 7, and the provisions of s 27 (completion of proceedings after retirement).

8   Aircraft and Shipbuilding Industries Act 1977 s 42(5)(a). 'Appointor' means, in the case of the president of the tribunal, the Lord Chancellor, and in the case of any other member, the Secretary of State: s 42(8).

9   Ibid s 42(5)(b).

10 Ibid s 42(5)(c).

11 Ibid s 42(6).

12 Ibid s 44(2). Such remuneration and allowances, and other expenses of the tribunal, are met in the first instance by the Secretary of State out of money provided by Parliament, but must be repaid to him on demand by British Shipbuilders: s 44(4). Any sums repaid to him must be paid into the Consolidated Fund: s 44(5). As to the Consolidated Fund see CONSTITUTIONAL LAW AND HUMAN RIGHTS vol 8(2) (Reissue) para 711 et seq; PARLIAMENT vol 34 (Reissue) para 952 et seq.

13 Aircraft and Shipbuilding Industries Act 1977 s 44(1). The staff must be paid such remuneration (whether by way of salary or fees) and allowances as the tribunal may determine: s 44(3). These payments are made and recovered as described in note 12 supra: s 44(4), (5).

648.   Conduct of arbitration proceedings.   In proceedings before the Aircraft and Shipbuilding Industries Arbitration Tribunal[1], the provisions of the Arbitration Act 1996 with respect to:

(1)   the administration of oaths and the taking of affirmations[2];

(2)   the correction in awards of mistakes and errors[3];

(3)   the summoning, attendance and examination of witnesses and the production of documents[4]; and

(4)   the costs of the reference and award[5],

apply with any necessary modifications[6].

Every order of the tribunal is enforceable as if it were an order of the High Court[7]. The tribunal may, at any stage of any proceedings before it, refer any question which arises (other than one which is primarily a question of law) to a person or persons appointed for the purpose for inquiry and report; such report may be adopted wholly or partly by the tribunal, and may be incorporated in an order of the tribunal[8].

Subject to the provisions set out above and to provisions relating to cases stated and appeals[9], the conduct of proceedings before the tribunal is governed by rules made by the Lord Chancellor[10]. Proceedings are instituted by serving[11] on the tribunal an originating application[12], which is served on each respondent named in it by the clerk of the tribunal by notice in the prescribed form[13]. Pleadings take the form of an applicant's statement[14] and respondent's answer[15]. Any party may apply for interlocutory directions[16], or the tribunal may give such directions of its own motion[17]. The time and place of the hearing is determined by the tribunal, with at least 21 days' notice to the parties[18]. It must be held in public[19], unless all the parties otherwise agree[20]. A party may appear in person or be represented by counsel or solicitor or, with leave, by any other person[21]. If a dispute is compromised the tribunal may make a consent order and further proceedings are stayed[22]. The tribunal's final decision is given in writing with reasons[23].

Proceedings may be dismissed for want of prosecution[24], and an application may be withdrawn by notice served on the clerk and accompanied by the written consent of every other party[25].

Subject to all the provisions described above, the tribunal may regulate its own procedure[26].

1   As to the tribunal see para 647 ante.
2   See the Arbitration Act 1996 s 38(5); and ARBITRATION.
3   See ibid s 57; and ARBITRATION.
4   See ibid ss 34, 43, 44; and ARBITRATION.
5   See ibid ss 59–65; and ARBITRATION.
6   Aircraft and Shipbuilding Industries Act 1977 s 42(7), Sch 7 para 2 (amended by the Arbitration Act 1996 s 107(1), Sch 3 para 32).
7   Aircraft and Shipbuilding Industries Act 1977 Sch 7 para 12.
8   Aircraft and Shipbuilding Industries Act 1977 Sch 7 para 13.
9   Ie ibid Sch 7 paras 3, 4: see para 649 post.
10   Ibid Sch 7 para 5. Such rules are made by statutory instrument subject to annulment in pursuance of a resolution of either House of Parliament: Sch 7 para 5. See the Aircraft and Shipbuilding Industries Arbitration Tribunal Rules 1977, SI 1977/1022.
11   As to the service of documents see ibid r 21.
12   Ibid r 2(1), Schedule Form 1. The application must name as respondents the parties and directly interested persons, and certify that it does not relate to Scottish proceedings: r 2(2). Directly interested persons may be joined to the proceedings by the tribunal, and it may also dismiss from the proceedings persons not directly interested: r 4.
      Applications must be numbered, listed and filed by the clerk, and the lists and files must be available for inspection: see rr 7–9.
13   Ibid r 3.
14   The statement is served on the tribunal, and then a copy is served by the clerk on each respondent with notice in the prescribed form: see ibid r 5. No further step may be taken in any proceedings before the expiration of time for service of an answer: r 22.
15   The answer is served on the tribunal, and then a copy is served by the clerk on the applicant: ibid r 6(1), (5). The respondent must include in his answer an address for service: r 6(4). A respondent must state which (if any) of the facts alleged by the applicant he denies, and set out any other matters or contentions; any facts which he does not deny he is taken to have admitted, but the tribunal may still require proof: r 6(2), (3).
16   Ibid r 10. As to the hearing of such applications see r 11.
17   Ibid r 12.
18   Ibid r 13(1), (2).
19   This does not apply to applications for interlocutory directions: ibid r 13(3).
20   Ibid r 13(3) and proviso. If the parties agree to a private hearing a member of the Council on Tribunals is entitled to attend: r 13(3) proviso. As to the Council on Tribunals see ADMINISTRATIVE LAW vol 1(1) (2001 Reissue) para 55 et seq.
21   Ibid r 15.
22   Ibid r 16. See also note 23 infra.

23 Ibid r 17(1). Orders of the tribunal are sealed: r 17(3). A copy of the decision must be sent to every party and a copy must be available for inspection: r 17(2).
24 Ibid r 19.
25 Ibid r 20.
26 Ibid r 23.

649. Special cases and appeals. The Aircraft and Shipbuilding Industries Arbitration Tribunal[1] may, and if so ordered by the Court of Appeal must, state in the form of a special case for determination by that court any question of law which may arise before it[2]. Application for a special case to be stated is made by notice in writing to the tribunal[3]. In certain cases[4] an appeal lies from the tribunal to the Court of Appeal on any question of law or fact[5].

1 As to the tribunal see para 647 ante.
2 Aircraft and Shipbuilding Industries Act 1977 s 42(7), Sch 7 para 3.
3 Aircraft and Shipbuilding Industries Arbitration Tribunal Rules 1977, SI 1977/1022, r 18(1). The tribunal clerk must serve a copy on every other party concerned: r 18(2). The tribunal must consider the application and notify its decision to the parties, giving reasons if it declines to state a case: r 18(3).
4 Appeal lies against a determination or order of the tribunal with respect to a claim by British Shipbuilders: (1) against the directors of a company to enforce a liability under the Aircraft and Shipbuilding Industries Act 1977 s 23 (repayment of dividends or interest); or (2) for compensation for loss arising from any transaction referred to the tribunal under s 28 (transfer of works), s 30 (dissipation of assets), or s 31 (onerous transactions): Sch 7 para 4(a), (b). See also para 645 ante.
5 Ibid Sch 7 para 4.

D. MISCELLANEOUS PROVISIONS

650. Unfair practices. A private company[1] engaged in shipbuilding or shiprepairing[2] may make a written complaint to the Secretary of State[3] that a practice employed by British Shipbuilders or one of its wholly owned subsidiaries in relation to shipbuilding or the provision of shipbuilding services, is unfair to the complainant, for a reason specified in the complaint[4]. The Secretary of State must send a copy of the complaint to the corporation and, after such period as he thinks reasonable, send a copy of any comments of the corporation to the complainant; if he considers that the complaint raises a question of substance and that the complainant has a reasonable case to make in support of it, the Secretary of State must afford the complainant and the corporation an opportunity to make representations on the matter to a person appointed by him[5]. The Secretary of State must consider the report of that person, and if it appears to the Secretary of State that the practice is unfair, he must give the corporation such directions[6] as appear to him to be requisite to secure the removal of the ground on which it is unfair[7].

1 Ie a person other than British Shipbuilders (see the text and note 4 infra), one of its wholly owned subsidiaries (see note 5 infra), or a body corporate the whole of whose equity share capital is owned by the Crown: Aircraft and Shipbuilding Industries Act 1977 s 47(1)(a)–(c), (2)(a)–(c). As to British Shipbuilders see para 637 ante. For the meaning of 'wholly owned subsidiary' see para 638 note 5 ante.
2 'Shiprepairing' includes refitting, converting and maintaining ships, and 'the provision of shiprepairing services' has a corresponding meaning: ibid s 47(2).
3 As to the Secretary of State see para 2 ante.
4 Aircraft and Shipbuilding Industries Act 1977 s 47(1), (2).
5 Ibid s 47(3).

6 For the general power of the Secretary of State to give directions to the corporation see para 639 ante.
7 Aircraft and Shipbuilding Industries Act 1977 s 47(4). He must furnish both the corporation and the complainant with a copy of the report of the appointed person and a statement of his (ie the Secretary of State's) conclusions on it: s 47(6). If directions are given to the corporation, he must furnish the complainant with a statement of them: s 47(5).

651. Pensions.

British Shipbuilders[1] may, in respect of such of the persons as are or have been employed by it or any of its wholly owned subsidiaries[2] as it may determine:

(1) pay such pensions[3] to or in respect of those persons;

(2) make such payments towards the provision of such pensions; or

(3) establish and maintain such schemes for the payment of such pensions,

as it may determine[4].

A scheme under head (3) above may provide that where a person participating in the scheme as an employee of the corporation or any of its wholly owned subsidiaries becomes a member of the corporation[5], his service as a member is to be treated for the purposes of the scheme as service as an employee[6]. However, if under the scheme any description of benefit may, or may in particular circumstances, be conferred only at the request or with the consent of the corporation, it may not make the provision set out above unless it also provides that except with the approval of the Secretary of State[7] and the Treasury, no such request or consent may be made or given in the case of a benefit for or in respect of a member of the corporation[8].

The Secretary of State, by regulations[9] made by statutory instrument[10], may make such provision in relation to any existing pension scheme[11] which provides for pensions to or in respect of persons who are or have been employed by a company which became a wholly owned subsidiary of the corporation, as appears to him expedient in consequence of its having become such a subsidiary[12]. Any persons having pension rights[13] under existing schemes (whether or not they are past or present employees as described above) must not be placed in any worse position by virtue of any such regulations[14]. If they are, the regulations are not invalid, but the Secretary of State must make the necessary amending regulations[15]. Any dispute as to whether such a person is or is not in a worse position under such regulations, including any question whether the position has been rectified by amending regulations, must be referred to and resolved by an employment tribunal[16].

1 As to British Shipbuilders see para 637 ante.
2 For the meaning of 'wholly owned subsidiary' see para 638 note 5 ante. References to a wholly owned subsidiary of the corporation include references to: (1) employment before the date of transfer (see para 645 ante) by a company which became a wholly owned subsidiary; and (2) employment under certain agreements for the rendering of personal services (see para 645 text and note 8 ante): Aircraft and Shipbuilding Industries Act 1977 s 49(15).
3 'Pension' in relation to any person means a pension, whether contributory or not, of any kind whatsoever payable to or in respect of him, and includes a gratuity so payable and a return of contributions or insurance premiums to a pension fund with or without interest or any other addition: ibid s 56(1).
4 Ibid s 49(1).
5 As to the appointment of members of the corporation see para 637 ante.
6 Aircraft and Shipbuilding Industries Act 1977 s 49(2).
7 As to the Secretary of State see para 2 ante.

8   Ibid s 49(3); Transfer of Functions (Minister for the Civil Service and Treasury) Order 1981, SI 1981/1670, art 2(2).

9   Such regulations may have effect from a date before their making, but not so as to put any person (other than the corporation or a wholly owned subsidiary) in a worse position: Aircraft and Shipbuilding Industries Act 1977 s 49(11).

10   The statutory instrument is subject to annulment in pursuance of a resolution of either House of Parliament: ibid s 49(4).

11   An 'existing pension scheme' is any pension scheme not made under ibid s 49(1): s 49(4). 'Pension scheme' includes any form of arrangements for the payment of pensions, whether subsisting by reason of an Act, trust, contract or otherwise, and also includes any customary practice under which pensions are paid: s 56(1).

12   Ibid s 49(4). In particular such regulations may make provision for:

    (1)   the complete or partial amalgamation of existing schemes with other existing schemes or with schemes established under s 49(1) (s 49(5)(a));

    (2)   amending, repealing or revoking (a) existing schemes, (b) any enactment relating to existing schemes or amalgamated schemes, or (c) any trust deed, rules or other instrument made for the purposes of an existing or amalgamated scheme (s 49(5)(b));

    (3)   complete or partial transfer of liabilities and obligations under existing schemes, or reducing or extinguishing such liabilities (s 49(5)(c));

    (4)   complete or partial transfer, or winding up, of any pension fund held for the purposes of an existing scheme (s 49(5)(d)); and

    (5)   supplemental or consequential matters (s 49(5)(e)).

See the Shipbuilding Industry (Pension Schemes) Regulations 1978, SI 1978/232. See also the Aircraft Industry (Pension Schemes) Regulations 1977, SI 1977/1329; and para 656 post.

The power to make regulations includes power to provide for the determination of any question of fact or of law which may arise in giving effect to them, and for regulating the practice and procedure to be followed (otherwise than in court proceedings) in connection with the determination of such questions: Aircraft and Shipbuilding Industries Act 1977 s 49(14). Nothing in s 49(4) or (5) authorises the making of provision for the diversion of any pension fund to purposes other than the payment of pensions to or in respect of persons to whom s 49(1) (see the text and notes 1–4 supra) applies: s 49(6).

13   'Pension rights' includes all forms of right to or eligibility for the present or future payment of a pension to or in respect of a person, and any expectation of the accruer of a pension to or in respect of a person under any customary practice, and also includes a right of allocation in respect of the present or future payment of a pension: ibid s 56(1).

14   Ibid s 49(7). However, regulations may make exceptional provisions to meet cases in which, in connection with or in anticipation of any provision of the Aircraft and Shipbuilding Industries Act 1977, pension rights have been created other than in the ordinary course: s 49(8).

15   Ibid s 49(9). He must do so as soon as possible after he is satisfied that the objective of s 49(7) is not satisfied, or after a determination under s 49(10) (see the text and note 16 infra): s 49(9).

16   Ibid s 49(10) (amended by the Employment Protection (Consolidation) Act 1978 s 159(2), Sch 16 para 28; and by virtue of the Employment Rights (Dispute Resolution) Act 1998 s 1(2)(a)). If the case requires, the dispute may be referred to and resolved by a tribunal established under the Industrial Tribunals (Northern Ireland) Order 1996, SI 1996/1921, art 3: see the Aircraft and Shipbuilding Industries Act 1977 s 49(10) (amended by the Industrial Tribunals (Northern Ireland) Order 1996, SI 1996/1921, art 26, Sch 1 para 6). Where by reason of any provision of regulations (other than under the Aircraft and Shipbuilding Industries Act 1977 s 49(8): see note 14 supra) loss is suffered by a person making contributions or paying pensions under an existing scheme, other than a wholly owned subsidiary, compensation is payable by the corporation, and if the amount of compensation cannot be agreed, it must be determined by arbitration: s 49(12). As to arbitration see para 647–649 ante.

652.   Compensation for loss of employment, emoluments and pensions.

Provision is made in the Aircraft and Shipbuilding Industries Act 1977 for the Secretary of State to make regulations[1] requiring British Shipbuilders[2] to pay compensation to or in respect of any employees of a company coming into public ownership who in consequence thereof suffer loss of employment, or loss or diminution of emoluments[3] or pension rights[4].

Such regulations must prescribe the procedure for making claims for compensation, and the manner in which and the person by whom any question whether or what compensation is payable is to be determined[5]. They must in particular contain provision enabling appeals from any determination, in such cases and subject to such conditions as may be prescribed, to be brought before an employment tribunal[6].

Regulations may make different provision in relation to different classes of person, and may have effect as from a date prior to their making, but not so as to put any person (other than the corporation or any wholly owned subsidiary[7]) in a worse position[8].

1   Such regulations must be made by statutory instrument: Aircraft and Shipbuilding Industries Act 1977 s 50(1). Any such statutory instrument is subject to annulment in pursuance of a resolution of either House of Parliament: s 50(5). As to the Secretary of State see para 2 ante.
2   As to British Shipbuilders see para 637 ante.
3   'Emoluments' includes any allowances, privileges or benefits, whether obtained legally or by customary practice: Aircraft and Shipbuilding Industries Act 1977 s 50(4).
4   Ibid s 50(1). See further, as to pensions and pension schemes para 651 ante. At the date at which this volume states the law, no such regulations had been made.
5   Ibid s 50(3)(a).
6   Ibid s 50(3)(b) (amended by the Employment Protection (Consolidation) Act 1978 s 159(2), Sch 16 para 28; and by virtue of the Employment Rights (Dispute Resolution) Act 1998 s 1(2)(a)). If the case requires, appeals may be brought before a tribunal established under the Industrial Tribunals (Northern Ireland) Order 1996, SI 1996/1921, art 3: see the Aircraft and Shipbuilding Industries Act 1977 s 50(3)(b) (amended by the Industrial Tribunals (Northern Ireland) Order 1996, SI 1996/1921, art 26, Sch 1 para 6).
7   For the meaning of 'wholly owned subsidiary' see para 638 note 5 ante.
8   Aircraft and Shipbuilding Industries Act 1977 s 50(2).

653.   Liability for subsidiaries.   If any sum required to be paid by a judgment or order by a wholly owned subsidiary[1] of British Shipbuilders[2] is not paid by that subsidiary within 14 days beginning on the date on which execution becomes leviable to enforce the judgment or order, the corporation is liable to pay the sum and the judgment or order may be enforced against the corporation[3]. When a company becomes a wholly owned subsidiary of the corporation, certain persons[4] who were liable under contracts of guarantee or indemnity in respect of that company cease to be so liable[5]. On the date of transfer[6], the assets of companies coming into public ownership were released from all existing charges[7]. Subject to certain exceptions[8], no person became entitled to exercise any right, or became subject to any obligation, in respect of a loan, on specified grounds connected with the passing of the Aircraft and Shipbuilding Industries Act 1977[9].

1   For the meaning of 'wholly owned subsidiary' see para 638 note 5 ante.
2   As to British Shipbuilders see para 637 ante.
3   Aircraft and Shipbuilding Industries Act 1977 s 53(1) (amended by the British Shipbuilders Act 1983 ss 2(4), 3(3), Schedule).
4   Ie persons who, immediately before the company became a wholly owned subsidiary: (1) were associated persons (see para 645 note 9 ante); or (2) controlled some other company or body corporate which controlled it: Aircraft and Shipbuilding Industries Act 1977 s 53(4).
5   Ibid s 53(3). See *Anglomar Shipping Co Ltd v Swan Hunter Shipbuilders Ltd and Swan Hunter Group Ltd, The London Lion* [1980] 2 Lloyd's Rep 456, CA.
6   See para 645 ante.

7   Aircraft and Shipbuilding Industries Act 1977 s 53(5).
8   See ibid s 53(7).
9   See ibid s 53(6).

654.   Service of notices.   Where any notice or other document is required or authorised to be given to or served on any person under the Aircraft and Shipbuilding Industries Act 1977[1], it may be given to or served on him: (1) by delivering it to him[2]; (2) by leaving it at his proper address[3]; (3) by sending it by post to him at that address[4]; or (4) in the case of certain specified notices[5], by sending it in a prepaid registered letter addressed to him at that address[6]. In the case of a body corporate, a document may be given to or served on its secretary or clerk[7], and, in the case of a partnership, it may be given to or served on a partner or a person having the control or management of the partnership business[8].

If the name or address of any person having an interest in premises to or on whom a document is to be given or served cannot after reasonable inquiry be ascertained, the document may be given or served: (a) by addressing it to him either by name or by the description of 'the owner' or, as the case may be, 'the occupier' of the premises and describing them; and (b) either by delivering it to some responsible person on the premises or by affixing it, or a copy of it, to some conspicuous part of the premises[9].

1   Aircraft and Shipbuilding Industries Act 1977 s 54(1).
2   Ibid s 54(2)(a).
3   Ibid s 54(2)(b). For this purpose and that of what is now the Interpretation Act 1978 s 7 (see STATUTES vol 44(1) (Reissue) para 1388) a person's proper address is his last known address, except that: (1) in the case of a body corporate or its secretary or clerk, it is the address of the registered or principal office of that body; and (2) in the case of a partnership or a person having the control or management of the partnership business, it is the address of the principal office of the partnership; the principal office of a company registered outside the United Kingdom or a partnership carrying on business outside the United Kingdom is its principal office within the United Kingdom: Aircraft and Shipbuilding Industries Act 1977 s 54(4). If a person has specified an address for the service of documents other than his proper address as defined supra, that specified address is also to be treated as his proper address: s 54(5). For the meaning of 'United Kingdom' see para 37 note 1 ante.
4   Ibid s 54(2)(c).
5   Ie notices required to be given under ibid ss 21, 26, 27, 29 and 31: see para 645 ante.
6   Ibid s 54(2)(d).
7   Ibid s 54(3)(a).
8   Ibid s 54(3)(b).
9   Ibid s 54(6).

655.   Construction credits.   The Secretary of State[1], with the consent of the Treasury, may guarantee the payment by any person who is an individual resident in, or a body corporate incorporated under the law of any part of the United Kingdom[2], any of the Channel Islands or the Isle of Man of any sum payable by that person in respect of principal or interest under arrangements (whether by way of loan or otherwise) entered into by that person for the purpose of financing the construction[3] to the order of that person in any member state of the European Community of a ship[4] or mobile offshore installation[5] of the qualifying size[6], and its equipment[7] to his order[8]. The aggregate of the liability of the Secretary of State under the guarantees together with the guarantees given under superseded legislation[9] may not exceed £1,400m, less the amounts which have been paid by him to meet a liability and have not been repaid to him[10].

The Secretary of State may make a loan to any person who is a creditor in respect of a sum the payment of which has been so guaranteed by the Secretary of State[11]. The aggregate of the loans outstanding may not at any time exceed the limit with respect to guarantees, less the amounts which have been paid by him to meet a liability and have not been repaid to him[12].

1   As to the Secretary of State see para 2 ante.

2   For the meaning of 'United Kingdom' see para 37 note 1 ante.

3   'Construction' includes the completion of a partially constructed ship or installation and the alteration of a ship or installation and of a partially constructed ship or installation: Industry Act 1972 s 10(9) (amended by the Shipbuilding Act 1979 s 2).

4   'Ship' includes every description of vessel used in navigation: Industry Act 1972 s 12(1).

5   'Mobile offshore installation' means any installation intended for underwater exploitation of mineral resources or exploration with a view to such exploitation and which can move by water from place to place without major dismantling or modification, whether or not it has its own motive power: ibid s 12(1).

6   A ship other than a tug is of the qualifying size if its gross tonnage, ascertained in accordance with regulations under the Merchant Shipping Act 1995 s 19 (as amended) (see SHIPPING AND NAVIGATION vol 43(1) (Reissue) para 172) is not less than 100 tons (Industry Act 1972 s 12(2)(a) (amended by the Merchant Shipping Act 1995 s 314(2), Sch 13 para 47)); a tug is of the qualifying size if it is of not less than 500 brake horsepower (Industry Act 1972 s 12(2)(b)); and an installation is of the qualifying size if it weighs not less than 100 tons excluding fuel and water (s 12(2)(c)).

7   'Equipment', in relation to a ship or installation, means the installation on or in it, or the provision for it, of fixed or movable equipment, or apparatus or furnishings of any kind: ibid s 12(1).

8   Ibid s 10(1) (amended by the Industry Act 1972 (Amendment) Regulations 1987, SI 1987/1807, reg 2). A guarantee or loan may be given on such terms and conditions as may be specified with the approval of the Treasury: Industry Act 1972 s 10(7). The Secretary of State, with the consent of the Treasury, may renew such a guarantee (including a guarantee previously so renewed) on the transfer of the liability to which it relates, or any part of that liability, from one body corporate to another within the same group: s 10(7A) (added by the Industry Act 1975 s 24(2)). Two bodies corporate are in the same group for this purpose if one is the other's holding company or both are subsidiaries of a third body corporate: Industry Act 1972 s 10(7B) (added by the Industry Act 1975 s 24(2)). In addition to construction credits (by way of guarantee) the Industry Act 1972 s 11 also provided for the making of grants by the Secretary of State towards the costs paid in the years 1972–1974 of the construction of certain ships. 'Holding company' and 'subsidiary' have the meanings assigned to them by the Companies Act 1985 s 736 (as substituted) (see COMPANIES vol 7(2) (1996 Reissue) para 827): Industry Act 1972 s 10(9) (amended by the Companies Consolidation (Consequential Provisions) Act 1985 s 30, Sch 2; and the Companies Act 1989 s 144(4), Sch 18 para 9).

9   Ie under the Shipbuilding Industry Act 1967 s 7 (repealed).

10   Industry Act 1972 s 10(2), (3) (s 10(2) amended by the Industry Act 1975 s 24). The original limit of £1,000m was raised to £1,400m by the Ships and Mobile Offshore Installations Construction Credits (Increase of Limit) Order 1975, SI 1975/138, art 2. The maximum may be raised to £1,800m by the Secretary of State by order contained in a statutory instrument approved by a resolution of the House of Commons: Industry Act 1972 s 10(3), (4) (s 10(3) amended by the Industry Act 1975 s 23). The liabilities of the Secretary of State do not include liability in respect of interest on any money which is the subject of a guarantee: Industry Act 1972 s 10(8).

11   Ibid s 10(5). Grants may be made by the Secretary of State with the consent of the Treasury, on such terms and conditions as he may determine, to any person who is or has been a creditor for the purpose of supplementing the interest receivable or received on the principal money the payment of which has been guaranteed under s 10 (as amended) or under the Shipbuilding Industry Act 1967 s 7 (repealed): Industry Act 1972 s 10A (added by the Industry Act 1975 s 25).

12   Industry Act 1972 s 10(6) (amended by the Industry Act 1975 s 24).

(vi) Aircraft Manufacture

656.   Privatisation of aircraft manufacturing industry: creation of British Aerospace Ltd. Under the Aircraft and Shipbuilding Industries Act 1977, the manufacture of aircraft and ships was taken into public ownership and two corporations, British Shipbuilders and British Aerospace, were formed[1]. The British Aerospace Act 1980, however, made provision for the vesting of the property, rights, liabilities and obligations of British Aerospace in a successor company, British Aerospace Ltd[2], as from the appointed day, that is, 1 January 1981[3], and for the dissolution of British Aerospace as from 31 December 1981[4].

The successor company was wholly owned by the Crown at the appointed day[5], and provision was made as to the initial government shareholding in the company[6], and the financial structure of the company and its subsidiaries (including the establishment and application of a 'statutory reserve', being the amount by which the government investment in British Aerospace exceeded the initial share capital of the successor company)[7].

The Secretary of State[8] is empowered to acquire voting shares in the successor company, or rights to subscribe for ordinary shares, or securities which can be converted into, or carry, rights to subscribe for shares, but may not dispose of them without the consent of the Treasury[9]. The Secretary of State was required to set a target investment limit for the government shareholding in the company as soon as it ceased to be wholly owned by the Crown, and was empowered from time to time, by order made by statutory instrument, to fix a new limit[10].

If a resolution is passed for the voluntary winding up of the successor company, or a winding-up order has been made by the court[11], the Secretary of State is liable, on the commencement of the winding up[12], to discharge certain outstanding liabilities of the successor company[13], and he becomes a creditor of the company to the extent of the amount he has paid[14].

Employment by British Aerospace was declared to be uninterrupted by the transfer to British Aerospace Ltd, and pension rights were expressly preserved[15].

1   See generally the Aircraft and Shipbuilding Industries Act 1977 (as amended); and para 637 et seq ante. British Aerospace was formed of the companies mentioned in s 19(1), Sch 1 Pt I. References in that Act to British Aerospace were generally removed by the British Aerospace Act 1980 ss 10(1), 15(2), Sch 3: see para 637 note 1 ante.

2   See the British Aerospace Act 1980 s 1(1), (2); and the British Aerospace (Nominated Company) Order 1980, SI 1980/1989.

3   See the British Aerospace Act 1980 ss 1, 14, Sch 1; and the British Aerospace (Appointed Day) Order 1980, SI 1980/1988. Provision was made for the continuation in force or effect after the appointed day of agreements and transactions entered into before that day (British Aerospace Act 1980 s 1(3), (6), Sch 1 para 1), for the continuity of certain proceedings (s 1(4)), and for the liability of the successor company under judgments or orders made before the appointed day (s 8). Specified government investment in British Aerospace was extinguished immediately before the appointed day: see s 2.
        Provision is made for the application of the Trustee Investments Act 1961 Sch 1 Pt IV para 3(b) (see TRUSTS vol 48 (Reissue) para 874); and in relation to the liability of the successor company to corporation tax (see INCOME TAXATION), and development land tax (now abolished): see the British Aerospace Act 1980 s 11, 12 (s 11 amended by the Taxation of Chargeable Gains Act 1992 s 290(1), Sch 10 para 4).

4   See the British Aerospace Act 1980 s 10; and the British Aerospace (Dissolution) Order 1981, SI 1981/1793. Transitional provision was also made: see the British Aerospace Act 1980 s 10, Sch 2.

5   See ibid s 1(2).

6   See ibid s 3 (amended by the Companies Consolidation (Consequential Provisions) Act 1985 s 30, Sch 2; and the Finance Act 1988 s 148, Sch 14 Pt XI), which provided for the issue of shares under the direction of the Secretary of State. As to the Secretary of State see para 2 ante. Any administrative expenses of the Secretary of State are paid out of money provided by Parliament: British Aerospace Act 1980 s 13.

7   See ibid s 4 (amended by the Companies Consolidation (Consequential Provisions) Act 1985 Sch 2).

8   The Secretary of State's functions in relation to the acquisition and disposal of shares, etc may be discharged by a nominee, who does so under the direction of the Secretary of State with the consent of the Treasury: see the British Aerospace Act 1980 s 6.

9   Ibid s 5(1)–(3). The Secretary of State's expenses are met out of money provided by Parliament: s 5(4). Any dividend or other sums received by him as a result of such acquisition must be paid into the Consolidated Fund: s 5(5). As to the Consolidated Fund see CONSTITUTIONAL LAW AND HUMAN RIGHTS vol 8(2) (Reissue) para 711 et seq; PARLIAMENT vol 34 (Reissue) para 952 et seq.

10   See the British Aerospace Act 1980 s 7. Any such limit was required to be lower than the one which it replaced: s 7(4)(a). The most recent limit is set by the British Aerospace Act 1980 (Government Shareholding) Order 1986, SI 1986/848, setting a target investment limit of nil: see art 2.

11   As to winding up generally see COMPANIES vol 7(3) (Reissue) para 2190 et seq.

12   Ie on the passing of the resolution or, as the case may be, on the making of the order: British Aerospace Act 1980 s 9(6).

13   Ibid s 9(1), (2) (s 9(2) amended by the Insolvency Act 1986 s 439(2), Sch 14). The liabilities are: (1) any obligation transferred to the successor company on the appointed day; and (2) any liability enforceable against the company under the British Aerospace Act 1980 s 8 (see note 3 supra): s 9(2). Any sums required by the Secretary of State to discharge any such liability are paid out of moneys provided by Parliament: s 9(3).

14   Ibid s 9(4), which further provides that the Secretary of State's claim is to be treated for the purposes of the winding up as a claim against the original liability. Any sums received by the Secretary of State in the winding up must be paid into the Consolidated Fund: s 9(5).

15   Ibid Sch 1 para 2. In the period during which the aircraft industry was in public ownership the same powers to establish and maintain pension schemes existed as have been previously described in relation to shipbuilding: see the Aircraft and Shipbuilding Industries Act 1977 s 49; and para 651 ante. See also the Aircraft Industry (Pension Schemes) Regulations 1977, SI 1977/1329, made under the Aircraft and Shipbuilding Industries Act 1977 s 49.

(vii) Scrap Metal Dealers

657. Registration of scrap metal dealers. No person may carry on business as a scrap metal dealer[1] in the area of a local authority[2] unless the appropriate particulars[3] relating to him are entered in the register maintained by the authority[4]. A person (other than a local authority in its own area[5]) carrying on or proposing to carry on business as a scrap metal dealer in the area of a local authority, on furnishing the authority in writing with the appropriate particulars, may apply to the authority to enter those particulars in the register, and the authority must then enter those particulars relating to the applicant in the register[6].

1   For the purposes of the Scrap Metal Dealers Act 1964, a person carries on business as a scrap metal dealer if he carries on a business which consists wholly or partly of buying and selling scrap metal (whether in the form in which it was bought or otherwise) other than a business in the course of which scrap metal is not bought except as materials for the manufacture of other articles and is not sold except as a by-product of such manufacture or as surplus materials bought but not required for such manufacture; and 'scrap metal dealer' (where that expression is used in the Act otherwise than in a reference to carrying on business as a scrap metal dealer) means a person who carries on business as a scrap metal dealer: s 9(1) (prospectively amended by the Vehicles (Crime) Act 2001 s 43, Schedule para 1(1), (2)(a)(c) as from a day to be appointed). 'Scrap metal' includes any old metal, and any broken, worn out, defaced or partly manufactured articles made wholly or

partly of metal and any metallic wastes, and also includes old, broken, worn out or defaced tooltips or dies made of any of the materials commonly known as hard metal or of cemented or sintered metallic carbides: Scrap Metal Dealers Act 1964 s 9(2). Scrap metal may also include new metal, eg offcuts: *Jenkins v A Cohen & Co Ltd* [1971] 2 All ER 1384 at 1388, [1971] 1 WLR 1280 at 1286, DC, per Ashworth J (per curiam). 'Article' includes any part of an article: Scrap Metal Dealers Act 1964 s 9(2). Any reference to metal, except in the expressions 'hard metal' and 'metallic carbides', is to be taken as a reference to any of the following metals: aluminium, copper, iron, lead, magnesium, nickel, tin and zinc, or, subject to s 9(4), to brass, bronze, gunmetal, steel, white metal or any other alloy of any of those metals: s 9(3). A substance being an alloy referred to in s 9(3) is not to be treated as being such an alloy if of its weight, 2% or more is attributable to gold or silver or any one or more of the following metals: platinum, iridium, osmium, palladium, rhodium and ruthenium: s 9(4).

2   'Local authority' means the council of a district or London borough or the Common Council of the City of London but, in relation to Wales, means the council of a county or county borough: ibid s 9(2) (amended by the Local Government Act 1972 s 272(1), Sch 30; and by the Local Government (Wales) Act 1994 s 22(3), Sch 9 para 6). For the purposes of the Scrap Metal Dealers Act 1964 s 1, a person carrying on business as a scrap metal dealer is treated as carrying on that business in the area of a local authority if, but only if: (1) a place in that area is occupied by him as a scrap metal store; or (2) no place is occupied by him as a scrap metal store, whether in that area or elsewhere, but he has his usual place of residence in that area; or (3) no place is occupied by him as a scrap metal store, whether in that area or elsewhere, but a place in that area is occupied by him wholly or partly for the purposes of that business: s 1(2)(a)(c). 'Place' includes any land, whether consisting of enclosed premises or not; and 'scrap metal store' means a place where scrap metal is received or kept in the course of the business of a scrap metal dealer: s 9(2). It is the duty of every local authority to enforce the provisions of s 1 with respect to persons carrying on business as scrap metal dealers in its area: s 1(9).

3   As to the appropriate particulars see ibid s 1(4)–(6); and para 658 post.

4   Ibid s 1(1). Every local authority must maintain a register of persons carrying on business in its area as scrap metal dealers: s 1(1). Any person who carries on business as a scrap metal dealer in contravention of s 1(1) is guilty of an offence, and liable on summary conviction to a fine not exceeding level 3 on the standard scale: s 1(7) (amended by virtue of the Criminal Justice Act 1982 ss 38(1), (6), (8), 46(1), (4)). As to the standard scale see para 16 note 21 ante.

5   As to the carrying on of business as a scrap metal dealer by a local authority in its area see the Scrap Metal Dealers Act 1964 s 1(10); and para 658 notes 11–12 post.

6   Ibid s 1(3).

658.   Registered particulars.
The appropriate particulars relating to a scrap metal dealer[1], in relation to the area of a local authority[2], are:

(1)   his full name[3];

(2)   his address[4];

(3)   the address of each place[5], if any, in the area which is occupied by the dealer as a scrap metal store[6];

(4)   the fact, if such is the case, that no place is occupied by him as a scrap metal store, whether in that area or elsewhere, but that he has his usual place of residence in that area[7]; and

(5)   the fact, if such is the case, that no place is occupied by him as a scrap metal store whether in that area or otherwise, but that a place in that area is occupied by him wholly or partly for the purposes of that business, together with the address of that place[8].

Except in the case of a local authority carrying on business as a scrap metal dealer in its own area[9], the entry of these particulars in the register maintained by a local authority must include a note of the day on which the entry is made, and at the end of a period of three years beginning with that day, and of each subsequent period of three years, the authority must cancel the entry unless the dealer applies before the end of the period for the registration to be continued for a further three-year period[10].

If any event occurs which involves an alteration of the registered particulars relating to a scrap metal dealer, the dealer must, within 28 days of the occurrence of the event in question, give notice of the alteration to the local authority, which must then make the necessary amendment[11]. Where a dealer ceases to carry on business as a scrap metal dealer he must give similar notice to the local authority, which must thereupon cancel the entry relating to him in the register[12].

1   For the meanings of 'scrap metal dealer' and 'scrap metal' see para 657 note 1 ante.
2   For the meaning of 'local authority' see para 657 note 2 ante.
3   Scrap Metal Dealers Act 1964 s 1(4)(a). In relation to any person who carries on, or proposes to carry on, the business of a scrap metal dealer in partnership with any other person, the particulars which that person is required to furnish include, in addition to those specified in s 1(4), the name under which the partnership is carried on, the name and place of residence of each other member of the partnership who is an individual and the name and registered or principal office of each other member of the partnership who is a body corporate: s 7(1)(b).
4   Ibid s 1(4)(b). If the dealer is an individual, the address is that of his usual place of residence, but if the dealer is a body corporate, the address is that of its registered principal office: s 1(4)(b)(i), (ii).
5   For the meaning of 'place' see para 657 note 2 ante.
6   Scrap Metal Dealers Act 1964 s 1(4)(c). For the meaning of 'scrap metal store' see para 657 note 2 ante.
7   Ibid s 1(4)(d).
8   Ibid s 1(4)(e).
9   As to the carrying on of such a business by a local authority in its area see ibid s 1(10); and notes 11–12 infra. As to the meaning of 'carrying on business as a scrap metal dealer' see para 657 note 1 ante.
10   See ibid s 1(6).
11   Ibid s 1(5)(a). Failure to comply with this requirement as to notice is an offence rendering the dealer liable on summary conviction to a fine not exceeding level 3 on the standard scale: s 1(7) (amended by virtue of the Criminal Justice Act 1982 ss 38(1), (6), (8), 46(1), (4)). In the case of a local authority carrying on business as a scrap metal dealer in its own area, if any event occurs which involves the amendment of its appropriate particulars it must thereupon amend the entry in the register: Scrap Metal Dealers Act 1964 s 1(5)(a), (10). As to the standard scale see para 16 note 21 ante.
12   Ibid s 1(5)(b). Failure to comply with this requirement as to notice is an offence rendering the ex-dealer liable on summary conviction to a fine not exceeding level 1 on the standard scale: s 1(8) (amended by virtue of the Criminal Justice Act 1982 ss 38(1), (6), (8), 46(1), (4)). In the case of a local authority ceasing to carry on business as a scrap metal dealer in its own area, it must thereupon cancel the entry in the register: Scrap Metal Dealers Act 1964 s 1(5)(b), (10).

659. Records of dealings. At each place[1] which he occupies as a scrap metal store[2] a scrap metal dealer[3] must[4] keep a book[5] in which he must enter certain particulars concerning all scrap metal received there[6], and all scrap metal either processed[7] at or dispatched from[8] that place[9]. As an alternative the dealer may instead keep two books[10], one to contain particulars concerning all scrap metal received at the place, and the other to contain particulars concerning all scrap metal either processed at, or dispatched from, the place; but he may use only one book for each of these purposes at any one place at any one time[11]. The relevant particulars must be entered immediately after[12] the receipt of the scrap metal at the place in question or, as the case may be, immediately after the processing or despatch of the scrap metal[13].

Failure to comply[14] with any of these requirements as to records of dealings is an offence[15].

1   For the meaning of 'place' see para 657 note 2 ante.

2   For the meaning of 'scrap metal store' see para 657 note 2 ante.

3   For the meaning of 'scrap metal dealer' and 'scrap metal' see para 657 note 1 ante.

4   This may not apply if he is a person to whom the Scrap Metal Dealers Act 1964 s 3 applies: see para 660 post.

5   This book must be a bound book kept exclusively for the purposes of entering the required particulars (see notes 6–7 infra) and must be retained by the dealer until the end of a two-year period beginning with the day on which the last entry was made in the book: ibid s 2(5). The book need not during the two-year period necessarily be kept at the store: *W Houston & Sons Ltd v Armstrong* [1970] 1 All ER 109, [1969] 1 WLR 1864, DC.

6   In the case of scrap metal received at a place the necessary particulars are as follows (Scrap Metal Dealers Act 1964 s 2(1)(a), (2)(a)–(f)):
    (1)   the description and weight of the scrap metal;
    (2)   the date and time of its receipt;
    (3)   if it is received from another person, the full name and address of that person;
    (4)   the price, if any, payable in respect of the receipt of the scrap metal, if that price has been ascertained at the time when the entry in the book relating to it is to be made;
    (5)   where head (4) supra does not apply, the value of the scrap metal at that time as estimated by the dealer; and
    (6)   in the case of scrap metal delivered at the place in question by means of a mechanically propelled vehicle bearing a registration mark (whether the vehicle belongs to the dealer or not), the registration mark borne by the vehicle.
    The description must be a fair one of the metal in question: *Jenkins v A Cohen & Co Ltd* [1971] 2 All ER 1384, [1971] 1 WLR 1280, DC.
    A registration mark borne by a vehicle is any mark displayed on the vehicle of a kind usually displayed on mechanically propelled vehicles for the purpose of complying with the provisions of what is now the Vehicle Excise Registration Act 1994 as to registration marks: Scrap Metal Dealers Act 1964 s 9(6) (amended by the Vehicle Excise and Registration Act 1994 s 63, Sch 3 para 1). As to the registration of vehicles see generally ROAD TRAFFIC vol 40(1) (Reissue) para 290 et seq.

7   'Processing', in relation to scrap metal, includes melting down and any other process by which the material ceases to be scrap metal, but does not include dismantling or breaking up, and 'processed' is construed accordingly: Scrap Metal Dealers Act 1964 s 2(7).

8   In the case of scrap metal either processed at or dispatched from the place the necessary particulars are as follows (ibid s 2(1)(b), (3)(a)–(d)):
    (1)   the description and weight of the scrap metal;
    (2)   the date of processing, or, as the case may be, dispatch of the scrap metal, and, if processed, the process applied;
    (3)   in the case of scrap metal dispatched on sale or exchange, the full name and address of the person to whom it is sold or with whom it is exchanged, and the consideration for which it is sold or exchanged;
    (4)   in the case of scrap metal processed or dispatched otherwise than on sale or exchange, the value of the scrap metal immediately before its processing or dispatch as estimated by the dealer.
    The description must be a fair one of the metal in question: *Jenkins v A Cohen & Co Ltd* [1971] 2 All ER 1384, [1971] 1 WLR 1280, DC.

9   Scrap Metal Dealers Act 1964 s 2(1)(a), (b). See also note 11 infra.

10   The keeping of each of these books must also conform with the requirements of ibid s 2(4), (5): see the text and notes 5 supra, 13 infra.

11   See ibid s 2(1) proviso. Where a place is occupied as a scrap metal store for the purposes of a business carried on in partnership, there must not be kept at that place in compliance with s 2(1) more than one book, or, in accordance with s 2(1) proviso, two books, and the requirements imposed on a person by s 2 in respect of that place, if complied with by a partner, are to be taken to be complied with by that person: s 7(2).

12   'Immediately after' means as soon as the deal is concluded: *Cox v Henderson* (1970) 114 Sol Jo 568, DC.

13   Scrap Metal Dealers Act 1964 s 2(4).

14   This may not apply in the case of a person to whom ibid s 3 applies: see para 660 post.

15   Ibid s 2(6). Such an offence is punishable on summary conviction with a fine not exceeding level 3 on the standard scale: s 2(6) (amended by virtue of the Criminal Justice Act 1982 ss 38(1), (6), (8), 46(1), (4)). As to the standard scale see para 16 note 21 ante.

660. Records by itinerant collectors etc. If a registered scrap metal dealer[1] satisfies the local authority[2] that he carries on or proposes to carry on the business of a scrap metal dealer[3] only as part of the business of an itinerant collector[4], the authority may make an order that the dealer be exempt[5] from the requirements[6] as to records of dealings[7]. If such an exemption is granted, when the dealer sells any scrap metal[8], he must obtain from the purchaser a receipt[9] which he must keep for two years[10] and which he must be able to produce on demand to any person authorised to require its production[11]. Any person failing to comply with any of the above requirements is guilty of an offence[12].

Special provisions as to records also apply in the case of a scrap metal dealer who does not occupy any place as a scrap metal store[13] but who is not exempted by a local authority order from the general requirements as to records[14], or who does occupy a place as a scrap metal store but in relation to whom there is no exempting order in force, and who receives scrap metal for the purposes of his scrap metal business otherwise than at the place he occupies as a scrap metal store and disposes of it in the course of that business without its being received at that place[15].

1   For the meaning of 'scrap metal dealer' see para 657 note 1 ante. Any reference to a person registered as a scrap metal dealer is a reference to a person in respect of whom the particulars required by the Scrap Metal Dealers Act 1964 s 1 (see paras 657–658 ante) are for the time being entered in a register maintained by a local authority under s 1: s 9(5).

2   For the meaning of 'local authority' see para 657 note 2 ante.

3   As to the meaning of 'carrying on business as a scrap metal dealer' see para 657 note 1 ante.

4   'Itinerant collector' means a person regularly engaged in collecting waste materials, and old, broken, worn out or defaced articles, by means of visits from house to house: Scrap Metal Dealers Act 1964 s 9(2). For the meaning of 'article' see para 657 note 1 ante.

5   The exemption afforded by the order remains active only as long as the order remains in force (see ibid s 3(1)), and the order may be revoked at any time by the local authority by which it was made (s 3(3)).

6   Ie the requirements of ibid s 2: see para 659 ante.

7   Ibid s 3(1). A local authority must not make such an order except after consultation with the chief officer of police for the police area (or, if more than one, for every police area) in which the area of the local authority, or any part of its area, is comprised: s 3(2). For the meaning of 'chief officer of police' see the Police Act 1996 s 101(1); the Interpretation Act 1978 s 5, Sch 1; and POLICE vol 36(1) (Reissue) para 205.

8   For the meaning of 'scrap metal' see para 657 note 1 ante.

9   The receipt must show the weight of the scrap metal comprised in the sale and the aggregate price at which it is sold: Scrap Metal Dealers Act 1964 s 3(1)(a).

10   The two-year period begins with the day on which the receipt was obtained: ibid s 3(1)(b).

11   Ibid s 3(1)(b). The authorised person is any constable: see s 6(1)(b), (3); and para 663 post.

12   Ibid s 3(4). Such an offence is punishable on summary conviction with a fine not exceeding level 3 on the standard scale: s 3(4) (amended by virtue of the Criminal Justice Act 1982 ss 38(1), (6), (8), 46(1), (4)). As to the standard scale see para 16 note 21 ante.

13   For the meaning of 'scrap metal store' see para 657 note 2 ante.

14   See the Scrap Metal Dealers Act 1964 s 3(5).

15   See ibid s 3(6).

661. Additional requirements imposed on convicted dealers. A person convicted of the offence of carrying on business as a scrap metal dealer[1] without the appropriate particulars relating to him being registered[2], or, the particulars being registered, of an offence connected with records of dealings[3], or any other offence which in the opinion of the convicting court involves dishonesty[4], may be made subject to additional requirements[5] by an order[6] made by the convicting court[7].

If any such requirement is contravened, the person to whom the order relates is guilty of an offence[8], and the convicting court may make a further order if it thinks fit[9].

1   As to the meaning of 'carrying on business as a scrap metal dealer'; and for the meanings of 'scrap metal dealer' and 'scrap metal' see para 657 note 1 ante.
2   Scrap Metal Dealers Act 1964 s 4(1)(a), which refers to a contravention of s 1(1) (see para 657 ante).
3   Ie convicted of an offence under ibid s 2 (see para 659 ante).
4   Ibid s 4(1)(b).
5   These are: (1) that at any place occupied by the dealer as a scrap metal store scrap metal may not be received between 6 pm and 8 am (ibid s 4(2)(a)); and (2) that all scrap metal received at that place must be kept, in the form in which it is received there, for a period of not less than 72 hours beginning with the time when it is so received (s 4(2)(b)). For the meanings of 'place' and 'scrap metal store' see para 657 note 2 ante.
6   The order must specify a period not exceeding two years for which it is to remain in force (if not revoked); and any such order may at any time, on the application of the person to whom it relates, be revoked by the court which made it: ibid s 4(3).
7   Ibid s 4(1).
8   Scrap Metal Dealers Act 1964 s 4(4). Such an offence is punishable on summary conviction with a fine not exceeding level 3 on the standard scale: s 4(4) (amended by virtue of the Criminal Justice Act 1982 ss 38(1), (6), (8), 46(1), (4)). As to the standard scale see para 16 note 21 ante.
9   Scrap Metal Dealers Act 1964 s 4(4).

662. Other offences relating to scrap metal. Apart from the offences already mentioned[1] it is an offence[2] for a scrap metal dealer[3] to acquire any scrap metal[4] from a person apparently under the age of 16, whether that person offers the scrap metal on his own or another person's behalf[5]. Any person who, on selling scrap metal to a scrap metal dealer, gives the dealer a false name or address also commits an offence[6].

1   See para 657 et seq ante.
2   Such an offence is punishable on summary conviction with a fine not exceeding level 1 on the standard scale: see the Scrap Metal Dealers Act 1964 s 5(1) (amended by virtue of the Criminal Justice Act 1982 ss 38(1), (6), (8), 46(1), (4)). As to the standard scale see para 16 note 21 ante.
3   For the meaning of 'scrap metal dealer' see para 657 note 1 ante.
4   For the meaning of 'scrap metal' see para 657 note 1 ante.
5   Scrap Metal Dealers Act 1964 s 5(1). It is a defence for the dealer to prove that the person from whom he acquired the scrap metal was in fact of or over the age of 16: Scrap Metal Dealers Act 1964 s 5(1) proviso.
6   Ibid s 5(2). A person guilty of such an offence is liable on summary conviction to a fine not exceeding level 1 on the standard scale: s 5(2) (amended by virtue of the Criminal Justice Act 1982 ss 38(1), (6), (8), 46(1), (4)).

663. Rights of entry and inspection. A constable has the right at all reasonable times to enter and inspect a place[1] for the time being entered on a local authority's register[2] as a place which is occupied by a scrap metal dealer[3] as a scrap metal store[4] or a place which is wholly or partly occupied by him for the purposes of his business[5]. He may also require production of, and may inspect, any scrap metal on the premises, and any book or receipt required to be kept[6], and may take copies of or extracts from any such book or receipt[7]. An officer of a local authority has the right to enter a place in its area which is not registered to ascertain whether it is being used as a scrap metal store[8].

A justice of the peace may issue a warrant authorising entry to a place by a constable or an officer of the local authority; and if necessary such entry may be made by force[9].

 A person who obstructs any of these rights of entry or inspection, or fails to produce any book or other document which a person has a right to inspect, commits an offence[10].

1 For the meaning of 'place' see para 657 note 2 ante.

2 Ie entered in a register under the Scrap Metal Dealers Act 1964 s 1 (see paras 657–658 ante): s 6(1)(a). For the meaning of 'local authority' see para 657 note 2 ante.

3 For the meanings of 'scrap metal dealer' and 'scrap metal' see para 657 note 1 ante.

4 For the meaning of 'scrap metal store' see para 657 note 2 ante.

5 Scrap Metal Dealers Act 1964 s 6(1)(a). Except under the authority of a warrant granted under s 6(3) (see the text and note 9 infra), no person is entitled to enter any place by force: s 6(4).

6 Ie the books and receipts required to be kept under ibid ss 2, 3: see paras 659–660 ante.

7 Ibid s 6(1)(b) (prospectively amended by the Vehicles (Crime) Act 2001 s 43, Schedule para 1(1), (2)(a)(c) as from a day to be appointed).

8 Scrap Metal Dealers Act 1964 s 6(2). The officer must be authorised in writing by the authority, and must have reasonable grounds for believing that the place is being used as a scrap metal store; he may require entry only at a reasonable time, and may be required to produce his written authority: s 6(2). The officer must not use force to gain entry: see note 5 supra.

9 Ibid s 6(3). The justice must be satisfied by information on oath that admission to a place specified in the information is reasonably required in order to secure compliance with the provisions of the Scrap Metal Dealers Act 1964, or to ascertain whether those provisions are being complied with, and the constable or officer of the local authority has the right of entry at any time within one month from the date of the warrant: s 6(3) (prospectively amended by the Vehicles (Crime) Act 2001 s 43, Schedule para 1(1), (3) as from a day to be appointed).

10 Scrap Metal Dealers Act 1964 s 6(5). A person guilty of such an offence is liable on summary conviction to a fine not exceeding level 1 on the standard scale: s 6(5) (amended by virtue of the Criminal Justice Act 1982 ss 38(1), (6), (8), 46(1), (4); and prospectively amended by the Vehicles (Crime) Act 2001 s 43, Schedule para 1(1), (4) as from a day to be appointed). As to the standard scale see para 16 note 21 ante.

664. Partnerships. In relation to any person who carries on, or proposes to carry on, the business of a scrap metal dealer[1] in partnership with any other person, the Scrap Metal Dealers Act 1964 has effect as if any reference to the occupation of a place[2] by a person as a scrap metal store[3] were a reference to the occupation of that place for the purposes of the partnership by that person, alone or jointly with a member of the partnership or by another member of the partnership alone[4].

1 As to the meaning of 'carrying on business as a scrap metal dealer'; and for the meanings of 'scrap metal dealer' and 'scrap metal' see para 657 note 1 ante.

2 For the meaning of 'place' see para 657 note 2 ante.

3 For the meaning of 'scrap metal store' see para 657 note 2 ante.

4 Scrap Metal Dealers Act 1964 s 7(1)(a). As to the appropriate particulars which a partnership is required to furnish to a local authority see s 7(1)(b); and para 658 note 3 ante; and as to the requirements imposed on a partnership as to the keeping of records see s 7(2); and para 659 note 11 ante.

665. Repeals. The Secretary of State[1] may by order[2] repeal any provision of a local Act not repealed by the Scrap Metal Dealers Act 1964[3], and may by that order make such amendments of that or any other local Act as appear to him to be necessary in consequence of the repeal, and any transitional provision as appears to him to be necessary or expedient in connection with the matter[4].

1 As to the Secretary of State see para 2 ante. As to the transfer of certain functions of the Secretary of State, so far as exercisable in relation to Wales, to the National Assembly for Wales see para 1 note 2 ante.

2   The power to make orders is exercisable by statutory instrument, any such instrument being subject to annulment in pursuance of a resolution of either House of Parliament: Scrap Metal Dealers Act 1964 s 10(4).

3   See ibid s 10(2), Schedule Pt II.

4   Ibid s 10(3). The Secretary of State must first consult any local authority or county council appearing to him to be concerned, and the provision must appear to him to be unnecessary having regard to the provisions of the Scrap Metal Dealers Act 1964 or to be inconsistent with the provisions of that Act: s 10(3). For the meaning of 'local authority' see para 657 note 2 ante.

(viii) Hairdressers and Barbers

A. IN GENERAL

666.   Registration in London.   The council of a London borough or the Common Council of the City of London[1] may by resolution appoint a day[2] after which no person may carry on the business[3] of a hairdresser or barber on any premises within the borough or, as the case may be, the City unless he is registered by the council in respect of those premises[4]. The council must register an applicant who provides particulars of his name and residence and the premises in respect of which he desires to be registered, and must issue to him a certificate of registration[5]. He must keep a copy of this certificate prominently displayed in the premises along with a copy of any relevant byelaws[6].

1   The Common Council is included by virtue of the Greater London Council (General Powers) Act 1967 s 20(1).

2   'The appointed day' in relation to a borough, or as the case may be, the City, means such day as may be fixed by resolution of the council: ibid s 21(7)(a). The council must cause to be published in a local newspaper circulating in the borough or the City notice of the passing of the resolution and of the day fixed by it, and of the general effect of the provisions of s 21(1)–(6) (see the text and notes 3–6 infra), and the day so fixed must not be earlier than the expiration of one month from the date of publication of the notice: s 21(7)(b). Either a copy of this newspaper containing any such notice, or a certified reproduction of part of it bearing the date of its publication and containing the notice, is evidence of the publication of the notice and of the date of publication: s 21(8).

3   A person is not deemed to carry on the business of a hairdresser or barber on any premises solely by reason that he visits those premises only by prior appointment with a customer who resides at or is an inmate of them for the purpose of attending to that customer: ibid s 21(1) proviso.

4   Ibid s 21(1), (7)(a). If any person carries on business in contravention of s 21(1), he is liable on summary conviction to a fine not exceeding level 3 on the standard scale, and a daily fine not exceeding £5 for each day on which an offence is continued after conviction: ss 20(1), 21(3) (s 21(3) amended by the Greater London Council (General Powers) Act 1983 s 3, Schedule; and by virtue of the Criminal Justice Act 1982 s 46(1), (4)). As to the standard scale see para 16 note 21 ante.

5   See the Greater London Council (General Powers) Act 1967 s 21(2). The obligation upon the council to register an applicant does not apply where planning permission is required for the carrying on of the business and has not been granted: see s 21(2) proviso.

6   See ibid s 21(4). Relevant byelaws are those made under the Public Health Act 1961 s 77, for the purpose of securing cleanliness of premises, instruments, equipment, clothing etc in a hairdresser's or barber's business: see the Greater London Council (General Powers) Act 1967 s 21(4); and para 667 post. Failure to display his certificate renders a person liable on summary conviction to a fine not exceeding level 2 on the standard scale and a daily fine not exceeding 50p: s 21(4) (amended by the Greater London Council (General Powers) Act 1983 s 3, Schedule; and by virtue of the Criminal Justice Act 1982 s 46(1), (4)). Where an offence punishable under s 21 (as amended) which has been committed by a body corporate is proved to have been committed with the consent or connivance of, or to be attributable to any neglect on the part of, any director, manager, secretary or other similar officer of the body corporate, or any person purporting to act in

such capacity, he as well as the body corporate is deemed to be guilty of that offence: s 21(5). The Public Health Act 1936 ss 287, 288, 341 (ss 287, 288 as amended) (which relate respectively to powers of entry, penalties for obstruction and the application of the Act to Crown property: see PROTECTION OF ENVIRONMENT AND PUBLIC HEALTH vol 38 (Reissue) paras 92, 98, 99), have effect as if the Greater London Council (General Powers) Act 1967 s 21 was contained in the Public Health Act 1936: Greater London Council (General Powers) Act 1967 s 21(6).

667. Regulation by local authorities. A local authority[1] may make byelaws for securing the cleanliness of premises[2] on which a hairdresser's or barber's business is carried on and the instruments, towels, materials and equipment used in that business, and the cleanliness of the hairdressers or barbers working in those premises in regard to themselves and their clothing[3]. The Secretary of State[4] is the confirming authority as respects these byelaws[5], and it is the duty of the local authority to enforce the byelaws it makes[6]. For the purpose of enforcing the byelaws the local authority has power of entry into premises[7].

1   'Local authority' in this context means the council of a district or London borough, the Common Council of the City of London, the Sub-Treasurer of the Inner Temple or the Under Treasurer of the Middle Temple, and includes the Council of the Isles of Scilly: Public Health Act 1961 s 2(3) (amended by the London Government Act 1963 s 40(2), Sch 11 Pt I para 33; and the Local Government Act 1972 s 272(1), Sch 30).

2   'Premises' includes messuages, buildings, land, easements and hereditaments of any tenure: Public Health Act 1936 s 343(1); definition applied by the Public Health Act 1961 s 1(4).

3   Ibid s 77(1). A hairdresser registered by a London borough council or the Common Council must display a copy of any such byelaws on his premises: see para 666 text and note 6 ante.

4   Ie the Secretary of State for the Environment: see the Secretary of State for the Environment Order 1970, SI 1970/1681, arts 2, 6; and CONSTITUTIONAL LAW AND HUMAN RIGHTS vol 8(2) (Reissue) para 452 et seq. As to the Secretary of State see para 2 ante. As to the transfer of certain functions of the Secretary of State, so far as exercisable in relation to Wales, to the National Assembly for Wales see para 1 note 2 ante.

5   Public Health Act 1961 s 77(3).

6   Ibid s 77(1).

7   See ibid s 77(2), applying the Public Health Act 1936 s 287 (as amended): see PROTECTION OF ENVIRONMENT AND PUBLIC HEALTH vol 38 (Reissue) para 98.

B. VOLUNTARY REGISTRATION

668. The Hairdressing Council. A body known as the Hairdressing Council is established in relation to the voluntary registration of hairdressers[1]. It consists of 15 members[2], comprising:

(1)   four employers or self-employed persons engaged in hairdressing[3] who are registered persons[4];

(2)   four employees engaged in hairdressing who are registered persons[5];

(3)   one person appointed by the President of the British Medical Association[6];

(4)   one person appointed by the President of the Royal College of Physicians of London[7]; and

(5)   five persons appointed by the members appointed under heads (1) and (2) above from among persons appearing to have wide experience of and shown capacity in industry, commerce, administration, finance or the practice of law or to have in some

other respect special knowledge or experience which would be of value to the council in the exercise and performance of its functions[8].

The council may do anything calculated to facilitate the proper discharge of its functions[9]. Its powers may be exercised notwithstanding any vacancy[10], and proceedings are not invalidated by any defect in the appointment of a member[11]. The council may make regulations with regard to its meeting and procedure[12].

The council must keep audited accounts of all sums received or paid by it[13]. It must set up an investigating committee and a disciplinary committee[14], and may appoint a registrar[15] and other officers and servants[16].

It may pay fees for attendance, and travelling and other allowances to members[17], pay remuneration, pensions and gratuities to officers and servants, and provide or maintain superannuation schemes for them[18]. The council has no powers, however, as regards negotiating questions of service, charges, wages or conditions of employment of hairdressers as between employer and employees or otherwise[19].

1   Hairdressers (Registration) Act 1964 s 1(1). The council is constituted in accordance with Sch 1 Pt I (paras 1–3); and the supplementary provisions contained in Sch 1 Pt II (paras 4–12) (relating to constitution, term of office, validity of proceedings), have effect with respect to the council: s 1(2). The council is a body corporate with perpetual succession and a common seal: Sch 1 para 4.
2   As to the tenure of office of members see ibid Sch 1 paras 6, 7. As to the first members appointed see Sch 1 paras 2, 5, 6(1). A member may resign at any time by notice addressed to the registrar (as to whom see the text and note 15 infra): Sch 1 para 8. A person appointed to fill a casual vacancy holds office during the remainder of the term in office of the person whom he has replaced; a vacancy other than a casual vacancy must be filled before the date on which the vacancy will occur: Sch 1 para 9.
3   'Hairdressing' means shaving, cutting, shampooing, tinting, dyeing, bleaching, waving, curling, straightening, setting, or dressing of the hair, upon the scalp or face, with or without the aid of any apparatus or appliance, preparation or substance; and the hand or vibro massage of the scalp or face: ibid s 15.
4   Ibid Sch 1 para 1(1). Two persons must be appointed by the National Hairdressers' Federation and two by the Incorporated Guild of Hairdressers, Wigmakers and Perfumers: Sch 1 para 1(1). Before those bodies make appointments they must consult together and ensure that not less than two of the appointees are engaged in ladies' hairdressing: Sch 1 para 3(1). 'Registered person' means a person who is registered under s 3 (see para 670 post): s 15.
5   Ibid Sch 1 para 1(2). These persons must be appointed by the Union of Shop, Distributive and Allied Workers: Sch 1 para 1(2). Not less than two of these appointees must be engaged in ladies' hairdressing: Sch 1 para 3(1).
6   Ibid Sch 1 para 1(3).
7   Ibid Sch 1 para 1(4). As to the Royal College of Physicians of London see MEDICINE, PHARMACY, DRUGS AND MEDICINAL PRODUCTS vol 30 (Reissue) para 48.
8   Ibid Sch 1 para 1(5).
9   Ibid Sch 1 para 10(1).
10   However, no business may be conducted unless there are at least five members present: ibid Sch 1 para 12.
11   Ibid Sch 1 para 10(3).
12   Ibid Sch 1 para 11.
13   Ibid s 13(1). The accounts are audited by auditors appointed by the council: s 13(1). No person may be appointed as an auditor unless he is eligible for appointment under the Companies Act 1989 s 25 (see COMPANIES vol 7(2) (1996 Reissue) para 956): Hairdressers (Registration) Act 1964 s 13(2) (amended by the Companies Act 1989 (Eligibility for Appointment as Company Auditor) (Consequential Amendments) Regulations 1991, SI 1991/1997, reg 2, Schedule para 12). Copies of the council's accounts must be furnished to any person on application and on payment of such reasonable sum as the council may determine: Hairdressers (Registration) Act 1964 s 13(3).

14 See ibid s 8; and para 672 post.
15 Ibid s 12(1), (2). The registrar holds and vacates office in accordance with the terms of his appointment: s 12(1).
16 See ibid Sch 1 para 10(2)(a).
17 See ibid Sch 1 para 10(2)(b).
18 See ibid Sch 1 para 10(2)(c), (d).
19 Ibid s 14.

669.   Register of hairdressers. The Hairdressing Council[1] must maintain a register of hairdressers[2], which it must publish as often as it thinks fit[3]. If the register is not published in any year the council must publish within that year any alterations in the register which have been made since its last publication[4].

1   As to the council see para 668 ante.
2   Hairdressers (Registration) Act 1964 s 2. That provision also provided for the establishment of the register at the time when the Act was passed. The register must contain the names, addresses, qualifications and such other particulars as may be prescribed of all persons who are entitled under the provisions of the Act to be registered and who apply in the prescribed manner to be so registered, and the form of hairdressing which such persons are qualified to practise: s 2. 'Prescribed' means prescribed by rules under the Act: s 15. For the meaning of 'hairdressing' see para 668 note 3 ante.
    The council may make rules with respect to the form and keeping of the register and the making of entries, alterations and corrections in it and, in particular:
    (1)   regulating the making of applications for registration and the supporting evidence (s 6(1)(a));
    (2)   providing for the notification to the council of any change in the particulars entitling a person to be registered (s 6(1)(b));
    (3)   prescribing fees for entry in, restoration to, and retention in, the register (s 6(1)(c), (d));
    (4)   authorising the registrar of the council to refuse to enter a name in or restore it to the register until the fee has been paid and to remove a name on non-payment of the retention fee after prescribed notices and warnings (s 6(1)(e));
    (5)   prescribing anything required or authorised to be prescribed by the provisions of the Act relating to the register (s 6(1)(f)).
    Rules under s 6 which provide for the erasure of a name from the register on failure to pay a fee must provide for its restoration to the register on the making of the prescribed application in that behalf and on payment of that fee and any additional fee prescribed in respect of the restoration: s 6(2). Rules which prescribe fees may provide for the charging of different fees in different classes of cases: s 6(3).
    Rules made under the Hairdressers (Registration) Act 1964 are not made by statutory instrument and are not dealt with in this title.
3   Ibid s 7(1), which additionally provided for the initial publication of the register within six months of 1 January 1966 (ie the appointed day: s 15).
4   Ibid s 7(2).

670.   Qualifications for registration. A person is entitled[1] to be registered by the Hairdressing Council[2] if he applies after the date appointed for the purpose by the council[3] and satisfies it that he has:
   (1)   served a period of apprenticeship[4], or attended a course of training approved[5] by it conducted at an institution so approved, or partly at one such institution and partly at another or others[6]; and
   (2)   that he has attained a reasonable and sufficient standard to qualify him to practise the form of hairdressing[7] in respect of which the application was made[8].

An applicant is also entitled to be registered if he satisfies the council that he was engaged in hairdressing, other than as an apprentice or while undergoing a course of training in hairdressing, for at least three years before the appointed day[9]. On registering any person the council must issue to him a certificate of registration[10].

1   Ie subject to the provisions of the Hairdressers (Registration) Act 1964 and any rules made under s 6 (see para 669 note 2 ante): s 3(1).
2   As to the council see para 668 ante.
3   Hairdressers (Registration) Act 1964 s 3(1).
4   Ibid s 3(1)(a)(i).
5   Ie approved under ibid s 4: see para 671 post.
6   Ibid s 3(1)(a)(ii).
7   For the meaning of 'hairdressing' see para 668 note 3 ante.
8   Hairdressers (Registration) Act 1964 s 3(1)(a)(i), (ii), (b).
9   Ibid s 3(2). For the meaning of 'appointed day' see para 669 note 3 ante.
10 Ibid s 3(3).

671.   Approval of courses, qualifications and institutions.   The Hairdressing Council[1] may approve:

(1)   any course of training which it considers is designed to confer sufficient knowledge and skill for the practice of hairdressing[2] on persons completing it[3];

(2)   any qualification which, as a result of an examination taken in conjunction with an approved course, is granted to candidates reaching a standard indicating in the council's opinion sufficient knowledge and skill to practise hairdressing[4]; and

(3)   any institution it considers properly organised and equipped for conducting the whole or any part of an approved course[5].

The council may refuse its approval or withdraw an approval previously given[6].

The power of approval conferred on the council includes power to approve a course of training prepared by it and conducted either under arrangements made by it or otherwise, and a qualification awarded by it as a result of an examination held under arrangements made by it[7]. If the council withdraws its approval this does not prejudice the registration or entitlement to registration of any person who was registered or entitled to registration by virtue of that approval immediately before it was withdrawn[8].

It is the council's duty to keep itself informed of the nature of the instruction given at approved institutions to persons attending approved courses and the examinations the passing of which may be prescribed[9] by it as being a condition of registration[10].

1   As to the council see para 668 ante.
2   For the meaning of 'hairdressing' see para 668 note 3 ante.
3   Hairdressers (Registration) Act 1964 s 4(1)(a).
4   Ibid s 4(1)(b).
5   Ibid s 4(1)(c).
6   Ibid s 4(1). The council must serve on the body or person affected notice of the giving, refusal or withdrawal of such an approval: s 4(1). Any reference in s 4 to a body or person affected, in relation to an approval, is a reference to the body or person who applied for the approval: s 4(4).
7   Ibid s 4(2)(a), (b).
8   Ibid s 4(3).
9   For the meaning of 'prescribed' see para 669 note 2 ante.
10 Hairdressers (Registration) Act 1964 s 5.

672.   Investigating and disciplinary committees.   The Hairdressing Council[1] must set up an investigating committee and a disciplinary committee[2]. The investigating committee is charged with the duty of conducting a preliminary investigation into any case where it is alleged that a person registered by the council is liable to have his name removed from the register[3] and of deciding whether the case should be referred to the disciplinary committee[4]. The disciplinary committee is charged with the duty of considering and determining any case referred to it by the investigating committee and any other case of which the disciplinary committee has cognisance[5].

Rules regulating the membership of each committee, the times and places of meetings, quorum and mode of summoning members of the disciplinary committee, are to be made by the council, but a person is not eligible for membership of either committee unless he is a member of the council[6]. The rules must ensure that no person who acted as a member of the investigating committee in respect of any case acts as a member of the disciplinary committee with respect to that case[7].

The council must make rules as to the procedure to be followed and the rules of evidence to be observed in proceedings before the disciplinary committee[8]. To advise this committee on questions of law there must in all proceedings before it be an assessor who must be a person who has a ten year general qualification[9].

1   As to the council see para 668 ante.
2   Hairdressers (Registration) Act 1964 s 8(1).
3   'The register' means the register of hairdressers to be maintained in pursuance of ibid s 2 (see para 669 ante): s 15.
4   Ibid s 8(1)(a).
5   Ibid s 8(1)(b). The committee has cognisance of other cases by virtue of s 9(3): see para 673 post.
6   Ibid s 8(2), Sch 2 para 1(1). Rules under the Hairdressers (Registration) Act 1964 are not made by statutory instrument, and are not dealt with in this work.
7   Ibid Sch 2 para 1(2).
8   Ibid Sch 2 para 2(1). In particular, under Sch 2 para 2(1)(a)–(e), the rules must:
    (1)   secure that notice of the proceedings is given at the specified time and in the specified manner, to the person alleged to be liable to have his name removed from the register;
    (2)   determine who, in addition to that person, is to be a party to the proceedings;
    (3)   secure that any party may be heard by the committee;
    (4)   enable any party to be represented by counsel or solicitor or (if the rules so provide and the party so elects) by a person of some other specified description; and
    (5)   require proceedings before the committee to be held in public except so far as may be provided by the rules.
    As respects proceedings for the registration of a person whose name was previously removed from the register by direction of the disciplinary committee, the council has power to make rules with respect to all or any of the matters mentioned in heads (1)–(5) supra, but is not required to do so; and separate rules may be made as respects such proceedings: Sch 2 para 2(2).
9   Ibid Sch 2 para 3(1) (amended by the Courts and Legal Services Act 1990 s 72(1), Sch 10 para 23). As to the meaning of a 'ten year general qualification' see s 71; and COURTS. The power of appointing an assessor for the disciplinary committee is exercisable by the council, but if no assessor appointed by it is available to act in any particular proceedings the committee may itself appoint an assessor: Hairdressers (Registration) Act 1964 Sch 2 para 3(2). Except in the case of an assessor so appointed by the committee, an assessor may be appointed under this provision either generally or for any particular proceedings or class of proceedings, and holds and vacates office in accordance with the terms of the instrument under which he is appointed: Sch 2 para 3(3).

673.   Removal from the register. The disciplinary committee[1] may direct that a person's name be removed from the register[2] where he is convicted by any court in the United Kingdom[3] of a criminal offence which in the committee's opinion renders him unfit to be registered, or it judges him guilty of serious negligence in any professional respect, or it is satisfied that his name has been fraudulently entered[4]. It must serve him with notice[5] of the direction[6]. Where the name of any person is removed from the register, he must deliver up to the Hairdressing Council[7] his certificate of registration within seven days of receiving notice of the removal[8].

A person whose name is removed is not entitled to be registered again except in pursuance of a direction given by the committee on his application[9].

1   As to this committee see para 672 ante.
2   For the meaning of 'the register' see para 672 note 3 ante.
3   For the meaning of 'United Kingdom' see para 37 note 1 ante.
4   Hairdressers (Registration) Act 1964 s 9(1).
5   'Notice' means notice in writing: ibid s 11(1). Any notice authorised or required to be served under the Hairdressers (Registration) Act 1964 may, without prejudice to any other method of service but subject to any provision to the contrary in rules under the Act, be served by post; and for the purpose of the application of s 11(2) to the Interpretation Act 1978 s 7 (which relates to service by post), the proper address of a person to whose registration such a notice relates is his address on the register: Hairdressers (Registration) Act 1964 s 11(2).
6   Ibid s 9(2).
7   As to the council see para 668 ante.
8   Hairdressers (Registration) Act 1964 s 10.
9   Ibid s 9(3). A direction under s 9 for the removal of a person's name from the register may prohibit an application under s 9(3) by that person until the expiration of a specified period from the date of the direction (and, where he has duly made such an application, from the date of his last application): s 9(3).

(ix) Employment Agencies

674.   Meaning of 'employment agency' and 'employment business'. 'Employment agency' means the business (whether or not carried on with a view to profit and whether or not carried on in conjunction with any other business) of providing services[1] (whether by the provision of information or otherwise) for the purpose of finding workers[2] employment with employers[3] or of supplying employers with workers for employment by them[4].

'Employment business' means the business (whether or not carried on with a view to profit and whether or not carried on in conjunction with any other business) of supplying persons (being persons in the employment of the person carrying on the business) to act for and under the control of other persons in any capacity[5].

However, neither 'employment agency' nor 'employment business' includes any arrangements, services, functions or business to which the Employment Agencies Act 1973 does not apply by virtue of certain specified exemptions[6].

1   This reference to providing services does not include a reference (1) to publishing a newspaper or other publication unless it is published wholly or mainly for the purpose mentioned in the text; (2) to the display by any person of advertisements on premises occupied by him otherwise than for that purpose; or (3) to providing a programme service within the meaning of the Broadcasting Act 1990 (see TELECOMMUNICATIONS AND BROADCASTING vol 45(1) (Reissue) para 253): Employment Agencies Act 1973 s 13(4)(a)–(c) (amended by the Cable and Broadcasting Act 1984 s 57, Sch 5; and subsequently by the Broadcasting Act 1990 s 203(1), Sch 20 para 18).
2   As from a day to be appointed, the term 'workers' is replaced by the term 'persons': Employment Agencies Act 1973 s 13(2) (amended, as from a day to be appointed, by the Employment Relations Act 1999 s 31, Sch 7 paras 1, 7).
3   'Employment' includes (1) employment by way of a professional engagement or otherwise under a contract for services; (2) the reception in a private household of a person under an arrangement by which that person is to assist in the domestic work of the household in

consideration of receiving hospitality and pocket money or hospitality only: Employment Agencies Act 1973 s 13(1). 'Worker' and 'employer' must be construed accordingly: s 13(1).

4   Ibid s 13(1), (2).
5   Ibid s 13(1), (3).
6   Ibid s 13(1). These exceptions are those that arise by virtue of s 13(7) (as amended): see para 676 post.

675. Prohibition orders. On application by the Secretary of State[1], an employment tribunal may by order prohibit a person from carrying on, or being concerned with the carrying on of any employment agency or employment business, or any specified description of employment agency or employment business[2]. Such an order (a 'prohibition order') may either prohibit a person from engaging in an activity altogether or prohibit him from doing so otherwise than in accordance with specified conditions[3]. A prohibition order must be made for a period beginning with the date of the order and ending on a specified date, or on the happening of a specified event, and in either case, not more than ten years later[4].

An employment tribunal may not make a prohibition order in relation to any person unless it is satisfied that he is, on account of his misconduct or for any other sufficient reason, unsuitable to do what the order prohibits[5].

Any person who, without reasonable excuse, fails to comply with a prohibition order is guilty of an offence[6].

On application by the person to whom a prohibition order applies, an employment tribunal may vary or revoke the order if it is satisfied that there has been a material change of circumstances since the order was last considered[7]. On such an application a tribunal may not so vary a prohibition order as to make it more restrictive[8].

An appeal lies to the Employment Appeal Tribunal on a question of law arising from any decision of, or arising in proceedings before, an employment tribunal in relation to the making of a prohibition order or the disposition of an application for variation or revocation of a prohibition order[9].

1   As to the Secretary of State see para 2 ante. As to the transfer of certain functions of the Secretary of State, so far as exercisable in relation to Wales, to the National Assembly for Wales see para 1 note 2 ante.
2   Employment Agencies Act 1973 s 3A(1) (ss 3A–3D added by the Deregulation and Contracting Out Act 1994 s 35, Sch 10 para 1(3); Employment Agencies Act 1973 s 3A(1), (4), (5), (6) amended by virtue of the Employment Rights (Dispute Resolution) Act 1998 s 1(2)(a)). 'Specified', in relation to a prohibition order, means specified in the order: Employment Agencies Act 1973 s 3A(9). For the meanings of 'employment agency' and 'employment business' see para 674 ante.
3   Ibid s 3A(2) (as added: see note 2 supra).
4   Ibid s 3A(3) (as added: see note 2 supra).
5   Ibid s 3A(4) (as added and amended: see note 2 supra), which is expressed to be subject to s 3A(5), (6) (as added and amended). For these purposes, where an employment agency or employment business has been improperly conducted, each person who was carrying on, or concerned with the carrying on of, the agency or business at the time, is deemed to have been responsible for what happened unless he can show that it happened without his connivance or consent and was not attributable to any neglect on his part: s 3A(7) (as so added).
    A tribunal may make a prohibition order in relation to a body corporate if it is satisfied that: (1) any director, secretary, manager or similar officer of the body corporate; (2) any person who performs on behalf of the body corporate the functions of a director, secretary, manager or similar officer, or (3) any person in accordance with whose directions or instructions the directors of the body corporate are accustomed to act, is unsuitable, on account of his misconduct or for any other sufficient reason, to do what the order

prohibits: s 3A(5) (as so added and amended). A person is not deemed to fall within head (3) supra by reason only that the directors act on advice given by him in a professional capacity: s 3A(8) (as so added). 'Director', in relation to a body corporate whose affairs are controlled by its members, means a member of the body corporate: s 3A(9) (as so added).

A tribunal may make a prohibition order in relation to a partnership if it is satisfied that any member of the partnership, or any manager employed by the partnership, is unsuitable, on account of his misconduct or for any other sufficient reason, to do what the order prohibits: s 3A(6) (as so added and amended).

6   Ibid s 3B (as added: see note 2 supra). A person guilty of such an offence is liable on summary conviction to a fine not exceeding level 5 on the standard scale: s 3B (as so added). Where any offence committed under the Employment Agencies Act 1973 by a body corporate is proved to have been committed with the consent or connivance of, or to have been attributable to any neglect on the part of, any director, manager, secretary or similar officer, or a person who was purporting to act in any such capacity, he as well as the body corporate is guilty of the offence and is liable to be proceeded against and punished accordingly: s 11. As to the standard scale see para 16 note 21 ante.

Notwithstanding the Magistrates' Courts Act 1980 s 127(1) (information to be laid within 6 months of offence: see MAGISTRATES) an information relating to a relevant offence which is triable by a magistrates' court in England and Wales may be so tried if it is laid at any time within 3 years after the date of the commission of the offence, and within 6 months after the date on which evidence sufficient in the opinion of the Secretary of State to justify the proceedings came to his knowledge: Employment Agencies Act 1973 s 11A(2) (s 11A added by the Employment Relations Act 1999 Sch 7 paras 1, 5). For this purpose a certificate of the Secretary of State or Lord Advocate (as the case may be) as to the date on which evidence came to his knowledge is conclusive evidence: Employment Agencies Act 1973 s 11A(4) (as so added). A relevant offence is one under s 3B (as added), ss 5(2), 6(2), 9(4)(b) (all as amended), or s 10(2), for which proceedings are instituted by the Secretary of State: s 11A(1) (as so added).

The court in which a person is convicted of an offence under the Employment Agencies Act 1973 may order him to pay to the Secretary of State a sum which appears to the court not to exceed the costs of the investigation which resulted in the conviction: s 11B (added by the Employment Relations Act 1999 Sch 7 paras 1, 5 as from a day to be appointed).

7   Employment Agencies Act 1973 s 3C(1) (as added (see note 2 supra); s 3C(1)–(4) amended by virtue of the Employment Rights (Dispute Resolution) Act 1998 s 1(2)(a)). The Secretary of State is a party to any proceedings before a tribunal with respect to such an application, and is entitled to appear and be heard accordingly: Employment Agencies Act 1973 s 3C(3) (as so added and amended).

When making a prohibition order or disposing of an application under s 3C (as added and amended), an employment tribunal may, with a view to preventing the making of vexatious or frivolous applications, by order prohibit the making of such an application, or further application, in relation to the prohibition order before such date as the tribunal may specify: s 3C(4) (as so added and amended).

8   Ibid s 3C(2) (as added and amended: see note 7 supra).

9   Ibid s 3D(1) (as added (see note 2 supra); s 3D(1), (2) amended by virtue of the Employment Rights (Dispute Resolution) Act 1998 s 1(2)(a)). No other appeal lies from a decision of an employment tribunal under the Employment Agencies Act 1973 s 3A or s 3C (both as added and amended) and the Tribunals and Inquiries Act 1992 (appeals from certain tribunals to the High Court: see ADMINISTRATIVE LAW vol 1(1) (2001 Reissue) para 72) does not apply to proceedings before an employment tribunal under those provisions: Employment Agencies Act 1973 s 3D(2) (as so added and amended).

676.   Exemptions from the Employment Agencies Act 1973. The following businesses, agencies and services are exempted from the application of the Employment Agencies Act 1973:

(1)   any business which is carried on exclusively for the purpose of obtaining employment[1] for persons formerly in the armed services or persons released from a custodial sentence passed by a criminal court in the United Kingdom, the Channel Islands or the Isle of Man[2];

(2)   any agency for the supply of nurses[3];

(3)   the business carried on by any county or district nursing association or other similar body, being an association or organisation established and existing wholly or mainly for the purpose of providing patients with the services of a nurse to visit them in their own homes without herself taking up residence there[4];

(4)   services which are ancillary to the letting on hire of any aircraft, vessel, vehicle, plant or equipment[5];

(5)   the exercise by a local authority[6] a police authority, the Service Authority for the National Criminal Intelligence Service, the Service Authority for the National Crime Squad[7] or a joint authority[8] of any of its functions[9];

(6)   the exercise by the Metropolitan Police Authority of any of its functions[10];

(7)   the exercise by the Broads Authority of any of its functions[11];

(8)   the exercise by a national park authority of any of its functions[12];

(9)   the exercise by the London Fire and Emergency Planning Authority of any of its functions[13];

(10)   services provided by any organisation[14] of employers[15] or of workers[16] for its members[17];

(11)   services provided in pursuance of arrangements made or a direction given under the Employment and Training Act 1973[18];

(12)   services provided by an appointments board or service controlled by one or more universities[19]; and

(13)   any prescribed[20] business or service, or prescribed class of business or service or business or service carried on or provided by prescribed persons or classes of person[21].

1   For the meaning of 'employment' see para 674 note 3 ante.

2   See the Employment Agencies Act 1973 s 13(7)(a) (amended by the Criminal Justice Act 1988 s 123(6), Sch 8 Pt I para 7). The business must be certified annually by or on behalf of the appropriate board of the Defence Council or the Secretary of State, as the case may be: see the Employment Agencies Act 1973 s 13(7)(a) (as so amended). For the meaning of 'United Kingdom' see para 37 note 1 ante. As to the Secretary of State see para 2 ante. As to the transfer of certain functions of the Secretary of State, so far as exercisable in relation to Wales, to the National Assembly for Wales see para 1 note 2 ante.

3   Ibid s 13(7)(b) (repealed by the Care Standards Act 2000 ss 111(2), 117(2), Sch 6 as from a day to be appointed). As to such agencies see the Nurses Agencies Act 1957; and MEDICINE, PHARMACY, DRUGS AND MEDICINAL PRODUCTS vol 30 (Reissue) para 489 et seq. This does not, however, exempt any other business carried on in conjunction with such an agency for the supply of nurses: Employment Agencies Act 1973 s 13(7) proviso (repealed by the Care Standards Act 2000 ss 111(2), 117(2), Sch 6 as from a day to be appointed).

4   Employment Agencies Act 1973 s 13(7)(c) (repealed by the Care Standards Act 2000 ss 111(2), 117(2), Sch 6 as from a day to be appointed).

5   Employment Agencies Act 1973 s 13(7)(d).

6   'Local authority', in relation to England, means a county council, the Common Council of the City of London, a district council or a London borough council and in relation to Wales, means a county council or a county borough council: ibid s 13(1) (definition amended by the Local Government Act 1985 s 102, Sch 17; and the Local Government (Wales) Act 1994 s 66(6), (8), Sch 16 para 41, Sch 18).

7   As to police authorities, the Service Authority for the National Criminal Intelligence Service and the Service Authority for the National Crime Squad see generally POLICE.

8   Ie a joint authority established under the Local Government Act 1985 Pt IV (ss 23–42) (as amended): see LOCAL GOVERNMENT vol 29(1) (Reissue) para 53 et seq.

9   Employment Agencies Act 1973 s 13(7)(f) (amended by the Local Government Act 1985 s 84, Sch 14 para 50; the Education Reform Act 1988 s 237(2), Sch 13 Pt I; the Police and

Magistrates' Courts Act 1994 s 43, Sch 4 Pt II para 50; the Police Act 1996 s 103, Sch 7 para 1(2)(i); and the Police Act 1997 s 134(1), Sch 9 para 26).

10   Employment Agencies Act 1973 s 13(7)(fa) (added by the Greater London Authority Act 1999 s 325, Sch 27 para 37).

11   Employment Agencies Act 1973 s 13(7)(ff) (added by the Norfolk and Suffolk Broads Act 1988 s 21, Sch 6 para 11). As to the Broads Authority see OPEN SPACES AND ANCIENT MONUMENTS vol 34 (Reissue) para 130.

12   Employment Agencies Act 1973 s 13(7)(fg) (added by the Environment Act 1995 s 78, Sch 10 para 11). As to national park authorities see OPEN SPACES AND ANCIENT MONUMENTS vol 34 (Reissue) para 157 et seq.

13   Employment Agencies Act 1973 s 13(7)(fh) (added by the Greater London Authority Act 1999 s 328, Sch 29 Pt I para 22). As to the London Fire and Emergency Planning Authority see FIRE SERVICES vol 18(2) (Reissue) para 17; LONDON GOVERNMENT.

14   'Organisation' includes an association of organisations: Employment Agencies Act 1973 s 13(1).

15   'Organisation of employers' means an organisation which consists wholly or mainly of employers and whose principal objects include the regulation of relations between employers and workers or organisations of workers: ibid s 13(1). For the meanings of 'employer' and 'worker' see para 674 note 3 ante.

16   'Organisation of workers' means an organisation which consists wholly or mainly of workers and whose principal objects include the regulation of relations between workers and employers or organisations of employers: ibid s 13(1). The organisation must genuinely be an organisation of workers, not merely a co-operative employment agency: see *McCabe v Edwards* [1981] ICR 468 at 476, DC, per Donaldson LJ.

17   Employment Agencies Act 1973 s 13(7)(g).

18   Ibid s 13(7)(ga) (added by the Trade Union Reform and Employment Rights Act 1993 s 49(2), Sch 8 para 4). This exception applies to arrangements made or a direction given under the Employment and Training Act 1973 s 10 (as substituted): see EMPLOYMENT vol 16 (2000 Reissue) para 605.

19   Employment Agencies Act 1973 s 13(7)(h).

20   'Prescribed' means prescribed by regulations made under the Employment Agencies Act 1973 by the Secretary of State: s 13(1). He has power to make regulations for prescribing anything which is to be prescribed under the Employment Agencies Act 1973: s 13(1). Regulations may make different provision in relation to different cases or classes of cases: s 12(3). Before making regulations he must consult with such bodies as appear to him to be representative of the interests concerned: s 12(2). After consultation with such bodies as appear to him to be concerned the Secretary of State may by order repeal or amend provisions of local Acts which appear to him to be unnecessary or inconsistent with the Employment Agencies Act 1973: see s 14(3).

The power to make regulations and orders under the Employment Agencies Act 1973 is exercisable by statutory instrument: s 12(4). Regulations under s 13(7)(i) (as substituted) (see the text and note 21 infra) or an order under s 14(3), are subject to annulment in pursuance of a resolution of either House of Parliament: s 12(6) (substituted by the Employment relations Act 1999 s 31, Sch 7 paras 1, 6).

21   See the Employment Agencies Act 1973 s 13(7)(i) (substituted by the Employment Relations Act 1999 Sch 7 paras 1, 8). The following bodies have been exempted under this head:

(1)   certain colleges for teacher training, other institutions of further education, charities, bodies comprising representatives of industrial training boards (defined in the Industrial Training Act 1982 s 1(2): see EMPLOYMENT vol 16 (2000 Reissue) para 609), together with representatives of any one or more of an organisation of employers, an organisation of workers or a body comprising representatives of two or more such organisations, and the British Council (see the Employment Agencies Act 1973 (Exemption) Regulations 1976, SI 1976/710);

(2)   the Crown Agents for Overseas Governments and Administrations, or any of its wholly owned subsidiaries (see the Employment Agencies Act 1973 (Exemption) (No 2) Regulations 1979, SI 1979/1741 (amended by SI 1984/978));

(3)   the Association of Dispensing Opticians Ltd, the Association of Meat Inspectors (Great Britain) Ltd, the Chartered Institute of Patent Agents, the Faculty of Actuaries in Scotland, the Incorporated Brewers' Guild, the Institute of Actuaries, the Institute of Careers Officers, the Institute of Chartered Accountants in England and Wales, the Institute of Chartered Accountants of Scotland, the Institute of Chartered Secretaries and Administrators, the Institute of Legal

Executives, the Institute of Marketing, the Institute of the Motor Industry, the Institute of Personnel Management, the Institute of Qualified Private Secretaries Ltd, the Law Society of Scotland, local law societies in England and Wales, the Pensions Management Institute, the Pharmaceutical Society of Great Britain, the Royal Society of Chemistry, the Society of Architectural and Associated Technicians, the Society of Business Economists, the Society of Chiropodists, the Law Society and Law Society Services Ltd (see the Employment Agencies Act 1973 (Exemption) (No 2) Regulations 1979, SI 1979/1741 (amended by SI 1984/978).

677. Conduct of employment agencies. The Secretary of State[1] may make regulations to secure the proper conduct of employment agencies[2] and employment businesses[3] and to protect the interests of persons availing themselves of the services of such agencies and businesses[4]. Any person who contravenes or fails to comply with such regulations is guilty of an offence[5]. Regulations made under this power[6] provide that employment agencies must abide by certain general obligations relating to their dealings with workers and employers[7], must comply with certain requirements as to advertising[8] and the keeping of records[9] and must notify employers (and, where appropriate, workers[10]) of their terms of business[11]. Special duties are imposed on agencies which arrange employment for persons aged under 18[12] or for workers coming to the United Kingdom or going abroad to work[13]. Provision is also made for safeguarding money received by agents on behalf of worker clients[14].

The regulations also make provision for the operation of employment businesses, which must also abide by certain general obligations[15] (including giving the hirer notice of terms of business and the worker notice of terms of employment) and comply with requirements as to advertising[16] and the keeping of records[17]. Special duties are imposed on businesses supplying workers to work abroad[18].

Any officer duly authorised in that behalf by the Secretary of State may, at all reasonable times, and on producing written evidence of his authority, if so required[19]:

(1)   enter any premises used or to be used for or in connection with the carrying on of an employment agency or business and any other premises which the officer has reasonable cause to believe are so used[20];

(2)   inspect those premises and any records or documents kept in pursuance of the Employment Agencies Act 1973 or any regulations made under that Act[21]; and

(3)   require any person on those premises to furnish him with information which he may require for ascertaining whether the provisions of the Act or of any regulations made under it are being complied with or for enabling the Secretary of State to exercise his functions[22].

Restrictions are placed upon the disclosure of any information obtained in the exercise of these powers[23].

1   As to the Secretary of State see para 2 ante. As to the transfer of certain functions of the Secretary of State, so far as exercisable in relation to Wales, to the National Assembly for Wales see para 1 note 2 ante.

2   For the meaning of 'employment agency' see para 674 ante.

3   For the meaning of 'employment business' see para 674 ante.

4   Employment Agencies Act 1973 s 5(1). As to the purposes for which regulations may be made see s 5(1)(a)–(ec) (s 5(1)(ea)–(ec) added by the Employment Relations Act 1999 s 31,

Sch 7 paras 1, 2(1), (2)). A reference in the Employment Agencies Act 1973 s 5(1)(ea)–(ec) (as so added) to services includes a reference to services in respect of persons seeking employment outside the United Kingdom and persons normally resident outside the United Kingdom seeking employment in the United Kingdom: s 5(1A) (added by the Employment Relations Act 1999 Sch 7 paras 1, 2(1), (3)). For the meaning of 'United Kingdom' see para 37 note 1 ante. As to the making of regulations and orders under the Employment Agencies Act 1973 see para 676 note 20 ante. In the case of regulations under s 5(1) (as amended), a draft must have been laid before and approved by each House of Parliament: s 12(5) (substituted by the Employment Relations Act 1999 Sch 7 paras 1, 6).

Any person who makes or causes to be made or knowingly allows to be made any entry in a record or other document required to be kept in pursuance of the Employment Agencies Act 1973 or of any regulations made under it which he knows to be false in a material particular is guilty of an offence: s 10(2). A person who commits such an offence is liable on summary conviction to a fine not exceeding level 5 on the standard scale: s 10(3) (amended by virtue of the Criminal Justice Act 1982 ss 38, 46). As to the standard scale see para 16 note 21 ante.

5 Employment Agencies Act 1973 s 5(2). A person guilty of such an offence is liable on summary conviction to a fine not exceeding level 5 on the standard scale: s 5(2) (amended by virtue of the Criminal Justice Act 1982 ss 38, 46). See also para 675 note 6 ante.

6 Ie the Conduct of Employment Agencies and Employment Businesses Regulations 1976, SI 1976/715. See also the Employment Agencies Act 1973 (Charging Fees to Au Pairs) Regulations 1981, SI 1981/1481.

7 See the Conduct of Employment Agencies and Employment Businesses Regulations 1976, SI 1976/715, reg 2.

8 See ibid reg 3.

9 See ibid reg 8, Schs 3, 4. As to the making of false entries in records see note 4 supra.

10 As to the notification of workers see para 678 text to note 13 post.

11 See the Conduct of Employment Agencies and Employment Businesses Regulations 1976, SI 1976/715, reg 4.

12 See ibid reg 5.

13 See ibid reg 6, Sch 1.

14 See ibid reg 7, Sch 2. As to the circumstances in which workers may be charged fees see para 678 post.

15 See ibid reg 9.

16 See ibid reg 10.

17 See ibid reg 12, Sch 6. As to the making of false entries in records see note 4 supra.

18 See ibid reg 11, Sch 5.

19 Employment Agencies Act 1973 s 9(1) (amended by the Employment Protection Act 1975 s 114, Sch 13 para 6).

20 Employment Agencies Act 1973 s 9(1)(a) (amended by the Deregulation and Contracting Out Act 1994 s 81, Sch 17).

As from a day to be appointed, head (1) in the text is substituted so as to refer simply to 'relevant business premises': Employment Agencies Act 1973 s 9(1)(a) (prospectively substituted by the Employment Relations Act 1999 s 31, Sch 7 paras 1, 4(1), (2)(a). 'Relevant business premises' means premises: (1) which are used, have been used or are to be used for or in connection with the carrying on of an employment agency or employment business; (2) which the officer has reasonable cause to believe are used or have been used for or in connection with the carrying on of an employment agency or employment business; or (3) which the officer has reasonable cause to believe are used for the carrying on of a business by a person who also carries on or has carried on an employment agency or employment business, if the officer also has reasonable cause to believe that records or other documents which relate to the employment agency or employment business are kept there: Employment Agencies Act 1973 s 9(1B) (added by the Employment Relations Act 1999 Sch 7 paras 1, 4(1), (3), (4) as from a day to be appointed).

A person who obstructs an officer in the exercise of his powers under the Employment Agencies Act 1973 s 9(1)(a) or (b) (or, as from a day to be appointed, s 9(1)(d): see note 21 infra), or who, without reasonable excuse, fails to comply with a requirement under s 9(1)(c) (or, as from a day to be appointed, s 9(1A): see note 21 infra), is guilty of an offence and liable on summary conviction to a fine not exceeding level 3 on the standard scale: see the Employment Agencies Act 1973 s 9(3) (amended by virtue of the Criminal

Justice Act 1982 ss 38, 46; and amended, as from a day to be appointed, by the Employment Relations Act 1999 Sch 7 paras 1, 4(5)(a)).

21   Employment Agencies Act 1973 s 9(1)(b). See also note 20 supra.

As from a day to be appointed, an authorised officer may take copies of records and other documents inspected under s 9(1)(b): s 9(1)(d) (added by the Employment Relations Act 1999 Sch 7 paras 1, 4(1), (2)(b) as from a day to be appointed). 'Document' includes information recorded in any form; and information is kept at premises if it is accessible from them: Employment Agencies Act 1973 s 9(1C) (added by the Employment Relations Act 1999 Sch 7 paras 1, 4(1), (3), (4) as from a day to be appointed).

As from a day to be appointed, if an officer seeks to inspect or acquire, in accordance with the Employment Agencies Act 1973 s 9(1)(b) or (c), a record or other document or information which is not kept at the premises being inspected, he may require any person on the premises to inform him where and by whom the record, other document or information is kept, and to make arrangements, if it is reasonably practicable for the person to do so, for the record, other document or information to be inspected by or furnished to the officer at the premises at a time specified by the officer: s 9(1A) (added by the Employment Relations Act 1999 Sch 7 paras 1, 4(1), (3), (4) as from a day to be appointed).

22   Employment Agencies Act 1973 s 9(1)(c). See also note 21 supra. A person is not required by this provision to answer any question tending to incriminate himself or, in the case of a person who is married, his wife or her husband: s 9(2). See also note 20 supra.

As from a day to be appointed, s 9(2) is substituted to provide that nothing in s 9 (as amended) requires a person to produce, provide access to or make arrangements for the production of anything which he could not be compelled to produce in civil proceedings before the High Court: s 9(2) (substituted by the Employment Relations Act 1999 Sch 7 paras 1 4(1), (4) as from a day to be appointed). A statement made by a person in compliance with a requirement under the Employment Agencies Act 1973 s 9 (as amended) may be used in evidence against him in criminal proceedings: s 9(2A) (added by the Employment Relations Act 1999 Sch 7 paras 1 4(1), (4) as from a day to be appointed). however, except in proceedings for an offence under the Perjury Act 1911 s 5 (false statements made otherwise than on oath: see CRIMINAL LAW, EVIDENCE AND PROCEDURE vol 11(1) (Reissue) para 304), no evidence relating to the statement may be adduced, and no question relating to it may be asked, by or on behalf of the prosecution unless evidence relating to it is adduced, or a question relating to it is asked, by or on behalf of the person who made the statement: Employment Agencies Act 1973 s 9(2B) (added by the Employment Relations Act 1999 Sch 7 paras 1 4(1), (4) as from a day to be appointed).

23   See the Employment Agencies Act 1973 s 9(4). No information so obtained may be disclosed except:

(1)   with the consent of the person furnishing the information, or, where furnished on behalf of another person, with the consent of that other person or with the consent of the person carrying on or proposing to carry on the employment agency or employment business concerned (s 9(4)(a)(i)); or

(2)   to the Secretary of State, or an officer or servant appointed by him, or a person exercising functions on his behalf, for the purposes of the exercise of their respective functions under the Act (s 9(4)(a)(ii) (renumbered by the Employment Protection Act 1975 ss 114, 125(3), Sch 13 para 6(3), Sch 18)); or

(3)   by the Secretary of State or such an officer, servant or person to the person carrying on or proposing to carry on the employment agency or employment business concerned, to any person in his employment, or, in the case of information relating to a person availing himself of the services of such an agency or business, to that person (Employment Agencies Act 1973 s 9(4)(a)(iii) (added by the Employment Protection Act 1975 ss 114, 125(3), Sch 13 para 6(3), Sch 18)); or

(4)   with a view to the institution of, or otherwise for the purposes of, any criminal proceedings pursuant to or arising out of the Act or for the purposes of any proceedings under the Employment Agencies Act 1973 s 3A, 3C or 3D (all as added and amended) (see para 675 ante) (s 9(4)(a)(iv) (renumbered by the Employment Protection Act 1975 ss 114, 125(3), Sch 13 para 6(3), Sch 18; and amended by the Deregulation and Contracting Out Act 1994 s 35, Sch 10 para 1(4); and prospectively amended by the Employment Relations Act 1999 ss 31, 44, Sch 7 paras 1, 4(6), Sch 9 Table 8 as from a day to be appointed)).

Any person who contravenes s 9(4)(a) (as amended) is guilty of an offence and liable on summary conviction to a fine not exceeding level 5 on the standard scale: Employment Agencies Act 1973 s 9(4)(b) (amended by virtue of the Criminal Justice Act 1982 ss 38, 46). See also para 675 note 6 ante.

678.   Charging of fees. A person carrying on an employment agency[1] or employment business[2] may not demand or directly or indirectly receive from any person any fee[3] for finding him employment or for seeking to find him employment[4], except in such cases or classes of case as are prescribed[5] by regulations[6]. Any person contravening this prohibition[7] is guilty of an offence[8].

The regulations made under the provisions described above provide that fees may be charged by agents for finding work for persons in specified professions in the entertainment industry[9], or for photographic and fashion models[10], except where the agent also charges a fee to the employer in question[11], or where the agent and the employer are connected with each other[12]. The charging of fees to au pairs is allowed but is subject to specific control[13]. Where the agent charges fees to workers, he must provide the worker with a written statement of his terms before seeking employment for him[14].

1   For the meaning of 'employment agency' see para 674 ante.

2   For the meaning of 'employment business' see para 674 ante.

3   'Fee' includes any charge however described: Employment Agencies Act 1973 s 13(1). As to the meaning of 'demand' in relation to a fee see *First Point International Ltd v Department of Trade and Industry* (1999) 164 JP 89, DC.

4   The collection and assessment of appraisal information is part of the process of seeking to find employment for a client, if the seeking of information is sufficiently proximate to what happens thereafter: see *First Point International Ltd v Department of Trade and Industry* (1999) 164 JP 89, DC.

5   For the meaning of 'prescribed' see para 676 note 20 ante.

6   Employment Agencies Act 1973 s 6(1). As from a day to be appointed, s 6(1) is substituted by the Employment Relations Act 1999 s 31, Sch 7 paras 1, 3, to provide that except in such cases or classes of case as the Secretary of State may prescribe: (1) a person carrying on an employment agency may not request or directly or indirectly receive any fee from any person for providing services (whether by the provision of information or otherwise) for the purpose of finding him employment or seeking to find him employment; (2) a person carrying on an employment business may not request or directly or indirectly receive any fee from an employee for providing services (whether by the provision of information or otherwise) for the purpose of finding or seeking to find another person, with a view to the employee acting for and under the control of that other person; (3) a person carrying on an employment business may not request or directly or indirectly receive any fee from a second person for providing services (whether by the provision of information or otherwise) for the purpose of finding or seeking to find a third person, with a view to the second person becoming employed by the first person and acting for and under the control of the third person: Employment Agencies Act 1973 s 6(1) (as prospectively substituted).

    As to the making of regulations and orders under the Employment Agencies Act 1973 see para 676 note 20 ante. In the case of regulations under s 6(1), a draft must have been laid before and approved by each House of Parliament: s 12(5) (substituted by the Employment relations Act 1999 s 31, Sch 7 paras 1, 6).

7   As to bodies completely exempted from the application of the Employment Agencies Act 1973 see para 676 ante.

8   Ibid s 6(2). A person guilty of such an offence is liable on summary conviction to a fine not exceeding level 5 on the standard scale: s 6(2) (amended by virtue of the Criminal Justice Act 1982 ss 38, 46). See also para 675 note 6 ante. As to the standard scale see para 16 note 21 ante.

9   Employment Agencies Act 1973 (Charging Fees to Workers) Regulations 1976, SI 1976/714, reg 3, Schedule para 1. 'Entertainment industry' means the production and presentation of films, television and sound broadcasts, and recordings, and of plays,

operas, ballets, musical and variety performances, and other similar means of entertainment whether taking place in theatres, concert halls, dance halls, clubs or any other places of public or private entertainment: reg 2(1). The specified professions referred to in the text are: (1) actors, singers, musicians, dancers and other performers; (2) composers, directors, assistant directors, production managers, assistant production managers, lighting cameramen, camera operators, make up artists, film editors, action arrangers and co-ordinators, costume and production designers, recording engineers, hairdressers, property masters, film continuity personnel, sound mixers and still photographers: Schedule para 1.

10 Ibid Schedule para 2.

11 Ibid reg 3(2)(a).

12 Ibid reg 3(2)(b). An agent and an employer are connected with each other in the following circumstances:

    (1)   where the agent, or a partner of his, or where the agent is a company, a director of it, is also the employer (reg 3(2)(b)(i));

    (2)   where the employer is a company controlled by any of the persons referred to in head (1) supra (reg 3(2)(b)(ii));

    (3)   where the employer, or a partner of his, or where the employer is a company, a director of it, is also the agent (reg 3(2)(b)(iii));

    (4)   where the agent is a company controlled by any of the persons referred to in head (3) supra (reg 3(2)(b)(iv)); or

    (5)   where the employer and the agent are both companies of which a third person has control (reg 3(2)(b)(v)).

For these purposes a company is controlled by a person if he exercises, is able to exercise or is entitled to acquire, control (whether direct or indirect) over the affairs of the company, and in particular if he possesses or is entitled to acquire the greater proportion of the share capital or voting power of the company: reg 3(3).

13 See the Employment Agencies Act 1973 (Charging Fees to Au Pairs) Regulations 1981, SI 1981/1481.

14 Conduct of Employment Agencies and Employment Businesses Regulations 1976, SI 1976/715, reg 4(2).

679–700. Discrimination by employment agencies. It is unlawful for an employment agency[1] to discriminate[2] either against a woman[3] or on racial grounds[4]:

(1)   in the terms on which the agency offers to provide any of its services[5]; or

(2)   by refusing or deliberately omitting to provide any of its services[6]; or

(3)   in the way it provides any of its services[7].

However, this provision does not apply if the discrimination only concerns employment which the employer could lawfully refuse to offer the person in question[8]. An employment agency or local education authority, education authority or other person is under no liability if it proves that it acted in reliance on a statement made by the employer to the effect that its action would not be unlawful[9], and that it was reasonable for the agency to rely on that statement[10].

It is unlawful for an employment agency to refuse a person any of its services:

(a)   because he is, or is not, a member of a trade union; or

(b)   because he is unwilling to accept a requirement to take steps to become or cease to be, or to remain or not to become a member of a trade union[11].

1 'Employment agency' means a person who, for profit or not, provides services for the purpose of finding employment for workers or supplying employers with workers: Sex discrimination Act 1975 s 82(1); Race Relations Act 1976 s 78(1). 'Employment' means employment under a contract of service or of apprenticeship or a contract personally to

execute any work or labour, and related expressions must be construed accordingly: Sex Discrimination Act 1975 s 82(1); Race Relations Act 1976 s 78(1).

2　As to the meaning of 'discrimination', 'discriminate' and related expressions see the Sex Discrimination Act 1975 s 5 (see DISCRIMINATION vol 13 (Reissue) para 310); and the Race Relations Act 1976 s 3 (see DISCRIMINATION vol 13 (Reissue) para 399 et seq).

3　'Woman' includes a female of any age: Sex Discrimination Act 1975 s 82(1).

4　As to the meaning of 'racial grounds', etc see the Race Relations Act 1976 s 3; and DISCRIMINATION vol 13 (Reissue) para 401.

5　Sex Discrimination Act 1975 s 15(1)(a); Race Relations Act 1976 s 14(1)(a). References to the services of an employment agency include guidance on careers and any other services related to employment: Sex Discrimination Act 1975 s 15(3); Race Relations Act 1976 s 14(3).

6　Sex Discrimination Act 1975 s 15(1)(b); Race Relations Act 1976 s 14(1)(b).

7　Sex Discrimination Act 1975 s 15(1)(c); Race Relations Act 1976 s 14(1)(c).

8　Sex Discrimination Act 1975 s 15(4); Race Relations Act 1976 s 14(4).

9　Ie would not, by virtue of the operation of the provision set out in the text and note 8 supra, be unlawful.

10　Sex Discrimination Act 1975 s 15(5); Race Relations Act 1976 s 14(5) (both amended by the Trade Union Reform and Employment Rights Act 1993 s 49(2), Sch 8 paras 8(b), 9(b)). A person who knowingly or recklessly makes such a statement which in a material respect is false or misleading commits an offence punishable on summary conviction with a fine not exceeding level 5 on the standard scale: Sex Discrimination Act 1975 s 15(6); Race Relations Act 1976 s 14(6) (both amended by virtue of the Criminal Justice Act 1982 ss 38, 46). As to the standard scale see para 16 note 21 ante.

11　See para 1143 post.

8. SHOPS

(1) DEREGULATION OF SHOPS

701. In general. The Shops Act 1950, the Shops (Airports) Act 1962 and the Shops (Early Closing Days) Act 1965 subjected shops to detailed restrictions in relation to hours of closing, conditions of employment, the hours of employment of young persons and relatively strict rules on Sunday trading. Such restrictions have now been abolished[1], except in the case of Sunday trading[2].

1 See the Employment Act 1989 ss 10, 29(4), Sch 3, Sch 7; the Deregulation and Contracting Out Act 1994 ss 23, 24, 81(1), Sch 17; and the Sunday Trading Act 1994 ss 1(2), 9(2), Sch 5.
2 As to Sunday trading see para 702 et seq post.

(2) SUNDAY TRADING

(i) In general

702. Restrictions on Sunday opening of large shops. Formerly, trading on Sunday was severely restricted[1]. The restricting provisions were repealed by the Sunday Trading Act 1994[2] and such restrictions as are now in force relate only to large shops[3]. A large shop must not be open on Sunday for the serving of retail customers[4]; but that prohibition does not apply if:

(1) it falls within a category of exempt shops[5];
(2) it is occupied by persons observing the Jewish Sabbath and a relevant notice has effect[6]; or
(3) a notice of proposed Sunday opening is in force and the shop is open only during the permitted opening hours under that notice[7].

If the above provisions[8] are contravened in relation to a shop, the occupier of the shop is liable on summary conviction to a fine not exceeding £50,000[9].

Where a person is charged with having contravened the above provisions[10] in relation to a large shop which was permitted to be open for the serving of retail customers on the Sunday in question during the permitted Sunday opening hours under the relevant notice, by reason of his having served a retail customer after the end of those hours, it is a defence to prove that the customer was in the shop before that time and left not later than half an hour after that time[11].

1 Ie by the Shops Act 1950 Pt IV (ss 47–67) (repealed).
2 Ie by the Sunday Trading Act 1994 ss 1(2), 9(2), Sch 5. Under the Sunday Trading Act 1994 the Secretary of State may by order made by statutory instrument: (1) repeal any provision of a local Act passed before or in the same session as the Sunday Trading Act 1994 if it appears to him that the provision is inconsistent with, or has become unnecessary in consequence of, any provision of the 1994 Act; and (2) amend any provision of such a local Act if it appears to him that the provision requires amendment in consequence of any provision of the 1994 Act or any repeal made by virtue of head (1) supra: s 6(1). Before he makes such an order repealing or amending any provision of a local Act, it is the Secretary of State's duty to consult each local authority which he considers would be affected by the repeal or amendment of that provision: Sunday Trading Act 1994 s 6(2). A statutory instrument containing such an order is subject to annulment in pursuance of a resolution of either House of Parliament: s 6(3).
     For these purposes, 'local authority' means any unitary authority or any district council, so far as it is not a unitary authority: s 8(1). 'Unitary authority' means: (a) the

council of any county, so far as it is the council for an area for which there are no district councils; (b) the council of any district comprised in an area for which there is no county council; (c) a county borough council; (d) a London borough council; (e) the Common Council of the City of London; or (f) the Council of the Isles of Scilly: s 8(2).

3   For these purposes, 'shop' means any premises where there is carried on a trade or business consisting wholly or mainly of the sale of goods (ibid s 1(1), Sch 1 para 1); and 'large shop' means a shop which has a relevant floor area exceeding 280 square metres (Sch 1 para 1). 'Relevant floor area', in relation to a shop, means the internal floor area of so much of the shop as consists of, or is comprised in, a building, but excluding any part of the shop which, throughout the week ending with the Sunday in question, is used neither for the serving of customers in connection with the sale of goods nor for the display of goods: Sch 1 para 1. 'Sale of goods' does not include: (1) the sale of meals, refreshments or intoxicating liquor for consumption on the premises on which they are sold; or (2) the sale of meals or refreshments prepared to order for immediate consumption off those premises: Sch 1 para 1. 'Intoxicating liquor' has the same meaning as in the Licensing Act 1964 (see INTOXICATING LIQUOR vol 26 (Reissue) para 3 note 10): Sunday Trading Act 1994 Sch 1 para 1.

4   Ibid Sch 1 para 2(1). For these purposes, 'retail customer' means a person who purchases goods retail: Sch 1 para 1. For the meaning of references to retail purchases see para 703 note 5 post. A shop may still be a large shop, even though only a small part of the whole shop is open to retail customers: *Haskins Garden Centres Ltd v East Dorset District Council* [1998] EGCS 71, DC.
     The Sunday Trading Act 1994 Sch 1 para 2(1) does not apply to any large shop situated in that part of the terminal area of the tunnel system located at the portals of the tunnels in the vicinity of Cheriton, Folkestone, that is within the area shown coloured blue on the deposited plan: Channel Tunnel (Sunday Trading Act 1994) (Disapplication) Order 1994, SI 1994/3286, art 3. 'The deposited plan' means the plan marked 'The Channel Tunnel (Sunday Trading Act 1994) (Disapplication) Order 1994', signed by authority of the Secretary of State for Transport, dated 22 November 1994 and deposited at the Department of the Environment, Transport and the Regions, Parliamentary Library, Room P3/001, 2 Marsham Street, London SW1P 3EB; and 'shop' has the same meaning as in the Sunday Trading Act 1994 (see note 3 supra): Channel Tunnel (Sunday Trading Act 1994) (Disapplication) Order 1994, SI 1994/3286, art 2; Interpretation Act 1978 s 17(2)(a).

5   See the Sunday Trading Act 1994 Sch 1 para 2(2)(a); and para 703 post.

6   See ibid Sch 1 para 2(2)(b); and para 706 post.

7   See ibid Sch 1 para 2(3); and para 704 post. The exemption so conferred does not apply where the Sunday is Easter Day or Christmas Day: Sch 1 para 2(4).

8   Ie ibid Sch 1 para 2(1): see supra.

9   Ibid Sch 1 para 7(1). As to the enforcement of the Sunday Trading Act 1994, and as to the general provisions relating to offences thereunder, see para 710 post.

10   See note 8 supra.

11   Sunday Trading Act 1994 Sch 1 para 8.

703.   Exempt shops. The general prohibition on large shops[1] opening on Sunday[2] does not apply to:

(1)   any shop which is at a farm and where the trade or business carried on consists wholly or mainly of the sale of produce from that farm;

(2)   any shop where the trade or business carried on consists wholly or mainly of the sale of intoxicating liquor[3];

(3)   any shop where the trade or business carried on consists wholly or mainly of the sale of any one or more of the following:
      (a)   motor supplies and accessories; or
      (b)   cycle supplies and accessories;

(4)   any shop which:
      (a)   is a registered pharmacy[4]; and
      (b)   is not open for the retail sale[5] of any goods other than medicinal products[6] and surgical appliances;

(5)   any shop at a designated airport[7] which is situated in an applicable part of the airport[8];

(6)   any shop in a railway station;

(7)   any shop at a service area[9];

(8)   any petrol filling station;

(9)   any shop which is not open for the retail sale of any goods other than food, stores or other necessaries required by any person for a vessel or aircraft on its arrival at, or immediately before its departure from, a port, harbour or airport; and

(10)   any stand[10] used for the retail sale of goods during the course of an exhibition[11].

In determining whether a shop falls within heads (1), (2) or (3) above, regard is to be had to the nature of the trade or business carried on there on weekdays as well as to the nature of the trade or business carried on there on Sunday[12].

1   For the meaning of 'large shop' see para 702 note 3 ante.

2   Ie the general prohibition in the Sunday Trading Act 1994 s 1(1), Sch 1 para 2(1): see para 702 ante.

3   For the meaning of 'intoxicating liquor' see para 702 note 3 ante.

4   For these purposes, 'registered pharmacy' has the same meaning as in the Medicines Act 1968 (see MEDICINE, PHARMACY, DRUGS AND MEDICINAL PRODUCTS vol 30 (Reissue) para 723 note 8): Sunday Trading Act 1994 Sch 1 para 1.

5   For these purposes, 'retail sale' means any sale other than a sale for use or resale in the course of a trade or business; and references to retail purchases are to be construed accordingly: ibid Sch 1 para 1.

6   For these purposes, 'medicinal product' has the same meaning as in the Medicines Act 1968 (see MEDICINE, PHARMACY, DRUGS AND MEDICINAL PRODUCTS vol 30 (Reissue) para 859): Sunday Trading Act 1994 Sch 1 para 1.

7   For these purposes, 'designated airport' means an airport designated by an order made by the Secretary of State, as being an airport at which there appears to him to be a substantial amount of international passenger traffic: ibid Sch 1 para 3(4). The power to make such an order is exercisable by statutory instrument: Sch 1 para 3(5). Any order made under the Shops (Airports) Act 1962 s 1(2) (repealed) and in force on 26 August 1994 (ie the commencement date of the Sunday Trading Act 1994 Sch 1: see para 708 note 1 post) has effect, so far as it relates to England and Wales, as if made also under the Sunday Trading Act 1994 Sch 1 para 3(4), and may be amended or revoked as it has effect for these purposes by an order under Sch 1 para 3(4): Sch 1 para 3(6). As to such orders see AVIATION vol 2 (Reissue) para 1235 note 13.

8   For these purposes, the applicable part is every part of a designated airport, except any part which is not ordinarily used by persons travelling by air to or from the airport: ibid Sch 1 para 3(3).

9   Ie within the meaning of the Highways Act 1980: see HIGHWAYS, STREETS AND BRIDGES vol 21 (Reissue) para 624 note 9.

10   For these purposes, 'stand', in relation to an exhibition, means any platform, structure, space or other area provided for exhibition purposes: Sunday Trading Act 1994 Sch 1 para 1.

11   Ibid Sch 1 paras 2(2)(a), 3(1). If a large shop is not exempt, it must comply with the requirements as to notice and the maximum of six hours' opening on a Sunday: see para 704 post.

12   Ibid Sch 1 para 3(2).

704. Notice of proposed Sunday opening. A person who is, or proposes to be, the occupier of a large shop[1] may give notice to the local authority[2] for the area in which the shop is situated:

(1)   stating that he proposes to open the shop on Sunday for the serving of retail customers[3]; and

(2)   specifying a continuous period of six hours, beginning no earlier than 10 am and ending no later than 6 pm, as the permitted Sunday opening hours in relation to the shop[4].

The occupier of a shop in respect of which such a notice has been given may, by a subsequent notice:

(a)   specify permitted Sunday opening hours that could be specified under head (2) above but are different from those specified in the earlier notice; or

(b)   cancel the earlier notice[5].

A notice under the above provisions:

(i)   does not take effect until the end of the period of 14 days beginning with the day on which it is given, unless the local authority agrees that it is to take effect at the end of a shorter period[6]; and

(ii)   ceases to have effect when superseded by a subsequent notice or cancelled as mentioned in head (b) above[7].

At any time when a large shop is open on Sunday for the serving of retail customers pursuant to such a notice, there must be displayed in a conspicuous position inside and outside the shop a further notice specifying the permitted Sunday opening hours[8]. If this requirement is contravened, the occupier of the shop is liable on summary conviction to a fine not exceeding level 2 on the standard scale[9].

1   For the meaning of 'large shop' see para 702 note 3 ante.
2   For the meaning of 'local authority' see para 702 note 2 ante.
3   For the meaning of 'retail customer' see para 702 note 4 ante; and for the meaning of 'retail sale' see para 703 note 5 ante.
4   Sunday Trading Act 1994 s 1(1), Sch 1 para 4(1). Where such a notice has effect in relation to a shop, Sch 1 para 2(1) (general prohibition on large shops opening on Sunday: see para 702 ante) does not apply in relation to the shop during the permitted Sunday opening hours specified in the notice (Sch 1 para 2(3)); but that exemption does not apply where the Sunday is Easter Day or Christmas Day (Sch 1 para 2(4)).
5   Ibid Sch 1 para 4(2).
6   Ibid Sch 1 para 4(3).
7   Ibid Sch 1 para 4(4).
8   Ibid Sch 1 para 6.
9   Ibid Sch 1 para 7(2). For the meaning of 'the standard scale' see para 16 note 21 ante. As to the enforcement of the Sunday Trading Act 1994, and as to the general provisions relating to offences thereunder, see para 710 post.

705.   Register of shops. Every local authority[1] must keep a register of shops[2] in respect of which a notice of Sunday opening[3] has effect[4]; and, in relation to every such shop, the register must contain particulars of:

(1)   the name, if any, and address of the shop; and

(2)   the permitted Sunday opening hours specified in the notice[5].

Any register so kept must be open to inspection by members of the public at all reasonable times and may be kept by means of a computer[6].

1   For the meaning of 'local authority' see para 702 note 2 ante.
2   For the meaning of 'shop' see para 702 note 3 ante.
3   Ie a notice under the Sunday Trading Act 1994 s 1(1), Sch 1 para 4: see para 704 ante.
4   Ibid Sch 1 para 5(1).
5   Ibid Sch 1 para 5(2).
6   Ibid Sch 1 para 5(3).

706.   Shops occupied by persons observing the Jewish Sabbath. A person of the Jewish religion[1] who is the occupier[2] of a large shop[3] may give to the local authority[4] for the area in which the shop is situated a notice signed by him stating:

(1)   that he is a person of the Jewish religion; and

(2)   that he intends to keep the shop closed for the serving of customers on the Jewish Sabbath[5].

Such a notice must be accompanied by a certificate signed by an authorised person[6] that the person giving the notice is a person of the Jewish religion[7]. If there is any change in the occupation of the shop in respect of which such a notice has effect, or in any partnership or among the directors of any company by which such a shop is occupied, the notice is to be taken to be cancelled at the end of the period of 14 days beginning with the day on which the change occurred, unless, during that period, or within such further time as the local authority[8] may allow, a fresh notice is given[8] in respect of the shop[9]. A person who, in a notice or certificate given for the above purposes, makes a statement which is false in a material respect and which he knows to be false or does not believe to be true is liable on summary conviction to a fine not exceeding level 5 on the standard scale[10].

Where such a notice is in force, the prohibition on the opening of a large shop on a Sunday does not apply[11].

Every local authority must keep a register containing particulars of the name, if any, and address of every shop in respect of which such a notice has effect[12]; and any register so kept must be open to inspection by members of the public at all reasonable times and may be kept by means of a computer[13].

1   These provisions also apply to persons who are members of any religious body regularly observing the Jewish Sabbath as they apply to persons of the Jewish religion; and accordingly: (1) references to persons of the Jewish religion are to be construed as including any person who is a member of such a body; and (2) in the application of those provisions to such persons, 'authorised person' means a minister of the religious body concerned: Sunday Trading Act 1994 s 1(1), Sch 2 para 9.

2   For these purposes, a shop occupied by a partnership or company is to be taken to be occupied by a person of the Jewish religion if, and only if, the majority of the partners or directors are persons of that religion: ibid Sch 2 para 8(2). Where the occupier of a shop is a partnership or company: (1) any notice under Sch 2 para 8(1) must be given by the majority of the partners or directors and, if not given by all of them, must specify the names of all of the other partners or directors; and (2) a certificate under Sch 2 para 8(3) (see infra) is required in relation to each of the persons by whom such a notice is given: Sch 2 para 8(4). For these purposes, 'shop' has the same meaning as in s 1(1), Sch 1 (see para 702 note 3 ante): Sch 2 para 8(12).

3   For these purposes, 'large shop' has the same meaning as in ibid Sch 1 (see para 702 note 3 ante): Sch 2 para 8(12).

4   For the meaning of 'local authority' see para 702 note 2 ante.

5   Sunday Trading Act 1994 Sch 2 paras 2(2)(b), 8(1).

6   For these purposes, 'authorised person', in relation to a notice under ibid Sch 2 para 8(1), means: (1) the minister of the synagogue of which the person giving the notice is a member; (2) the secretary of that synagogue, within the meaning given in the Marriage Act 1949 Pt IV (ss 53–57) (as amended) (see REGISTRATION CONCERNING THE INDIVIDUAL vol 39(2) (Reissue) para 520 note 5); or (3) any other person nominated for these purposes by the President of the London Committee of Deputies of the British Jews (otherwise known as the Board of Deputies of British Jews): Sunday Trading Act 1994 Sch 2 para 8(12).

7   Ibid Sch 2 para 8(3).

8   Ie under ibid Sch 2 para 8(1): see supra.

9   Ibid Sch 2 para 8(7). Where a fresh notice is given under Sch 2 para 8(1) by reason of a change of the kind mentioned in Sch 2 para 8(7), the local authority may dispense with the certificate required by Sch 2 para 8(3) (see supra) in the case of any person in respect of whom such a certificate has been provided in connection with a former notice in respect of that shop or any other shop in the area of the local authority: Sch 2 para 8(8). A notice given under Sch 2 para 8(1) in respect of any shop must be cancelled on application in that behalf being made to the local authority by the occupier of the shop: Sch 2 para 8(9).

10   Ibid Sch 2 para 8(10). For the meaning of 'the standard scale' see para 16 note 21 ante. As to the enforcement of the Sunday Trading Act 1994, and as to the general provisions relating to offences thereunder, see para 710 post. Where a person is convicted of such an offence, the local authority may cancel any notice under Sch 2 para 8(1) to which the offence relates: Sch 2 para 8(11).

11   See ibid Sch 1 para 2(2)(b); and para 702 ante.

12   Ibid Sch 2 para 8(5).

13   Ibid Sch 2 para 8(6).

707.   Control of loading and unloading at large shops on Sunday morning.

A local authority[1] may by resolution designate its area as a loading control area with effect from a date specified in the resolution, which must be a date at least one month after the date on which the resolution is passed[2].

Where a large shop[3] is the subject of a notice to open on Sunday[4] and is situated in an area so designated, the occupier must not load or unload, or permit any other person to load or unload, goods from a vehicle at the shop before 9 am on Sunday in connection with the trade or business carried on in the shop, unless the loading or unloading is carried on:

(1)   with the consent[5] of the local authority for the area in which the shop is situated; and

(2)   in accordance with any conditions[6] subject to which that consent is granted[7].

A person who contravenes the above provisions is liable on summary conviction to a fine not exceeding level 3 on the standard scale[8].

1   For the meaning of 'local authority' see para 702 note 2 ante.

2   Sunday Trading Act 1994 s 2(1). A local authority may by resolution revoke any designation so made: s 2(2). Before making or revoking any such designation, it is the duty of a local authority to consult persons appearing to it to be likely to be affected by the proposed designation or revocation, whether as the occupiers of shops or as local residents, or persons appearing to the local authority to represent such persons: s 2(3). Where a local authority makes or revokes such a designation, it must publish notice of the designation or revocation in such manner as it considers appropriate: s 2(4).

3   For the meaning of 'large shop' see para 702 note 3 ante.

4   Ie a notice under the Sunday Trading Act 1994 s 1(1), Sch 1 para 4: see para 704 ante.

5   An application for such consent must be made in writing and must contain such information as the local authority may reasonably require: ibid s 2(5), Sch 3 para 4. An applicant for such a consent must pay such reasonable fee in respect of his application as the local authority may determine: Sch 3 para 5. Where an application is duly made to the local authority for such a consent, the authority must grant the consent unless it is satisfied that the loading or unloading of goods from vehicles before 9 am on Sunday at the shop to which the application relates, in connection with the trade or business carried on at the shop, has caused, or would be likely to cause, undue annoyance to local residents: Sch 3 para 6(1). The authority must determine the application and notify the applicant in writing of its decision within the period of 21 days beginning with the day on which the application is received by the authority (Sch 3 para 6(2)); and, in a case where a consent is granted, such notification must specify the conditions, if any, subject to which the consent is granted (Sch 3 para 6(3)). Where a local authority grants such a consent, it may cause a notice giving details of that consent to be published in a local newspaper circulating in its area: Sch 3 para 8. Where the local authority is satisfied that the loading or unloading authorised by virtue of such a consent has caused undue annoyance to local residents, it may revoke the consent: Sch 3 para 7(b).

6   Such a consent may be granted subject to such conditions as the local authority considers appropriate: ibid Sch 3 para 3(1). The local authority may at any time vary the conditions subject to which a consent is granted, and must give notice of the variation to the person to whom the consent was granted: Sch 3 para 3(2).

7   Ibid Sch 3 paras 1, 2.

8   Ibid Sch 3 para 9. For the meaning of 'the standard scale' see para 16 note 21 ante. As to the enforcement of the Sunday Trading Act 1994, and as to the general provisions relating

to offences thereunder, see para 710 post. Where the occupier of a shop in respect of which such a consent is granted is convicted of an offence under Sch 3 para 9 by reason of his failure to comply with the conditions subject to which the consent was granted, the local authority may revoke the consent: Sch 3 para 7(a).

708. Leases entered into before 26 August 1994. Where any lease or agreement, however worded, entered into before 26 August 1994[1] has the effect of requiring the occupier of a shop[2] to keep the shop open for the serving of retail customers[3]:

(1) during normal business hours; or

(2) during hours to be determined otherwise than by or with the consent of the occupier,

that lease or agreement is not to be regarded as requiring, or as enabling any other person to require, the occupier to open the shop on Sunday for the serving of retail customers[4].

1 Ie the date on which the Sunday Trading Act 1994 s 3 came into force. Sections 1, 6–8, 9(1), (3), (4) came into force on 5 July 1994 (ie the date of Royal Assent). Schedules 1, 2 were brought into force on 26 August 1994: s 9(3); Sunday Trading Act 1994 Appointed Day Order 1994, SI 1994/1841, art 2. The remaining provisions of the Sunday Trading Act 1994 also came into force on 26 August 1994: Sunday Trading Act 1994 s 9(3); Sunday Trading Act 1994 Appointed Day Order 1994, SI 1994/1841, art 2.
2 For these purposes, 'shop' has the same meaning as in the Sunday Trading Act 1994 s 1(1), Sch 1 (see para 702 note 3 ante): s 3(3).
3 For these purposes, 'retail customer' has the same meaning as in ibid Sch 1 (see para 702 note 4 ante): s 3(3)
4 Ibid s 3(1). Section 3(1) does not affect any lease or agreement: (1) to the extent that it relates specifically to Sunday and would otherwise have the effect of requiring Sunday trading of a kind which before 26 August 1994 would have been lawful by virtue of any provision of the Shops Act 1950 Pt IV (ss 47–67) (repealed); or (2) to the extent that it is varied by agreement after 26 August 1994: Sunday Trading Act 1994 s 3(2).

(ii) Rights of Shop Workers

709. In general. Special statutory protection is given[1] in relation to Sunday working for shop and betting workers.

Workers qualifying as protected shop workers and protected betting workers, that is to say workers already in employment on 25 August 1994 as shop workers or, as the case may be, on 2 January 1995 as betting workers, or whose contracts do not require Sunday working[2], are protected from being required to work on Sundays[3]. In addition, all shop or betting workers are given an option not to work on Sundays[4].

Protected or opted-out shop or betting workers have a right not to be discriminated against for refusal to work on Sundays[5]; and the dismissal of such a worker for such a refusal is automatically unfair[6], as is any later selection for redundancy on that ground[7].

1 Ie by the Employment Rights Act 1996 Pt IV (ss 36–43) (as amended): see EMPLOYMENT vol 16 (2000 Reissue) para 245 et seq.
2 See EMPLOYMENT vol 16 (2000 Reissue) para 245.
3 See EMPLOYMENT vol 16 (2000 Reissue) para 246.
4 See EMPLOYMENT vol 16 (2000 Reissue) para 247.
5 See the Employment Rights Act 1996 s 45; and EMPLOYMENT vol 16 (2000 Reissue) para 251.
6 See ibid s 101; and EMPLOYMENT vol 16 (2000 Reissue) para 502.
7 See ibid s 105(1), (4) (as amended); and EMPLOYMENT vol 16 (2000 Reissue) para 496. In addition, dismissal for asserting statutory rights by such a worker is automatically unfair: see s 104 (as amended); and EMPLOYMENT vol 16 (2000 Reissue) para 507.

(iii) Enforcement

710.   In general.   It is the duty of every local authority[1] to enforce within its area the provisions[2] of the Sunday Trading Act 1994[3]. For the purposes of such duties, it is the duty of every local authority to appoint inspectors[4]. An inspector appointed by a local authority has a right, on producing, if so required, some duly authenticated document showing his authority, at all reasonable hours:

(1)   to enter any premises within the area of the local authority, with or without a constable, for the purpose of ascertaining whether there is or has been any contravention of certain provisions[5] of the 1994 Act;

(2)   to require the production of, inspect and take copies of any records, in whatever form they are held, relating to any business carried on on the premises which appear to him to be relevant for the purposes of head (1) above;

(3)   where those records are kept by means of a computer, to require the records to be produced in a form in which they may be taken away; and

(4)   to take such measurements and photographs as he considers necessary for the purposes of head (1) above[6].

Any person who intentionally obstructs an inspector so appointed acting in the execution of his duty is liable on summary conviction to a fine not exceeding level 3 on the standard scale[7].

The following general provisions apply to any offence under the 1994 Act[8]:

(a)   where the commission by any person of an offence is due to the act or default of some other person, that other person is guilty of the offence, and a person may be charged with, and convicted of, the offence on that basis, whether or not proceedings are taken against the first-mentioned person[9];

(b)   where an offence committed by a body corporate is proved to have been committed with the consent or connivance of, or to be attributable to any neglect on the part of, any director, manager, secretary or other similar officer of the body corporate, or any person who was purporting to act in any such capacity, he, as well as the body corporate, is guilty of the offence and is liable to be proceeded against and punished accordingly[10];

(c)   it is a defence for the person charged with an offence to prove that he took all reasonable precautions and exercised all due diligence to avoid the commission of the offence by himself or by a person under his control[11].

1   For the meaning of 'local authority' see para 702 note 2 ante.
2   Ie the provisions of the Sunday Trading Act 1994 ss 1(1), 2(5), Sch 1 (see paras 702–704 ante), Sch 2 Pt II (paras 8–10) (see para 706 ante) and Sch 3 (see para 707 ante).
3   Ibid Sch 2 para 1.
4   Ibid Sch 2 para 2.
5   Ie ibid Schs 1, 3.
6   Ibid Sch 2 para 3.
7   Ibid Sch 2 para 4. For the meaning of 'the standard scale' see para 16 note 21 ante.
8   The specific offences created by the Sunday Trading Act 1994 are considered in their particular contexts in para 702 et seq ante.
9   Ibid Sch 2 para 5.

10 Ibid Sch 2 para 6(1). Where the affairs of a body corporate are managed by its members, Sch 2 para 6(1) applies in relation to the acts and defaults of a member in connection with his functions of management as if he were a director of the body corporate: Sch 2 para 6(2).

11 Ibid Sch 2 para 7(1). If in any case the defence provided by Sch 2 para 7(1) involves the allegation that the commission of the offence was due to the act or default of another person, the person charged is not, without leave of the court, entitled to rely on that defence unless, at least seven clear days before the hearing, he has served on the prosecutor a notice in writing giving such information identifying or assisting in the identification of that other person as was then in his possession: Sch 2 para 7(2).

711–800.   Other powers of enforcement. Although given specific powers to enforce the restrictions on Sunday opening[1], a local authority may also use its general power to bring civil proceedings in its own name[2] and apply for an injunction to restrain breaches of the legislation by a particular offender, especially where that offender is deliberately and flagrantly flouting the law and intends to carry on doing so[3].

1   See para 702 et seq ante.

2   See the Local Government Act 1972 s 222(1); and LOCAL GOVERNMENT vol 29(1) (Reissue) para 440.

3   *Stoke-on-Trent City Council v B & Q (Retail) Ltd* [1984] AC 754, [1984] 2 All ER 332, HL. Although the cases cited here were decided under the Shops Act 1950 (repealed), the principles should apply equally to the Sunday Trading Act 1994. There is no need for the council to have exhausted its specific criminal powers first: *Runnymede Borough Council v Ball* [1986] 1 All ER 629, [1986] 1 WLR 353, CA (a planning case). Such an action is not defeated by the defendant's claim to have a defence to any criminal proceedings since that goes, not to jurisdiction, but to the discretion whether to grant the injunction; further, the court has a discretion to grant such an interlocutory injunction without requiring the council to give an undertaking in damages: *Kirklees Metropolitan Borough Council v Wickes Building Supplies Ltd* [1993] AC 227, [1992] 3 All ER 717, HL. This matter used to be of great significance under the Shops Act 1950 Pt IV (ss 47–67) (repealed) governing Sunday trading which was subject to widespread breach and was only backed specifically by criminal fines of level 4 on the standard scale, insufficient to deter breaches, given the profits to be made. There should now be less likelihood of such cases arising given that: (1) there is now a more liberal regime on Sunday opening; and (2) the maximum penalty for breach of the current regime is raised (see para 702 ante). For the meaning of 'the standard scale' see para 16 note 21 ante.

9. PROMOTION OF TRADE AND ASSISTANCE TO INDUSTRY

(1) PROMOTION OF TRADE

(i) Export and Investment Guarantees

801. The provision of financial facilities and assistance. The Secretary of State[1] may make arrangements[2] to provide financial facilities and assistance[3] with a view to facilitating, directly or indirectly, supplies by persons carrying on business[4] in the United Kingdom of goods or services to persons carrying on business outside the United Kingdom, and to make arrangements for the purpose of rendering economic assistance to countries outside the United Kingdom[5]. He may also make arrangements to facilitate the performance of, or to reduce or avoid losses arising under, obligations created or arising in connection with matters as to which he has exercised his powers[6].

1 As to the Secretary of State see para 2 ante; as to the exercise of functions in Wales see para 1 note 3 ante.
2 Transactions entered into in pursuance of such arrangements, or arrangements of the kinds described in paras 802–803 post, may be on such terms as the Secretary of State considers appropriate: Export and Investment Guarantees Act 1991 s 4(1).
3 Such facilities and assistance may be provided in any forum, including guarantees, insurance, grants or loans: ibid s 1(4). A guarantee includes an indemnity: s 4(3)(b).
4 'Business' includes a profession; a reference to persons 'carrying on business' in relation to things done outside the United Kingdom includes persons carrying on any other activities; a reference to things done in or outside the United Kingdom is to things done wholly or partly in or, as the case may be, outside the United Kingdom: ibid s 4(3)(a), (c), (4). As to the meaning of 'carry on business' see para 63 et seq ante.
5 Ibid s 1(1), (2). References to the United Kingdom include references to the Isle of Man and the Channel Islands: s 4(4). For the meaning of 'United Kingdom' generally see para 37 note 1 ante. All the functions of the Secretary of State under ss 1–7, except the power to make orders under ss 5–6, must be exercised and performed through the Export Credits Guarantee Department, which continues to be a department of the Secretary of State: s 13(1). The powers of the Secretary of State under ss 1–3 are exercisable only with the consent of the Treasury; such consent may be given in relation to particular cases or such description of cases as may be specified in the consent: s 4(2).
6 Ibid s 1(3).

802. Insurance in respect of overseas losses. The Secretary of State[1] may make arrangements[2] for insuring any person carrying on business in the United Kingdom[3] against risks of losses resulting directly or indirectly from war, expropriation, restrictions on remittances and other similar events, in connection with (1) any investment of resources by the insured in enterprises carried on outside the United Kingdom; or (2) guarantees given by the insured in respect of any investment of resources by others in such enterprises in which the insured has any interest[4]. Arrangements may also be made for insuring persons providing such insurance[5].

1 As to the Secretary of State see para 2 ante.
2 As to such arrangements see para 801 note 2 ante.
3 As to references to persons carrying on business in the United Kingdom see para 801 note 5 ante.
4 Export and Investment Guarantees Act 1991 s 2(1). References to a person carrying on business in the United Kingdom and to the insured include any company controlled directly or indirectly by him: s 2(3). See also INSURANCE vol 25 (Reissue) para 777. As to the exercise of this power by the Secretary of State see para 801 note 5 ante.
5 Ibid s 2(2).

803.   Management of the Export Credits Guarantee Department portfolio. The Secretary of State[1] may make any arrangements[2] which, in his opinion, are in the interests of the proper financial management of the Export Credits Guarantee Department portfolio (the 'ECGD portfolio')[3]. In pursuance of such arrangements, the Secretary of State may enter into any form of transaction, including (1) lending; and (2) providing and taking out insurance and guarantees[4]. In pursuance of such an arrangement, however, he may not enter into a transaction for the purpose of borrowing money, although he is not precluded from entering into a transaction by reason of its involving borrowing[5].

1   As to the Secretary of State see para 2 ante.
2   Such arrangements may be made in anticipation of further rights being acquired or liabilities beings incurred by the Secretary of State: Export and Investment Guarantees Act 1991 s 3(5). As to such arrangements see further para 801 note 2 ante.
3   Ibid s 3(1), which refers simply to 'the ECGD portfolio'. The 'ECGD portfolio' means the rights and liabilities to which the Secretary of State is entitled or subject by virtue of the exercise of his powers under the Export and Investment Guarantees Act 1991 or the old law or in consequence at arrangements made in the exercise of those powers: s 3(6). The 'old law' means the Export and Investment Guarantees Act 1978 (repealed) and any earlier enactment from which any provision of that Act was derived: Export and Investment Guarantees Act 1991 s 15(2).
4   Ibid s 3(2). The Secretary of State may alter arrangements made under ss 1, 2, (see paras 801–802 ante) or under the old law (see note 3 supra) or make new or further arrangements: s 3(5). Arrangements made under s 3 may be made in anticipation of further rights being acquired or liabilities beings incurred by the Secretary of State: s 3(5). As to the exercise of these powers by the Secretary of State see para 801 note 5 ante. As to the meaning of 'guarantee' see para 801 note 3 ante.
5   Ibid s 3(3).

804.   Information relating to credit and investment insurance. The Secretary of State[1] may provide, and charge for (1) information relating to credit or investment insurance; (2) services ancillary to the provision of such credit and insurance; and (3) such other goods and services as may be specified by order[2].

1   As to the Secretary of State see para 2 ante.
2   Export and Investment Guarantees Act 1991 s 5(1). The power to make an order is exercisable only with the consent of the Treasury: s 5(2). The power to make an order is exercisable by statutory instrument, and no such order may be made unless a draft of it has been laid before and approved by resolution of the House of Commons: s 15(3). At the date at which this volume states the law, no such order had been made.

805.   Limits to Secretary of State's commitments. The aggregate amount of the Secretary of State's[1] commitments[2] at any time under arrangements relating to exports and insurance[3] must not exceed £35,000m in the case of commitments in sterling, and 30,000 million special drawing rights[4] in the case of foreign currency commitments[5]. The aggregate amount of commitments in connection with the management of the ECGD portfolio[6] must not exceed £15,000m in the case of commitments in sterling, and 10,000m special drawing rights in the case of foreign currency commitments[7]. The Secretary of State may by order, with the consent of the Treasury, increase or further increase these limits[8], but may not exercise this power in respect of any limit on more than three occasions[9].

1   As to the Secretary of State see para 2 ante.
2   The Secretary of State's commitments under any arrangements are his rights and liabilities relating to those arrangements: Export and Investment Guarantees Act 1991 s 6(5)(a). The

amount of any commitments must be ascertained in accordance with the principles determined from time to time by the Secretary of State with the consent of the Treasury: s 6(5)(b).

3 Ie arrangements under ibid ss 1, 2 other than arrangements for giving grants under s 1(3) (see para 801 ante), and arrangements under the old law (as to which see para 803 note 3 ante) other than arrangements for giving grants: s 6(2).

4 The figure was raised from 15,000m to 25,000m by the Export and Investment Guarantees (Limit on Foreign Currency Commitments) Order 1998, SI 1998/1675, and to 30,000m by the Export and Investment Guarantees (Limit on Foreign Currency Commitments) Order 2000, SI 2000/2087. The accounts of the International Monetary Fund have been denominated in special drawing rights since 1972 following the enactment of the International Monetary Fund Act 1968 (repealed). The text of the amendments made to the Articles of Agreement of the Fund relating to special drawing rights is set out in Cmnd 3662.

5 Export and Investment Guarantees Act 1991 s 6(1)(a), (b). 'Foreign currency' means any currency other than sterling, including special drawing rights and any other units of account defined by reference to more than one currency: s 6(5)(c). Whether any commitments are in sterling or foreign currency is to be determined by reference to the currency in which the amount of the commitment is measured, rather than the currency of payment: s 6(5)(d). The equivalent in special drawing rights of the amount of any commitment in foreign currency must be ascertained at intervals determined from time to time by the Secretary of State with the consent of the Treasury, and in accordance with principles so determined: s 6(5)(e). A determination under s 6(5)(e) may provide for leaving out of account for the purposes of the limit in s 6(1)(b) or s 6(3)(b) (see the text and note 7 infra) any amount by which the limit would otherwise be exceeded to the extent that the amount is attributable to (1) a revaluation under s 6(5)(e) of commitments; or (2) the fulfilment of an undertaking which, if fulfilled when it was given, would not have caused the limit to be exceeded: s 6(6).

6 Ie under ibid s 3. See para 803 ante.

7 Ibid s 6(3)(a), (b).

8 Ibid s 6(4), (7). The limits in s 6(1) (see the text and notes 1–5 supra) may be increased by a sum not exceeding £5,000m or 5,000m special drawing rights, and in s 6(3) (see the text and notes 6–7 supra) by a sum not exceeding £3,000m or 2,000m special drawing rights: s 6(4)(a), (b). No such order may be made unless a draft of it has been laid before and approved by resolution of the House of Commons: s 15(3).

9 Ibid s 6(4).

806. Annual report of the Secretary of State. The Secretary of State[1] must prepare and lay before Parliament an annual report on the discharge of his functions under the provisions described in the immediately preceding paragraphs[2]. A separate return must be prepared as soon as is practicable after 31 March each year showing the aggregate amounts of the commitments in sterling and in foreign currency on that date for the purposes of the relevant statutory limits[3]. That return must also be laid before Parliament[4]. Any such return must also give such further information as to the amounts of the commitments for the purposes of those limits as the Secretary of State may determine for that return[5].

1 As to the Secretary of State see para 2 ante.

2 Export and Investment Guarantees Act 1991 s 7(1), (5).

3 Ibid s 7(2). The limits referred to are those in s 6(1), (3): see para 805 ante.

4 Ibid s 7(5).

5 Ibid s 7(3).

(ii) Transfer or Delegation of Export Credits Guarantee Department Functions

807. Provision for transfer of the Export Credits Guarantee Department. The Secretary of State[1] may make a scheme or schemes for the transfer to any person or persons of such property, rights and liabilities as are specified in or determined in accordance with the scheme[2]. Such a scheme may apply to property wherever situated and to property, rights and liabilities whether or not otherwise capable of being transferred or assigned by the Secretary of State or Her Majesty[3]. A scheme comes into force on a day specified in or determined under the scheme, and the property, rights and liabilities are transferred and vest on that day[4].

No scheme may provide for the transfer of any rights or liabilities relating to a person's employment but specified regulations[5] apply to the transfer of property, rights or liabilities by virtue of such a scheme[6]. Where, by operation of the regulations in relation to a transfer of property, rights or liabilities a person ceases to be employed in the civil service and becomes employed by a transferee, he will not be treated as having retired on redundancy for the purposes of a specified superannuation scheme[7] and his ceasing to be employed in the civil service is not an occasion of redundancy for the purposes of the agreed redundancy procedures of the civil service[8].

1   As to the Secretary of State see para 2 ante.
2   Export and Investment Guarantees Act 1991 s 8(1). The property, rights and liabilities are those (1) to which the Secretary of State, or, in the case of copyright, Her Majesty, is entitled or subject immediately before the day on which the scheme comes into force; and (2) which then subsisted for the purposes of or in connection with or are otherwise attributable to the exercise of functions under Pt I (ss 1–7) or the old law (as to which see para 803 note 3 ante): s 8(1)(a), (b). Any property, rights or liabilities are to be taken to fall within s 8(1)(b) if the Secretary of State so certifies: s 8(2).
3   Ibid s 8(3). The scheme may contain such supplementary, incidental, transitional or consequential provisions as appear to the Secretary of State to be appropriate: s 8(5).
4   Ibid s 8(4). A certificate by the Secretary of State that anything specified has vested on any day in any person by virtue of a scheme is conclusive for all purposes: s 8(6), Schedule para 1.
    Any agreement made, transaction effected or other thing (not contained in an enactment) which:
    (1)   has been made, effected or done by or in relation to the Secretary of State;
    (2)   relates to any property, rights or liability transferred under a scheme; and
    (3)   is in force or effective immediately before the day on which the scheme comes into force,
    has effect on or after that day as if made, effected or done by the transferee: Schedule para 2(1), (2). References to the Secretary of State relating to or affecting any property, right or liability of the Secretary of State, contained in specified descriptions of documents, are taken on or after that day to refer to the transferee: Schedule para 2(3). 'Transferee' means any person to whom anything is transferred by virtue of a scheme under s 8: s 8(7).
5   Ie the Transfer of Undertakings (Protection of Employment) Regulations 1981, SI 1981/1794 (as amended): see paras 1303, 1394, 1418 et seq post; and EMPLOYMENT vol 16 (2000 Reissue) para 387 et seq.
6   Export and Investment Guarantees Act 1991 s 9(1). The regulations apply whether or not the transfer would, apart from s 9(1), be a relevant transfer for the purposes of those regulations: s 9(1).
7   Ie any scheme under the Superannuation Act 1972 s 1 (as amended): see SOCIAL SECURITY AND PENSIONS vol 44(2) (Reissue) para 875.
8   Export and Investment Guarantees Act 1991 s 9(2).

808. Vehicle companies. The Secretary of State[1] may, with the consent of the Treasury[2]:

(1)   subscribe for or otherwise acquire shares in or securities of a vehicle company[3] or acquire rights so to subscribe[4];

(2)   by direction to a company formed or acquired for the purpose of becoming a transferee, require it, in consequence of the transfer by a scheme of property, rights or liabilities[5], to issue to him or to some other specified person such shares or securities as may be specified[6];

(3)   from time to time by direction to a vehicle company require it to issue to him or some other specified person such shares or securities as may be specified[7]; or

(4)   make loans to a vehicle company on such terms and conditions as he may determine[8].

He may not subscribe for or otherwise acquire shares in or securities of a vehicle company, or acquire rights so to subscribe, unless all relevant shares[9] are to be held by or on behalf of the Crown[10], or at any time give a direction or make a loan to a vehicle company unless all relevant shares are then held by or on behalf of the Crown[11]. A scheme of transfer of property, rights and liabilities may, as between any vehicle companies or between a vehicle company and the Secretary of State, confer or impose rights and liabilities in connection with any of the matters as to which the Secretary of State may exercise his statutory powers[12].

1   As to the Secretary of State see para 2 ante.
2   Export and Investment Guarantees Act 1991 s 10(7).
3   'Vehicle company' means a company formed or acquired for the purpose of becoming a transferor or holding shares in a company formed or acquired for that purpose: ibid s 10(1). For the meaning of 'transferee' see para 807 note 4 ante.
4   Ibid s 10(2)(a). The Secretary of State may not dispose of any such shares or securities without the consent of the Treasury: s 10(7).
5   Ie under a scheme made under ibid s 8: see para 807 ante.
6   Ibid s 10(2)(b). A direction under s 10(2)(b) or s 10(2)(c) may require any shares to which it relates to be issued as fully or partly paid up: s 10(3).
7   Ibid s 10(2)(c); and see note 6 supra.
8   Ibid s 10(2)(d).
9   'Relevant shares' means the issued shares of a vehicle company or, if it is a subsidiary of another vehicle company, the issued shares of that other company: ibid s 10(5)(b).
10   Shares are held by or on behalf of the Crown where the Crown or any person acting on its behalf has a legal interest in them: ibid s 10(5)(a).
11   Ibid s 10(4).
12   Ibid s 10(6).

809.   Insurance of Secretary of State against losses.   The Secretary of State[1] may make arrangements with any transferee[2] under which the transferee insures the Secretary of State against risks of losses arising in consequence of arrangements made, before the date on which any scheme of transfer comes into force[3], under specified statutory provisions[4] or the old law[5].

1   As to the Secretary of State see para 2 ante.
2   For the meaning of 'transferee' see para 807 note 4 ante.
3   Ie a scheme under the Export and Investment Guarantees Act 1991 s 8: see para 807 ante.
4   Ie ibid Pt I (ss 1–7).
5   Ibid s 11(1). For the meaning of 'old law' see para 803 note 3 ante. The Secretary of State must from time to time determine, in relation to such classes of risk determined by him as might be insured by him, whether it is expedient in the national interest for him to exercise his powers under s 1 to make arrangements for reinsuring persons providing insurance for risks of that class: s 11(2). In exercising his duty under s 11(2) the Secretary of State must consult the Export Guarantees Advisory Council: s 11(4). The council referred to is established under s 13(2); its function is to give to the Secretary of State, at his request, advice in respect of any matter relating to the exercise of his functions under the Act: s 13(3). Section 11 is without prejudice to any power of the Secretary of State under Pt I: s 11(3).

810.   Functions of the Secretary of State.   All the functions of the Secretary of State[1] under Part I of the Export and Investment Guarantees

Act 1991[2] are exercised and performed through the Export Credits Guarantee Department, which is a department of the Secretary of State[3].

The Secretary of State may, however, make arrangements for certain functions[4] to be exercised on his behalf by any transferee[5] or any other person, instead of through the Export Credits Guarantees Department, on such terms and conditions as he may determine[6].

Any sums required by the Secretary of State for making payments or for defraying his administrative expenses under the Act are paid out of money provided by Parliament[7], and any sums received by him by virtue of the Act must be paid into the Consolidated Fund[8].

1 As to the Secretary of State see para 2 ante.
2 Ie the Export and Investment Guarantees Act 1991 ss 1–7. However, this does not apply to the power to make orders under s 5 or s 6 (see paras 804, 805 text and notes 8–9 ante): s 13(1).
3 Ibid s 13(1).
4 Ie the functions to which ibid s 12 applies, namely the Secretary of State's power to make arrangements under s 1 (see para 801 ante) and any of his functions under such arrangements, or arrangements under the old law, including, so far as they relate to any such arrangements, arrangements made by virtue of s 3(4): s 12(2). For the meaning of 'old law' see para 803 note 3 ante.
5 For the meaning of 'transferee' see para 807 note 4 ante.
6 Export and Investment Guarantees Act 1991 s 12(1); s 12 does not affect any requirement for the consent of the Treasury: s 12(3).
7 If any sum required by the Secretary of State for fulfilling his liabilities is not so provided, it must be charged on and paid out of the Consolidated Fund: ibid s 14(2). As to the Consolidated Fund see CONSTITUTIONAL LAW AND HUMAN RIGHTS vol 8(2) (Reissue) para 711 et seq; and PARLIAMENT vol 34 (Reissue) para 952 et seq.
8 Ibid s 14(1).

(iii) Exploratory Expenditure

811. Reimbursement of expenditure. The Secretary of State[1] may, with the consent of the Treasury, enter into an agreement with any person carrying on business[2] in the United Kingdom[3], the Channel Islands or the Isle of Man, or with a company controlled by such a person[4], under which the Secretary of State undertakes that if the other party to the agreement or a company controlled by that party:

(1)   incurs expenditure approved by the Secretary of State in considering whether to make an investment of resources of a description so approved in an enterprise carried on or proposed to be carried on in a country other than the United Kingdom, the Channel Islands and the Isle of Man; or

(2)   incurs expenditure approved by the Secretary of State in considering whether to participate in the management of such an enterprise,

and decides not to participate (whether by making an investment or otherwise), the Secretary of State must pay to the other party such sum, not exceeding the amount of the expenditure, as may be provided by the agreement[5].

Any such agreement may include such terms as the Secretary of State considers appropriate in the circumstances[6].

1 Ie the Secretary of State for Foreign and Commonwealth Affairs: see CONSTITUTIONAL LAW AND HUMAN RIGHTS vol 8(2) (Reissue) paras 459–460.
2 'Business' includes a profession: Overseas Development and Co-operation Act 1980 s 3(5)(a).

3   For the meaning of 'United Kingdom' see para 37 note 1 ante.

4   References to a company controlled by a person are references to a company so controlled directly or indirectly, and include cases where the person having control is also a company: Overseas Development and Co-operation Act 1980 s 3(5)(b).

5   Ibid s 3(1). Any expenses incurred by the Secretary of State by virtue of s 3 must be defrayed out of money provided by Parliament: s 3(3). Any sum received by him by virtue of an agreement under s 3 must be paid into the Consolidated Fund: s 3(4). As to the Consolidated Fund see CONSTITUTIONAL LAW AND HUMAN RIGHTS vol 8(2) (Reissue) para 711 et seq; and PARLIAMENT vol 34 (Reissue) para 952 et seq.

6   Ibid s 3(2).

(iv) Worker-controlled Enterprises

812. Worker-controlled enterprises. For five years beginning on 22 November 1976[1] a power was conferred on the Secretary of State[2] to make grants to relevant bodies[3] to assist them to provide advice about the organisation of common ownership enterprises[4] and co-operative enterprises[5] or to make loans to common ownership enterprises and co-operative enterprises[6]. The power has lapsed and not been renewed, but regulations[7] governing the terms upon which a relevant body could make an assisted loan remain in force.

A loan or grant may be made by the designated district authority[8] of an inner urban area with a special social need for the establishment of a common ownership or co-operative enterprise where the authority considers that such a body would benefit the designated district[9].

1   Ie the date on which the Industrial Common Ownership Act 1976 received royal assent and came into force.

2   As to the Secretary of State see para 2 ante.

3   'Relevant body' means a body appearing to the Secretary of State to be constituted for the purpose of encouraging the development of common ownership enterprises (see note 4 infra) or co-operative enterprises (see note 5 infra): Industrial Common Ownership Act 1976 s 1(5).

4   'Common ownership enterprise' is defined by ibid s 2(1) as a body as to which the registrar (ie the Chief Registrar of Friendly Societies: s 2(5)) has given, and has not revoked, a certificate stating that he is satisfied:

    (1)   that it is a company which has no share capital, is limited by guarantee and is a bona fide co-operative society, or a registered industrial or provident society;

    (2)   that its memorandum, articles of association or rules include provisions which secure:

        (a)   that only persons employed by, or by a subsidiary of, the body may be members, and that (subject to any provision about membership qualifications made by the members by reference to age, length of service or other factors which do not discriminate by reference to politics or religion) all such persons may be members with equal voting rights;

        (b)   that the body's assets are applied only for the purposes of its objects, which do not include the making over of assets to any member except for value and except in pursuance of arrangements for sharing the body's profits among its members;

        (c)   that any surplus assets on winding up or dissolution are not distributed among the members but are transferred to such a common ownership enterprise or such a central fund maintained for the benefit of common ownership enterprises as may be determined by the members or are held for charitable purposes; and

    (3)   that the body is controlled by a majority of the people working for it and of the people working for its subsidiaries, if any.

    If it appears to the registrar or the Secretary of State that a body in respect of which he has given a certificate in pursuance of s 2 has ceased to be a common ownership enterprise or a co-operative enterprise, he may revoke the certificate: s 2(4).

    'Company' means a company as defined by the Companies Act 1985 s 735 (see COMPANIES vol 7(1) (1996 Reissue) para 11 note 1), or a company registered under that

Act; and a body is a subsidiary of another body if it is a subsidiary of the other body as defined by the Companies Act 1985 s 736 (as substituted) or for the purposes of the Friendly and Industrial and Provident Societies Act 1968: Industrial Common Ownership Act 1976 s 2(5) (amended by the Companies Consolidation (Consequential Provisions) Act 1985 s 30, Sch 2; and the Companies Act 1989 s 144(4), Sch 18 para 15). For the meaning of 'charitable purposes' see CHARITIES vol 5(2) (2001 Reissue) para 1 et seq. The registrar may charge such fee as the Treasury may determine for any certificate which he proposes to give, and any sum received by him in respect of such a fee must be paid into the Consolidated Fund: Industrial Common Ownership Act 1976 s 2(3). For tax relief on interest paid on a loan made to acquire an interest in a common ownership enterprise see the Income and Corporation Taxes Act 1988 ss 361, 363; and INCOME TAXATION vol 23 (Reissue) para 1045 et seq. As to the Consolidated Fund see CONSTITUTIONAL LAW AND HUMAN RIGHTS vol 8(2) (Reissue) para 711 et seq; and PARLIAMENT vol 34 (Reissue) para 952 et seq.

5   Industrial Common Ownership Act 1976 s 1(1). 'Co-operative enterprise' means a body as to which the Secretary of State has given, and has not revoked, a certificate stating that (1) having regard to the provision which is made by the body's written constitution as to the manner in which its income is to be applied for the benefit of its members and all other relevant provisions of the constitution, the body is in substance a co-operative association; and (2) the body is controlled by a majority of the people working for it and of the people working for its subsidiaries, if any: s 2(2). As to the revocation of such a certificate see s 2(4); and note 4 supra.

6   Ibid s 1(1), (2). Sums payable to the Secretary of State by way of repayment of or interest on a loan are payable into the Consolidated Fund: s 1(4).

7   Ie the Industrial Common Ownership (Loans) Regulations 1977, SI 1977/1386 (amended by SI 1989/992), made under the Industrial Common Ownership Act 1976 s 1(3). Any statutory instrument made by virtue of s 1(3) is subject to annulment in pursuance of a resolution of either House of Parliament: s 1(3).

8   'Designated district authority', in relation to a designated district, means the council of that district or the council of the county or region which includes that district: Inner Urban Areas Act 1978 ss 1(2), 17(1). 'Designated district' means any district specified as such a district by an order under s 1(1); 'county' includes Greater London, and 'district' includes a London borough; and any reference to the council of a county or district is to be construed accordingly: s 17(1). As to inner urban areas generally see TOWN AND COUNTRY PLANNING vol 46 (Reissue) para 1258 et seq.

9   See ibid ss 1(1), 3; and TOWN AND COUNTRY PLANNING vol 46 (Reissue) para 1260.

(v) Development of Tourism

813.   The British Tourist Authority and other tourist boards. For the purpose of promoting the development of tourism to and within Great Britain[1], four tourist boards[2] have been established[3]. These bodies are known respectively as the British Tourist Authority[4], the English Tourist Board[5], the Scottish Tourist Board[6] and the Wales Tourist Board[7]. Each tourist board is a body corporate having perpetual succession and a common seal[8]. The Greater London Authority is under a duty to promote tourism in Greater London[9].

1   For the meaning of 'Great Britain' see para 31 note 2 ante.

2   'Tourist board' means any body established by the Development of Tourism Act 1969 s 1, namely the four bodies mentioned in the text: s 1(6).

3   Ibid s 1(1).

4   Ibid s 1(1). The British Tourist Authority consists of a chairman and not more than five other members appointed by the Secretary of State, together with the chairmen of the other three tourist boards: s 1(2). The Secretary of State here concerned is the Secretary of State for Culture, Media and Sport. As to the Secretary of State generally see para 2 ante but note that the powers of the Secretary of State for Trade and Industry under this Act were transferred to the Secretary of State for Employment (Transfer of Functions (Tourism and Small Businesses) Order 1985, SI 1985/1778) and then to the Secretary of State for National Heritage (Transfer of Functions (National Heritage) Order 1992, SI 1992/1311). As to the appointment and resignation of members of tourist boards and the declaration of

offices to be vacant see the Development of Tourism Act 1969 s 1(5), Sch 1 paras 3–5, 18. As to their remuneration and pensions see Sch 1 paras 6–9, 17 (amended by virtue of the Transfer of Functions (Minister for the Civil Service and Treasury) Order 1981, SI 1981/1670, art 2(2)). Members receiving remuneration are disqualified for membership of the House of Commons: House of Commons Disqualification Act 1975 s 1(1)(f), Sch 1 Pt III; and see PARLIAMENT vol 34 (Reissue) para 610. The Department of National Heritage was renamed the Department for Culture, Media and Sport by the Secretary of State for Culture, Media and Sport Order 1997, SI 1997/1744; and the Secretary of State is now styled accordingly.

5   Development of Tourism Act 1969 s 1(1). The English Tourist Board consists of a chairman and not more than six other members appointed by the Secretary of State: s 1(3). As to the Secretary of State see note 4 supra.

6   Ibid s 1(1). The Scottish Tourist Board consists of a chairman and not more than six other members appointed by the Secretary of State for Scotland: s 1(3).

7   Ibid s 1(1). The Wales Tourist Board consists of a chairman and not more than six other members appointed by the National Assembly for Wales, to which the functions of the Secretary of State for Wales under the Act, so far as exercisable in relation to Wales, were transferred by the National Assembly for Wales (Transfer of Functions) Order 1999, SI 1999/672, art 2, Sch 1: Development of Tourism Act 1969 s 1(3). As to the National Assembly for Wales see para 1 note 3 ante; and as to the Welsh Tourist Board's alternative Welsh name see the Alternative Names in Welsh Order 1994, SI 1994/2889.

8   Development of Tourism Act 1969 Sch 1 paras 1, 15, 16. As to the proceedings of a board see Sch 1 paras 12–14. As to staff see Sch 1 paras 10, 11. A board is not regarded as the servant or agent of the Crown, and is not exempt from taxes etc: see Sch 1 para 2.

9   Greater London Authority Act 1999 s 378. The Authority has a duty to advise certain bodies on matters relating to tourism: s 379. The Authority's functions under these provisions may be delegated: s 380. Grants may be paid by the Secretary of State to the Authority for its tourism functions: s 381. Definitions for these provisions are contained in s 382. See generally LONDON GOVERNMENT.

814.   Functions of tourist boards.

The function of the British Tourist Authority[1] is to encourage people to visit Great Britain[2], to encourage people living in Great Britain to take their holidays there, and to encourage the provision and improvement of tourist amenities and facilities[3] in Great Britain[4]. Each of the other tourist boards[5] has the same functions as respects its respective country[6].

Each tourist board has power to do anything for the purpose of discharging these functions or anything which is incidental or conducive to their discharge[7] and in particular (but without prejudice to the generality of the above provisions) power:

(1)   to promote or undertake publicity in any form[8];

(2)   to provide advisory and information services[9];

(3)   to promote or undertake research[10];

(4)   to establish committees to advise them in the performance of their functions[11]; and

(5)   to contribute to or reimburse expenditure incurred by any other person or organisation carrying on the activities listed in heads (1) to (3) above[12].

None of the tourist boards except the British Tourist Authority has power, otherwise than with the agreement of that authority, to carry on any activities outside the United Kingdom[13] for the purpose of encouraging people to visit Great Britain or any part of it[14]. Except as otherwise provided[15], none of the tourist boards has power to give financial assistance for the carrying out of, or itself to carry out, any project for providing or improving tourist amenities or facilities in Great Britain[16]. Notwithstanding this provision, the Wales Tourist Board may, with the consent of the

National Assembly for Wales, carry on activities outside the United Kingdom for the purpose of encouraging people to visit Wales[17].

In discharging their functions, the English Tourist Board, the Scottish Tourist Board and the Wales Tourist Board must have regard to the desirability of fostering and, in appropriate cases, co-operating with organisations discharging functions corresponding to those of the boards in relation to particular areas within the countries for which the boards are respectively responsible[18]. Each tourist board must also have regard to the desirability of undertaking appropriate consultation with the other tourist boards and with persons and organisations who have knowledge of, or are interested in, any matters affecting the discharge of its functions[19].

1   As to the British Tourist Authority see para 813 ante.
2   For the meaning of 'Great Britain' see para 31 note 2 ante.
3   'Tourist amenities and facilities' means, in relation to any country, amenities and facilities for visitors to that country and for other people travelling within it on business or pleasure: Development of Tourism Act 1969 s 2(9).
4   Ibid s 2(1).
5   For the meaning of 'tourist board' see para 813 note 2 ante.
6   Development of Tourism Act 1969 s 2(1).
7   Ibid s 2(2).
8   Ibid s 2(2)(a).
9   Ibid s 2(2)(b).
10 Ibid s 2(2)(c).
11 Ibid s 2(2)(d).
12 Ibid s 2(2)(e). A tourist board may charge for its services and receive contributions towards its expenses in carrying out any of its functions (s 2(7)), but it may not borrow money except with the consent of the relevant minister and (except for the Wales Tourist Board) the Treasury (s 2(8)). 'The relevant minister' means, in relation to the British Tourist Authority and the English Tourist Board, the Secretary of State (see s 1(6); and para 813 note 4 ante), in relation to the Scottish Tourist Board, the Secretary of State for Scotland and, in relation to the Wales Tourist Board, the Secretary of State for Wales (s 1(6)). As to the transfer of functions of the Secretary of State for Wales to the National Assembly for Wales see para 813 note 7 ante. Treasury approval under s 2(8) is no longer required in relation to the Wales Tourist Board: see the National Assembly for Wales (Transfer of Functions) Order 1999, SI 1999/672, art 2, Sch 1. After consultation with a tourist board, the relevant minister may give to it directions of a general character as to the exercise of its functions: Development of Tourism Act 1969 s 19(1).
13 For the meaning of 'United Kingdom' see para 37 note 1 ante.
14 Development of Tourism Act 1969 s 2(3). However, this does not prevent a tourist board from carrying out activities on behalf of the British Tourist Authority: s 2(3).
15 Ie by ibid ss 3, 4: see para 815 post.
16 Ibid s 2(4).
17 Tourism (Overseas Promotion) (Wales) Act 1992 s 1(1), (2); National Assembly for Wales (Transfer of Functions) Order 1999, SI 1999/672, Sch 1. This does not affect the British Tourist Authority's power to carry on activities outside the United Kingdom for the purpose of encouraging people to visit Wales, nor does it prevent the Wales Tourist Board from acting on behalf of the authority as mentioned in the Development of Tourism Act 1969 s 2(3) (see note 14 supra): Tourism (Overseas Promotion) (Wales) Act 1992 s 1(3). The Tourism (Overseas Promotion) (Scotland) Act 1984 makes parallel provision for the Scottish Tourist Board.
18 Development of Tourism Act 1969 s 2(5). Without prejudice to s 2(1)–(4), each of the boards mentioned has power to provide such organisations with financial and other assistance: s 2(5).
19 Ibid s 2(6).

815.   Tourist projects.   After consultation with the other tourist boards[1], the British Tourist Authority[2] may prepare schemes providing for the giving of financial assistance by those boards for specified classes of projects which in the authority's opinion will provide or improve tourist amenities and facilities[3] in Great Britain[4]. Subject to the provisions of any scheme and to certain directions[5], a tourist board, in making a grant or loan, may impose such terms and conditions as it thinks fit, including conditions for the repayment of a grant in specified circumstances[6]. Such a scheme must be submitted to the Secretary of State, who may by order confirm it with or without modification[7].

In accordance with arrangements approved by the relevant minister and the Treasury, a tourist board may give financial assistance for the carrying out of any project which in the board's opinion will provide or improve tourist amenities and facilities in the country for which it is responsible[8], and with the approval of the minister and (except in the case of the Wales Tourist Board) the Treasury may carry out any such project[9].

1 For the meaning of 'tourist board' see para 813 note 2 ante.
2 As to the British Tourist Authority see para 813 ante.
3 For the meaning of 'tourist amenities and facilities' see para 814 note 3 ante.
4 Development of Tourism Act 1969 s 3(1). For the meaning of 'Great Britain' see para 31 note 2 ante. A scheme under s 3 may provide for financial assistance to be given by way of grant or loan or by any combination of those methods: s 3(3). Such a scheme may be varied or revoked by a subsequent scheme prepared, submitted and confirmed in like manner or, subject to s 3(6) (see note 7 infra), by an order made by the Secretary of State after consultation with the authority and the other tourist boards: s 3(5). As to the Secretary of State see para 813 note 4 ante.
5 Ie directions under ibid s 19: see note 6 infra.
6 Ibid s 3(4). As to the means of securing compliance with conditions see Sch 2 (amended by the Criminal Law Act 1977 s 65, Sch 13; and the Criminal Justice Act 1982 ss 38, 46). A tourist board may by notice require any person who has received such a grant, and any person acting on his behalf, to furnish to the board specified information, or to produce for examination specified books, records or other documents, for the purpose of enabling it to determine whether any condition for making the grant is satisfied or is being complied with, or whether the grant has become repayable in whole or in part in accordance with any such condition: Development of Tourism Act 1969 Sch 2 para 1(1). As to the service of such a notice see Sch 2 para 1(2), (3). Failure to comply with a notice is an offence punishable on summary conviction with a fine not exceeding level 5 on the standard scale (as to which see para 16 note 21 ante): Sch 2 para 1(4) (amended by virtue of the Criminal Justice Act 1982 ss 38, 46).
   Subject to the provisions of the Development of Tourism Act 1969 s 3, and to the provisions of Pt II (financial assistance for hotel development), the relevant minister (defined in para 814 note 12 ante) may, with the approval of the Treasury, give to a tourist board directions as to (1) the matters with respect to which that board must be satisfied before making a loan under the scheme; (2) the terms on which and the conditions subject to which any such loan is to be made; (3) the conditions to be imposed in making any grant under the scheme: s 19(2)(a)–(c). Such directions may distinguish between different classes of case: s 19(2) (amended by the Statute Law (Repeals) Act 1998 s 1(1), Sch 1 Pt IV). Without prejudice to the provisions of head (1) supra, directions under that head may require a tourist board to be satisfied that the applicant cannot obtain a loan for the purpose in question from any other source, whether on terms which are more or less favourable than those of any loan which might be made by the board: Development of Tourism Act 1969 s 19(3). A tourist board must give effect to any directions given to it under s 19: s 19(4).
7 Ibid s 3(2). If a scheme is so confirmed it then has effect: s 3(2). Any power of the Secretary of State to make orders under s 3 is exercisable by statutory instrument, and any order under s 3(2) must set out the scheme which the order confirms: s 3(6). No order may be made under s 3 except with the consent of the Treasury and unless a draft of the order has been laid before Parliament and approved by a resolution of each House: s 3(6). At the date at which this volume states the law, no such order had been made.
8 Ibid s 4(1)(a). Such financial assistance may be given by way of grant or loan or, if the project is being or is to be carried out by a company incorporated in Great Britain, by subscribing for or otherwise acquiring shares or stock in the company, or by any combination of those methods: s 4(2). In making such a grant or loan a tourist board may, subject to the arrangements, impose such terms and conditions as it thinks fit, including

conditions for the repayment of a grant in specified circumstances, and Sch 2 (as amended: see note 6 supra) has effect for securing compliance with such conditions: s 4(3). A tourist board must not dispose of any shares or stock so acquired by it by virtue of s 4 except (1) after consultation with the company in which the shares or stock are held, and; (2) with the approval of the relevant minister and (except for the Wales Tourist Board) the Treasury: s 4(4); National Assembly for Wales (Transfer of Functions) Order 1999, SI 1999/672, art 2, Sch 1.

9   Development of Tourism Act 1969 s 4(1)(b); National Assembly for Wales (Transfer of Functions) Order 1999, SI 1999/672, Sch 1.

816.   Other duties and powers. It is the duty of a tourist board[1] to advise any minister or public body[2] on such matters relating to tourism in Great Britain[3] (in the case of the British Tourist Authority), or the part of Great Britain with which the board is concerned (in the case of the other boards), as the minister or body may refer to it or as the board thinks fit[4].

At the request of any corresponding body established under the law of Northern Ireland, any of the Channel Islands or the Isle of Man[5] and on such terms as may be agreed upon between the British Tourist Authority and that body, the authority has power to carry on activities outside the United Kingdom[6] and those islands for encouraging people to visit Northern Ireland or those islands[7].

A tourist board has power to enter into and carry out agreements with the minister responsible for overseas development[8] under which, at his expense, the board acts as the instrument by means of which technical assistance is furnished by him to overseas countries[9].

1   For the meaning of 'tourist board' see para 813 note 2 ante.
2   'Public body' includes any local authority or statutory undertaker, and any trustees, commissioners, board or other persons who, as a public body and not for their own profit, act under any enactment for the improvement of any place or the production or supply of any commodity or service: Development of Tourism Act 1969 s 5(2).
3   For the meaning of 'Great Britain' see para 31 note 2 ante.
4   Development of Tourism Act 1969 s 5(1).
5   As to the Channel Islands and the Isle of Man see COMMONWEALTH AND DEPENDENCIES vol 6 (Reissue) para 838 et seq.
6   For the meaning of 'United Kingdom' see para 37 note 1 ante.
7   Development of Tourism Act 1969 s 5(3).
8   'The minister responsible for overseas development' means the Secretary of State for the time being discharging the functions conferred by the Overseas Development and Co-operation Act 1980 s 1 (provision of assistance to or for the benefit of overseas countries): s 2(6). The Secretary of State concerned is the Secretary of State for International Development: see the Transfer of Functions (International Development) Order 1997, SI 1997/1749; and CONSTITUTIONAL LAW AND HUMAN RIGHTS vol 8(2) (Reissue) para 459 et seq.
9   Overseas Development and Co-operation Act 1980 s 2(1)(a), Sch 1 Pt I.

817.   Accounts and information. Each tourist board[1] must keep proper accounts and other records in relation to the accounts and must prepare in respect of each of its financial years[2] a statement of account in such form as the relevant minister[3] may with the approval of the Treasury determine[4]. The statement must be submitted to him at such time as he may with such approval direct[5]. Each tourist board must provide him with such information relating to its activities or proposed activities as he from time to time requires[6]. As soon as possible after the end of each financial year, each tourist board must make to the relevant minister a report dealing with its activities during that year, and he must lay a copy of the report before each House of Parliament[7].

1	For the meaning of 'tourist board' see para 813 note 2 ante.
2	'Financial year' means a 12 month period ending with 31 March in each year: Development of Tourism Act 1969 s 6(7).
3	For the meaning of 'relevant minister' see para 814 note 12 ante.
4	Development of Tourism Act 1969 s 6(1).
5	Ibid s 6(2). The relevant minister must, on or before 30 November in any year, transmit to the Comptroller and Auditor General the statement of account prepared by each tourist board for the last financial year: s 6(3). The Comptroller and Auditor General must examine and certify each such statement and lay copies before Parliament together with his report: s 6(4). In relation to statements of account prepared by the Wales Tourist Board for financial years beginning in and after 1999, the functions of the Comptroller and Auditor General under s 6(3), (4) are transferred to the Auditor General for Wales, who must lay his report and the copy statements of account before the National Assembly for Wales: National Assembly for Wales (Transfer of Functions) Order 1999, SI 1999/672, art 2, Sch 1.
6	Development of Tourism Act 1969 s 6(5). For this purpose the board must permit any person authorised in that behalf by the minister to inspect and make copies of its accounts, books, documents or papers and must afford to that person such explanation of each as he may reasonably require: s 6(5).
7	Ibid s 6(6).

818. Registration of hotels etc and notification of prices.

Provision may be made by Order in Council[1] for the registration[2] by tourist boards[3] of hotels[4] and other establishments in Great Britain[5] at which sleeping accommodation is provided by way of trade or business[6]. An order may make provision[7] in particular:

(1)	as to the form and contents of the register or registers to be maintained and the establishments to be registered[8];

(2)	for requiring the person carrying on an establishment which is required to be registered to furnish specified information, at specified times, to the body responsible for registering it[9];

(3)	for the charging of annual or other periodical fees for registration[10];

(4)	for the issue and display of certificates of registration and the display of signs indicating that the establishment is registered[11];

(5)	for the inspection of establishments and for powers of entry for that purpose[12];

(6)	for exemptions from any of the requirements of the order[13];

(7)	for securing compliance with any requirement by the imposition of a penalty not exceeding level 4 on the standard scale[14].

Provision may also be made by order for requiring the display by hotels and other establishments of information with respect to the prices charged there for sleeping accommodation or otherwise for securing that such information is brought to the notice of persons seeking to avail themselves of the accommodation[15].

1	Such an order is subject to annulment in pursuance of a resolution of either House of Parliament and may be revoked or varied by a subsequent order: Development of Tourism Act 1969 s 17(6). At the date at which this volume states the law, no such order had been made. An order may contain such supplementary and incidental provisions as appear to be necessary or expedient, and may authorise the relevant ministers (defined in para 814 note 12 ante) to make regulations as respects England and Scotland, and the National Assembly for Wales as respects Wales, for purposes specified in the order: see s 17(4); and the National Assembly for Wales (Transfer of Functions) Order 1999, SI 1999/672, art 2, Sch 1.
2	A tourist board maintaining a register has power to publish or make available for publication (gratuitously or for consideration) any information furnished to it, and any information as to any classification or grade accorded to any establishment: Development of Tourism Act 1969 s 17(7).

3 For the meaning of 'tourist board' see para 813 note 2 ante.
4 For the meaning of 'hotel' in an order made under the Development of Tourism Act 1969 s 18 see note 15 infra.
5 For the meaning of 'Great Britain' see para 31 note 2 ante.
6 Development of Tourism Act 1969 s 17(1).
7 An order and any regulations made under it may make different provision for different cases and provision may be made for an order to come into force at different times in relation to, or to different parts of, England, Scotland and Wales respectively: ibid s 17(5).
8 Ibid s 17(2)(a). If provision is made for the classification or grading of the establishments entered in a register, provision may also be made for (1) requiring the criteria in accordance with which classification or grading is carried out to be determined from time to time by the British Tourist Authority (as to which see para 813 ante) after consultation with the other tourist boards and other organisations representative of trade and consumer interests likely to be affected; (2) the publication of any criteria so determined; and (3) enabling the person carrying on a registered establishment to make representations to the board concerned before any classification or grade is accorded or altered or cancelled: s 17(3).
9 Ibid s 17(2)(b).
10 Ibid s 17(2)(c).
11 Ibid s 17(2)(d).
12 Ibid s 17(2)(e).
13 Ibid s 17(2)(f).
14 Ibid s 17(2)(g) (amended by virtue of the Criminal Justice Act 1982 ss 40, 46). Since the amendment referred to applies only to the power conferred by the Development of Tourism Act 1969 to make subordinate legislation including the imposition of fines for summary offences, and not to instruments previously made in exercise of that power, the fines contained in the relevant order (see note 15 infra) are not, it is thought, to be read as being converted to references to the standard scale, but remain as the amounts originally specified. As to the standard scale see para 16 note 21 ante.
15 Ibid s 18(1). The provisions of s 17(2)(e)–(g), (4)–(6) apply to such an order: s 18(2). See the Tourism (Sleeping Accommodation Price Display) Order 1977, SI 1977/1877. That order defines 'hotel' as any establishment in Great Britain at which sleeping accommodation is provided by way of trade or business which for the purposes of letting has not fewer than four bedrooms or eight beds (including beds situated in dormitories) excluding any normally in the same occupation for more than 21 consecutive nights, and at which accommodation is offered (whether for one night or for a longer period) to anyone able and willing to pay and in a fit state to be received; however, this excludes any establishment which is a bona fide members' club and provides such accommodation as a benefit of membership, and any establishment where accommodation is normally provided for a price which includes the provision of other services which are not merely ancillary to the provision of accommodation: art 2.
   At each hotel there must be prominently displayed in the reception area or (if there is none) at the entrance, where it can easily be read by a person seeking accommodation, a legible notice stating the current prices (specifically including any service charge and specifically including or specifically excluding a specified amount of value added tax, if payable) for rooms for one or two adults and of a bed for one adult in a dormitory or shared room: art 3(1), (2). If accommodation is only provided inclusive of meals, this must be stated: art 3(3). Where there are different prices within each category of accommodation, only the highest and lowest for each category need be stated (disregarding any room or bed which is normally in the same occupation for more than 21 consecutive nights): art 3(4). Additional information may be included, but not so as to detract from the prominence required to be given to the above information: art 3(5). Failure without reasonable excuse to display such a notice is an offence punishable on summary conviction with a fine not exceeding £200: art 4.
   A duly authorised weights and measures inspector may enter and inspect premises to determine whether these provisions are being complied with: see art 5(1). Wilful obstruction of the inspector is an offence punishable on summary conviction with a fine not exceeding £100: art 5(2). As to absences by bodies corporate see art 6. The Secretary of State for Trade and Industry may by regulations exclude any class of establishment from the order: see art 7. As to penalties see further note 14 supra.

819. Financial provisions. The relevant minister[1] may pay to a tourist board[2] such sums in respect of its expenditure as he may with the consent of the Treasury determine[3]. Any sums required by a relevant minister for making such payments and any other expenses of his must be defrayed out of money provided by Parliament[4]. Any sums received by a tourist board (1) in repayment of or as interest on any loan made by it; (2) in repayment of any grant made by it; or (3) as a dividend on or otherwise in respect of any shares or stock acquired by it, must be paid to the relevant minister[5].

1   For the meaning of 'relevant minister' see para 814 note 12 ante.
2   For the meaning of 'tourist board' see para 813 note 2 ante.
3   Development of Tourism Act 1969 s 20(1).
4   Ibid s 20(2).
5   Ibid s 20(3). Any sums received by a relevant minister under s 20(3) must be paid into the Consolidated Fund: s 20(4). As to the Consolidated Fund see CONSTITUTIONAL LAW AND HUMAN RIGHTS vol 8(2) (Reissue) para 711 et seq; and PARLIAMENT vol 34 (Reissue) para 952 et seq.

(vi) Industrial Design

820.   Furtherance of industrial design.   In order to promote the improvement of design in the products of British industry, the President of the Board of Trade in 1944 appointed a Council of Industrial Design[1]. The Secretary of State[2], with the approval of the Treasury, may make grants out of money provided by Parliament to the council and to any association or body the objects of which include promoting the improvement of design in any industry or activities appearing to him to be conducive to it and as to which he is satisfied that it does not carry on any business for the purposes of making a profit[3].

1   See 406 HC Official Report (5th series) col *1612*.
2   As to the Secretary of State see para 2 ante.
3   Industrial Organisation and Development Act 1947 s 11.

(2) ASSISTANCE TO INDUSTRY

(i) Promotion of Local Employment

821.   Powers for providing employment.   The Industrial Development Act 1982[1] confers powers upon the Secretary of State[2] principally for the designation of development areas, special development areas and intermediate areas[3], the provision of grants for project investment in development areas[4], financial assistance for industry in assisted areas[5], premises and sites[6], improvement of basic services[7], and the establishment of the Industrial Advisory Board[8].

1   The Industrial Development Act 1982 is extensively amended by the Co-operative Development Agency and Industrial Development Act 1984. For transitional provisions see the Co-operative Development Agency and Industrial Development Act (Commencement) Order 1984, SI 1984/1845 (amended by SI 1986/128). The Industrial Development Act 1982 (as amended) consolidated, with certain exceptions, the Local Employment Act 1972, the Industry Act 1972 Pts I, II, the Industry Act 1980 s 18 and the Industry Act 1981 s 6.
2   As to the Secretary of State see para 2 ante.
3   See the Industrial Development Act 1982 s 1 (as amended); and para 822 post.
4   See ibid s 2 (as substituted); and paras 822, 825 post. No such grants are, however, payable unless application for approval of a project was received on or before 31 March 1988: see para 825 post.
5   See ibid s 7; and paras 822, 825 post.
6   See ibid s 14 (as amended); and paras 833, 837 post.

7   See ibid s 13; and paras 834, 837 post.
8   See ibid s 10; and paras 832, 837 post.

822.   Development areas. The Secretary of State[1] may by order[2] specify any area of Great Britain[3] as a development area[4]. In making such an order he must have regard to all the circumstances, actual and expected, including the state of employment and unemployment, population changes and migration, and the objectives of regional policies[5].

An order may describe a development area by reference to any of the following kinds of area or any combination of those areas:

(1)   wards;

(2)   travel to work areas (being areas by reference to which the Secretary of State publishes unemployment records);

(3)   any other area which has been created by, or exists or existed for the purposes of, any Act or statutory instrument, whenever passed or made,

and any reference in such an order to a named area or combination of areas is to be construed as a reference to that area as it exists on the date on which the order comes into force[6].

This power is not exercisable for the purposes of regional development grant[7].

1   The Secretary of State is in practice the Secretary of State for Trade and Industry: see para 3 note 2 ante.

2   The order referred to is one made or having effect as if made under the Industrial Development Act 1982 s 1: s 18(1). An order under s 1 must be made by statutory instrument subject to annulment in pursuance of a resolution of either House of Parliament: s 1(7). It may contain such transitional provisions as respects regional development grants under Pt II (ss 2–6) (as substituted): see para 825 et seq post) as appear to the Secretary of State appropriate in connection with any variation effected by the order in the areas which are assisted areas of any particular category but no provision having the effect of reducing the amount of grant payable on current projects is to be made except in the case of anticipatory projects: s 1(5) (amended by the Co-operative Development Agency and Industrial Development Act 1984 s 5(2), Sch 1 Pt II para 4(a)); but see text and note 7 infra. These transitional provisions may include provision for the attribution of part of an anticipatory project to the period before the variation takes effect and its approval in accordance with the attribution: see the Industrial Development Act 1982 s 1(6) (substituted by the Co-operative Development Agency and Industrial Development Act 1984 Sch 1 Pt II para 4(b)). At the date at which this volume states the law, the order currently in force under this section is the Assisted Areas Order 2000, SI 2000/2038.

   For the purposes of the Industrial Development Act 1982 Pt II, a development area (or part of it) could formerly be designated by order as a special development area: s 1(2); Regional Development Grants (Termination) Act 1988 s 1(4)(b). 'Development area' and 'special development area' mean an area for the time being so specified or designated by an order made, or having effect as if made, under the Industrial Development Act 1982 s 1: s 18(1). Further provision relating to orders for the designation of special development areas is contained in s 1(7), (8) (s 1(8) amended by the Co-operative Development Agency and Industrial Development Act 1984 Sch 1 Pt II para 4(c)); but such provision is now superfluous.

3   For the meaning of 'Great Britain' see para 31 note 2 ante.

4   Industrial Development Act 1982 s 1(1)(a). See also text and note 7 infra.

5   Ibid s 1(3). See also note 2 supra, and text and note 7 infra.

6   Ibid s 1(4) (substituted by the Co-operative Development Agency and Industrial Development Act 1984 s 4). See also note 2 supra, and text and note 7 infra.

7   Regional Development Grants (Termination) Act 1988 s 1(1), which provides that the power conferred by the Industrial Development Act 1982 s 1(1) is not exercisable for the purposes of Pt II (as substituted); see paras 825–827 post.

823.   Intermediate areas. The Secretary of State[1] may by order[2] specify any area of Great Britain[3] as an intermediate area[4]. In making such an order he must have regard to all the circumstances actual and expected, including the state of employment and unemployment, population changes and migration and the objectives of regional policies[5].

An order may describe a development area by reference to any of the following kinds of area or any combination of those areas:

(1)   wards;

(2)   travel to work areas (being areas by reference to which the Secretary of State publishes unemployment records);

(3)   any other area which has been created by, or exists or existed for the purposes of, any Act or statutory instrument, whenever passed or made,

and any reference in such an order to a named area or combination of areas is to be construed as a reference to that area as it exists on the date on which the order comes into force[6].

This power is not exercisable for the purposes of regional development grant[7].

1   The Secretary of State is in practice the Secretary of State for Trade and Industry: see para 3 note 2 ante.

2   As to the making of such orders see para 822 note 2 ante.

3   For the meaning of 'Great Britain' see para 31 note 2 ante.

4   Industrial Development Act 1982 ss 1(1)(b). 'Intermediate area' means an area for the time being so specified or designated by an order made, or having effect as if made, under s 1: s 18(1).

The status as an intermediate area is important as regards the provision of premises and basic services (see paras 833–834 post) and the amount of grant which may be made for the clearance of derelict land (see para 879 post). However, regional development grants are not payable in intermediate areas.

5   Ibid s 1(3).

6   Ibid s 1(4) (substituted by the Co-operative Development Agency and Industrial Development Act 1984 s 4). See also note 2 supra, and text and note 7 infra.

7   Regional Development Grants (Termination) Act 1988 s 1(1), which provides that the power conferred by the Industrial Development Act 1982 s 1(1) is not exercisable for the purposes of Pt II (ss 2–6) (as substituted: see para 825 note 2 post): see paras 825–827 post.

824.   Inner urban areas. The Secretary of State[1] may by order specify as a designated district any district which includes the whole or part of an inner urban area in respect of which there exists a special social need[2]. A designated district authority[3] may then give financial assistance in the form of loans for the acquisition of or for works on land[4], or loans and grants for the establishment of common ownership or co-operative enterprises[5].

If the designated district authority by resolution declares an area within the designated district to be an improvement area[6] the authority may give further assistance in the form of loans or grants to improve amenities[7] or grants for converting or improving industrial or commercial buildings[8].

Where the Secretary of State and other ministers concerned consider that a concerted effort is required to alleviate a special social need in any inner urban area, they may arrange with the designated district authority[9] and other appropriate persons what action should be taken[10], and the Secretary of State may by order specify the area as a special area[11]. The authority may then make loans for site preparation[12] and grants towards rent[13] or loan interest[14].

Further, the Secretary of State may by order designate an inner urban area as an urban development area with its own urban development corporation[15], and the area may be designated as an enterprise zone[16].

1   The Secretary of State is the Secretary of State for the Environment or, in Wales, the National Assembly for Wales: see TOWN AND COUNTRY PLANNING vol 46 (Reissue) para 10.
2   See the Inner Urban Areas Act 1978 s 1; and TOWN AND COUNTRY PLANNING vol 46 (Reissue) para 1258.
3   'Designated district authority' in relation to a designated district means the council of that district or the council of the county or region which includes that district: ibid s 1(2).
4   See ibid s 2; and TOWN AND COUNTRY PLANNING vol 46 (Reissue) para 1259.
5   See ibid s 3; and TOWN AND COUNTRY PLANNING vol 46 (Reissue) para 1260.
6   See ibid s 4, Schedule paras 1–3; and TOWN AND COUNTRY PLANNING vol 46 (Reissue) paras 1261, 1264.
7   See ibid s 5; and TOWN AND COUNTRY PLANNING vol 46 (Reissue) para 1262.
8   See ibid s 6 (as amended); and TOWN AND COUNTRY PLANNING vol 46 (Reissue) para 1263.
9   Ie the council of that district or council of the county or region which includes that district, or both: see ibid s 7(1)(a).
10   See ibid s 7; and TOWN AND COUNTRY PLANNING vol 46 (Reissue) para 1265.
11   See ibid s 8; and TOWN AND COUNTRY PLANNING vol 46 (Reissue) para 1266.
12   See ibid s 9; and TOWN AND COUNTRY PLANNING vol 46 (Reissue) para 1267.
13   See ibid s 10; and TOWN AND COUNTRY PLANNING vol 46 (Reissue) para 1268.
14   See ibid s 11; and TOWN AND COUNTRY PLANNING vol 46 (Reissue) para 1269.
15   See the Local Government, Planning and Land Act 1980 s 134 (as amended), s 135; and TOWN AND COUNTRY PLANNING vol 46 (Reissue) para 1270 et seq. Where land is in both an urban development area and a designated district the urban development authority has many of the powers of a designated district authority: see s 162; and TOWN AND COUNTRY PLANNING vol 46 (Reissue) para 1276.
16   See ibid s 179, Sch 32 (both as amended); and TOWN AND COUNTRY PLANNING vol 46 (Reissue) para 1335 et seq.

(ii) Regional Development Grants

825. Powers of the Secretary of State. Under the Industrial Development Act 1982 the Secretary of State[1] had the power to make grants ('regional development grants')[2]. However, by virtue of the Regional Development Grants (Termination) Act 1988, no such grants are payable after 31 March 1988[3], except where application for approval of a project was received on or before that date[4]. An application may nonetheless be treated as received on that date if the Secretary of State is satisfied that the application was posted by first class letter before that date[5]. The following restrictions are imposed on the payment of grants for projects for which an application for approval is received after 12 January 1988[6]:

(1)   grant is only payable in respect of capital expenditure[7] on the provision of an asset, if the asset is provided before the closing date for grant purposes or, where the asset is not provided before that date, if, and to the extent that, expenditure on its provision is defrayed before that date[8];

(2)   grant is only payable in respect of the provision of a job, if the job is provided before the closing date for grant purposes[9];

(3)   grant will not, however, be payable in respect of capital expenditure on the provision of assets or in respect of the provision of jobs unless a claim for its payment is received by the Secretary of State before the closing date for claim purposes[10];

(4)   no adjustment will be made which would effectively increase the

amount of grant beyond the amount payable on the basis of the determination made on the approval of the project[11].

The Secretary of State had the power to specify the qualifying activities, and the prescribed percentages, amounts and limits for the purposes of the Industrial Development Act 1982[12]. However, by virtue of the Regional Development Grants (Termination) Act 1988 those powers are no longer exercisable[13]. This is in consequence of the termination and restriction of payment of grants after specified dates[14].

In addition, the Secretary of State has a separate statutory power to make grants, out of money provided by Parliament, to certain bodies[15] for the purpose of assisting them to promote industrial or commercial development in the area with which they are concerned[16]. In making such a grant the Secretary of State may impose such conditions as he thinks fit including, in particular:

(a) a condition requiring the recipient to keep proper accounts and records in respect of the application of the grant[17];

(b) a condition requiring the recipient to submit to the Secretary of State such periodic statements of accounts and reports relating to the application of the grant as the Secretary of State may direct[18];

(c) a condition requiring the recipient to repay the whole or any part of the grant if any condition of the grant is not complied with[19].

1 As to the Secretary of State see para 2 ante.
2 See the Industrial Development Act 1982 Pt II (ss 2–6) (substituted by the Co-operative Development Agency and Industrial Development Act 1984 s 5(1), Sch 1 Pt I).
3 Regional Development Grants (Termination) Act 1988 s 1(1).
4 Ibid s 1(2).
5 Ibid s 1(3).
6 See ibid s 2(1). These restrictions do not, however, apply in the case of projects commenced on or before 12 January 1988: s 2(1). For these purposes, a project is treated as commencing when, under the project, the first asset or job is provided or, if earlier, expenditure is first defrayed on the provision of an asset: s 2(7). An application received after 12 January 1988 is nonetheless treated as received on that date if the Secretary of State is satisfied that the application was posted by first-class or second-class letter not later than that date: s 2(8).
7 The definitions of 'asset', 'expenditure', 'jobs', 'provision' and 'provide' contained in the Industrial Development Act 1982 s 2(7) (as substituted: see note 2 supra) apply to those terms as used in the Regional Development Grants (Termination) Act 1988: s 2(9).
8 Ibid s 2(3). Any reference, in relation to a project, to the closing date for grant purposes, is a reference to the second anniversary of the date on which the project was approved: s 2(2)(a).
9 Ibid s 2(4). As to the meaning of 'job' see note 7 supra.
10 Ibid s 2(5). Any reference, in relation to a project, to the closing date for claim purposes is a reference to the third anniversary of the date on which the project was approved or, if the Secretary of State has specified an earlier date in the approval, the date so specified: s 2(2)(b).
11 Ibid s 2(6).
12 Ie the Industrial Development Act 1982 s 5(1)–(8) (as substituted: see note 2 supra).
13 See the Regional Development Grants (Termination) Act 1988 s 1(4)(c).
14 See text and notes 1–4 supra.
15 Ie (1) the Devon and Cornwall Development Bureau; (2) the North of England Development Council; (3) the North West Industrial Development Association; (4) the Yorkshire and Humberside Development Association; and (5) any other body, whether corporate or unincorporate, whose principal object appears to the Secretary of State to be the promotion of industrial or commercial development in an area in England: Miscellaneous Financial Provisions Act 1983 s 2(2). The Secretary of State must obtain the consent of the Treasury before making a grant to any body other than one named in heads (1)–(4) supra: see s 2(3). The Secretary of State, for these purposes, is the Secretary of State

for the Environment or, in Wales, the Secretary of State for Wales: see CONSTITUTIONAL
LAW AND HUMAN RIGHTS vol 8(2) (Reissue) para 453 et seq; TOWN AND COUNTRY
PLANNING vol 46 (Reissue) para 10.
16   Ibid s 2(1).
17   Ibid s 2(4)(a).
18   Ibid s 2(4)(b). The Secretary of State must lay before each House of Parliament a copy of
      every statement submitted to him in compliance with a condition of this kind: s 2(5).
19   Ibid s 2(4)(c).

826.   Directions as to assets.   The Secretary of State[1] may give general
directions or directions concerning a particular case, as respects the
determination of:

(1)   any question as to the classification of an asset as between the
        following classes, that is to say, machinery or plant, buildings or
        works[2];

(2)   any questions as to the area in which as asset is to be treated as
        situated or used[3];

(3)   any question as to the area in which a job is to be treated as carried
        out[4];

(4)   any question whether, and in what circumstances, a project is to be
        treated as providing an asset or a job[5];

(5)   the number of jobs a project is to be treated as providing where
        some of them are less than full-time[6].

1   As to the Secretary of State see para 2 ante.
2   Industrial Development Act 1982 s 5(9)(a) (substituted by the Co-operative Development
     Agency and Industrial Development Act 1984 s 5(1), Sch 1 Pt I).
3   Industrial Development Act 1982 s 5(9)(b) (as substituted: see note 2 supra).
4   Ibid s 5(9)(c) (as substituted: see note 2 supra).
5   Ibid s 5(9)(d) (as substituted: see note 2 supra).
6   Ibid s 5(9)(e) (as substituted: see note 2 supra).

827.   Enforcement of conditions.   The Secretary of State[1] may by notice
require any person who has received a regional development grant[2], or any
person acting on his behalf, to supply information and produce records for
inspection to enable the Secretary of State to determine whether any
condition[3] of the grant is being complied with or whether the grant has
become repayable[4]. Any person duly authorised by the Secretary of State, on
production if required of written evidence of his authority, may at all
reasonable times enter and inspect premises where any asset[5] in respect of
which a grant has been made is or should be and require any person
appearing to be in charge to produce or identify the asset for inspection[6]. An
authorised person has similar power as regards a job in respect of which a
grant has been made, to enter premises where the job is being or should be
carried out, and require the identification of the place of work of the person
employed to carry out that job[7].
    Any person who, without reasonable excuse, fails to comply with any
condition subject to which a grant was made to him requiring him to inform
the Secretary of State of any event by which the grant becomes repayable, in
whole or in part, is liable on summary conviction to a fine[8]. The payment of
grants is now terminated except in specified circumstances[9].

1   As to the Secretary of State see para 2 ante.
2   As to grants see para 825 ante.
3   The Secretary of State was empowered to impose conditions on the making of a grant, in
     particular for the repayment of grant in the event of non-compliance with another

condition of the grant: see the Industrial Development Act 1982 s 6(1), (2) (substituted by the Co-operative Development Agency and Industrial Development Act 1984 s 5(1), Sch 1 Pt I).

4 Industrial Development Act 1982 s 6(3), Sch 1 para 1(1) (s 6(3) as substituted: see note 3 supra). The notice may impose time limits: see Sch 1 para 1(2), (3). As to service see Sch 1 para 1(4). A person who in purported compliance with such a notice knowingly or recklessly makes a statement or produces a document which is false in a material particular is guilty of an offence and liable, on summary conviction, to a fine not exceeding the prescribed sum or, on conviction on indictment, to a fine or imprisonment for a term not exceeding two years or both: Sch 1 para 3(1). A person who without reasonable excuse fails to comply with such a notice is guilty of an offence and liable on summary conviction to a fine not exceeding level 5 on the standard scale: Sch 1 para 3(2). As to the commission of offences by officers of bodies corporate see Sch 1 para 5. As to the standard scale see para 16 note 21 ante. For the meaning of 'the prescribed sum' see the Magistrates' Courts Act 1980 s 32 (as amended); and CRIMINAL LAW, EVIDENCE AND PROCEDURE vol 11(2) (Reissue) para 806; MAGISTRATES.

5 'Asset' means machinery, plant, buildings or works, and 'machinery', 'plant', 'building' and 'works' include any part of machinery, plant, building or works respectively: ibid s 2(7) (substituted by the Co-operative Development Agency and Industrial Development Act 1984 Sch 1 Pt I).

6 Industrial Development Act 1982 Sch 1 para 2(1) (so numbered by the Co-operative Development Agency and Industrial Development Act 1984 s 5(2), Sch 1 Pt II para 5). A person who wilfully obstructs any person in the exercise of a right of entry under the Industrial Development Act 1982 Sch 1 para 2 (as amended) or fails to comply with such a requirement to produce or identify assets is guilty of an offence and liable on summary conviction to a fine not exceeding level 3 on the standard scale: Sch 1 para 3(3). As to the commission of offences by officers of bodies corporate see Sch 1 para 5.

7 Ibid Sch 1 para 2(2) (added by the Co-operative Development Agency and Industrial Development Act 1984 Sch 1 Pt II para 5). For the penalty for obstructing a person in the exercise of this power see note 6 supra.

8 Industrial Development Act 1982 Sch 1 para 4(1). If he is convicted summarily the fine must not exceed the statutory maximum: Sch 1 para 4(1). As to the statutory maximum see para 16 note 21 ante.

9 Regional Development Grants (Termination) Act 1988 s 1; see para 825 ante.

(iii) Financial Assistance for Industry

828. Industry in assisted areas. For specified purposes[1] the Secretary of State[2] may, with the consent of the Treasury, provide financial assistance[3] where, in his opinion[4]: (1) such assistance is likely to provide, maintain or safeguard employment in any part of the assisted areas[5]; and (2) the undertakings for which the assistance is provided are or will be wholly or mainly in those areas[6].

1 For these purposes see the Industrial Development Act 1982 s 7(2); and para 830 post. As to the tax treatment of grants under ss 7, 8, see the Income and Corporation Taxes Act 1988 s 93; and INCOME TAXATION.

2 As to the Secretary of State see para 2 ante.

3 As to the nature of this financial assistance see the Industrial Development Act 1982 s 7(3), (4); and para 831 post.

4 Ibid s 7(1).

5 Ibid s 7(1)(a). 'The assisted areas' means the development areas, the intermediate areas and Northern Ireland: s 7(6). As to development areas and intermediate areas see paras 822–823 ante.

6 Ibid s 7(1)(b).

829. Industry generally. For specified purposes[1] the Secretary of State[2] may, with the consent of the Treasury, provide financial assistance[3] where, in his opinion[4]:

(1) the financial assistance is likely to benefit the economy of the United Kingdom, or of any part or area of the United Kingdom[5];

(2)　　it is in the national interest that financial assistance should be provided on the scale, and in the form and manner, proposed[6]; and

(3)　　the financial assistance cannot, or cannot appropriately, be so provided otherwise than by him[7].

The aggregate of the sums paid[8] by him, other than sums paid in respect of foreign currency guarantees[9], and his liabilities under any guarantees[10] given by him, less any sum received by him by way of repayment of loans, or repayment of principal sums paid to meet guarantees, may not at any time exceed £2, 300m[11]. The aggregate of his liabilities under foreign currency guarantees[12] and any sums paid by him in respect of such guarantees[13], less any sums received by him by way of repayment of principal sums paid to meet foreign currency guarantees, may not at any time exceed 1,000m special drawing rights[14].

The sums which the Secretary of State pays or undertakes to pay by way of financial assistance in respect of any one project, excluding sums paid or to be paid in respect of foreign currency guarantees, may not exceed £10m, except so far as any excess has been authorised by a resolution of the House of Commons[15].

1　Ie for the purposes set out in the Industrial Development Act 1982 s 7(2): see para 830 post.

2　As to the Secretary of State see para 2 ante.

3　For the financial assistance which may be given see the Industrial Development Act 1982 s 7(3), applied by s 8(2); see para 831 post. See also s 8(2), (3); and para 831 notes 1, 4 post.

4　Ibid s 8(1).

5　Ibid s 8(1)(a). For the meaning of 'United Kingdom' see para 37 note 1 ante.

6　Ibid s 8(1)(b).

7　Ibid s 8(1)(c).

8　Ie under ibid s 8. As to taxation see para 828 note 1 ante.

9　Ibid s 8(4)(a). 'Foreign currency guarantee' means a guarantee given under s 8 or under the Industry Act 1972 s 8 (repealed) by the Secretary of State under which his liability is measured in a foreign currency, whether or not it is to be discharged in such a currency; for this purpose a liability measured in sterling but expressed to be subject to a limit in a foreign currency is taken to be measured in such a currency, and a liability measured in foreign currency but expressed to be subject to a limit in sterling is taken to be measured in sterling: Industrial Development Act 1982 s 8(11). 'Foreign currency' means any currency other than sterling, including special drawing rights, and 'guarantee' includes any form of insurance: ss 8(11), 9(7). As to special drawing rights see para 805 note 4 ante.

10　Ibid s 8(4)(b). Liabilities in respect of interest on a principal sum so guaranteed are excluded, as are liabilities under foreign currency guarantees: s 8(4)(b).

11　Ibid s 8(4), (5). The Secretary of State may, on not more than four occasions, by order made with the consent of the Treasury, increase the limit by a specified sum not exceeding £200m: s 8(5). Such an order must be made by statutory instrument, a draft of which has been approved by resolution of the House of Commons: s 8(10). The first order, raising the limit from £1,900m to £2,100m, was the Financial Assistance for Industry (Increase of Limit) Order 1996, SI 1996/569; subsequently the limit was raised to £2,300m by the Financial Assistance for Industry (Increase of Limit) Order 2000, SI 2000/995.

12　Industrial Development Act 1982 s 8(6)(a). Liability in respect of interest on a principal sum guaranteed under s 8 or under the Industry Act 1972 s 8 (repealed) is excluded: Industrial Development Act 1982 s 8(6)(a).

13　Ibid s 8(6)(b).

14　Ibid s 8(6), (7); this is subject to the supplementary provisions of s 9 as to limits on foreign currency liabilities: s 8(6). On not more than four occasions the Secretary of State may, by order made with the consent of the Treasury, increase, or further increase, the limit by a specified amount not exceeding 500m special drawing rights: s 8(7). Such an order must be made by statutory instrument, a draft of which has been approved by resolution of the House of Commons: s 8(10). At the date at which this volume states the law, no such order had been made.

The amount to be taken into account under s 8(6) at any time in respect of a liability, if the amount of the liability is not expressed in special drawing rights, is the equivalent at that time in special drawing rights of the amount of the liability: s 9(1). That equivalent is determined by the Secretary of State by reference to: (1) the day on which the guarantee is given, and (2) the last day of each quarter at the end of which the guarantee remains in force, having regard to what appears to be the appropriate rate of exchange: s 9(2). A determination under head (1) supra takes effect from the date from which it was made, and remains in force until the end of the quarter in which the guarantee was given, unless it ceases to be required at an earlier date: s 9(3). A determination made under head (2) supra takes effect as from the end of the quarter and remains in force throughout the following quarter, unless it ceases to be required at an earlier date: s 9(4). 'Quarter' means a quarter ending with 31 March, 30 June, 30 September or 31 December in any year: s 9(7).

The amount to be taken into account under s 8(6) in respect of a sum paid or received by the Secretary of State otherwise than in special drawing rights is an amount determined by him, by reference to the day of payment or receipt and having regard to what appears to him the appropriate rate of exchange, as being the equivalent in special drawing rights of that sum: s 9(5).

The limit imposed by s 8(6) may be exceeded if the excess is attributable only to, or to a combination of, the following (s 9(6)):

(a)   a quarterly revaluation (s 9(6)(a));
(b)   the Secretary of State's liability under a guarantee given in pursuance of a previous undertaking so far as the amount taken into account for the purposes of the limit in respect of the liability exceeds what it would have been if determined by reference to the day on which the undertaking was given (s 9(6)(b));
(c)   a payment made by the Secretary of State under a guarantee, so far as the amount to be taken into account for the purposes of the limit in respect of the payment exceeds what it would have been if determined by reference to the day on which the guarantee was given (s 9(6)(c)).

A quarterly revaluation is a determination made or having effect as if made under head (2) supra: s 9(7).

15 Ibid s 8(8). This does not apply where the Secretary of State is satisfied that the payment or undertaking is urgently needed at a time when it is impracticable to obtain the approval of the House of Commons, in which case he must lay a statement concerning the financial assistance before each House of Parliament: s 8(9).

830. Purposes for which assistance may be given. The specified purposes for which financial assistance for industry[1] may be provided are:

(1)   to promote the development or modernisation of an industry[2];

(2)   to promote the efficiency of an industry[3];

(3)   to create, expand or sustain productive capacity in an industry, or in undertakings in an industry[4];

(4)   to promote the reconstruction, reorganisation or conversion of an industry or of undertakings in an industry[5];

(5)   to encourage the growth of, or the proper distribution of undertakings in, an industry[6]; and

(6)   to encourage arrangements for ensuring that any contraction of an industry proceeds in an orderly way[7].

1   Ie under the Industrial Development Act 1982 s 7(1) or s 8(1): see paras 828–829 ante.
2   Ibid s 7(2)(a). Unless the context otherwise requires, 'industry' includes any description of commercial activity, and references to an industry include references to any section of an industry: s 7(5).
3   Ibid s 7(2)(b).
4   Ibid s 7(2)(c).
5   Ibid s 7(2)(d).
6   Ibid s 7(2)(e).
7   Ibid s 7(2)(f).

831.   Nature of financial assistance.   Financial assistance for industry[1] may be given on any terms or conditions, and by any description of investment or lending or guarantee, or by making grants[2]. In particular, assistance may be given by:

(1)   investment by acquisition of loan or share capital in any company, including an acquisition effected by the Secretary of State through another company formed for the purpose of giving[3] such assistance[4];

(2)   investment by the acquisition of any undertaking or of any assets[5];

(3)   a loan, whether secured or unsecured, and whether or not carrying interest, or interest at a commercial rate[6]; or

(4)   any form of insurance or guarantee to meet any contingency, and in particular to meet default on payment of a loan, or of interest on a loan, or non-fulfilment of a contract[7].

1   Ie under the Industrial Development Act 1982 s 7(1) or s 8(1): see paras 829–830 ante.
2   Ibid s 7(3). The Secretary of State may not, however, under s 8 use any money for the acquisition or assistance of banks or insurance companies: s 8(2). As to the Secretary of State see para 2 ante.
3   Ie under ibid Pt III (ss 7–10), or the Industry Act 1972 Pt II (ss 7–9) (repealed).
4   Industrial Development Act 1982 s 7(3)(a). Assistance under this head may not be given unless the Secretary of State is satisfied that it cannot, or cannot appropriately, be given in any other way, and in giving financial assistance under this head he may not acquire any shares or stock in a company without its consent: ss 7(4), 8(3). Such restrictions would not apply to the acquisition of shares or stock under particular powers contained in another Act. See eg the British Leyland Act 1975 (repealed), which authorised the Secretary of State to acquire shares in British Leyland Motor Corporation Ltd up to a maximum expenditure of £265m.
5   Industrial Development Act 1982 s 7(3)(b).
6   Ibid s 7(3)(c).
7   Ibid s 7(3)(d).

832.   The Industrial Development Advisory Board.   The Industrial Development Advisory Board[1] ('the board') consists of a chairman and not fewer than six nor more than 12 other members[2], and must include persons who appear to the Secretary of State[3] to have wide experience of, and to have shown capacity in, industry, banking, accounting and finance[4]. The board is appointed by the Secretary of State to advise him with respect to the exercise of his functions[5] as to financial assistance for industry[6]. If it makes a recommendation with respect to any matter at his request and he exercises his functions contrary to that recommendation, he must, if the board so requests, lay a statement as to the matter before Parliament[7].

1   The board was originally established on 11 October 1972 under the Industry Act 1972 s 9(1) (repealed), and is continued by the Industrial Development Act 1982 s 10(1).
2   Ibid s 10(2).
3   As to the Secretary of State see para 2 ante.
4   Industrial Development Act 1982 s 10(3).
5   Ie his functions under ibid ss 7, 8: see para 828 et seq ante.
6   Ibid s 10(1).
7   Ibid s 10(4).

(iv)   General Assistance for Industry

833.   Provision of premises and sites.   In addition to particular powers given to the Urban Regeneration Agency[1] and the Welsh Development Agency[2] to provide and manage sites and premises for industrial or commercial undertakings, the Secretary of State[3] has specified powers in order to provide or facilitate the provision of premises in any development area[4] or intermediate area[5] for occupation by undertakings[6] carried on or to be carried on there or for otherwise meeting the requirements of such undertakings, including requirements arising from the needs· of persons employed or to be employed in them[7]. These powers are:

(1)   to acquire land[8] by agreement or, if so authorised, compulsorily[9];

(2)   to erect buildings and carry out works on land belonging to the Secretary of State[10]; and

(3)   by agreement with the persons interested in any other land, to erect buildings and carry out works on the land on such terms, including terms as to repayment of expenditure incurred by the Secretary of State, as may be specified[11].

Any person duly authorised in writing by the Secretary of State may, at any reasonable time, enter any land to survey it in connection with the exercise of these powers to acquire land[12]. Where land acquired by the Secretary of State under these powers[13] is situated in a locality which is not a development area or an intermediate area, he may exercise in relation to it the following powers[14]:

(a)   to preserve and maintain the land and any buildings or works on it, and to erect buildings and carry out works on it[15];

(b)   where there are buildings on the land, to acquire by agreement other land contiguous or adjacent to it for the purpose of erecting on it extensions to those buildings, or of erecting on it other buildings to be used with buildings on the land already acquired as part of a single undertaking[16];

(c)   to provide means of access, services and other facilities for meeting the requirements of undertakings carried on, or to be carried on, on the land, including requirements arising from the needs of persons employed or to be employed[17].

The Secretary of State may modernise, adapt or reconstruct any buildings or other works on land acquired by him under any of these powers[18].

1   See para 847 post.

2   As to the agency and its functions see para 856 et seq post. The English Industrial Estates Corporation, which was abolished by the Leasehold Reform, Housing and Urban Development Act 1993 s 184(1) (Leasehold Reform, Housing and Urban Development Act 1993 (Commencement Order No 4) 1994, SI 1994/935, art 3), held similar powers. Its role has been absorbed by the Urban Regeneration Agency, established by the 1993 Act.

3   As to the Secretary of State see para 2 ante.

4   As to development areas see para 822 ante.

5   As to intermediate areas see para 823 ante.

6   'Undertaking' means any trade or business or any other activity providing employment: Industrial Development Act 1982 s 17(2).

7   Ibid s 14(1). Where a locality ceases to be a development area or intermediate area, the fact that it is no longer such an area does not prejudice the completion by the Secretary of State of buildings or works begun before that time in the locality under s 14(1), or the exercise by him in relation to land in the locality of his powers under s 14(1) so far as may be necessary to fulfil any agreement entered into by him before that time: s 17(3)(a). The Secretary of State is in practice the Secretary of State for Trade and Industry.

8   'Land' includes messuages, tenements and hereditaments, houses and buildings of any tenure: ibid s 17(1).

9   Ibid s 14(1)(a). The Secretary of State may not acquire under this power any buildings other than industrial buildings, except for redevelopment or as part of a larger property which in his opinion would be incomplete without them: s 14(2). Further, the Acquisition of Land Act 1981 applies in relation to the compulsory purchase of land by the Secretary

of State under the Industrial Development Act 1982 s 14; but notwithstanding anything in s 14, where at the time of publication of notice of the preparation of a draft compulsory purchase order the land is in use for the purposes of any undertaking, and that undertaking provides employment which is substantial having regard to the extent of the land used for its purposes and the nature of the undertaking, the Secretary of State may not be authorised to acquire compulsorily the interest of the person carrying on the undertaking: s 14(5). 'Industrial building' means a building (1) which is used or designed for use for carrying on, in the course of a trade or business, a process for or incidental to: (a) the making of any article or part of any article, (b) the altering, repairing, ornamenting, finishing, cleaning, washing, freezing, packing or canning, or adapting for sale, or breaking up or demolition, of any article, or (c) the getting, dressing, or preparation for sale of minerals or the extraction or preparation for sale of oil or brine; or (2) which is used or designed for use for carrying on, in the course of a trade or business, scientific research: s 14A(1) (added by the Housing and Planning Act 1986 s 49(1), Sch 11 Pt I para 25(1), (3)). Premises which (i) are used or designed for use for providing services or facilities ancillary to the use of other premises for the carrying on of any such process or research as is mentioned above, and (ii) are or are to be comprised in the same building or the same curtilage as those other premises, are themselves to be treated as used or designed for use for the carrying on of such a process or, as the case may be, of such research: Industrial Development Act 1982 s 14A(2) (as so added). 'Article' means an article of any description, including a ship or vessel; 'building' includes part of a building; 'minerals' includes all minerals and substances in or under land of a kind ordinarily worked for removal by underground or surface working, except that it does not include peat cut for purposes other than sale; and 'scientific research' means any activity in the fields of natural or applied science for the extension of knowledge: s 14A(3) (as so added).

10   Ibid s 14(1)(b).
11   Ibid s 14(1)(c).
12   Ibid s 14(6) (amended by the Planning (Consequential Provisions) Act 1990 s 4, Sch 2 para 57), which further applies the Town and Country Planning Act 1990 ss 324(8), 325(1)–(6), (8), (9) (as amended) to such powers of entry as they apply to the Town and Country Planning Act 1990 s 324 (as amended). See TOWN AND COUNTRY PLANNING vol 46 (Reissue) para 33 et seq.
13   This includes corresponding powers under the Local Employment Act 1972 s 5 (repealed): Industrial Development Act 1982 s 14(4).
14   Ibid s 14(4).
15   Ibid s 14(4)(a).
16   Ibid s 14(4)(b).
17   Ibid s 14(4)(c).
18   Ibid s 14(3). Where the execution of such work will interrupt the use of the buildings or works by any undertaking, the Secretary of State may acquire other land by agreement, and erect buildings and carry out works on it, or on land previously acquired by him, for the purpose of providing premises for the occupation of that undertaking or of otherwise meeting its requirements: s 14(3).

834.   Improvement of basic services.   Where it appears to the minister in charge of any government department that adequate provision has not been made for the needs of any development area[1] or intermediate area[2] in respect of a basic service[3] for which the department is responsible, and it is expedient with a view to contributing to the development of industry in that area that the service should be improved, he may, with the consent of the Treasury, make grants or loans towards the cost of the improvements to such persons and in such manner as appears to him appropriate[4].

1   As to development areas see para 822 ante.
2   As to intermediate areas see para 823 ante.
3   'Basic service' means the provision of facilities for transport, whether by road, rail, water or air, or of power, lighting, heating, water, or sewerage and sewage disposal facilities, or any other service or facility on which the development of the area in question, and in particular of industrial undertakings in it, depends: Industrial Development Act 1982 s 13(2). For the meaning of 'undertaking' see para 833 note 6 ante.
4   Ibid s 13(1). These powers are in addition to any other powers of a Minister of the Crown to make grants or loans: s 13(3). Where at any time a locality ceases to be a development

area or an intermediate area, the fact that it is no longer such an area does not prejudice the making of any grant or loan in any case in which the application for the grant or loan was received by the Secretary of State before that time: s 17(3)(b). Nor does it prejudice the continued operation of any agreement relating to such a grant or loan or of any other agreement relating to grants or loans entered into under Pt IV (ss 11–17) (as amended), or corresponding provisions of the Local Employment Act 1972: Industrial Development Act 1982 s 17(3)(c). As to the Secretary of State see para 2 ante.

835.   Advice for businesses. The Secretary of State[1] may make provision for the giving of advice, whether free of charge or otherwise, to persons carrying on or proposing to carry on a business[2]. Not later than six months after the end of any financial year in which this power is used he must prepare and lay before Parliament a report on the exercise during the year of this power[3].

1   As to the Secretary of State see para 2 ante.
2   Industrial Development Act 1982 s 11(1).
3   See ibid s 11(2).

836.   Promotion of careers in industry. The Secretary of State[1] may make such grants[2] or loans[3] to any body as he considers appropriate[4] for the purpose of assisting in:

(1)   the promotion of the practice of engineering[5],
(2)   the encouragement and improvement of links between industry, or any part of industry, and bodies or individuals concerned with education[6],
(3)   the encouragement of young persons and others to take up careers in industry, or in any part of industry, and to pursue appropriate educational courses[7].

He may also, with the approval of the Treasury, guarantee obligations, arising out of loans, incurred by any body established by royal charter[8], and the members of which are appointed by him[9] and which is, in his opinion, concerned with promoting the practice of engineering[10].

1   As to the Secretary of State see para 2 ante.
2   Grants may be made on such conditions as the Secretary of State may determine with the approval of the Treasury: Industrial Development Act 1982 s 12(2).
3   Loans may be made at such rates of interest as the Secretary of State may determine with the approval of the Treasury: ibid s 12(2). He may not, however, determine a rate of interest in respect of a loan which is lower than the lowest rate for the time being determined by the Treasury under the National Loans Act 1968 s 5 (see CONSTITUTIONAL LAW AND HUMAN RIGHTS vol 8(2) (Reissue) para 736), in respect of comparable loans out of the National Loans Fund: Industrial Development Act 1982 s 12(3).
4   Ibid s 12(1).
5   Ibid s 12(1)(a).
6   Ibid s 12(1)(b).
7   Ibid s 12(1)(c).
8   Ibid s 12(5)(a).
9   Ibid s 12(5)(b).
10 Ibid s 12(4).
     As to the provision of information by public bodies for the purposes of the provision of services under s 12 see the Learning and Skills Act 2000 s 138; and EDUCATION vol 15(2) (Reissue) para 955.

837.   Annual reports and statements of account of the Secretary of State. For each financial year the Secretary of State[1] must prepare and lay before Parliament[2] a report on the discharge of his functions:

(1)   relating to assisted areas[3], regional development grants[4], financial

assistance for industry[5], the provision of premises and sites[6] and the improvement[7] of basic services[8], and

(2)   in relation to credits and grants for the construction of ships and offshore installations[9], including any function in respect of guarantees given by him under the Shipbuilding Industry Act 1967[10].

The Secretary of State may discharge this duty in any year by making a report on any of his functions mentioned in heads (1) and (2) above and one or more separate reports on the remaining functions[11].

For every financial year the Secretary of State must prepare a statement of accounts, in such form as the Treasury may direct, showing the financial results for the year as respects his activities in the execution of certain of the statutory provisions[12] (other than activities in respect of grants)[13]. He must transmit the statement to the Comptroller and Auditor General, on or before 30 November after the financial year in question, for examination and certification[14]. Copies of every such statement, together with the report of the Comptroller and Auditor General, must be laid before Parliament by the Secretary of State[15].

1   As to the Secretary of State see para 2 ante.
2   The report must be laid not later than six months after the end of the financial year to which it relates: Industrial Development Act 1982 s 15(1) (amended by the Housing and Planning Act 1986 s 49(2), Sch 12 Pt III; and, as from a date to be appointed, by the Leasehold Reform, Housing and Urban Development Act 1993 s 187(2), Sch 22). In the application of the Industrial Development Act 1982 s 15 (as amended) in relation to a financial year beginning before 28 January 1983, any reference in s 15(1) (as so amended) to a provision of the Act includes a reference to the enactment re-enacted in that provision: s 15(4).
3   Ie under ibid Pt I (s 1): see paras 822–823 ante.
4   Ie under ibid Pt II (ss 2–6) (as substituted): see para 825 et seq ante.
5   Ie under ibid Pt III (ss 7–10): see para 828 et seq ante. The report relating to Pt III must contain a statement showing the total amount of the liabilities of the Secretary of State, excluding any liability in respect of interest on a principal sum, under guarantees given by him under Pt III or the Industry Act 1972 Pt II (ss 7–9) (repealed), or, as the case may be, Pt III (ss 10–12) (as amended) of that Act, including any liabilities under guarantees given by him under the Shipbuilding Industry Act 1967 s 7 (repealed): Industrial Development Act 1982 s 15(3).
6   Ie under ibid s 14: see para 833 ante.
7   Ie under ibid s 13: see para 834 ante.
8   Ibid s 15(1)(a).
9   Ie under the Industry Act 1972 Pt III: see para 655 ante.
10 Industrial Development Act 1982 s 15(1)(c).
11 Ibid s 15(2).
12 Ie ibid ss 13, 14: see paras 833–834 ante.
13 Ibid s 16(1) (amended by the Industrial Development Act 1985 ss 4(2), 6(3), Schedule).
14 Industrial Development Act 1982 s 16(2).
15 Ibid s 16(3).

838.   Disclosure of information by the government. The Treasury must keep a macro-economic model suitable for demonstrating the likely effects on economic events in the United Kingdom[1] of different assumptions about the following matters: (1) government economic policies[2]; (2) economic events outside the United Kingdom[3]; and (3) such other matters, if any, as appear likely to the Treasury from time to time to have a substantial effect on economic events in the United Kingdom[4].

The model must enable forecasts[5] to be made of:

(a)   the level of gross domestic product;

   (b)   unemployment;

   (c)   the balance of payments on current account;

   (d)   the general index of retail prices; and

   (e)   average earnings;

and of any such other economic variables, if any, from time to time as are appropriate in the opinion of the Treasury[6]. The model must be maintained on a computer[7] and must be available to members of the public to make forecasts based on their own assumptions, using the computer during office hours on payment of such reasonable fee as the Treasury may determine[8]. The Treasury must publish, not less than twice a year, forecasts produced with the aid of the model as to such matters and based on such alternative assumptions as appear to it to be appropriate[9].

   The Treasury must, from time to time, publish an analysis of errors in such forecasts that would have remained even if the assumptions set out in the forecasts and on which they were based had been correct[10].

1   For the meaning of 'United Kingdom' see para 37 note 1 ante.
2   Industry Act 1975 s 27, Sch 5 para 1(a).
3   Ibid Sch 5 para 1(b).
4   Ibid Sch 5 para 1(c).
5   References to forecasts under ibid Sch 5 para 2 are references to forecasts relating to successive periods of three months and not to shorter periods: Sch 5 para 3. Any forecast must indicate, where possible, the margin of error attaching to it: Sch 5 para 7.
6   Ibid Sch 5 para 2.
7   Ibid Sch 5 para 4.
8   Ibid Sch 5 para 5.
9   Ibid Sch 5 para 6.
10 Ibid Sch 5 para 8.

(v) British Technology Group Ltd

839.   Dissolution of the National Research Development Corporation and the National Enterprise Board. All the property, rights and liabilities[1] to which the National Research Development Corporation or the National Enterprise Board was entitled before 6 January 1992 (the appointed day)[2] are now vested in British Technology Group Ltd[3], the successor company[4] nominated by the Secretary of State[5]. Immediately before 6 January 1992 the reserve established by the corporation[6] and any liability of the board to the Secretary of State in respect of its public dividend capital[7] were extinguished[8].

   The corporation and the board were to continue in existence after the appointed day until the Secretary of State was satisfied, in the case of either body, that nothing remained to be done under the relevant transitional provisions and, after consulting the body and the successor company, by order dissolved the body in question[9]. They were dissolved on 1 July 1996[10].

   Any agreement made, transaction effected or other thing done by, to or in relation to the board or the corporation, which was in force or effective before the appointed day, has effect as if it were so made, effected, or done by, to or in relation to the successor company, and as if the successor company were the same person in law as the board or corporation[11]. An agreement in force immediately before the appointed day which (1) confers or imposes rights or liabilities which vest in the successor company, and (2) refers to a member or officer of the corporation or board, has effect in relation to anything to be done after that day, as if the reference were to an appointed or corresponding officer of the successor company[12].

Provision was made for the modification of contracts of employment by substituting references to the successor company for references to the corporation and the board[13], for the inclusion of rights and liabilities relating to pensions, allowances and gratuities in those rights and liabilities which vested in the successor company[14], and for employment with the board or the corporation to be treated as employment with the successor company[15].

1   References to property, rights and liabilities of the National Research Development Corporation or the National Enterprise Board are references to all such property, rights and liabilities, whether or not capable of being transferred or assigned by the corporation or board: British Technology Group Act 1991 s 1(3). References to the property of the corporation or the board are references to property whether situated in the United Kingdom or elsewhere, and references to rights and liabilities of the corporation or the board are references to rights to which they are entitled or liabilities to which they are subject whether under the law of the United Kingdom or any part of it, or under the law of any country or territory outside the United Kingdom: s 1(4). For the meaning of 'United Kingdom' see para 37 note 1 ante.

2   Ie the day appointed for the purposes of ibid s 1(1) (see note 5 infra): see the British Technology Group Act 1991 (Appointed Day) Order 1991, SI 1991/2721.

3   See the British Technology Group Act 1991 (Nominated Company) Order 1991, SI 1991/2722. That order nominated the British Technology Group plc, which subsequently re-registered as a private company on 31 March 1992: see the British Technology Group Act 1991 (Government Shareholding) Order 1992, SI 1992/1437, note (a). A director of British Technology Group Ltd is disqualified for membership of the House of Commons: House of Commons Disqualification Act 1975 s 1(1)(f), Sch 1 Pt III (amended by the British Technology Group Act 1991 s 1(6), Sch 1 para 5).

4   On the appointed day, the successor company was required to be formed and registered under the Companies Act 1985, limited by shares and wholly owned by the Crown: British Technology Group Act 1991 s 1(2). A company is regarded as wholly owned by the Crown at any time when each of the issued shares of the company is held by, or by a nominee of, the Treasury or the Secretary of State: s 16(2).

5   Ibid s 1(1). As to the power conferred on the board and the corporation to make preparations for the vesting of the property, rights and liabilities see Sch 1 para 1. The Secretary of State here concerned is the Secretary of State for Trade and Industry: see para 2 ante.

6   Ie the reserve established under the Development of Inventions Act 1967 s 10 (repealed): British Technology Group Act 1991 s 2(1)(a).

7   Ibid s 2(1)(b). Section 2(1) does not operate to extinguish any liability of the board under the Industry Act 1975 Sch 2 para 5(3) or (3A) (repealed) which accrued before 6 January 1992: British Technology Group Act 1991 s 2(2).

8   Ibid s 2(1).

9   Ibid s 11. As to the transitional provisions see Sch 3. The period between the appointed day and the day of dissolution is known as the 'transitional period': s 11(1).

10 National Enterprise Board (Dissolution) Order 1996, SI 1996/1448.

11 British Technology Group Act 1991 Sch 1 para 2. Accordingly, references (1) in any agreement (written or not), deed, bond or instrument, (2) in any process or other document issued, prepared or employed for the purpose of any proceeding before any court or other tribunal or authority, and (3) in any other document (other than an enactment) relating to or affecting any property, right or liability of the corporation or board which vests in the successor company, are taken as referring to the successor company: Sch 1 para 2.

12 Ibid Sch 1 para 3.

13 Ibid Sch 1 para 4(1)(a).

14 Ibid Sch 1 para 4(1)(b).

15 Ibid Sch 1 para 4(2).

840.   Government holding in successor company.   As a consequence of the provisions vesting the property, rights and liabilities of the National Research Development Corporation and the National Enterprise Board in the successor company[1], provision was made for:

(1) the initial issue and allotment of securities and rights to the Treasury or the Secretary of State or to their nominees[2];

(2) the power of the Treasury and the Secretary of State or their nominees to . acquire securities and rights in the successor company[3];

(3) consultation with representatives of United Kingdom universities prior to offering such securities for sale[4]; and

(4) the setting by order of a target investment limit for the government shareholding in the successor company[5].

The first target investment limit was required to be set at the level of the government holding of ordinary voting rights (disregarding any temporary suspension of voting rights) at the time the order was made[6]; thereafter, new limits might be set provided that each such limit was lower than the one which it replaced[7]. The Secretary of State and the Treasury were placed under a duty to secure that the government shareholding did not carry voting rights exceeding the target investment limit[8]. Since the government shareholding in the successor company at the time of the making of the first order comprised one special rights redeemable preference share carrying nil voting rights, the first target investment limit was set at nil[9], and no further orders could be made[10].

1   Ie British Technology Group Ltd; see the British Technology Group Act 1991 ss 1(2), 16(1); and para 839 text and notes 3–5 ante.

2   See ibid s 3. As to the power of the Treasury and the Secretary of State to exercise their functions through nominees see s 5. As to the Secretary of State see para 2 ante.

3   See ibid s 4. For the meaning of 'United Kingdom' see para 37 note 1 ante.

4   See ibid s 7.

5   See ibid s 6(1), (2); and text and notes 6–10 infra.

6   Ibid s 6(3), (7).

7   Ibid s 6(4).

8   See ibid s 6(5). However, this did not prohibit the taking up of rights as an existing holder of shares or other securities, provided that, if the target investment limit was thereby exceeded, the Secretary of State or the Treasury complied as soon as reasonably practicable with s 6(5): s 6(6).

9   British Technology Group Act 1991 (Government Shareholding) Order 1992, SI 1992/1437.

10 See text and notes 6–7 supra.

841.   Financial structure of successor company; borrowing by successor company.   If the aggregate nominal value of the issued securities[1] of the successor company[2] is less than the amount of the reserve and public dividend capital extinguished by the British Technology Group Act 1991[3], a sum equal to the amount of the difference must be carried by the successor company to a reserve (the 'statutory reserve')[4]. The successor company may apply the statutory reserve only in paying up unissued shares of the company to be allotted to its members as fully paid bonus shares[5].

For the purposes of any statutory accounts[6] of the successor company:

(1) all the property, rights and liabilities to which the National Research Development Corporation or the National Enterprise Board was entitled or subject immediately before the end of the last financial year[7] of the corporation or the board ending before 6 January 1992[8] are to be taken to have been vested in the successor company, and to have been so vested immediately after the end of that year[9];

(2) the value or amount of any asset or liability of the corporation or

board taken to have been vested in the successor company by virtue of head (1) above is to be taken to be the value or the amount assigned to that asset or liability for the purposes of the corresponding statement of accounts prepared in respect of the financial year referred to under that head[10].

The British Technology Group Act 1991 conferred on the Secretary of State a power to make loans to the successor company[11].

Any powers conferred on the Secretary of State by the successor company's articles of association restricting the sums of money which the company and its subsidiaries may borrow or raise are exercisable in the national interest, notwithstanding any rule of law and the provisions of any enactment[12].

1   Ie issued in pursuance of the British Technology Group Act 1991 s 3: see further para 840 ante.
2   Ie British Technology Group Ltd: see para 839 text and notes 3–5 ante.
3   Ie by virtue of the British Technology Group Act 1991 s 2: see para 839 ante.
4   Ibid s 8(1).
5   Ibid s 8(2). An exception was provided by that provision so that the statutory reserve might be applied as if it were profits available for distribution, as directed by the Secretary of State with the consent of the Treasury; but the power to make such a direction is not exercisable at any time after the company ceased to be wholly owned by the Crown: ss 8(2), (3), 16(2). As to distributions to be made out of profits within the meaning of the Companies Act 1985 s 263(1) see COMPANIES vol 7(1) (1996 Reissue) para 701.
      No part of the statutory reserve may count as an undistributable reserve of the successor company for the purposes of s 264(3)(d) (see COMPANIES vol 7(1) (1996 Reissue) para 702), but for the purpose of determining under s 264 whether the company may make a distribution at any time, any amount standing to the credit of the reserve (excluding any amount which under the British Technology Group Act 1991 s 8(2) is authorised to be, but has not yet been, applied as if it were profits available for distribution) is to be treated for the purposes of the Companies Act 1985 s 264(3)(c) as if it were unrealised profits of the company: British Technology Group Act 1991 s 8(4).
6   Ie any accounts prepared by the successor company for the purposes of any provisions of the Companies Act 1985, including group accounts: British Technology Group Act 1991 s 8(7).
7   'Financial year' in relation to the corporation means a year ending on 31 March; in relation to the board it means the accounting year as defined in the Industry Act 1975 s 37(1) (repealed): British Technology Group Act 1991 s 16(1).
8   Ie the appointed day for the vesting of the property, rights and liabilities of the corporation and the board in the successor company: see para 839 note 2 ante.
9   British Technology Group Act 1991 s 8(5)(a).
10 Ibid s 8(5)(b). The amount to be included in respect of any item is to be determined as if anything done by the corporation or the board had been done by the successor company, and, accordingly, the amount to be included in any reserves as representing the successor company's accumulated realised profits is to be determined as if any profits realised and retained by the corporation or board had been realised and retained by the company: s 8(6).
11 See ibid s 9. This power was exercisable only while the successor company was wholly owned by the Crown: s 9(1).
12 Ibid s 10(1). Any alteration of the articles of association of the successor company which has the effect of conferring or extending the power mentioned in s 10(1) after the company ceased to be wholly owned by the Crown must be disregarded: s 10(2).

842.   Corporation tax liability of successor company. The successor company[1] is to be treated for the purposes of the Corporation Tax Acts[2] as if it were the same person as the National Research Development Corporation or the National Enterprise Board[3]. However, the company's chargeable gains are to be computed without regard to any allowable losses of the corporation or the board[4]. Shares issued by the successor company must be treated as if they had been issued wholly in consideration of a subscription paid to that company of an amount equal to the nominal value of the shares[5]. Any debenture[6] issued by the company must be treated as if it had been issued wholly in consideration of a loan made to that company of an amount equal to the principal sum payable under the debenture and wholly and exclusively for the purposes of the trade carried on by the company[7].

1   Ie the British Technology Group Ltd: see para 839 text and notes 3–5 ante.
2   For the meaning of 'Corporation Tax Acts' see the Interpretation Act 1978 s 5, Sch 1; and INCOME TAXATION.
3   British Technology Group Act 1991 s 12(1).
4   Ibid s 12(2) (amended by the Taxation of Chargeable Gains Act 1992 s 290(1), Sch 10 para 25). See CAPITAL GAINS TAXATION vol 5(1) (Reissue) para 148.
5   British Technology Group Act 1991 s 12(3).
6   'Debenture' includes debenture stock: ibid s 16(1).
7   Ibid s 12(4).

843.   Application of Trustee Investments Act 1961.   For the purpose of applying the Trustee Investments Act 1961[1] in relation to investment in shares or debentures of the successor company[2] during the calendar year in which the appointed day[3] falls (the first investment year), or during any year following that year, the successor company will be deemed to have paid a dividend in any year preceding the first investment year which is included in the relevant five years[4], and in the first investment year, if that year is included in the relevant five years and the company does not in fact pay such a dividend in that year[5].

1   Ie the Trustee Investments Act 1961 Sch 1 Pt IV para 3(b), which provides that shares and debentures of a company are not to count as wider-range and narrower-range investments respectively within the meaning of the Act unless the company has paid dividends in each of the five years immediately preceding that in which the investment is made; see TRUSTS vol 48 (2000 Reissue) paras 907–908. The Trustee Investments Act 1961 was repealed by the Trustee Act 2000 as from 1 February 2001 (see the Trustee Act 2000 (Commencement) Order 2001, SI 2001/49) and replaced by the general power of investment under Pt II (ss 3–7) of that Act; see TRUSTS vol 48 (2000 Reissue) paras 924–926.
2   Ie the British Technology Group Ltd: see para 839 text and notes 3–5 ante.
3   As to the appointed day see para 839 text and note 2 ante.
4   Ie the five years immediately preceding the year in which the investment in question is made or proposed to be made: British Technology Group Act 1991 s 13(2).
5   Ibid s 13(1).

(vi)   The Urban Regeneration Agency

844.   Creation of the Urban Regeneration Agency.   The English Industrial Estates Corporation ceased to exist on 25 April 1994[1] and all the property, rights and liabilities to which it was entitled or subject immediately before that date became the property, rights and liabilities of the Urban Regeneration Agency ('the agency')[2]. The functions of the corporation are conferred upon the agency[3].

1   Leasehold Reform, Housing and Urban Development Act 1993 s 184(1); Leasehold Reform, Housing and Urban Development Act 1993 (Commencement No 4) Order 1994, SI 1994/935.
2   Leasehold Reform, Housing and Urban Development Act 1993 ss 184(2), 185.
3   See ibid s 158(1). The agency is not to be regarded as the servant or agent of the Crown or as enjoying any status, immunity or privilege of the Crown, and its property is not to be regarded as the property of, or property held on behalf of, the Crown: s 158(3).

845.   Constitution of the Urban Regeneration Agency. The Urban Regeneration Agency consists of such number of members, being not less than six, as the Secretary of State[1] may, from time to time, appoint[2]. He must appoint one member as chairman and may, if he thinks fit, appoint another as deputy chairman[3]. A member of the agency may resign his office by notice in writing to the Secretary of State[4] and the Secretary of State may remove a member from office if he is satisfied that the member:

(1)   is unable or unfit to carry out the functions of a member[5],

(2)   has not complied with the terms of his appointment[6], or

(3)   has become bankrupt or made an arrangement with his creditors[7].

A member of the agency is disqualified for membership of the House of Commons[8].

The agency must pay to its members such remuneration and such allowances as the Secretary of State may determine[9]. The agency may:

(a)   pay such pensions, allowances or gratuities to or in respect of any persons who have been or are its members as the Secretary of State may determine[10];

(b)   make such payments as he determines towards provision for the payment of pensions, allowances or gratuities to or in respect of any such persons[11].

With the consent of the Secretary of State, the agency must appoint a chief executive[12] who is responsible to the agency for the general exercise of its functions[13]. The agency may, with the approval of the Secretary of State, appoint staff[14] and, with the consent of the Secretary of State, pay to members of its staff such remuneration and allowances as it may determine[15]. Anything authorised or required to be done by the agency may be done by any member of the agency, or of its staff, or by any committee or sub-committee, authorised for the purpose by the agency[16].

The Secretary of State may give directions as to the exercise by the agency of its power[17] to regulate procedure and such directions may be of a general or particular nature, and may be varied or revoked by subsequent directions[18]. A member of the agency or any committee or sub-committee who is directly or indirectly interested in any matter brought up for consideration at a meeting of the agency, or of the committee or sub-committee, must disclose the nature of his interest to the meeting[19].

The application of the seal of the agency is authenticated by the signature of any member of the agency or of its staff who has been duly authorised, whether generally or specially, for the purpose[20]. Every document purporting to be an instrument issued by the agency and duly sealed with the agency seal or signed on behalf of the agency must be received in evidence and, unless the contrary is proved, is deemed to be an instrument so issued[21].

1   The Secretary of State here concerned, formerly the Secretary of State for the Environment, and then the Secretary of State for the Environment, Transport and the Regions, is now the Secretary of State for Transport, Local Government and the Regions: see the Secretaries of State for Transport, Local Government and the Regions and for Environment, Food and Rural Affairs Order 2001, SI 2001/2568.

2   Leasehold Reform, Housing and Urban Development Act 1993 s 158(2), Sch 17 para 1(1).

3   Ibid Sch 17 para 1(2). Subject to these provisions, a member of the agency holds and vacates office in accordance with the terms of his appointment: Sch 17 para 1(3). A person who ceases to be a member of the agency is eligible for re-appointment: Sch 17 para 1(4).

4   Ibid Sch 17 para 1(5). A person ceases to be chairman or deputy chairman of the agency if he resigns as such by notice in writing to the Secretary of State or if he ceases to be a member of the agency: Sch 17 para 1(7).

5   Ibid Sch 17 para 1(6)(a).
6   Ibid Sch 17 para 1(6)(b).
7   Ibid Sch 17 para 1(6)(c).
8   House of Commons Disqualification Act 1975 s 1, Sch 1 Pt II (amended for this purpose, by the Leasehold Reform, Housing and Urban Development Act 1993 Sch 17 para 8); see PARLIAMENT vol 34 (Reissue) para 610.
9   Leasehold Reform, Housing and Urban Development Act 1993 Sch 17 para 2(1). If, when a person ceases to be a member of the agency, the Secretary of State determines that there are special circumstances which make it right that he should receive compensation, the agency must pay to him a sum by way of compensation of such an amount as the Secretary of State determines: Sch 17 para 2(3). Treasury approval is required for any determination of the Secretary of State under these provisions: Sch 17 para 2(4).
10 Ibid Sch 17 para 2(2)(a).
11 Ibid Sch 17 para 2(2)(b).
12 Ibid Sch 17 para 3(2).
13 Ibid Sch 17 para 3(1).
14 Ibid Sch 17 para 3(3). The terms and condition of appointment of any person appointed by the agency under these provisions are to be determined by the agency, with the consent of the Secretary of State: Sch 17 para 3(4). Treasury approval is required for the giving of such consent: see Sch 17 para 3(8).
15 Ibid Sch 17 para 3(5). The agency may (1) pay such pensions, allowances or gratuities to or in respect of any persons who have been or are members of its staff; (2) make such payments towards provision for the payment of pensions, allowances or gratuities to or in respect of any such persons, as it may, with the consent of the Secretary of State, determine: Sch 17 para 3(6). Treasury approval is required for the giving of consent under Sch 17 para 3(5) or (6): Sch 17 para 3(8). Any reference to pensions, allowances or gratuities to or in respect of any such persons as are mentioned includes a reference to payments by way of compensation to or in respect of any members of the agency's staff who suffer loss of office or employment or diminution of emoluments: Sch 17 para 3(7).
16 Ibid Sch 17 para 4.
17 Subject to these provisions, the agency may regulate both its own procedure, including quorum, and that of any committee or sub-committee: ibid Sch 17 para 5(1). With the consent of the Secretary of State, persons who are not members of the agency may be appointed as members of a committee or sub-committee of the agency, but any such committee or sub-committee may not consist entirely of persons who are neither members of the agency or its staff: Sch 17 para 5(4). The agency may pay to any person who is a member of a committee or sub-committee but who is not a member of the agency such remuneration and allowances as the Secretary of State may, with Treasury approval, determine: Sch 17 para 5(5).
18 Ibid Sch 17 para 5(2). The validity of any proceedings of the agency or of any committee or sub-committee of it is not affected by (1) a vacancy amongst the members of the agency, committee or sub-committee; (2) a defect in the appointment of a member of the agency, committee or sub-committee; or (3) a contravention of directions under these provisions, or of Sch 17 para 6(2) (see note 19 infra): Sch 17 para 5(3).
19 Ibid Sch 17 para 6(1). Where the matter in respect of which such a disclosure is made is a contract or agreement of any description, the member must not take part in any deliberation or decision of the agency, committee or sub-committee with respect to that matter: Sch 17 para 6(2). Where the matter in respect of which such disclosure is made is one other than a contract or agreement, the member may take part in any deliberation or decision of the agency, committee or sub-committee with respect to the matter unless the rest of the members decide that the interest disclosed might prejudicially affect the member's consideration of the matter: Sch 17 para 6(3).
20 Ibid Sch 17 para 7(1).
21 Ibid Sch 17 para 7(2).

846.   Objects of the Urban Regeneration Agency. The main object of the Urban Regeneration Agency is to secure the regeneration of land in England which is land of one or more of the following descriptions[1]:

(1)   vacant or unused[2];
(2)   situated in an urban area which is underused or ineffectively used[3];
(3)   contaminated, derelict, neglected or unsightly[4]; or
(4)   likely to become derelict, neglected, or unsightly by reason of actual

or apprehended collapse at the surface as the result of the carrying out of relevant operations[5] which have ceased to be carried out[6], and which the agency, having regard to guidance and acting in accordance with directions given by the Secretary of State[7], determines to be suitable for regeneration[8].

The agency also has the object of securing the development of land in England which it determines[9] to be suitable for such development[10].

The objects of the agency are to be achieved in particular by the following means, or by such of them as seem to the agency to be appropriate in any particular case, namely:

(a)   by securing that land and buildings are brought into effective use[11];

(b)   by developing, or encouraging the development of, existing and new industry and commerce[12];

(c)   by creating an attractive and safe environment[13];

(d)   by facilitating the provision of housing and providing, or facilitating the provision of, social and recreational facilities[14].

1   Leasehold Reform, Housing and Urban Development Act 1993 s 159(1)(a), (2).
2   Ibid s 159(2)(a).
3   Ibid s 159(2)(b).
4   Ibid s 159(2)(c).
5   'Relevant operations' has the same meaning as in the Derelict Land Act 1982 s 1(11) (see para 877 note 4 post): Leasehold Reform, Housing and Urban Development Act 1993 s 159(2).
6   Ibid s 159(2)(d).
7   Ie directions given under ibid s 167. As to the Secretary of State see para 845 note 1 ante.
8   Ibid s 159(1)(b).
9   Ie having regard to guidance given by the Secretary of State under ibid s 167(1) (see para 847 text and note 16 post), acting in accordance with directions given by him under s 167(2) (see para 848 text and note 7 post), and with his consent: s 159(3)(a)–(c). As to consents generally see para 847 note 9 post.
10 Ibid s 159(3).
11 Ibid s 159(4)(a).
12 Ibid s 159(4)(b).
13 Ibid s 159(4)(c).
14 Ibid s 159(4)(d).

847.   General powers of the Urban Regeneration Agency. Subject to the provisions of the Leasehold Reform, Housing and Urban Development Act 1993[1], for the purpose of achieving its objects the Urban Regeneration Agency may[2].

(1)   acquire, hold, manage, reclaim, improve and dispose of land, plant, machinery, equipment, and other property[3];

(2)   carry out the development or redevelopment of land, including the conversion or demolition of existing buildings[4];

(3)   carry out building and other operations[5];

(4)   provide means of access, services, or other facilities for land[6];

(5)   seek to ensure the provision of water, electricity, gas, sewerage and other services[7];

(6)   carry on any business or undertaking for the purpose of its objects[8];

(7)   with the consent of the Secretary of State[9], form or acquire interests in bodies corporate[10];

(8)   act with other persons, whether in partnership or otherwise[11];

(9)   give financial assistance to other persons[12];

(10) act as agent for other persons[13];

(11) provide advisory or other services and facilities[14]; and

(12) generally do anything necessary or expedient for the purposes of its objects or for purposes incidental to those purposes[15].

The agency must have regard to guidance from time to time given by the Secretary of State in deciding which land is suitable for regeneration or development, and which of its functions it is to exercise for securing the regeneration or development of any particular land and how it is to exercise those functions[16]. A transaction between a person and the agency is not invalidated by reason only of the agency's failure to observe its objects or the requirement to exercise its functions for the purpose of achieving its objects, and such a person is not concerned to see or inquire whether there has been any such failure[17].

1 Ie the Leasehold Reform, Housing and Urban Development Act 1993 Pt III (ss 158–185).
2 Ibid s 160(1). Section 160(1) relates only to the capacity of the agency as a statutory corporation, and nothing in ss 159, 160 (see the text and notes 3–15 infra, and paras 846 ante, 848 post) authorises it to disregard any enactment or rule of law: s 160(3).
3 Ibid s 160(1)(a). 'Improve', in relation to land, includes refurbish, equip and fit out: s 160(4). In ss 160–185, 'land' includes land which does not fall within s 159(1) or (3) (see para 846 ante): s 160(4).
4 Ibid s 160(1)(b).
5 Ibid s 160(1)(c).
6 Ibid s 160(1)(d).
7 Ibid s 160(1)(e).
8 Ibid s 160(1)(f).
9 As to the Secretary of State see para 845 note 1 ante. Any consent of the Secretary of State under ibid Pt III may (1) be given unconditionally or subject to conditions; (2) be given in relation to a particular case or such descriptions of case as may be specified in the consent; and (3) except in relation to anything done or agreed to be done on the authority of the consent, be varied or revoked by a notice given by the Secretary of State to the agency: s 166.
10 Ibid s 160(1)(g).
11 Ibid s 160(1)(h).
12 Ibid s 160(1)(i).
13 Ibid s 160(1)(j).
14 Ibid s 160(1)(k).
15 Ibid s 160(1)(l).
16 Ibid s 167(1).
17 Ibid s 168(1).

848. Restrictions on powers of the Urban Regeneration Agency. The Urban Regeneration Agency is not empowered[1]:

(1) to provide housing otherwise than by acquiring existing housing accommodation and making it available on a temporary basis for purposes incidental to the purposes of its objects[2];

(2) to acquire an interest in a body corporate which at the time of the acquisition is carrying on a trade or business, if the effect of the acquisition would be to make the body corporate a subsidiary[3] of the agency[4]; or

(3) except with the consent of the Secretary of State[5], to dispose of any land otherwise than for the best consideration which can reasonably be obtained[6].

Without prejudice to any provision requiring the consent of the Secretary of State for anything to be done, he may give directions to the agency for restricting the exercise by it of any of its functions, or for requiring it to exercise those functions in any manner specified in the directions[7].

1 Ie notwithstanding the provisions of the Leasehold Reform, Housing and Urban Development Act 1993 ss 159, 160: see paras 846–847 ante.

2   Ibid s 160(2)(a).

3   'Subsidiary' has the meaning given by the Companies Act 1985 s 736 (as substituted) (see COMPANIES vol 7(2) (1996 Reissue) para 827): Leasehold Reform, Housing and Urban Development Act 1993 s 160(4).

4   Ibid s 160(2)(b).

5   As to the Secretary of State see para 845 note 1 ante. As to consents generally see para 847 note 9 ante.

6   Leasehold Reform, Housing and Urban Development Act 1993 s 160(2)(c). As to the meaning of 'land' in this provision see para 847 note 3 ante.

7   Ibid s 167(2). Directions may be of a general or particular nature and may be varied or revoked by subsequent directions: s 167(3). A transaction between a person and the agency is not invalidated by reason only that it was carried out in contravention of directions under s 167(2) and a person is not concerned to see or inquire whether any directions have been given or complied with: s 168(2).

849. Finances. After consultation with the Urban Regeneration Agency, the Secretary of State[1] may, with Treasury approval, determine the financial duties of the agency[2]. The Secretary of State may, with Treasury approval, out of money provided by Parliament, pay to the agency, in respect of the exercise of its functions and in respect of its administrative expenses, such sums as he may with such approval determine[3].

The agency may borrow temporarily, by way of overdraft or otherwise, such sums as it may require for meeting its obligations and exercising its functions[4]:

(1)   in sterling from the Secretary of State[5]; or

(2)   with the consent of the Secretary of State or in accordance with a general authority given by him, either in sterling or in a currency other than sterling from a person other than the Secretary of State[6].

The agency may borrow otherwise than by way of temporary loan such sums as it may require[7]:

(a)   in sterling from the Secretary of State[8]; or

(b)   with the consent of the Secretary of State, in a currency other than sterling, from a person other than the Secretary of State[9].

The aggregate of borrowed sums[10] must not exceed £200m or such greater sum not exceeding £300m as the Secretary of State may by order specify[11].

The Treasury may guarantee, in such manner and on such on conditions as it thinks fit, the repayment of the principal of, and the payment of interest on, any sums which the agency borrows from a person other than the Secretary of State[12]. Immediately after a guarantee is given[13], the Treasury must lay a statement of the guarantee before each House of Parliament, and where any sum[14] is issued for fulfilling a guarantee so given, the Treasury must lay before each House of Parliament a statement relating to that sum, as soon as possible after the end of each financial year[15], beginning with that in which the sum was issued and ending with that in which all liability in respect of the principal of the sum and in respect of interest on it is finally discharged[16].

Where it appears to the Secretary of State, after consultation with the Treasury and the agency, that the agency has a surplus, whether on capital or on revenue account[17], he may, with Treasury approval and after consulting with the agency, direct the agency to pay to him such sum (not exceeding the amount of the surplus) as may be specified in the direction[18]. The whole or part of any payment made to the Secretary of State, if with Treasury approval he so determines, must be treated as made:

    (i)   by way of repayment of such part of the principal of loans which the Secretary of State has power to lend to the agency[19]; and

    (ii)   in respect of the repayments due at such times,

as may be so determined[20].

1   As to the Secretary of State see para 845 note 1 ante.

2   Leasehold Reform, Housing and Urban Development Act 1993 s 158(2), Sch 18 para 2(1). Different determinations may be made in relation to different functions of the agency: Sch 18 para 2(1). The Secretary of State must give the agency notice of every determination, which may (1) relate to a period beginning before the date on which it is made; (2) contain incidental or supplemental provisions; and (3) be varied or revoked by a subsequent determination: Sch 18 para 2(2).

3   Ibid Sch 18 para 3(1). The payment may be made on such terms as the Secretary of State may, with Treasury approval, determine: Sch 18 para 3(2).

4   Ibid Sch 18 para 4(1).

5   Ibid Sch 18 para 4(1)(a). The Secretary of State may lend to the agency any sums it has power to borrow from him under Sch 18 para 4(1) or (2): Sch 18 para 4(3). The Treasury may issue to him out of the National Loans Fund any sums necessary to enable him to make such loans: Sch 18 para 4(4). Loans must be repaid to him at such times and by such methods, and interest on the loans must be paid to him at such times and at such rates, as he may determine: Sch 18 para 4(5). All such sums received must be paid into the National Loans Fund: Sch 18 para 4(6). Treasury approval is required for the making of any loan under Sch 18 para 4(3) or the raking of any determination under Sch 18 para 4(5): Sch 18 para 4(7). As to the National Loans Fund see generally CONSTITUTIONAL LAW AND HUMAN RIGHTS vol 8(2) (Reissue) paras 727–739.

6   Ibid Sch 18 para 4(1)(b). Treasury approval is required for the giving of any consent or authority under Sch 18 para 4(1) or (2): Sch 18 para 4(7). As to consents generally see para 847 note 9 ante.

7   Ibid Sch 18 para 4(2). See also notes 5–6 supra.

8   Ibid Sch 18 para 4(2)(a).

9   Ibid Sch 18 para 4(2)(b). See also note 6 supra.

10 'Borrowed sums' means sums borrowed by the agency under ibid Sch 18 para 4, less any repayments made or treated as made: Sch 18 para 7(2).

11 Ibid Sch 18 para 7(1). No such order may be made unless a draft has been laid before and approved by resolution of the House of Commons: Sch 18 para 7(3). At the date at which this volume states the law, no such order had been made.

12 Ibid Sch 18 para 5(1).

13 Ie under ibid Sch 18 para 5.

14 Any sums required by the Treasury for fulfilling a guarantee under these provisions must be charged on and issued out of the Consolidated Fund: ibid Sch 18 para 5(3). If any sums are issued in fulfilment of a guarantee given under these provisions, the agency must make to the Treasury, at such times and in such manner as the Treasury may from time to time direct, payments of such amounts as the Treasury so directs or towards repayment of the sums so issued and payment of interest, at such rates as the Treasury so directs, on what is outstanding for the time being in respect of the sums issued: Sch 18 para 5(4). Any sums received by the Treasury pursuant to such payments must be paid into the Consolidated Fund: Sch 18 para 5(5). As to the Consolidated Fund see CONSTITUTIONAL LAW AND HUMAN RIGHTS vol 8(2) (Reissue) para 711 et seq; and PARLIAMENT vol 34 (Reissue) para 952 et seq.

15 The first financial year of the agency began with 10 November 1993 (the coming into force of ibid Sch 18) and ended with 31 March 1994: Sch 18 para 1(a); Leasehold Reform, Housing and Urban Development Act 1993 (Commencement and Transitional Provisions No 3) Order 1993, SI 1993/2762. Subsequent financial years are successive periods of 12 months from 1 April 1994: Leasehold Reform, Housing and Urban Development Act 1993 Sch 18 para 1(b).

16 Ibid Sch 18 para 5(2).

17 Ie after making allowance by way of transfer to reserve or otherwise for its future requirements: ibid Sch 18 para 6(1).

18 Ibid Sch 18 para 6(1), (a). Any sum received by the Secretary of State under these provisions must, subject to the provisions relating to repayment of loans (see note 20 infra), be paid into the Consolidated Fund: Sch 18 para 6(3).

19 Ie under ibid Sch 18 para 4(3): see note 5 supra.

20 Ibid Sch 18 para 6(4). Any sum treated under these provisions as a repayment of a loan must be paid by the Secretary of State into the National Loans Fund: Sch 18 para 6(5).

850. Accounts and reports. The Secretary of State[1] must prepare, in respect of each financial year[2], an account of the sums issued to him to make loans to the Urban Regeneration Agency[3], sums received in repayment of such loans[4] and the disposal by him of such funds, and the surplus funds paid into the National Loans Fund and the Consolidated Fund[5], in such form and manner as the Treasury may direct[6]. The Secretary of State must send the account to the Comptroller and Auditor General before the end of November next following the end of that year[7]. The Comptroller and Auditor General must examine, certify and report on the account, and lay copies of it and of his report before each House of Parliament[8].

The agency must keep proper accounts and other records in relation to them[9]. The accounts and records must show, in respect of the financial year to which they relate, a true and fair view of the agency's activities[10]. The agency must prepare in respect of each financial year a statement of accounts complying with any requirement which the Secretary of State, with Treasury approval, has notified in writing to the agency, relating to the information to be contained in the statement, the manner in which the information is to be presented and the methods and principles according to which the statement is to be prepared[11]. The agency's accounts and statements of accounts must be audited by an auditor to be appointed annually by the Secretary of State[12]. As soon as the accounts and statement of accounts of the agency for any financial year have been audited, it must send a copy of the statement, together with a copy of any report made by the auditor on the statement of accounts to the Secretary of State[13]. As soon as possible after the end of each financial year, the agency must: (1) make to the Secretary of State a report dealing generally with its operations during that year; and (2) include in the report a copy of its audited statement of accounts for that year and such information as the Secretary of State may specify[14].

In addition, the agency must provide the Secretary of State with such information relating to its activities as he may require, and for that purpose: (a) must permit any person authorised by him to inspect and make copies of the accounts, books, documents or papers of the agency; and (b) must afford such explanation of them as that person or the Secretary of State may reasonably require[15].

1   As to the Secretary of State see para 845 note 1 ante.
2   As to the financial years of the agency see para 849 note 15 ante.
3   Ie under the Leasehold Reform, Housing and Urban Development Act 1993 s 158(2), Sch 18 para 4(4); see para 849 note 5 ante.
4   Ie under ibid Sch 18 para 4(5): see para 849 note 5 ante.
5   Ibid Sch 18 para 8(1). As to the surplus funds see Sch 18 para 6; and para 849 text and notes 17–20 ante.
6   Ibid Sch 18 para 8(4).
7   Ibid Sch 18 para 8(2).
8   Ibid Sch 18 para 8(3).
9   Ibid Sch 18 para 9(1).
10 Ibid Sch 18 para 9(2).
11 Ibid Sch 18 para 9(3). Subject to any requirement notified to the agency in preparing any such statement of accounts, the agency must follow such course as may for the time being be approved by the Secretary of State with Treasury consent: Sch 18 para 9(4).
12 Ibid Sch 18 para 10(1). A person is not qualified for appointment as an auditor unless he is eligible for appointment as a company auditor under the Companies Act 1989 Pt II

(ss 24–54); and if the agency were a body to which the Companies Act 1985 s 384 (as substituted) (duty to appoint auditors) applies (see COMPANIES vol 7(2) (1996 Reissue) para 1027), a person would not be ineligible for appointment as company auditor of the agency by reason of the Companies Act 1989 s 27 (ineligibility on ground of lack of independence): Leasehold Reform, Housing and Urban Development Act 1993 Sch 18 para 10(2).

13   Ibid Sch 18 para 11.
14   Ibid Sch 18 para 12(1). The Secretary of State must lay a copy of the report before each House of Parliament: Sch 18 para 12(2).
15   Ibid Sch 18 para 13.

851. Vesting of land by order. The Secretary of State[1] may by order[2] provide that land[3] specified in the order which is vested in a local authority[4], statutory undertakers[5], or other public body, or in a wholly owned subsidiary of a public body, is to vest in the Urban Regeneration Agency[6].

Such an order may not specify land vested in statutory undertakers which is used for the purpose of carrying on their statutory undertakings or which is held for that purpose[7]. In the case of land vested in statutory undertakers, the power to make such an order is exercised by the Secretary of State and the appropriate minister[8]. In addition, no such order may be made in relation to a universal service provider within the meaning of the Postal Services Act 2000[9].

Compensation under the Land Compensation Act 1961[10] is assessed with reference to values current on the date the order comes into force[11].

1   As to the Secretary of State see para 845 note 1 ante.
2   Such an order must be made by statutory instrument, but no such order may be made unless a draft of the order has been laid before and approved by resolution of each House of Parliament: Leasehold Reform, Housing and Urban Development Act 1993 s 161(9).
3   As to the meaning of 'land' in this provision see para 847 note 3 ante.
4   'Local authority' means a county council, a district council, a London Borough Council or the Common Council of the City of London: Leasehold Reform, Housing and Urban Development Act 1993 s 161(7).
5   'Statutory undertakers', except where the context otherwise requires, means:
    (1)   persons authorised by any enactment to carry on any railway, light railway, tramway, road transport, water transport, canal, inland navigation, dock, harbour, pier or lighthouse undertaking, or any undertaking for the supply of hydraulic power;
    (2)   British Shipbuilders, the Civil Aviation Authority and the British Coal Corporation;
    (3)   a person who holds a licence under the Transport Act 2000 Pt I Ch I (air traffic services) to the extent that the person is carrying out activities authorised by the licence;
    (4)   any other authority, body or undertakers specified in an order made by the Secretary of State;
    (5)   any wholly owned subsidiary of any person, authority or body mentioned in heads (1)–(4) supra;
and 'statutory undertaking' must be construed accordingly: Leasehold Reform, Housing and Urban Development Act 1993 s 161(7) (amended by the Coal Industry Act 1994 s 67(1), (8), Sch 9 para 45, Sch 11 Pt IV as from the dissolution date to be appointed under s 23(2), to remove the British Coal Corporation from the definition; the Transport Act 2000 s 37, Sch 5 para 17; and the Postal Services Act 2000 (Consequential Modifications No 1) Order 2001, SI 2001/1149, art 3(2), Sch 2). An order made under head (3) supra must be made by statutory instrument which is subject to annulment in pursuance of a resolution of either House of Parliament: Leasehold Reform, Housing and Urban Development Act 1993 s 161(10). 'Wholly owned subsidiary' has the meaning given by the Companies Act 1985 s 736 (as substituted) (see COMPANIES vol 7(2) (Reissue) para 827): Leasehold Reform, Housing and Urban Development Act 1993 s 161(7).
6   Ibid s 161(1). An order has the same effect as a declaration under the Compulsory Purchase (Vesting Declarations) Act 1981 except that, in relation to such an order, the enactments mentioned in the Leasehold Reform, Housing and Urban Development

Act 1993 Sch 19 will have effect with modifications as specified in that Schedule: s 161(4). See generally COMPULSORY ACQUISITION OF LAND.

7   Ibid s 161(2).
8   Ibid s 161(3). The 'appropriate minister':
   (1)   in relation to statutory undertakers who are or are deemed to be statutory undertakers for the purpose of any provision of the Town and Country Planning Act 1990 Pt XI (ss 262–283) (as amended), must be construed as if that expression is contained in that Part;
   (2)   in relation to any other statutory undertakers, must be construed in accordance with an order made by the Secretary of State,
   and the reference to the Secretary of State and the appropriate minister must be similarly construed: Leasehold Reform, Housing and Urban Development Act 1993 s 161(7). An order under head (2) supra is made by statutory instrument which is subject to annulment in pursuance of a resolution of either House of Parliament: s 161(10). If any question arises as to which minister is the appropriate minister in relation to any statutory undertakers, that question must be determined by the Treasury: s 161(8).
9   Ibid s 161(6A) (added by the Postal Services Act 2000 (Consequential Modifications No 1) Order 2001, SI 2001/1149, art 3(1), Sch 1 para 98(1), (2)).
10 Ie the Land Compensation Act 1961 (as amended) as applied by the Leasehold Reform, Housing and Urban Development Act 1993 s 161(4), Sch 19.
11 Ibid s 161(5). No compensation is payable, by virtue of an order under s 161(1), under the Land Compensation Act 1961 Pt IV (ss 23–29) (repealed; revived by the Planning and Compensation Act 1991 s 66, Sch 14; amended by the Leasehold Reform, Housing and Urban Development Act 1993 ss 181, 187(2), Sch 22): Leasehold Reform, Housing and Urban Development Act 1993 s 161(6).

852.   Acquisition of land.   The Urban Regeneration Agency may, for the purpose of achieving its objects, or for purposes incidental to that purpose:

   (1)   acquire land by agreement or, on being authorised by the Secretary of State[1], compulsorily[2];

   (2)   be authorised by the Secretary of State to acquire compulsorily, by means of a compulsory purchase order[3], such new rights over land[4] as are specified in that order[5];

   (3)   where such land forms part of a common, open space or fuel or field garden allotment, acquire, by agreement or, on being authorised by the Secretary of State to do so, compulsorily, land for giving in exchange for the land or, as the case may be, rights acquired[6].

1   As to the Secretary of State see para 845 note 1 ante.
2   Leasehold Reform, Housing and Urban Development Act 1993 s 162(1). The Acquisition of Land Act 1981 applies, subject to modifications, to the compulsory acquisition of land under these provisions: Leasehold Reform, Housing and Urban Development Act 1993 ss 162(4), 169, Sch 20 Pt I. For land purchased by agreement, the provisions of the Compulsory Purchase Act 1965 Pt I (ss 1–32) (as amended), so far as applicable, other than s 31 (as amended), apply to such acquisition and in that Part as so applied 'land' has the meaning given by the Interpretation Act 1978: Leasehold Reform, Housing and Urban Development Act 1973 s 162(6). See generally COMPULSORY ACQUISITION OF LAND.
3   'Compulsory purchase order' has the same meaning as in the Acquisition of Land Act 1981 (see s 2(1)): Leasehold Reform, Housing and Urban Development Act 1993 s 162(7). See generally COMPULSORY ACQUISITION OF LAND.
4   For these purposes 'new rights over land' means rights over land which are not in existence when the order specifying them is made: ibid s 162(7).
5   Ibid s 162(2). The Acquisition of Land Act 1981 Sch 3 (as amended) applies to compulsory acquisitions of such rights, but with the modification that the reference in para 4(3) to 'statutory undertakers' includes a reference to the agency: Leasehold Reform, Housing and Urban Development Act 1993 s 162(6). See generally COMPULSORY ACQUISITION OF LAND.
6   Ibid s 162(3).

853. Power to enter and survey land. Any person duly authorised in writing by the Urban Regeneration Agency may at any reasonable time enter any land[1] for the purpose of surveying it, or estimating its value, in connection with any proposal to acquire that land or any other land or any claim for compensation in respect of such an acquisition[2]. The power to survey includes the power to search and bore the land for the purpose of ascertaining the nature of the subsoil or the presence of minerals in it[3]. A person who is authorised to enter any land must, if so required, produce evidence of his authority before entry[4], and may not demand admission as of right to any land which is occupied unless 28 days' notice of the intended entry is given to the occupier by the agency[5].

Any person who wilfully obstructs a person acting in exercise of his powers of entry is guilty of an offence and is liable on summary conviction to a fine not exceeding level 2 on the standard scale[6].

If any person who is admitted into a factory, workshop or workplace discloses to any person any information obtained by him in it as to any manufacturing process or trade secret, he is guilty of an offence[7].

Where land is damaged in the exercise of a right of entry or in the making of any survey, compensation in respect of that damage may be recovered by any person interested in the land from the agency[8].

1   As to the meaning of 'land' in this provision see para 847 note 3 ante.
2   Leasehold Reform, Housing and Urban Development Act 1993 s 163(1).
3   Ibid s 163(2). No person may carry out any works under these provisions unless notice of his intention to do so was included in the notice required to be given by the agency to the occupier (see text and notes 4–5 infra): s 163(10). The authority of the appropriate minister is required for the carrying out of any such works if the land in question is held by statutory undertakers and they object to the proposed works on the ground that the execution of the works would be seriously detrimental to the carrying on of their undertaking: s 162(11). 'Appropriate minister' has the same meaning as in the Town and Country Planning Act 1990 ss 265, 336(1), and 'statutory undertakers' has the same meaning as in s 262 (as amended): Leasehold Reform, Housing and Urban Development Act 1993 s 163(11).
4   Ibid s 163(3)(a).
5   Ibid s 163(3)(b).
6   Ibid s 163(4). As to the standard scale see para 16 note 21 ante
7   Ibid s 163(5). No offence is committed if such disclosure is made by a person in the course of performing his duty in connection with the purpose for which he is authorised to enter the premises: s 163(6). A person guilty of the offence is liable on summary conviction to a fine not exceeding the statutory maximum, or on conviction on indictment to imprisonment for a term not exceeding two years or a fine, or both: s 163(7). As to the statutory maximum see para 16 note 21 ante.
8   Ibid s 163(8). The provisions of the Town and Country Planning Act 1990 s 118 (determination of claims for compensation) (see TOWN AND COUNTRY PLANNING vol 46 (Reissue) para 706) apply in relation to such compensation as they do in relation to Pt IV (ss 107–118) (as amended): Leasehold Reform, Housing and Urban Development Act 1993 s 163(9).

854. Financial assistance. The consent of the Secretary of State[1] is required for the exercise of the power of the Urban Regeneration Agency to give financial assistance[2]. Such assistance may only be given in respect of qualifying expenditure[3] and on such terms and conditions as the agency, with the Secretary of State's consent, considers appropriate[4]. Financial assistance may be given in any form and may, in particular, be given by way of: (1) grants; (2) loans; (3) guarantees; or (4) incurring expenditure for the benefit of the person assisted, but the agency may not, in giving financial assistance, purchase loan or share capital in a company[5].

1   As to the Secretary of State see para 845 note 1 ante. As to consents generally see para 847 note 9 ante.
2   Leasehold Reform, Housing and Urban Development Act 1973 s 164(1). The Secretary of State's consent may only be given with Treasury approval: s 164(4).
3   Ibid s 164(1)(a). 'Qualifying expenditure' is expenditure incurred in connection with any of the following matters: (1) the acquisition of land; (2) the reclamation, improvement or refurbishment of land; (3) the development or redevelopment of land, including the conversion or demolition of existing buildings; (4) the equipment or fitting out of land; (5) the provision of means of access, services or other facilities for land; (6) environmental improvements: s 164(2). As to the meaning of 'land' in this provision see para 847 note 3 ante.
4   Ibid s 164(1)(b). The terms and conditions may include, in particular, provision as to: (1) the circumstances in which the assistance must be repaid, or otherwise made good, to the agency, and the manner in which that is to be done; (2) the circumstances in which the agency is entitled to recover the proceeds or part of the proceeds of any disposal of land in respect of which the assistance was provided: s 164(5). Any person receiving financial assistance must comply with the terms and conditions on which it is given and compliance may be enforced by the agency: s 164(6).
5   Ibid s 164(3).

855.   Connection of private streets to highway.   For the purpose of achieving its objects or for purposes incidental to that purpose[1], the Urban Regeneration Agency may serve a notice (a 'connection notice')[2] on the local highway authority[3] requiring the authority to connect a private street to an existing highway, whether or not it is a highway which for the purpose of the Highways Act 1980 is a highway maintainable at the public expense[4]. Before serving a connection notice the agency must consult the highway authority about the proposed contents of the notice[5]. Within the period of two months beginning with the date on which the connection notice was served, the local highway authority may appeal against the notice to the Secretary of State[6]. After considering any representations made to him by the agency and the local highway authority, the Secretary of State must determine an appeal by setting aside or confirming the connection notice, with or without modifications[7]. Where a connection notice becomes effective[8], the local highway authority must carry out the works specified in the notice within such period as may be specified, and may recover from the agency the expenses reasonably incurred by the authority in doing so[9].

1   As to the objects of the agency see para 846 ante.
2   A connection notice must specify: (1) the private street and the existing highway; (2) the works which appear to the agency to be necessary to make the connection; and (3) the period within which those works should be carried out: Leasehold Reform, Housing and Urban Development Act 1993 s 165(2).
3   'Local highway authority' has the same meaning as in the Highways Act 1980: Leasehold Reform, Housing and Urban Development Act 1993 s 165(9). See further HIGHWAYS, STREETS AND BRIDGES.
4   Ibid s 165(1).
5   Ibid s 165(3).
6   Ibid s 165(4). As to the Secretary of State see para 845 note 1 ante.
7   Ibid s 165(5).
8   Ie where (1) no appeal is made within the period of 2 months, upon expiry of that period; (2) where an appeal is made within that period but is withdrawn before it has been determined by the Secretary of State, on the date following the expiry of the period of 21 days beginning with the date on which the Secretary of State is notified of the withdrawal; (3) where an appeal is made and the connection notice is confirmed by a determination, on such date as the Secretary of State may specify in the determination: ibid s 165(6).
9   Ibid s 165(7). If the local highway authority does not carry out the works specified in the notice within the period so specified, the agency may itself carry out or complete those works or arrange for another person to do so: s 165(8).

(vii) Industry in Wales

A. CONSTITUTION, FUNCTIONS AND POWERS OF THE WELSH DEVELOPMENT AGENCY

856. Constitution and purposes of the Welsh Development Agency. The Welsh Development Agency was established in 1975[1] for the purpose of:

(1)   furthering the economic and social development of Wales or any part of Wales, and in that connection providing, maintaining and safeguarding employment[2],

(2)   promoting efficiency in business and international competitiveness in Wales[3], and

(3)   furthering the improvement of the environment in Wales, having regard to existing amenity[4].

The agency consists of a chairman, a deputy chairman and between seven and 13[5] other members[6], all appointed by the Secretary of State[7]. Provision is made for the remuneration of members and staff[8], the payment of compensation[9] and the payment of pensions[10]. The agency has a chief executive[11], and is a body corporate[12] with a common seal[13].

The agency may establish such committees for the discharge of any of its functions, or for giving it advice about the discharge of its functions, as it considers appropriate[14]. The members of a committee are appointed by the agency and may be members of the agency or, with the approval of the Secretary of State, persons who are not members[15].

Subject to any directions given by the Secretary of State[16], and to restrictions on the participation of a member who has an interest in any contract or matter which is before the agency[17], the agency determines its own quorum and arrangements relating to its meetings, and those of its committees[18].

1   See the Welsh Development Agency Act 1975 s 1(1). The Welsh Industrial Estates Corporation, which had been established by the Local Employment Act 1960 s 8 (repealed), and continued by the Local Employment Act 1972 s 10 (repealed), was dissolved, and its property, rights and liabilities vested in the agency: Welsh Development Agency Act 1975 s 7(1) (amended by the Planning (Consequential Provisions) Act 1990 s 4, Sch 2 para 34(1)). As to the transfer of staff from the corporation to the agency and compensation for loss of employment see the Welsh Development Agency Act 1975 s 7(2), Sch 2 (amended by the Employment Protection (Consolidation) Act 1978 s 159(2), Sch 16 para 22); and the Welsh Development Agency (Compensation) Regulations 1976, SI 1976/2107. Land in Wales held for the purposes of the Local Employment Act 1972 was vested in the agency by the Welsh Development Agency Act 1975 s 8. The agency may appoint agents and form committees (see the text and notes 14–15 infra).

2   Ibid s 1(2)(a) (amended by the Industry Act 1980 s 1(3)(a) and the Government of Wales Act 1998 s 126(2)(a)).

3   Welsh Development Agency Act 1975 s 1(2)(b) (amended by the Government of Wales Act 1998 s 126(2)(b)). 'Business' includes any industrial, commercial or professional activities (whether or not with a view to profit) and the activities of any government department or any local or other public authority: Welsh Development Agency Act 1975 s 27(1) (amended by the Government of Wales Act 1998 s 128, Sch 14 para 10).

4   Welsh Development Agency Act 1975 s 1(2)(d).

5   The Secretary of State may by order increase the maximum number of other members from nine: ibid s 2(1) (amended by the Government of Wales Act 1998 Sch 14 para 3). The number has been increased to 13 by the Welsh Development Agency (Membership) Order 1998, SI 1998/2490.

6   Welsh Development Agency Act 1975 s 2(1) (amended by the Development of Rural Wales Act 1976 s 23(1), (2) and the Government of Wales Act 1998 Sch 14 para 3). The members must include persons appearing to the Secretary of State to have wide experience of, and to have shown capacity in, industry, commerce, banking, accountancy, finance, the

organisation or representation of workers, administration, local government or environmental matters: Welsh Development Agency Act 1975 s 2(3). The Secretary of State must be satisfied, before and from time to time after making such an appointment, that no member (or prospective member) has or will have any financial interest likely to affect prejudicially the performance of his functions as a member; the member (or prospective member) in question must furnish the Secretary of State with information as required by the Secretary of State for carrying out this duty: s 2(10), Sch 1 para 1. The Secretary of State is in practice the Secretary of State for Wales; but the functions of the Secretary of State have been transferred to the National Assembly for Wales by the National Assembly for Wales (Transfer of Functions) Order 1999, SI 1999/672, art 2, Sch 1. As to the National Assembly for Wales see para 1 note 3 ante. Any expenses of the Secretary of State incurred in consequence of the Act must be defrayed out of money provided by Parliament: Welsh Development Agency Act 1975 s 21.

7   Ibid s 2(2) (amended by the Government of Wales Act 1998 s 152, Sch 18 Pt IV).

A member, chairman or deputy chairman holds office in accordance with the terms of his appointment and may resign by written notice to the Secretary of State: Welsh Development Agency Act 1975 Sch 1 paras 2, 3. The terms of appointment of a member becoming or ceasing to become chairman or deputy chairman may be varied by the Secretary of State: Sch 1 para 4. If the chairman or deputy chairman ceases to be a member, he ceases also to hold that office: Sch 1 para 5. The Secretary of State may declare vacant the office of member or chief executive by reason of: (1) absence without permission for more than three consecutive months; (2) bankruptcy or the making of an arrangement with creditors; (3) incapacity through physical or mental illness; or (4) other inability or unfitness to discharge the functions of a member: Sch 1 para 6(1), (2). Such a declaration must be notified in such manner as the Secretary of State thinks fit, and thereupon takes effect: Sch 1 para 6(3). Members and officers are eligible for re-appointment: Sch 1 para 7. Members are disqualified for membership of the House of Commons: House of Commons Disqualification Act 1975 s 1(1)(f), Sch 1 Pt II (amended for this purpose by the Welsh Development Agency Act 1975 Sch 1 para 13); see PARLIAMENT vol 34 (Reissue) para 610.

8   The agency must pay its members and staff such remuneration and reasonable allowances as the Secretary of State may determine with the approval of the Treasury: ibid Sch 1 para 9; Transfer of Functions (Minister for the Civil Service and Treasury) Order 1981, SI 1981/1670. Unless it is satisfied that adequate machinery already exists, the agency must seek consultation with appropriate organisations with a view to concluding agreements establishing machinery for the negotiation of terms and conditions of employment, with provision for arbitration: Welsh Development Agency Act 1975 Sch 1 para 12(3) (amended by the Government of Wales Act 1998 ss 128, 152, Sch 14 para 12, Sch 18).

9   Where a person ceases to be a member otherwise than on expiry of his term of office, the Secretary of State may, if it appears to him that there are special circumstances making it right to do so, with the approval of the Treasury, direct the agency to pay compensation to that person: Welsh Development Agency Act 1975 Sch 1 para 11 (amended by the Government of Wales Act 1998 Sch 14 para 12, Sch 18); Transfer of Functions (Minister for the Civil Service and Treasury) Order 1981.

10 The agency must make such provision as may be determined by the Secretary of State with the approval of the Treasury, for the payment of pensions, allowances or gratuities (including refunds of pension contributions with or without interest or other additions) to past or present members: Welsh Development Agency Act 1975 Sch 1 para 10 (amended by the Government of Wales Act 1998 Sch 14 para 12, Sch 18); Transfer of Functions (Minister for the Civil Service and Treasury) Order 1981. See also the Pensions Increase (Welsh Development Agency) Regulations 1978, SI 1978/211, made under the Pensions (Increase) Act 1971 s 5 (as amended). In the case of such of its employees as the Secretary of State may determine with the approval of the Treasury, the agency must also make provision for the payment of or towards such pensions, allowance and gratuities, or provide and maintain schemes for such payment: Welsh Development Agency Act 1975 Sch 1 para 12(1); Transfer of Functions (Minister for the Civil Service and Treasury) Order 1981. If an employee becomes a member his service as a member is treated for the purposes of such a scheme as service as an employee: Welsh Development Agency Act 1975 Sch 1 para 12(2).

11 See ibid s 2(4). The first appointment was made by the Secretary of State; subsequent appointments are made, with his approval, by the agency: s 2(5). The chief executive is a member of the agency, but may not be chairman or deputy chairman: s 2(6), (7). Subject to

s 2(4), (5), the agency appoints its staff with the consent as to numbers of the Secretary of State and with the approval of the Treasury: Sch 1 para 8 (amended by the Government of Wales Act 1998 Sch 14 para 12, Sch 18); Transfer of Functions (Minister for the Civil Service and Treasury) Order 1981 art 2(2). As to remuneration etc see text and notes 8–10 supra.

12 Welsh Development Agency Act 1975 Sch 1 para 17. The agency is not to be regarded as the servant or agent of the Crown or as enjoying any status, immunity or privilege of the Crown; nor is its property to be regarded as property of or held on behalf of the Crown: s 2(8). Except as provided by Sch 1 para 20 (see infra) in relation to stamp duty, the agency is not exempt from any tax, duty, rate, levy or other charge, whether general or local: s 2(9). Stamp duty is not chargeable on any instrument certified to the Inland Revenue Commissioners as made or executed for the purpose of the transfer to the agency of securities or other property held by or on behalf of the Crown or by a company all of whose shares are owned by or on behalf of the Crown or by a wholly owned subsidiary of such a company: Sch 1 para 20(1). No instrument is deemed to be duly stamped unless it is stamped with the duty for which it would otherwise be liable or it has been stamped in accordance with the Stamp Act 1891 s 12 (as amended) with a particular stamp denoting that it is not chargeable with any duty or that it is duly stamped: Welsh Development Agency Act 1975 Sch 1 para 20(2). See STAMP DUTIES AND STAMP DUTY RESERVE TAX vol 44(1) (Reissue) para 1111. 'Wholly owned subsidiary' has the same meaning as in the Companies Act 1985 s 736 (as substituted) (see COMPANIES vol 7(2) (1996 Reissue) para 827): Welsh Development Agency Act 1975 s 27(1) (definition amended by the Companies Consolidation (Consequential Provisions) Act 1985 s 30, Sch 2; and the Companies Act 1989 s 144(4), Sch 18 para 13).

13 The fixing of the common seal must be authenticated by signature of the chairman or some other person authorised for the purpose by the agency: Welsh Development Agency Act 1975 Sch 1 para 18. A document purporting to be duly executed must be received in evidence and deemed to be executed unless the contrary is proved: Sch 1 para 19. A certificate signed by the chief executive of the agency that any document purporting to be made or issued by or on behalf of the agency was so made or issued is conclusive evidence of that fact: Sch 1 para 19A (paras 19A, 19B added by the Government of Wales Act 1998 Sch 14 para 12). A person dealing with the agency need not inquire as to whether necessary directions, approvals, authorities or consents have been given to the agency, or whether such directions have been complied with, and in favour of any such person, the validity of anything done is not affected by anything contained in such a direction, approval, authority or consent, or by the fact that it has not been given: Welsh Development Agency Act 1975 Sch 1 para 19B (as so added).

14 Ibid s 6(1).

15 Ibid s 6(2).

16 Ie directions under ibid s 1: see para 857 post.

17 A member of the agency or any committee of the agency who is in any way interested in a contract made or to be made by the agency or in any other matter falling to be considered by the agency or the committee must disclose the nature of his interest at a meeting of the agency or the committee, and the disclosure must be recorded in the minutes: ibid Sch 1 para 15(1). In relation to a contract the member must not participate in any deliberation or decision, and in relation to any other matter he must not so participate if the agency or committee decides that the interest might prejudicially affect his consideration of the matter: Sch 1 para 15(2). Notice that he is a member of a specified body corporate or firm and is to be regarded as interested in any contract with or matter concerning that body or firm after the date of the notice, is sufficient disclosure of his interest: Sch 1 para 15(3). Disclosure need not be made in person at a meeting provided that the member takes reasonable steps to ensure that the disclosure is made by a notice which is taken into consideration and read at a meeting: Sch 1 para 15(4).

18 Ibid Sch 1 para 14. The validity of proceedings is not affected by any vacancy among members, a defect in their appointment or non-compliance with Sch 1 para 15 (see note 17 supra): Sch 1 para 16.

857. Functions of the Welsh Development Agency. The functions of the Welsh Development Agency are:

(1)   to promote Wales as a location for businesses[1], or assist or concert its promotion as such a location[2];

(2)   to provide finance for persons carrying on or intending to carry on businesses[3];

(3)   to carry on businesses and to establish and carry on new ones[4];

(4)   otherwise to promote or assist the establishment, growth, modernisation or development of businesses, or a particular business or particular businesses[5];

(5)   to make land available for development[6];

(6)   to provide sites, premises, services and facilities for businesses[7];

(7)   to manage sites and premises for businesses[8];

(8)   to bring derelict land[9] into use or improve its appearance[10],

(9)   to undertake the development and redevelopment of the environment[11]; and

(10)   to promote private ownership of interests in businesses by the disposal of securities and other property held by the agency or any of its subsidiaries[12].

In exercising its functions the agency must have regard to the requirements of agriculture and efficient land management[13]. It may do anything, whether in Wales or elsewhere, which is calculated to facilitate the discharge of functions specified above or is incidental or conducive to their discharge[14]. However, nothing authorises the disregard by the agency of any enactment or rule of law[15].

The Secretary of State[16] may give the agency directions of a general or specific character as to the exercise of its functions[17], but must first consult the agency[18]. After consulting such local authorities, national park authorities and other bodies as appear to have an interest, the agency must from time to time prepare and submit to the Secretary of State for his approval[19] programmes for the performance of such of its functions as he may direct[20].

The agency has power to:

(a)   make such charge for its services as it thinks fit[21];

(b)   accept any gift made to it for the purpose of any of its functions, and subject to the terms of the gift and the statutory provisions, apply it for those purposes[22]; and

(c)   carry out or commission the carrying out of such inquiries, investigations or researches concerning its functions as it may deem necessary or expedient for the performance of its functions[23].

1   'Business' includes any industrial, commercial or professional activities (whether or not with a view to profit) and the activities of any government department or any local or other public authority: Welsh Development Agency Act 1975 s 27(1) (definition added by the Government of Wales Act 1998 s 128, Sch 14 para 10(2)).

2   Welsh Development Agency Act 1975 s 1(3)(a) (amended by the Government of Wales Act 1998 s 126(3)(a)). The agency may appoint a local authority or national park authority, the development corporation of a new town or any other body or person to act as its agent in carrying out its functions under the Welsh Development Agency Act 1975 s 1(3)(a), (da), (f)–(i) (see heads (1), (5)–(9) in the text) or s 21C (see para 860 post): s 5(1) (amended by the Environment Act 1995 s 78, Sch 10 para 13(2); and by the Government of Wales Act 1998 Sch 14 para 4). Any such authority, corporation, body or person, on being requested by the agency, may place the services of any of its staff at the agency's disposal, on such terms as may be agreed with the agency: Welsh Development Agency Act 1975 s 5(2). As to development corporations of new towns see TOWN AND COUNTRY PLANNING vol 46 (Reissue) para 1093 et seq.

3   Ibid s 1(3)(b) (amended by the Government of Wales Act 1998 s 126(3)(b)).

4   Welsh Development Agency Act 1975 s 1(3)(c) (as amended: see note 3 supra). The agency may only exercise these functions through subsidiaries: s 1(5). 'Subsidiary' means a subsidiary as defined by the Companies Act 1985 s 736 (as substituted) (see COMPANIES

vol 7(2) (Reissue) para 827): Welsh Development Agency Act 1975 s 27(1) (amended by the Companies Consolidation (Consequential Provisions) Act 1985 s 30, Sch 2).

5 Welsh Development Agency Act 1975 s 1(3)(d) (amended by the Industry Act 1980 ss 1(3)(c), 21(1), Sch 2; and by the Government of Wales Act 1998 s 126(3)(c)).

6 Welsh Development Agency Act 1975 s 1(3)(da) (added by the Government of Wales Act 1998 s 126(3)(d)). As to the powers of the agency to acquire land see para 858 post.

7 Welsh Development Agency Act 1975 s 1(3)(f) (as amended: see note 3 supra). For the purpose of providing or managing sites, premises and facilities the agency must exercise its powers in accordance with arrangements approved by the Secretary of State: s 9(1) (amended by the Government of Wales Act 1998 Sch 14 para 5). The agency has power to modernise, adapt or reconstruct buildings: Welsh Development Agency Act 1975 s 9(2). In appropriate circumstances justifying the giving of special assistance, the Secretary of State may authorise the agency to provide premises rent free for such time as he thinks appropriate: see s 9(3) (as so amended). He may also authorise it to undertake or assist in the provision of means of access or other services or facilities in or for an area where this appears to him expedient for the purpose of contributing to or supporting the development of industry there: s 10 (as so amended).

8 Ibid s 1(3)(g); and see note 7 supra.

9 'Land' has the meaning given to it by the Interpretation Act 1978 Sch 1: Welsh Development Agency Act 1975 s 27(1) (definition substituted by the Government of Wales Act 1998 Sch 14 para 10(3)).

10 Welsh Development Act 1975 s 1(3)(h) (as amended: see note 3 supra). As to derelict land generally see s 16 (as substituted); and para 863 post.

11 Ibid s 1(3)(i).

12 Ibid s 1(3)(j) (added by the Industry Act 1980 s 1(3)(b); and amended by the Government of Wales Act 1998 s 126(3)(d)).

13 Welsh Development Agency Act 1975 s 1(4).

14 Ibid s 1(6). In particular the agency may (1) acquire, hold and dispose of securities; (2) form bodies corporate; (3) form partnerships; (4) make loans; (5) guarantee obligations arising out of loans or otherwise; (6) make grants; (7) act as agent; (8) acquire and dispose of land, plant, machinery, equipment and other property; (9) manage land, develop land, carry out works on land and maintain or assist in maintaining works; (10) make land, plant, machinery, equipment and other property available for use by other persons; (11) provide or assist in providing advisory or other services or facilities in relation to any of its functions; and (12) promote or assist in promoting publicity relating to its functions: s 1(7). As to restrictions on the agency's powers see ss 19, 20 (both as amended); and paras 864–865 post.

Unless the Secretary of State otherwise directs under s 1(9) (see text and note 17 infra), the powers mentioned in heads (1)–(5) supra may only be exercised in connection with the functions mentioned in heads (2) and (3) in the text, and the power mentioned in head (6) supra may only be exercised in connection with those functions in accordance with a programme approved by the Secretary of State under s 1(15): s 1(8) (amended by the Government of Wales Act 1998 s 126(4)).The power to acquire land under head (8) supra (as to which see the Welsh Development Agency Act 1975 s 21A (as added); and para 858 post) includes power to acquire land to provide premises for the occupation of an undertaking the use of whose buildings has been interrupted by works of modernisation, adaptation or reconstruction as mentioned in note 7 supra, or otherwise to meet the requirements of such an undertaking, and for that purpose the agency may erect buildings and carry out works on land so acquired: s 9(2).

15 Ibid s 1(16).

16 As to the Secretary of State see para 856 note 6 ante.

17 Welsh Development Agency Act 1975 s 1(9). It is the duty of the agency to give effect to any such directions: s 1(9). Any direction may be varied or revoked by a subsequent direction: s 1(13). The directions may extend to directions as to the making and terms of a transfer of securities or other property held by the agency or its subsidiaries to the Secretary of State or his nominee: Industry Act 1980 s 2(1)(c). The Secretary of State must lay a copy of a direction before each House of Parliament within 28 days, or later with a statement of the reason why a copy was not so laid within 28 days: Welsh Development Agency Act 1975 s 1(11) (amended by the Industry Act 1980 s 1(3)(d), Sch 2). The agency's annual report must set out any directions given during the year: Welsh Development Agency Act 1975 s 1(12). If an annual report sets out a direction a copy of which has not been laid in accordance with s 1(11), a statement of the reason why a copy

was not so laid must be annexed to the report by the Secretary of State, and s 1(11) does not in that case apply: s 18(1), Sch 3 para 9(3) (amended by the Industry Act 1980 Sch 2). As to the annual report see para 870 post.

18　Welsh Development Agency Act 1975 s 1(10).

19　The Secretary of State may approve a scheme in whole or in part, with or without modifications, or may refuse to approve it: ibid s 1(15).

20　Ibid s 1(14) (amended by the Environment Act 1995 s 78, Sch 10 para 13(1); and the Government of Wales Act 1998). This duty includes in particular a duty to prepare and submit schemes for the improvement, development or redevelopment of the environment in Wales: see s 15; and para 863 post.

21　Ibid s 4(a).

22　Ibid s 4(b).

23　Ibid s 4(c).

858.　Powers of Welsh Development Agency to acquire land.　Certain powers of the Welsh Development Agency[1] are powers to acquire land by agreement; and to acquire land compulsorily if authorised to do so by the Secretary of State[2]. Where the agency so acquires or has so acquired land, it has power to acquire by agreement or compulsorily any adjoining land which is required for the purpose of executing works for facilitating its development or use, and where the land forms part of a common, an open space or a fuel or field garden allotment, any land required for the purpose of being given in exchange for it[3]. The agency may acquire rights over land by the creation of new rights as well as by acquiring rights already in existence[4]. Before acquiring land under these provisions for the purpose of the specified statutory function[5] the agency must (1) consider whether the land would or would not be made available for development if it did not act; (2) consider the fact that planning permission has or has not been granted in respect of the land or is likely or unlikely to be granted; (3) (in a case where no planning permission has been granted in respect of the land) consult every relevant local authority[6]; and (4) consider the needs of those engaged in building, agriculture and forestry and of the community in general[7].

Where the agency has acquired land for the purpose of any of its functions, it may appropriate it to the purpose of any of its other functions[8]. Where the agency has acquired or appropriated land for the purpose of the specified statutory function, it must, until it either disposes of the land or appropriates it to the purpose of any of its other functions, manage it and turn it to account[9].

On the completion by the agency of a compulsory acquisition of land under these provisions, all private rights of way, and rights of laying down, erecting, continuing or maintaining any apparatus on, under or over the land, are extinguished and any such apparatus vests in the agency[10]. Any person who suffers loss by the extinguishment of a right or the vesting of any apparatus is entitled to compensation from the agency[11].

The erection, construction or carrying out, or maintenance, of any building or work on land which has been acquired by the agency under these provisions, whether done by the agency or by a person deriving title under the agency, is authorised if it is done in accordance with planning permission even if it involves interference with certain interests or rights[12], or a breach of a restriction as to the user of land arising by virtue of a contract[13]. Provision is made for the payment of compensation in respect of any interference or breach[14].

Specific provision is made as to (a) the use and development of consecrated ground and burial grounds[15]; (b) the use and development of land for open spaces[16]; (c) extinguishment of rights of way, and rights as to apparatus, of statutory undertakers[17]; (d) rights of entry[18]; (e) provision of information[19]; (f) regulations as to forms of documents[20]; (g) local inquiries[21]; (h) Crown land[22]; and (i) offences by corporations[23].

If the Secretary of State certifies that possession of a house which has been acquired by the agency under these provisions, and is for the time being held by the agency for the purposes for which it was acquired, is immediately required for those purposes, nothing in the Rent (Agriculture) Act 1976, the Rent Act 1977 or the Housing Act 1988 may prevent the agency from obtaining possession of the house[24].

The Secretary of State may make regulations for the keeping by the agency of a register recording acquisitions, holdings and disposals of land[25].

1 Ie under the Welsh Development Agency Act 1975 ss 1(7)(h), 16(3)(b). As to the Welsh Development Agency see para 856 ante.
2 Ibid s 21A(1) (s 21A added by the Government of Wales Act 1998 s 127, Sch 13 para 2). Provisions of the Acquisition of Land Act 1981 apply, with specified modifications, to compulsory purchase under the Welsh Development Agency Act 1975 s 21A: Sch 4 paras 1–3 (Sch 4 added by the Government of Wales Act 1998 Sch 13 para 3). Provisions of the Compulsory Purchase Act 1965 apply in relation to the acquisition of land by agreement under the Welsh Development Agency Act 1975 s 21A: Sch 4 paras 4, 9 (as so added).
3 Ibid s 21A(2) (as added: see note 2 supra).
4 Ibid s 21A(3) (as added: see note 2 supra).
5 Ie under ibid s 1(3)(da) (as added); see para 857 ante.
6 'Relevant local authority' is the council of any county, county borough or district, any joint planning board, or any national park authority in whose area the land or any part of it is situated: ibid s 21A(5) (as added: see note 2 supra).
7 Ibid s 21A(4) (as added: see note 2 supra).
8 Ibid s 21A(6) (as added: see note 2 supra).
9 Ibid s 21A(7) (as added: see note 2 supra).
10 Ibid Sch 4 para 5(1) (as added: see note 2 supra). This does not apply to any right vested in, or apparatus belonging to, statutory undertakers for the purpose of the carrying on of their undertaking: Sch 4 para 5(2) (as so added). However, it does have effect in relation to any right or apparatus not falling within Sch 4 para 5(2) subject to any direction given by the agency before the completion of the acquisition that para 5(1) is not to apply, and to any agreement which may be made (whether before or after the completion of the acquisition) between the agency and the person in or to whom the right or apparatus is vested or belongs: Sch 4 para 5(3) (as so added).
11 Ibid Sch 4 para 5(4) (as added: see note 2 supra). Compensation is determined under the Land Compensation Act 1961: Welsh Development Agency Act 1975 Sch 4 para 5(5) (as so added).
12 Ie any easement, liberty, privilege, right or advantage annexed to land and adversely affecting other land, including any natural right to support: ibid Sch 4 para 6(3) (as added: see note 2 supra).
13 Ibid Sch 4 para 6(1) (as added: see note 2 supra). However, nothing in this provision authorises interference with any right of way or any right of laying down, erecting, continuing or maintaining apparatus on, under or over land which is vested in or belongs to statutory undertakers for the purpose of the carrying on of their undertaking: Sch 4 para 6(2) (as so added). Neither is any act or omission authorised on the part of any person which is actionable at the suit of any person on any grounds other than an interference or breach: Sch 4 para 6(7) (as added: see note 2 supra).
14 See ibid Sch 4 para 6(4)–(6) (as added: see note 2 supra).
15 Ibid Sch 4 paras 7, 10 (as added: see note 2 supra).
16 Ibid Sch 4 paras 8, 10 (as added: see note 2 supra).
17 Ibid Sch 4 paras 11–13 (as added: see note 2 supra).
18 Ibid Sch 4 paras 14, 15 (as added: see note 2 supra).
19 Ibid Sch 4 paras 18, 19 (as added: see note 2 supra).

20 Ibid Sch 4 para 20 (as added: see note 2 supra).
21 Ibid Sch 4 para 21 (as added: see note 2 supra).
22 Ibid Sch 4 para 22 (as added: see note 2 supra).
23 Ibid Sch 4 para 23 (as added: see note 2 supra).
24 Ibid Sch 4 para 16 (as added: see note 2 supra). As to the Acts mentioned in the text see
    further AGRICULTURE; HOUSING; LANDLORD AND TENANT.
25 Ibid Sch 4 para 17 (as added: see note 2 supra).

859.   Disposal of land by agency.   In exercising any power under the Welsh Development Agency Act 1975 to dispose of land, the Welsh Development Agency may not dispose of land for a consideration less than the best that can reasonably be obtained except as provided by statute[1], or with the consent of the Secretary of State[2].

1   Ie under the Welsh Development Agency Act 1975 s 16(7) (see para 863 post). As to the
    Welsh Development Agency see para 856 ante.
2   Ibid s 21B (added by the Government of Wales Act 1998 s 127, Sch 13 para 2).

860.   Powers to advise on land matters.   If requested to do so by a public authority, the Welsh Development Agency may advise the authority about disposing of any of the authority's land in Wales to other persons, and assist the authority in disposing of the land[1]. In this context, 'public authority' means (1) a government department; (2) the National Assembly for Wales; (3) a county council, county borough council or community council; (4) a national park authority; (5) a development corporation for a new town; (6) a health authority, special health authority or NHS trust; (7) a body corporate established by or under an enactment for the purpose of carrying on under national ownership any industry or part of an industry; (8) any statutory undertakers; or (9) any other public authority, body or undertakers specified in an order made by the Secretary of State[2].
     The agency may assist (a) the council of a county or county borough in Wales in making an assessment of land in its area which is, in its opinion, available and suitable for development; (b) a joint planning board in Wales in making an assessment of land in its district which is, in its opinion, available and suitable for development; or (c) a national park authority for a national park in Wales in making an assessment of land in the national park which is, in its opinion, available and suitable for development[3].

1   Welsh Development Agency Act 1975 s 21C(1) (s 21C added by the Government of Wales
    Act 1998 s 127, Sch 13 para 2). As to the Welsh Development Agency see para 856 ante.
2   Welsh Development Agency Act 1975 s 21C(2) (as added: see note 1 supra). For the
    meaning of 'statutory undertakers' see para 861 note 3 post.
3   Ibid s 21C(3) (as added: see note 1 supra).

861.   Powers of entry.   Any duly authorised person[1] may at any reasonable time enter any land[2] (1) for the purposes of surveying it[3], or estimating its value, in connection with any proposal to acquire[4] that land or any other land; or (2) in connection with any claim for compensation in respect of any such acquisition[5]; or (3) for the purpose of surveying it in order to enable the Welsh Development Agency[6] to determine whether to make an application for planning permission for the carrying out of development of that land[7]. Admission as of right to occupied land may not be demanded except on 24 hours' notice[8] to the occupier[9].
     It is the duty of a person exercising a power of entry to take reasonable care to avoid damage or injury to plant, machinery, equipment, livestock, crops or enclosures, and on leaving the land to secure it as effectively against

unauthorised entry as he found it[10]. Where any land is damaged in the exercise of a power of entry, compensation may be recovered by any person interested in the land from the agency or the Secretary of State[11].

A person who intentionally obstructs a person acting in the exercise of the powers described above is guilty of an offence and liable on summary conviction to a fine not exceeding level 3 on the standard scale[12]. If any person who is admitted into a factory, workshop or workplace in the exercise of a power of entry under these provisions discloses to any person any information obtained by him there as to any manufacturing process or trade secret, then unless the disclosure is made in the course of performing his duty in connection with the purpose for which he was authorised to enter the premises, he is guilty of an offence[13] and liable on summary conviction to a fine not exceeding the statutory maximum, or on conviction on indictment to imprisonment for up to two years or a fine or both[14].

1   The authority must be given in writing by the agency: Welsh Development Agency Act 1975 s 21A(8), Sch 4 para 14(1) (s 21A and Sch 4 added by the Government of Wales Act 1998 s 127, Sch 13 paras 2, 3 respectively). Evidence of it must be produced if required by the occupier of the land or anyone acting on his behalf: Welsh Development Agency Act 1975 Sch 4 para 15(1)(a) (as so added).

2   As to the meaning of 'land' see para 857 note 9 ante.

3   The power to survey land includes power to search and bore in order to ascertain the nature of the subsoil or the presence of minerals or contaminants in it: Welsh Development Agency Act 1975 Sch 4 para 14(3) (as added: see note 1 supra). No works may be carried out under Sch 4 para 14(3) unless notice of the intention to do so was included in the notice required by Sch 4 para 15(1)(b) (see text and notes 8–9 infra): Sch 4 para 15(5)(a). If the land in question is held by statutory undertakers who object to the proposed works on the ground that the carrying out of those works would be seriously detrimental to the carrying on of their undertakings, the works must not be carried out without the authority of the appropriate minister: Sch 4 para 15(5)(b).

    'Statutory undertakers' means (1) persons authorised by virtue of any enactment to carry on any railway, light railway, tramway, road transport, water transport, canal, inland navigation, dock, harbour, pier or lighthouse undertaking, or any undertaking for the supply of hydraulic power; and (2) the Civil Aviation Authority, any universal service provider in connection with the provision of a universal postal service, and any other authority, body or undertakers which by virtue of any enactment are to be treated as statutory undertakers for the purposes of the Town and Country Planning Act 1990: Welsh Development Agency Act 1975 s 27(1) (definition amended by the Gas Act 1986 s 67(4), Sch 9 Pt I; the Water Act 1989 s 190(1), Sch 25 para 51; the Electricity Act 1989 s 112(4), Sch 18; the Planning (Consequential Provisions) Act 1990 s 4, Sch 2 para 34(3)(b); the Coal Industry Act 1994 s 67(1), (8), Sch 9 para 16, Sch 11 Pt II; and the Postal Services Act 2000 (Consequential Modifications No 1) Order 2001, SI 2001/1149, art 3(1), Sch 1 para 40). 'Appropriate minister', in relation to any statutory undertakers in relation to whom it is defined by the Town and Country Planning Act 1990 s 265 or any other Act, has the meaning assigned by the Act so defining it: Welsh Development Agency Act 1975 s 27(1) (definition amended by the Planning (Consequential Provisions) Act 1990 Sch 2 para 34(3)(a)).

4   Ie under the Welsh Development Agency Act 1975 s 21A (as added): see para 858 ante.

5   Ibid Sch 4 para 14(1)(a), (b) (as added: see note 1 supra).

6   As to the Welsh Development Agency see para 856 ante.

7   Welsh Development Agency Act 1975 Sch 4 para 14(2) (as added: see note 1 supra).

8   The Local Government Act 1972 ss 231, 233 (service of documents on and by local authorities) apply as if the agency were a local authority: Welsh Development Agency Act 1975 s 25 (substituted by the Government of Wales Act 1998 Sch 14 para 9); see LOCAL GOVERNMENT.

9   Welsh Development Agency Act 1975 Sch 4 para 15(1)(b) (as added: see note 1 supra).

10 Ibid Sch 4 para 15(6) (as added: see note 1 supra).

11 Ibid Sch 4 para 15(3) (as added: see note 1 supra). As to the Secretary of State see para 856 note 6 ante. Except in so far as may be otherwise provided by regulations made by the Secretary of State under Sch 4 para 15(4) (as so added), any question of disputed

compensation under Sch 4 para 15(3) must be referred to and determined by the Lands Tribunal; and the provisions of the Land Compensation Act 1961 ss 2, 4 apply to the determination of any such question, subject to any necessary modifications and to the provisions of any regulations so made: Welsh Development Agency Act 1975 Sch 4 para 15(4) (as so added). See COMPULSORY ACQUISITION OF LAND.

12   Ibid Sch 4 para 15(2) (as added: see note 1 supra). As to the standard scale see para 16 note 21 ante.

13   Ibid Sch 4 para 15(7) (as added: see note 1 supra).

14   Ibid Sch 4 para 15(8) (as added: see note 1 supra). As to the statutory maximum see para 16 note 21 ante.

862.   Power to obtain information. If the Welsh Development Agency[1], with a view to performing any of its functions relating to any land[2], considers that it ought to have information connected with that or any other land, it may serve[3] a notice on one or more of the following:

(1)   the occupier of the land;

(2)   any person who has an interest in the land either as freeholder, mortgagee or lessee, or who directly or indirectly receives rent for the land;

(3)   any person who, in pursuance of an agreement between himself and a person interested in the land, is authorised to manage the land or to arrange for the letting of it[4].

The notice must specify the land and the function of the agency in question, and the provision which confers the function[5]. It must require the recipient to furnish to the agency within a period specified in it (which must not be less than 14 days beginning with the day on which the notice is served) the nature of his interest in the land, and the name and address of each person whom the recipient of the notice believes to be the occupier of the land and of each person whom he believes to be a person who has an interest in the land or is authorised to manage or let the land[6].

Refusal or failure without reasonable excuse to give such information, or knowingly or recklessly making a false statement in complying with the notice, is an offence punishable on summary conviction by a fine not exceeding level 4 on the standard scale[7].

The council of every county and county borough in Wales, every joint planning board for a district in Wales, and every national park authority for a national park in Wales must supply the agency with such information as the Secretary of State[8] may by regulations prescribe (being information which the agency may need for performing its functions), and with such certificates supporting the information as the Secretary of State may specify in the regulations[9]. Unless the agency directs otherwise[10], if a local planning authority in Wales receives an application for planning permission, it must as soon as practicable after receipt send a copy of the application to the agency[11], and on the grant of planning permission relating to land in Wales, the local planning authority or the Secretary of State (if it was granted by him) must as soon as practicable send a copy of the notification of the planning permission to the agency[12].

1   As to the Welsh Development Agency see para 856 ante.

2   As to the meaning of 'land' see para 857 note 9 ante.

3   As to the service of notices or documents see para 861 note 8 ante.

4   Welsh Development Agency Act 1975 s 21A(8), Sch 4 para 18(1) (s 21A and Sch 4 added by the Government of Wales Act 1998 s 127, Sch 13 paras 2, 3 respectively).

5   Welsh Development Agency Act 1975 Sch 4 para 18(1) (as added: see note 4 supra).

6   Ie who is a person mentioned in head (2) or (3) in the text: ibid Sch 4 para 18(2) (as added: see note 4 supra).

7 Ibid Sch 4 para 18(3) (as added: see note 4 supra). As to the standard scale see para 16 note 21 ante.
8 As to the Secretary of State see para 856 note 6 ante
9 Welsh Development Agency Act 1975 Sch 4 para 19(1) (as added: see note 4 supra).
10 Ibid Sch 4 para 19(4) (as added: see note 4 supra).
11 Ibid Sch 4 para 19(2) (as added: see note 4 supra).
12 Ibid Sch 4 para 19(3) (as added: see note 4 supra).

863. The environment and derelict land. The Welsh Development Agency[1] must prepare and submit to the Secretary of State[2] programmes, for implementation by the agency itself, by the agency acting jointly with any other authority or person, or through persons or authorities acting on behalf of the agency, for the improvement, development or redevelopment of the environment in Wales[3].

Where it appears to the agency that steps should be taken for the purpose of reclaiming or improving land[4] which is derelict, neglected or unsightly[5], or of enabling such land to be brought into use[6], then, with the consent of the Secretary of State, it may[7]:

(1) make grants to any person in respect of relevant expenditure[8] incurred by that person, of such amounts and payable at such times and subject to such conditions as the agency may from time to time determine[9];

(2) after consultation with such local authorities[10] or other bodies as appear to it to have an interest, acquire that land, or any other land[11]; and

(3) carry out any works on such land or other land[12].

After carrying out works on land so acquired, the agency may dispose of it free of charge to a local authority or the development corporation of a new town for the purpose of its use as a public open space[13].

1 As to the Welsh Development Agency see para 856 ante.
2 As to the Secretary of State see para 856 note 6 ante.
3 Welsh Development Agency Act 1975 s 15(1) (amended by the Environment Act 1995 s 78, Sch 10 para 13(3); and by the Government of Wales Act 1998 s 128, Sch 14 para 7). This is part of the agency's duty under the Welsh Development Agency Act 1975 s 1(14) (see para 857 text and note 20 ante): s 15(1). The agency may make payments to other authorities or persons, of such amount and in such manner as it may, with the approval of the Secretary of State and the Treasury, determine, for carrying out work which it considers will contribute to the purposes of such a programme: s 15(2) (amended by the Government of Wales Act 1998 Sch 14 para 7).
4 As to the meaning of 'land' see para 857 note 9 ante.
5 Welsh Development Agency Act 1975 s 16(1)(a), (2)(a) (s 16 substituted by the Derelict Land Act 1982 s 2(1), (2), (4)). These powers also apply, except as regards the power under the Welsh Development Agency Act 1975 s 16(3)(a) (as so substituted) (see text and note 7 infra), to land which is not actually derelict, neglected or unsightly, but which is likely to become so by reason of actual or apprehended collapse of the surface due to relevant operations which have ceased to be carried out: see s 16(2)(b) (as so substituted). 'Relevant operations' means underground mining operations other than operations for the purpose of the working and getting of coal, or of coal and other minerals worked with coal, or for the purpose of getting any product from coal in the course of working and getting coal: s 16(9) (as so substituted).
6 Ibid s 16(1)(b) (as substituted: see note 5 supra).
7 The agency's powers in this regard are in addition to and not in derogation from any other power conferred by the Welsh Development Agency Act 1975: s 16(3) (as substituted: see note 5 supra). Thus it has power to acquire land under s 1(7)(h), and power to survey land under Sch 14 para 14: see paras 857–858 ante.
8 'Relevant expenditure' means expenditure incurred, with the agency's approval, in or in connection with (1) the carrying out, for the purpose specified in text and notes 4–6 supra, of any works to which ibid s 16(1) (as substituted: see note 5 supra) applies; (2) the

carrying out of a survey of such land to determine whether such works should be undertaken (whether or not such works are carried out); and (3) the acquisition of such land by a local authority in whose area it is situated: s 16(4) (as so substituted). For the meaning of 'local authority' see note 10 infra.

9   Ibid s 16(1), (3)(a) (as substituted: see note 5 supra). Grants may made in such manner as appears to the agency to be requisite: s 16(5) (as so substituted). The maximum amount of a grant (to a person other than a local authority in whose area the land is situated) is 80% of the relevant expenditure, or, in the case of a periodical grant in respect of costs from time to time incurred or treated as incurred in respect of the borrowing of money to defray the relevant expenditure, 80% of the costs so incurred or treated as incurred: s 16(6) (as so substituted). The figure of 80% may be altered by the Secretary of State by order with the consent of the Treasury: s 16(6) (as so substituted). A statutory instrument containing such an order is subject to annulment by a resolution of either House of Parliament, and such an order may make such transitional provision as appears to the Secretary of State to be necessary or expedient: ss 16(8) (as so substituted), 28(1) (amended by the Government of Wales Act 1998 Sch 14 para 11).

10   'Local authority' means a county council or county borough council: Welsh Development Agency Act 1975 s 16(9) (as substituted: see note 5 supra; amended by the Local Government (Wales) Act 1994 s 66(6), Sch 16 para 48; and by the Environment Act 1995 s 120(3), Sch 24). In relation to land in a national park for which a national park authority is the local planning authority, 'local authority' includes a national park authority: Environment Act 1995 s 70, Sch 9 para 7. As to national parks see OPEN SPACES AND ANCIENT MONUMENTS vol 34 (Reissue) paras 148–199.

11   Welsh Development Agency Act 1975 s 16(3)(b) (as substituted: see note 5 supra; amended by the Government of Wales Act 1998 s 152, Sch 18 Pt III).

12   Welsh Development Agency Act 1975 s 16(3)(c) (as substituted: see note 5 supra).

13   Ibid s 16(7) (as substituted: see note 5 supra). As to new town development corporations see TOWN AND COUNTRY PLANNING vol 46 (Reissue) para 1093 et seq.

864.   Power to operate media businesses.

Neither the Welsh Development Agency[1] nor any of its subsidiaries[2] may[3] (1) commence a business of publishing newspapers, magazines or other periodicals for sale to the public in the United Kingdom[4], or (2) become the holder of a relevant licence[5]. This does not apply, however, to periodicals wholly or mainly concerned with the activities of the agency or any of its subsidiaries[6].

Neither the agency nor any of its subsidiaries may acquire any of the share capital of a body corporate[7] if a substantial part of the undertaking of that body corporate, or of a group of companies of which it is the holding company[8], consists of carrying on (a) a business such as is mentioned in head (1) above[9], or (b) activities connected with the provision of a service under a relevant licence[10].

If the agency or any of its subsidiaries acquires any of the share capital of a body corporate which carries on any such business as is mentioned in head (1) above, it is the duty of the agency or subsidiary to exercise its voting power with a view to securing that the body corporate disposes of the business as soon as practicable[11]. Similarly, if the agency or a subsidiary acquires any of the share capital of a body corporate which has any interest, direct or indirect, in a body corporate which carries on such a business, it is the duty of the agency or subsidiary to exercise its voting power with a view to securing that the capital of the body corporate which carries on that business is disposed of as soon as practicable[12]. However, the Secretary of State[13] may direct that the agency or subsidiary is not under such a duty for the duration of the direction[14], if he is of the opinion that without such a direction serious commercial injury would be caused to any newspaper, magazine or periodical concerned[15].

If the agency or a subsidiary acquires any of the share capital of a body corporate which is the holder of a relevant licence, it must consult the appropriate authority[16] as to the steps it is to take with regard to that share capital, and obey any direction given by the appropriate authority[17].

It is the duty of the agency and any subsidiary to use any power to control or influence the carrying on of a business as mentioned in head (1) above or of the activities of the holder of a relevant licence only in relation to financial or commercial matters[18].

1   As to the Welsh Development Agency see para 856 ante.
2   For the meaning of 'subsidiary' see para 857 note 4 ante.
3   Welsh Development Agency Act 1975 s 19(1), which is subject to s 19(2) (see text and note 6 infra).
4   Ibid s 19(1)(a). For the meaning of 'United Kingdom' see para 37 note 1 ante.
5   Ibid s 19(1)(b) (substituted by the Broadcasting Act 1990 s 203(1), Sch 20 para 24(a)). 'Relevant licence' means a licence granted by the Independent Television Commission or the Radio Authority under the Broadcasting Act 1990 Pt I (ss 1–71) or Pt III (ss 83–126) or the Broadcasting Act 1996 Pt I (ss 1–39) or Pt II (ss 40–72): Welsh Development Agency Act 1975 s 19(11) (substituted by the Broadcasting Act 1990 Sch 20 para 24(f); amended by the Broadcasting Act 1996 s 148(1), Sch 10 para 27). See TELECOMMUNICATIONS AND BROADCASTING.
6   Welsh Development Agency Act 1975 s 19(2).
7   Ibid s 19(3) (amended by the Industry Act 1980 s 21, Sch 2).
8   'Holding company' means a holding company as defined in the Companies Act 1985 s 736 (as substituted) (see COMPANIES vol 7(2) (1996 Reissue) para 827): Welsh Development Agency Act 1975 s 27(1) (definition amended by the Companies Consolidation (Consequential Provisions) Act 1985 s 30, Sch 2).
9   Welsh Development Agency Act 1975 s 19(3)(i).
10 Ibid s 19(3)(ii) (substituted by the Broadcasting Act 1990 Sch 20 para 24(b)).
11 Welsh Development Agency Act 1975 s 19(5).
12 Ibid s 19(6).
13 As to the Secretary of State see para 856 note 6 ante.
14 Welsh Development Agency Act 1975 s 19(7).
15 Ibid s 19(8).
16 'Appropriate authority' means, in relation to a licence granted under the Broadcasting Act 1990 Pt I or the Broadcasting Act 1996 Pt I, the Independent Television Commission, and in relation to a licence granted under the Broadcasting Act 1990 Pt III or the Broadcasting Act 1996 Pt II, the Radio Authority: Welsh Development Agency Act 1975 s 19(11) (as substituted and amended: see note 5 supra).
17 Ibid s 19(9) (amended by the Broadcasting Act 1990 Sch 20 para 24(c)).
18 Welsh Development Agency Act 1975 s 19(10) (amended by the Broadcasting Act 1990 Sch 20 para 24(e)).

865. Other restrictions on powers of Welsh Development Agency. Neither the Welsh Development Agency[1] nor any of its subsidiaries[2] may acquire any of the share capital of a body corporate, except with the consent of the Secretary of State[3] or in accordance with any general authority given by him[4], if:

(1)   its acquisition would entitle the agency to exercise or control the exercise of 30 per cent or more of the votes at any general meeting of the body corporate[5], or

(2)   the value of the consideration for its acquisition, together with the value of any consideration paid for share capital of that body corporate already held by the agency or any of its subsidiaries, would exceed £1m[6].

Head (1) above does not restrict the acquisition of share capital which gives a right to vote exercisable only in restricted circumstances[7], and the fact that the agency holds share capital of that kind must be disregarded for the purpose of determining whether it is prevented from acquiring further share capital of the same body corporate[8].

1   As to the Welsh Development Agency see para 856 ante.
2   For the meaning of 'subsidiary' see para 857 note 4 ante.
3   As to the Secretary of State see para 856 note 6 ante.
4   Welsh Development Agency Act 1975 s 20(1).
5   Ibid s 20(1)(a).
6   Ibid s 20(1)(b) (amended by the Industry Act 1980 s 6(3)).
7   Welsh Development Agency Act 1975 s 20(2).
8   Ibid s 20(4).

B.   THE WELSH INDUSTRIAL DEVELOPMENT ADVISORY BOARD

866.   The Welsh Industrial Development Advisory Board. The Secretary of State[1] must appoint a board called 'the Welsh Industrial Development Advisory Board' to advise him with respect to the exercise of his functions relating to the giving of financial assistance to industry in assisted areas[2]. The board consists of a chairman and between four and seven other members[3]. The members must include persons who appear to the Secretary of State to have wide experience of, and to have shown capacity in, industry, banking, accounting, finance or the organisation or representation of workers[4]. If the board makes a recommendation with respect to any matter at the request of the Secretary of State but he exercises his functions contrary to it, he must, if the board so requests, lay a statement as to the matter before Parliament[5].

1   As to the Secretary of State see para 856 note 6 ante.
2   Welsh Development Agency Act 1975 s 13(1) (amended by the Industrial Development Act 1982 s 19(1), Sch 2 Pt II para 13). The functions referred to are those under the Industrial Development Act 1982 s 7, as to which see paras 828, 830–831 ante. The National Assembly for Wales has power to make provision for the transfer of the functions of the board, and to require attendance of members or members of the staff of the board to attend proceedings of the Assembly and produce documents, and the Secretary of State has power to make provision about the accounts and audit of the board and reports on its functions: see the Government of Wales Act 1998 ss 28, 74, 144, Sch 4 para 12, Sch 5 para 1, Sch 17 para 1. As to the National Assembly for Wales see para 1 note 3 ante.
3   Welsh Development Agency Act 1975 s 13(2).
4   Ibid s 13(3).
5   Ibid s 13(4) (amended by the Industrial Development Act 1982 Sch 2 Pt II para 13).

C.   FINANCIAL PROVISIONS RELATING TO THE WELSH DEVELOPMENT AGENCY

867.   Financial duties of the Welsh Development Agency. After consulting the Welsh Development Agency[1], the Secretary of State[2] may, with the approval of the Treasury, determine the financial duties of the agency[3]. Such a determination may (1) relate to a period beginning before the date on which it was made; (2) contain incidental or supplemental provisions; and (3) be varied by a subsequent determination[4].

1   As to the Welsh Development Agency see para 856 ante.
2   As to the Secretary of State see para 856 note 6 ante.
3   Welsh Development Agency Act 1975 s 17(1) (amended by the Government of Wales Act 1998 s 128, Sch 14 para 8). Different determinations may be made in relation to different functions and activities: Welsh Development Agency Act 1975 s 17(1). The Secretary of State must notify every determination to the agency: s 17(2).
4   Ibid s 17(2)(a)–(c).

868.   Financing of the Welsh Development Agency. The Secretary of State[1] may, with the consent of the Treasury, pay to the Welsh Development Agency[2] out of money provided by Parliament such sums ('public dividend capital') in respect of certain of the agency's functions[3] as he thinks fit[4]. In consideration of receiving public dividend capital the agency must make a payment to the Secretary of State of an amount proposed by the agency and agreed[5] by the Secretary of State in respect of each accounting year except where the agency satisfies the Secretary of State that it is inappropriate to do so[6].

The Secretary of State may pay the agency, out of money provided by Parliament, such sums as he may, with the consent of the Treasury, determine in respect of administrative expenses relating to any of the agency's functions, and in respect of the exercise of its functions, other than those to which the public dividend capital relates[7].

The agency may borrow only:

(1)   from its wholly owned subsidiaries[8], or

(2)   for the purpose of the exercise of any of its functions,

         (a)   in sterling from the Secretary of State[9], or

         (b)   with the consent of the Secretary of State and the approval of the Treasury, or in accordance with any general authority given by the Secretary of State with the approval of the Treasury, in any currency from any other person[10].

It is the agency's duty to ensure that no wholly owned subsidiary of it borrows money otherwise than from the agency or from another such subsidiary, except with the consent of the Secretary of State and the approval of the Treasury[11].

The Treasury may guarantee the repayment of principal, the payment of interest, and the discharge of any other financial obligations in connection with any sums borrowed by the agency from any person other than the Secretary of State[12]. Immediately after giving such a guarantee, the Treasury must lay a statement of it before each House of Parliament[13]. Where any sum is required[14] for fulfilling a guarantee, the Treasury must lay before each House of Parliament a statement as to that sum for each financial year, beginning with the year in which the sum was issued and ending with the year in which all liability in respect of the sum and interest on it is discharged[15]. If any sums are issued in fulfilment of a guarantee, the agency must make to the Treasury, at such time and in such manner as the Treasury directs, payments of such amounts as the Treasury so directs in or towards repayment of those sums and payments of interest at a rate directed by the Treasury, on what is outstanding in respect of those sums[16].

The aggregate amount outstanding, otherwise than by way of interest, in respect of:

(i)   the general external borrowing[17] of the agency and its subsidiaries[18],

(ii)   sums issued by the Treasury in fulfilment of guarantees and not repaid to the Treasury,

(iii)   sums paid to the agency by the Secretary of State out of money provided by Parliament less repayments and less sums paid to the agency for administrative expenses, and

(iv)   loans guaranteed by the agency,

must not exceed £2,000m[19].

1   As to the Secretary of State see para 856 note 6 ante.

2   As to the Welsh Development Agency see para 856 ante.

3   Ie the functions under the Welsh Development Agency Act 1975 s 1(3)(b), (c): see para 857 heads (2)–(3) ante.

4   Ibid s 18(1), Sch 3 para 1(1). The Secretary of State may not make a payment without the approval of the Treasury: Sch 3 para 1(5). Capital debt may in certain circumstances be treated as an addition to public dividend capital: see para 869 note 11 post.

5   The Secretary of State may not make a payment or signify agreement without the approval of the Treasury: ibid Sch 3 para 1(5).

6   Ibid Sch 3 para 1(3). The agency may, with the approval of the Secretary of State, and must if with the approval of the Treasury he requires it to do so, make payments in reduction of the public dividend capital: Sch 3 para 1(3A) (added by the Industry Act 1980 s 4(3)). Sums received by the Secretary of State must be paid into the Consolidated Fund: Welsh Development Agency Act 1975 Sch 3 para 1(3), (3A) (Sch 3 para 1(3A) as added). As to the Consolidated Fund see CONSTITUTIONAL LAW AND HUMAN RIGHTS vol 8(2) (Reissue) para 711 et seq; PARLIAMENT vol 34 (Reissue) para 952 et seq. 'Accounting year' means the period of 12 months ending with 31 March in any year: s 27(1).

7   Ibid Sch 3 para 2 (amended by the Industry Act 1980 s 21(1), Sch 2). As to the functions for which public dividend capital is payable see text and notes 1–4 supra.

8   Welsh Development Agency Act 1975 Sch 3 para 3(1)(b). As to the meaning of 'wholly owned subsidiary' see para 856 note 12 ante.
     The Secretary of State may, with the approval of the Treasury, lend to the agency any sum which it is empowered to borrow, and the Treasury may issue to the Secretary of State any sums necessary for him to do so out of the National Loans Fund: Sch 3 para 4(1). Any such loan must be repaid at such times and by such methods, with interest paid at such times and rates, as the Secretary of State may from time to time direct; sums received by him must be paid into the National Loans Fund: Sch 3 para 4(2). He must in respect of each financial year prepare an account of sums so issued or repaid to him and the disposal of those sums, and must send that account to the Auditor General for Wales before the end of the following November; the Auditor General must examine, certify and report on the account and lay copies of it and of his report before the National Assembly for Wales: Sch 3 para 4(3) (modified by the National Assembly for Wales (Transfer of Functions) Order 1999, SI 1999/672, art 2, Sch 1). The statement must include particulars of the sums paid to the agency or into the Consolidated Fund under the Welsh Development Agency Act 1975 Sch 3 para 1 (as amended) (see text and notes 1–6 supra): Sch 3 para 1(4). The Secretary of State may not make a loan or give a direction except with the approval of the Treasury, and the form of account and the manner of preparing it must be such as the Treasury may direct: Sch 3 para 4(4). As to the National Loans Fund see generally CONSTITUTIONAL LAW AND HUMAN RIGHTS vol 8(2) (Reissue) paras 727–739.

9   Ibid Sch 3 para 3(1)(a), (2)(a) (amended and substituted respectively by the Industrial Development Act 1985 s 5).

10   Welsh Development Agency Act 1975 Sch 3 para 3(1)(a), (2)(b) (as amended and substituted: see note 9 supra).

11   Ibid Sch 3 para 5.

12   Ibid Sch 3 para 6(1) (amended by the Miscellaneous Financial Provisions Act 1983 s 4, Sch 2). The guarantee may be given in such manner and on such conditions as the Treasury thinks fit: Welsh Development Agency Act 1975 Sch 3 para 6(1).

13   Ibid Sch 3 para 6(2).

14   Any sum so required must be charged on and issued out of the Consolidated Fund: ibid Sch 3 para 6(3).

15   Ibid Sch 3 para 6(2).

16   Ibid Sch 3 para 6(4). Any sums so received must be paid into the Consolidated Fund: Sch 3 para 6(5).

17   'General external borrowing' means (1) in relation to the agency, sums borrowed by it other than (a) sums borrowed from a body corporate which at the time of the loan is one of its subsidiaries, or (b) sums mentioned in head (iii) in the text; (2) in relation to a subsidiary of the agency, sums borrowed by it (whether or not it was such a subsidiary when any such sum was borrowed), other than sums borrowed from the agency or another subsidiary: ibid s 18(5) (amended by the Industry Act 1980 Sch 2). 'General external borrowing' does not, however, include any debt assumed by the agency under the Welsh Development Agency Act 1975 Sch 3 para 7 (as amended): s 18(5); see para 869 post.

18   For the meaning of 'subsidiary' see para 857 note 4 ante.

19   Welsh Development Agency Act 1975 s 18(2), (3) (s 18(2) as amended; see note 17 supra; s 18(3) amended by the Welsh Development Agency Act 1997 s 1; and the Welsh Development Agency (Financial Limit) Order 2000, SI 2000/1147). Orders further increasing the amount must be laid in draft before, and approved by a resolution of, the

House of Commons: Welsh Development Agency Act 1975 s 18(3A) (added by the Welsh Development Agency Act 1997 s 1). However, functions under the Welsh Development Agency Act 1975 are transferred to the National Assembly for Wales (see para 1 note 3 ante), by which SI 2000/1147 was made.

869. Publicly owned property and capital debt. Nothing in the Welsh Development Act 1975 or in any other enactment, including, subject to express contrary provision, an enactment contained in an Act passed after that Act, prevents the transfer to the Welsh Development Agency[1] or its nominees of any publicly owned[2] securities or other publicly owned property[3]. However, such securities or property may be so transferred only with the consent[4] of the Secretary of State or in accordance with any general authority[5] given by him[6].

On any acquisition by the agency of property held by or on behalf of the Crown or by a company all of whose shares are held by or on behalf of the Crown or by a wholly owned subsidiary of such a company[7], the agency assumes a debt to the Secretary of State of such amount[8] as may be notified in writing by him to the agency, with the approval of the Treasury[9]. The rate of interest payable on so much of the agency's capital debt[10] as the Secretary of State does not direct to be treated as an addition to the agency's public dividend capital[11], the date from which interest is to begin to accrue, the arrangements for paying off the principal and the other terms of the debt, are such as the Secretary of State may, with the approval of the Treasury, from time to time determine[12].

1   As to the Welsh Development Agency see para 856 ante.
2   Securities and other property are publicly owned for these purposes if they are held (1) by or on behalf of the Crown; (2) by a company all of whose shares are held by or on behalf of the Crown or by a wholly owned subsidiary of such a company; (3) by any corporation constituted by or under any enactment under which an industry or part of an industry is carried on by it under national ownership or control; or (4) by a wholly owned subsidiary of such a corporation: Welsh Development Agency Act 1975 s 27(2). As to the meaning of 'wholly owned subsidiary' see para 856 note 12 ante.
3   Ibid s 14(1).
4   Where the Secretary of State has given such a consent and the consideration for the transfer exceeds £1m, he must lay before each House of Parliament a statement specifying (1) the securities to be transferred, (2) the transferor, (3) the consideration, and (4) the date of his consent: ibid s 14(4). As to the Secretary of State see para 856 note 6 ante.
5   The Secretary of State must lay a copy of any such general authority before each House of Parliament: ibid s 14(3).
6   Ibid s 14(2).
7   Ibid s 18(1), Sch 3 para 7(2) (amended by the Industry Act 1980 s 21, Sch 2). This does not, however, apply to the transfer of property on the dissolution of the Welsh Industrial Estates Corporation (see the Welsh Development Agency Act 1975 s 7 (as amended); and para 856 note 1 ante): Sch 3 para 7(2).
8   The amount to be notified is the aggregate of (1) the consideration given when the property was first brought into public ownership, and (2) the costs and expenses of and incidental to its being brought into public ownership: ibid Sch 3 para 7(3). If it appears to the Secretary of State that there has been such a change in circumstances since the property was first brought into public ownership that its true value would not be reflected by reference to heads (1) and (2) supra, he may, with the approval of the Treasury, determine the amount to be notified: Sch 3 para 7(4).
9   Ibid Sch 3 para 7(1).
10 'Capital debt' is not defined, but it is presumed, from the heading to ibid Sch 3 para 7 and the context of the provision here described, to refer to the debt assumed by the agency under Sch 3 para 7(1), (2) (as amended): see text and notes 7–9 supra.
11 For the meaning of 'public dividend capital' see para 868 text and notes 1–4 ante. The Secretary of State may direct that so much of the debt assumed by the agency as he may, with the approval of the Treasury, determine, is to be treated as an addition to the public dividend capital: ibid Sch 3 para 1(2).

12 Ibid Sch 3 para 7(6). Different rates and dates may be determined with respect to different portions of the debt: Sch 3 para 7(6). Any sums received by the Secretary of State under this provision must be paid into the National Loans Fund: Sch 3 para 7(7). As to the National Loans Fund see generally CONSTITUTIONAL LAW AND HUMAN RIGHTS vol 8(2) (Reissue) paras 727–739.

870.   Accounts, reports and the provision of information.   The Welsh Development Agency[1] must keep proper accounts and records and must prepare a statement of account in respect of each accounting year[2], in such form and manner as the Secretary of State[3] may determine with the approval of the Treasury[4], and submit it to the Secretary of State at such time as he may direct[5]. The Secretary of State must transmit that statement to the Auditor General for Wales on or before 30 November following the end of the accounting year in question[6]; the Auditor General must examine and certify it and lay copies of it before the National Assembly for Wales together with his report[7].

The agency must make, as soon as possible after the end of each accounting year, a report to the Secretary of State dealing with the operation of the agency during that year[8]; and the Secretary of State must lay a copy before each House of Parliament[9].

The agency must provide the Secretary of State with such information relating to its activities or proposed activities as he may from time to time require, and for that purpose must permit any person authorised by the Secretary of State or the Auditor General for Wales to inspect and make copies of its accounts, books, documents or papers, and must afford such explanations as that person may reasonably require[10].

1   As to the Welsh Development Agency see para 856 ante.
2   For the meaning of 'accounting year' see para 868 note 6 ante.
3   As to the Secretary of State see para 856 note 6 ante.
4   Welsh Development Agency Act 1975 s 18(1), Sch 3 para 8(1).
5   Ibid Sch 3 para 8(2).
6   Ibid Sch 3 para 8(3) (modified by the National Assembly for Wales (Transfer of Functions) Order 1999, SI 1999/672, art 2, Sch 1). As to the Auditor General for Wales see CONSTITUTIONAL LAW AND HUMAN RIGHTS.
7   Welsh Development Agency Act 1975 Sch 3 para 8(4) (as modified: see note 6 supra).
8   Ibid Sch 3 para 9(1).
9   Ibid Sch 3 para 9(2). See also s 1(11), (12), Sch 3 para 9(3) (as amended); and para 857 note 17 ante.
10 Ibid Sch 3 para 8(5) (as modified: see note 6 supra).

(viii)   Transfer of Control of Important Manufacturing Undertakings

871.   Prohibition orders.   The Secretary of State[1] may make a prohibition order if it appears to him (1) that there is a serious and immediate probability of a change of control[2] of an important manufacturing undertaking[3]; and (2) that that change of control would be contrary to the interests[4] of the United Kingdom or of any substantial part of it[5]. The order must specify the undertaking[6], prohibit the change of control[7] and prohibit or restrict the doing of things which would in the opinion of the Secretary of State constitute or lead to it[8], and may make such incidental or supplementary provision as appears to him to be necessary or expedient[9]. The order, which must be made by statutory instrument[10], must be laid before Parliament after being made[11].

Nothing in a prohibition order has effect so as to apply to any person in relation to his conduct outside the United Kingdom unless he is a citizen of the United Kingdom and Colonies[12], a body corporate incorporated in the United Kingdom[13] or a person carrying on business in the United Kingdom either alone or in partnership with others[14], but in a case falling within any of these categories the order may extend to acts or omissions outside the United Kingdom[15].

No criminal proceedings lie against a person on the ground that he has committed, or aided, abetted, counselled or procured the commission of, or conspired or attempted to commit, or incited others to commit, any contravention of a prohibition order[16]. However, this does not limit any person's right to bring civil proceedings in respect of any contravention or apprehended contravention of such an order, and, without prejudice to that right, compliance with such an order may be enforced by civil proceedings by the Crown for an injunction or any other appropriate relief[17].

1 As to the Secretary of State see para 2 ante.

2 For the meaning of 'change of control' see para 872 post.

3 Industry Act 1975 ss 11(1), 13(1)(a). 'Important manufacturing undertaking' means an undertaking which, in so far as it is carried out in the United Kingdom, is wholly or mainly engaged in manufacturing industry and appears to the Secretary of State to be of special importance to the United Kingdom or to any substantial part of it: s 11(2). 'Manufacturing industry' means activities described in any of the minimum list headings in Orders III to XIX of the Standard Industrial Classification: Industry Act 1975 s 37(1). In determining the extent to which an undertaking is engaged in manufacturing industry, the following activities are treated as manufacturing industry so far as they relate to products manufactured or to be manufactured by the undertaking, namely: research, transport, distribution, machinery repair and maintenance, sales and marketing, storage, mining and quarrying, production and distribution of energy and heating, administration, staff training and packaging: s 37(3). 'Standard Industrial Classification' means the revised edition published by HM Stationery Office in 1968 of the publication of that name prepared by the Central Statistical Office of the Chancellor of the Exchequer: s 37(1) (definition substituted by the Co-operative Development Agency and Industrial Development Act 1984 s 5(2), Sch 1 Pt II para 1; and subsequently amended by the Transfer of Functions (Economic Statistics) Order 1989, SI 1989/992, art 6(4), Sch 2 para 2(a)). For the meaning of 'United Kingdom' see para 37 note 1 ante.

4 'Interests' means interests which relate to public policy, public security or public health: Industry Act 1975 s 13(7) (added by the Industry Act 1975 (Prohibition and Vesting Order) Regulations 1998, SI 1998/3035, reg 2).

5 Industry Act 1975 s 13(1)(b).

6 Ibid s 13(1).

7 Ibid s 13(1)(i).

8 Ibid s 13(1)(ii).

9 Ibid s 13(1).

10 Ibid s 38(1). Any power to make an order under the Act includes power to make an order varying or revoking a previous order: s 38(2).

11 Ibid s 15(1). Unless approved by each House it ceases to have effect after 28 days, but without prejudice to anything previously done by virtue of it or to the making of a new order: s 15(1). No account is taken of any period during which Parliament is dissolved or prorogued or both Houses are adjourned for more than four days: s 15(2).

12 Ibid s 18(1)(a). As to categories of citizenship see BRITISH NATIONALITY AND IMMIGRATION.

13 Ibid s 18(1)(b). A body corporate is deemed not to be resident in the United Kingdom if it is not incorporated there: s 18(2). As to incorporation by registration under the Companies Act 1985 see COMPANIES vol 7(1) (1996 Reissue) para 7 et seq; and as to companies formed outside England and Wales see COMPANIES vol 7(2) (1996 Reissue) para 1771 et seq.

14 Industry Act 1975 s 18(1)(c).

15 Ibid s 18(1).

16 Ibid s 17(1).

17 Ibid s 17(2).

872.   Meaning of 'change of control'. There is a change of control of an important manufacturing undertaking[1] only upon the happening of a relevant event[2]. 'Relevant event' means any event as a result of which:

(1)   the person carrying on the whole or part of the undertaking ceases to be resident in the United Kingdom[3];

(2)   a person not resident there acquires the whole or part of the undertaking[4];

(3)   a body corporate resident there but controlled[5] by a person not resident there acquires the whole or part of the undertaking[6];

(4)   a person not resident there becomes able to exercise or control the exercise of 30, 40 or 50 per cent of votes that may be cast at a general meeting of a body corporate carrying on the whole or part of the undertaking or such a percentage of votes in any other body corporate which is in control of such a body[7]; or

(5)   a person resident there and able to exercise or control the exercise of 30, 40 or 50 per cent of those votes in a body corporate carrying on the whole or part of the undertaking or in any other body corporate which is in control of such a body ceases to be resident there[8].

1   For the meaning of 'important manufacturing undertaking' see para 871 note 3 ante.
2   Industry Act 1975 s 12(1).
3   Ibid s 12(2)(a). As to residence of a body corporate see para 871 note 13 ante. For the meaning of 'United Kingdom' see para 37 note 1 ante.
4   Ibid s 12(2)(b).
5   For these purposes a body corporate or an individual entitled to cast 30% or more of the votes that may be cast at a general meeting of a body corporate is in control of that body: ibid s 12(3)(a). Control of a body corporate which has control of another body corporate gives control of the latter body: s 12(3)(b). Any power to direct the holder of shares or stock in a body corporate as to the exercise of his votes at a general meeting of that body is treated as entitlement to cast the votes in respect of those shares or that stock: s 12(4). Two or more persons acting together in concert may be treated as a single person for the purposes of any of the provisions of Pt II (ss 11–20) (as amended) as to change of control: s 12(5).
6   Ibid s 12(2)(c).
7   Ibid s 12(2)(d), (6).
8   Ibid s 12(2)(e), (6).

873.   Vesting orders. The Secretary of State[1] may make a vesting order, with the approval of the Treasury, if (1) the conditions for the making of a prohibition order[2] are satisfied[3]; or (2) a prohibition order has been made in relation to an important manufacturing undertaking[4]; or (3) he has learnt of circumstances which appear to him to constitute a change of control[5] of such an undertaking and is satisfied that the change is contrary to the interests[6] of the United Kingdom or of any substantial part of it[7].

The order, which may only be made if he is satisfied that it is necessary in the national interest[8] and that, having regard to all the circumstances, that interest cannot, or cannot appropriately, be protected in any other way[9], directs that on a specified day (a) certain share capital and loan capital[10], or (b) any assets which are employed in the undertaking, are to vest in himself or in his nominees, and may contain such incidental or supplementary provision as appears to him to be necessary or expedient[11]. It may also contain provisions by virtue of which rights, liabilities or incumbrances to which assets or capital which will vest under it are subject[12] will be extinguished in consideration of the payment of compensation[13], will be transferred to the Secretary of State[14] or will be charged on the compensation[15]. If the order provides for the vesting of assets employed in an undertaking it may prohibit or set aside any transfer of those assets or of any right in respect of them[16]. A vesting order setting aside a transfer must give a right to compensation[17].

The order, which must be made by statutory instrument[18], may not be made unless a draft has been laid before, and approved by a resolution of, each House of Parliament[19], and until a compensation order has also been laid before each House[20].

1   The Secretary of State is in practice the Secretary of State for Trade and Industry, as to whom see para 2 ante.
2   As to prohibition orders see para 871 ante. The conditions referred to are those set out in heads (1) and (2) in the text thereto.
3   Industry Act 1975 s 13(2)(a).
4   Ibid s 13(2)(b). For the meaning of 'important manufacturing undertaking' see para 871 note 3 ante.
5   For the meaning of 'change of control' see para 872 ante. The change of control must have occurred on or after 1 February 1975: ibid s 13(2)(c).
6   For the meaning of 'interests' see para 871 note 4 ante.
7   Industry Act 1975 s 13(2)(c). For the meaning of 'United Kingdom' see para 37 note 1 ante.
8   'The national interest' means the national interest in relation to public policy, public security or public health: ibid s 13(8) (added by the Industry Act 1975 (Prohibition and Vesting Order) Regulations 1998, SI 1998/3035, reg 2)
9   Industry Act 1975 s 13(3).
10 Ie (1) where the Secretary of State considers that the interests of the United Kingdom or of any substantial part of it cannot, or cannot appropriately, be protected unless all the share capital of the relevant body corporate vests, the share capital and so much of any of its loan capital as is specified in the order; and (2) in any other case, that part of the share capital of any relevant body corporate which, when the order is laid before Parliament under ibid s 15(3), appears to him to be involved in the change of control: s 13(4). 'Relevant body corporate' means (a) a body corporate incorporated in the United Kingdom carrying on there as the whole or a major part of its business there the whole or part of an important manufacturing undertaking, or (b) a body corporate incorporated in the United Kingdom which is the holding company of a group of companies carrying on there as the whole or the major part of its business there the whole or part of such an undertaking, and as to which one of two conditions is satisfied: s 13(5). These conditions are (i) that it appears to the Secretary of State that there is a serious and immediate probability of the happening of an event in relation to the company which would constitute a change of control of the undertaking, or (ii) that he has learnt of circumstances relating to the company which appear to constitute a change of control of the undertaking on or after 1 February 1975: s 13(6). 'Holding company' means a holding company as defined by the Companies Act 1985 s 736 (as substituted) (see COMPANIES vol 7(2) (1996 Reissue) para 827): Industry Act 1975 s 37(1) (amended by the Companies Consolidation (Consequential Provisions) Act 1985 s 30, Sch 2).
11 Industry Act 1975 s 13(2) (amended by the British Technology Group Act 1991 s 17(2), Sch 2 Pt I). This includes provisions to safeguard any capital which is to vest and any assets of a body corporate (or of its subsidiary) whose capital is to vest, and to prohibit or set aside any transfers of it or of rights in respect of it: Industry Act 1975 s 16(3). A vesting order setting aside a transfer entitles the body corporate or subsidiary to recover any transferred assets: s 16(5). 'Subsidiary' means a subsidiary as defined by the Companies Act 1985 s 736 (as substituted) (see COMPANIES vol 7(2) (1996 Reissue) para 827): Industry Act 1975 s 37(1) (amended by the Companies Consolidation (Consequential Provisions) Act 1985 Sch 2).
12 Industry Act 1979 s 16(1).
13 Ibid s 16(1)(a). As to compensation see s 19 (as amended); and para 875 post.
14 Ibid s 16(1)(b) (s 16(1)(b), (4) amended by the British Technology Group Act 1991 Sch 2 Pt I).
15 Industry Act 1975 s 16(1)(c).
16 Ibid s 16(2). It also entitles the Secretary of State to recover any transferred capital or assets: s 16(4) (as amended: see note 14 supra). The transfers to which s 16 (as amended)

applies include transfers made before a draft of the order is laid before Parliament but after the Secretary of State has served notice on the person concerned of his intention to lay the draft: s 16(7). 'The person concerned' means (1) in the case of an order such as is mentioned in head (a) in the text, the relevant body corporate, and (2) in the case of an order such as is mentioned in head (b) in the text, the person carrying on the undertaking: s 16(8). The notice must be published in the London Gazette: s 16(9).

Any notice or other document required or authorised under the Act to be served on any person may be served either by delivering it to him or by leaving it at his proper address or by sending it by post: s 36(1). Notice is duly served on a body corporate or a firm if it is served on the secretary or clerk of the body corporate or a partner of the firm: s 36(2). For the purpose of s 36 and what is now the Interpretation Act 1978 s 7, Sch 2 para 3 (see STATUTES vol 44(1) (Reissue) para 1388), the proper address (1) of a secretary or clerk of a body corporate, is the registered or principal office of the body corporate; (2) of the partner of a firm, is the principal office of the firm; and (3) of any other person, is his last known address: Industry Act 1975 s 36(3).

17   See ibid s 16(6).

18   See para 871 text and note 10 ante.

19   Industry Act 1975 s 15(3). The draft may not be so laid (a) in a case under head (1) in the text, after the end of three months from the service of a notice under s 16(7) (see note 16 supra); (b) in a case under head (2), after the end of three months from the making of the prohibition order (unless the circumstances mentioned in head (1) or head (3) exist when the draft is laid before Parliament); (c) in a case under head (3), after the end of three months from the date when the Secretary of State learnt of circumstances there mentioned: s 15(4). On the expiry of 28 days from the laying of the draft in a House, the order proceeds in that House, whether or not it has been referred to a committee under Standing Orders relating to private Bills, as if its provisions would require to be enacted by a public Bill which cannot be referred to a committee: s 15(5). In reckoning these 28 days no account is taken of periods during which Parliament is dissolved or prorogued or the House is adjourned for more than four days: s 15(6).

20   See ibid s 19(1); and para 875 post.

874.   Extension of vesting orders. Where 30 per cent or more of the share capital of a body corporate vests in the Secretary of State[1] or his nominees by virtue of a vesting order[2], the Secretary of State must serve[3] on the holders of the rest of the share capital, and on any other persons who to his knowledge have a present or prospective right to subscribe for shares in the body corporate, a notice informing them of the making of the order and of their right to require the order to extend to their share capital or rights[4]. The recipient of such a notice may within three months of its date serve on the Secretary of State a counter-notice requiring the order so to extend[5], whereupon, from the date of the counter-notice, the vesting order has effect as if the share capital or rights specified in the counter-notice had been specified in the vesting order[6].

1   As to the Secretary of State see para 2 ante.

2   As to vesting orders see para 873 ante.

3   The notice must be served within 28 days of the making of the order: Industry Act 1975 s 14(1). As to the service of notices see para 873 note 16 ante.

4   Ibid s 14(1), (4) (amended by the British Technology Group Act 1991 s 17(2), Sch 2 Pt I).

5   Industry Act 1975 s 14(2).

6   Ibid s 14(3).

875.   Compensation orders. No vesting order[1] may be made until there has also been laid before both Houses of Parliament a compensation order providing for the payment of compensation for the acquisition of the capital or assets and for any extinguishment or transfer of rights, liabilities or incumbrances[2]. The order:

(1)   must identify the persons or descriptions of persons to be compensated and determine their rights and duties in relation to any compensation paid to them[3],

(2)   must specify the manner in which it is to be paid[4];

(3)   must provide for the payment of interest on compensation in respect of the relevant period[5],

(4)   may make different provision in relation to different descriptions of capital or assets and different rights, liabilities or incumbrances[6], and

(5)   may contain incidental and supplementary provisions[7].

The order must be made by statutory instrument[8] and is subject to special parliamentary procedure[9].

Compensation may be paid out of money provided by Parliament[10] or by the issue of government stock[11].

1   As to vesting orders see paras 873–874 ante.
2   Industry Act 1975 s 19(1).
3   Ibid s 19(3)(a).
4   Ibid s 19(3)(b). See also note 11 infra.
5   Ibid s 19(3)(c). 'The relevant period' means (1) in relation to capital or assets, the period commencing with the date of vesting and ending with the date of payment of compensation, and (2) in relation to rights, liabilities and incumbrances, the period commencing with the date of their extinguishment and ending on the date of payment: s 19(3) (amended by the British Technology Group Act 1991 s 17(2), Sch 2 Pt I).
6   Industry Act 1975 s 19(3)(d).
7   Ibid s 19(3)(e).
8   See para 871 text and note 10 ante.
9   Industry Act 1975 s 19(2). As to special parliamentary procedure see PARLIAMENT vol 34 (Reissue) para 912 et seq. The Statutory Orders (Special Procedure) Act 1945 s 6(2) proviso is modified for this purpose by the Industry Act 1975 s 19(5).
10   Ibid s 19(4)(a).
11   Ibid s 19(4)(b). 'Government stock' means stock the principal of which and the interest on which is charged on the National Loans Fund with recourse to the Consolidated Fund: s 19(4)(b). The power conferred by s 19(3)(b) is a power to provide for compensation by one or both of the means specified in s 19(4): s 19(4). As to the National Loans Fund see generally CONSTITUTIONAL LAW AND HUMAN RIGHTS vol 8(2) (Reissue) paras 727–739. As to the Consolidated Fund see CONSTITUTIONAL LAW AND HUMAN RIGHTS vol 8(2) (Reissue) para 711 et seq; PARLIAMENT vol 34 (Reissue) para 952 et seq..

876.   Disputes as to vesting and compensation orders. A procedure is prescribed for the determination of any dispute which arises out of a vesting order[1] or compensation order[2] to which one of the parties is the Secretary of State[3] or a body corporate the whole or part of whose share capital has vested by virtue of the order in him or his nominees[4], either if the order requires it to be submitted to arbitration[5] or if one of the parties wishes it to be so submitted[6]. Where the procedure applies to a dispute arising out of an order it applies also to any dispute arising out of a related order[7].

If a party to such a dispute serves on the other party or parties to the dispute, at a time when no proceedings relating to it have been commenced in any court, a notice that he wishes it to be determined by arbitration, the Secretary of State must by order[8] establish a tribunal[9] to determine the dispute[10]. The tribunal's procedure is determined by rules to be made by the Lord Chancellor[11], although certain of the statutory arbitration provisions apply[12]. The tribunal may refer any question arising (other than a question which is primarily one of law) to a person appointed by it for the purpose, for inquiry and report[13]. The tribunal's order is enforceable as if it were an order of the High Court[14]. Appeal lies to the Court of Appeal on any question of law or fact from any determination or order of the tribunal with respect to compensation[15] on the setting aside by a vesting order of any transfer of capital or assets[16]. The tribunal may, and if so ordered by the Court of Appeal must, state in the form of a special case for determination by that court any question of law arising in the proceedings[17].

1   As to vesting orders see paras 873–874 ante.
2   As to compensation orders see para 875 ante.
3   As to the Secretary of State see para 2 ante.
4   Industry Act 1975 s 20(3) (amended by the British Technology Group Act 1991 s 17(2), Sch 2 Pt I). That amendment removed from the Industry Act 1975 s 20(3) a reference to the National Enterprise Board, but omitted to make further changes necessary in order to make sense of the provision after the removal of that reference; the provision is here treated as if those changes had been made.
5   Ibid s 20(3)(a).
6   Ibid s 20(3)(b).
7   Ibid s 20(3). For this purpose a vesting order and a compensation order are related if they relate to the same capital or assets: s 20(4).
8   The order must be made by statutory instrument: see para 871 text and note 11 ante. It must be laid before each House of Parliament: ibid s 20(1), Sch 3 para 2.
9   The tribunal is a court of record with an official seal which is judicially noticed: ibid Sch 3 para 3. It sits, as the Lord Chancellor directs, either as a single tribunal or in two or more divisions, and consists of a president, who must have a seven year general qualification within the meaning of the Courts and Legal Services Act 1990 s 71 (see COURTS), appointed by the Lord Chancellor, and two other members appointed by the Secretary of State, with respectively business and financial experience: Industry Act 1975 Sch 3 para 4 (amended by the Courts and Legal Services Act 1990 s 71(2), Sch 10 para 39).
    The members of a tribunal hold office for such period as may determined at the time of appointment, and are eligible for re-appointment; however, a member may resign on giving one month's written notice to the appointor, or the appointor may declare the member's office vacant on the ground of unfitness to continue, or his office may become vacant on bankruptcy or the making of an arrangement with creditors: Industry Act 1975 Sch 3 para 6(1) (renumbered and amended by the Judicial Pensions and Retirement Act 1973 s 26(10), Sch 6 para 52). No appointment as president may be such as to extend beyond the appointee's 70th birthday; but this may be extended by authorisation under the Judicial Pensions and Retirement Act 1993 s 26(4)–(6): Industry Act 1975 Sch 3 para 6(2) (added by the Judicial Pensions and Retirement Act 1993 Sch 6 para 52). If a member becomes by reason of illness or other infirmity temporarily incapable of performing his duties, his appointor must appoint some other fit person in his place for any period not exceeding six months at a time: Industry Act 1975 Sch 3 para 7. A member's appointor is the Lord Chancellor or the Secretary of State, as described above: Sch 3 para 8. A tribunal may appoint such officers as it considers necessary for assisting it in the proper execution of its duties: Sch 3 para 11. Members are paid such remuneration and allowances as the Secretary of State, with the approval of the Treasury, may determine; an officer and any person to whom the dispute is referred under Sch 3 para 27 (see text and note 13 infra), may be paid such remuneration and allowances as the Secretary of State, with the approval of the Treasury, may determine; the Secretary of State must pay any such remuneration or allowances, and must defray any other expenses out of money provided by Parliament: Sch 3 para 12; Transfer of Functions (Minister for the Civil Service and Treasury) Order 1981, SI 1981/1670. Members are disqualified for membership of the House of Commons: House of Commons Disqualification Act 1975 s 1(1)(f), Sch 1 Pt II (amended for this purpose by the Industry Act 1975 Sch 3 para 9); see PARLIAMENT vol 34 (Reissue) para 610. The tribunal is under the direct supervision of the Council on Tribunals: Tribunals and Inquiries Act 1992 s 1(1)(a), Sch 1 para 25; cf ADMINISTRATIVE LAW vol 1(1) (2001 Reissue) para 55 et seq.
10 Industry Act 1975 Sch 3 para 1. Where a dispute has been submitted to a tribunal, any other dispute of the kind described in the text must be determined by the same tribunal: s 20(2).
11 Ibid Sch 3 para 17(1). At the date at which this volume states the law, no such rules had been made. They must be made by statutory instrument, which is subject to annulment in

pursuance of a resolution of either House of Parliament: Sch 3 para 17(1), (2). Separate provision is made in relation to procedure in Scotland: see Sch 3 paras 18–25, 26(b).

12 See ibid Sch 3 para 14 (amended by the Arbitration Act 1996 s 107(1), Sch 3 para 30), which provides that the provisions of the Arbitration Act 1996 Pt I (ss 1–84) with respect to oaths and affirmations, the correction of errors in awards, the summoning, attendance and examining of witnesses, the production of documents, and costs (see ARBITRATION) apply with necessary modifications, but no other provisions of that Part apply.

13 See the Industry Act 1975 Sch 3 para 27. Such report may be adopted wholly or partly by the tribunal and, if adopted, may be incorporated in an order of the tribunal: Sch 3 para 27.

14 Ibid Sch 3 para 26(a). See PRACTICE AND PROCEDURE.

15 Ie under ibid s 16(6): see para 873 text to note 17 ante.

16 Ibid Sch 3 para 16.

17 Ibid Sch 3 para 15. For the procedure see CPR Pt 52 Practice Direction para 18; and PRACTICE AND PROCEDURE.

(ix) Utilisation of Derelict Land

877. Powers relating to derelict land. Derelict land is land in England[1] which is derelict, neglected or unsightly[2] and, in relation to a local authority[3] in whose area it is situated, land which is not derelict, neglected or unsightly but is likely to become so through actual or apprehended collapse of the surface as the result of the carrying out of relevant operations[4] which have ceased to be carried out[5].

In relation to such land, the Secretary of State[6] may, with the consent of the Treasury, make grants[7] out of money provided by Parliament to any persons in respect of relevant expenditure[8] incurred by them, where it appears to him that steps should be taken for the purpose of reclaiming or improving any such land[9], or enabling it to be brought into use[10].

1 The Derelict Land Act 1982 s 1 extends only to England: s 1(13). Similar powers in respect of Wales are exercisable by the Welsh Development Agency: see the Welsh Development Agency Act 1975 s 16 (substituted by the Derelict Land Act 1982 s 2(1)); and para 863 ante.

2 Derelict Land Act 1982 s 1(2)(a).

3 'Local authority' means a county, district or London borough council, or the Common Council of the City of London: ibid s 1(11) (amended by the Local Government Act 1985 s 102(2), Sch 17; and by the Environment Act 1995 s 120(3), Sch 24). In relation to land in a national park for which a national park authority is the local planning authority, 'local authority' in the Derelict Land Act 1982 includes a national park authority: Environment Act 1995 s 70, Sch 9 para 7. 'National park' means an area designated by an order made under the National Parks and Access to the Countryside Act 1949 s 5(3) (see OPEN SPACES AND ANCIENT MONUMENTS vol 34 (Reissue) para 148): Derelict Land Act 1982 s 1(11). By the Norfolk and Suffolk Broads Act 1988 s 2(6), Sch 3 Pt II para 43 (amended by the Environment Act 1995 s 78, Sch 10 para 27), the Broads Authority is to be treated for the purposes of the Derelict Land Act 1982 as a national park authority, and the Broads (as defined by the Norfolk and Suffolk Broads Act 1988 s 2(3)) as a national park for which it is the local planning authority.

4 'Relevant operations' means underground mining operations other than operations for the purpose of the working and getting of coal, or of coal and other minerals worked with coal, or for the purpose of getting any product from coal in the course of working and getting coal: Derelict Land Act 1982 s 1(11).

5 Ibid s 1(2)(b).

6 It appears that the Secretaries of State here concerned are the Secretary of State for Trade and Industry (see para 2 ante) and the Secretary of State for Transport, Local Government and the Regions (see para 845 note 1 ante). The Secretary of State may appoint the Urban Regeneration Agency to act as his agent: Leasehold Reform, Housing and Urban Development Act 1993 s 175(1), (2)(a). As to the Urban Regeneration Agency see para 844 et seq ante.

7 As to grants see para 879 post.

8   'Relevant expenditure' means expenditure incurred with the approval of the Secretary of State after 30 August 1982 in or in connection with (1) the carrying out, for the purpose mentioned in the text, of any works on the derelict land or any other land; (2) the carrying out of a survey of the derelict land to determine whether works for that purpose should be undertaken (whether or not such works are carried out); and (3) in relation to a local authority in whose area the derelict land is situated, the acquisition for that purpose of the derelict land or any other land: Derelict Land Act 1982 ss 1(3), 5(3). The Secretary of State may appoint the Urban Regeneration Agency to act as his agent: see note 6 supra.

9   Ibid s 1(1)(a).

10 Ibid s 1(1)(b).

878.   Derelict land clearance areas.   The Secretary of State[1] may by order[2] specify any locality in England[3] as a derelict land clearance area[4] if (1) he is of the opinion that the economic situation in the locality is such that the making of the order would be particularly appropriate with a view to contributing to the development of industry in the locality[5], or (2) the Treasury has consented to the making of the order[6]. The effect of an area being so specified is that it is then eligible for grants[7] at the same level as those payable in relation to land in a development area[8] or intermediate area[9].

1   As to the Secretary of State see para 877 note 6 ante.

2   Such an order must be made by statutory instrument which is subject to annulment in pursuance of a resolution of either House of Parliament: Derelict Land Act 1982 s 1(10). Localities must be specified by reference to areas created or existing for other purposes: s 1(10) (amended by the Industrial Development Act 1982 s 19(1), Sch 2 Pt II para 19 (applying s 1(4) of that Act); and the Co-operative Development Agency and Industrial Development Act 1984 s 5(2), Sch 1 Pt II para 3).

3   As to the extent of the Derelict Land Act 1982 see para 877 note 1 ante.

4   Ibid s 1(7).

5   Ibid s 1(8)(a). See the Derelict Land Clearance Area Order 1984, SI 1984/778; and the Wakefield (Derelict Land Clearance Area) Order 1987, SI 1987/1653. These provisions replace similar provisions in the Local Employment Act 1972 s 8 (repealed) which in turn replaced the Local Employment Act 1970 s 3(1) (repealed). Under those Acts the following orders were made, which continue in force as if made under the Derelict Land Act 1982 s 1, by virtue of the Interpretation Act 1978 s 17(2)(b): the Derelict Land Clearance Areas Order 1970, SI 1970/309 (amended by SI 1972/421; and SI 1974/1372); the Derelict Land Clearance Areas Order 1978, SI 1978/691 (amended by SI 1979/334; and SI 1980/1890); the Derelict Land Clearance Areas Order 1980, SI 1980/1890; and the Derelict Land Clearance Areas Order 1982, SI 1982/935.

6   Derelict Land Act 1982 s 1(8)(b). See also note 5 supra.

7   As to grants see para 879 post.

8   'Development area' means an area specified as such by an order made, or having effect as if made, under the Industrial Development Act 1982 s 1 (as amended) (see para 822 ante): Derelict Land Act 1982 s 1(11) (amended by the Industrial Development Act 1982 Sch 2 Pt II para 19). The current such order is the Assisted Areas Order 1993, SI 1993/1877 (amended by SI 1993/1894).

9   Derelict Land Act 1982 s 1(7). 'Intermediate area' means an area specified as such by such an order as is mentioned in note 8 supra: s 1(11). As to such areas see para 823 ante.

879.   Grants.   In England[1] the Secretary of State[2] may make grants to any person of such amounts and payable at such times and subject to such conditions as he may from time to time determine in respect of relevant expenditure[3] incurred by that person with regard to derelict land[4]. Grants may be made in such manner as appears to the Secretary of State to be requisite[5]. Grants must not exceed the prescribed percentage[6], depending on whether or not the land is situated in a development area[7], an intermediate area[8] or a derelict land clearance area[9], and on whether the applicant is a local authority[10] or other person[11]. Similar, but separate, provision is made as to the prescribed percentage[12] where the land is not situated in any such area[13]. The fact that a locality ceases to be a development area, intermediate area or derelict land clearance area, or that an area ceases to be an area of outstanding natural beauty or comprised in a national park, does not affect the amount of grant which may be made provided that the relevant expenditure was approved by the Secretary of State before the time of the cessation[14].

1   As to the extent of the Derelict Land Act 1982 see para 877 note 1 ante.
2   As to the Secretary of State see para 877 note 6 ante.
3   For the meaning of 'relevant expenditure' see para 877 note 8 ante.
4   Derelict Land Act 1982 s 1(1). For the meaning of 'derelict land' see para 877 ante. The Secretary of State may appoint as his agent the Urban Regeneration Agency: see para 877 note 6 ante.
5   Ibid s 1(4).
6   Ie (1) the prescribed percentage of the relevant expenditure, or (2) in the case of a periodical grant in respect of costs from time to time incurred or treated as incurred in respect of the borrowing of money to defray the relevant expenditure, the prescribed percentage of the costs so incurred or treated as so incurred: ibid s 1(5)(a), (b). As to the amount of the prescribed percentage see note 11 infra.
7   For the meaning of 'development area' see para 878 note 8 ante.
8   For the meaning of 'intermediate area' see para 878 note 9 ante.
9   The Derelict Land Act 1982 s 1(5) refers specifically only to development areas and intermediate areas, but, by virtue of s 1(7), where an area has been specified as a derelict land clearance area it is to be treated for grant purposes as if it were a development area or an intermediate area: see para 878 ante.
10 For the meaning of 'local authority' see para 877 note 3 ante.
11 Derelict Land Act 1982 s 1(5). Where the land is situated in a development area, an intermediate area or a derelict land clearance area there is no limit to the amount of relevant expenditure which can be given by way of grant to a local authority, but in the case of any other person the prescribed percentage of relevant expenditure which may be given by grant is 80% or such other limit as may be so prescribed by order made by the Secretary of State with the consent of the Treasury: Derelict Land Act 1982 s 1(5) (definition of 'prescribed percentage' amended by the Leasehold Reform, Housing and Urban Development Act 1993 s 187(1), Sch 21 para 8). As to orders see para 878 note 2 ante. Orders under the Derelict Land Act 1982 s 1(5) (as so amended) may make such transitional provision as appears necessary or expedient: s 1(10).
12 The prescribed percentage is described in terms similar to those set out in note 6 supra: ibid s 1(6)(a), (b). As to the amount of the prescribed percentage see note 13 infra.
13 Ibid s 1(6). The prescribed percentage is (1) where the land is in a national park or an area of outstanding natural beauty and the applicant is a local authority in whose area the land is situated, 75%; and (2) in any other case, 50%: s 1(6). For the meaning of 'national park' see para 877 note 3 ante. 'Area of outstanding natural beauty' means an area designated as such by an order made under the National Parks and Access to the Countryside Act 1949 s 87 (as amended) (see OPEN SPACES AND ANCIENT MONUMENTS vol 34 (Reissue) para 152): Derelict Land Act 1982 s 1(11).
14 Ibid s 1(9).

(3) DEVELOPMENT COUNCIL LEGISLATION

(i) Development Councils

880.   Establishment and purpose of development councils.   A development council may be established for any industry by order[1] made by the Secretary of State[2] or the minister concerned ('the appropriate minister')[3]. Before making such an order, the appropriate minister must consult any organisation appearing to him to be representative of substantial numbers of persons carrying on business in the industry and such organisations representative of persons employed in the industry as appear to him to be appropriate[4]. An order may not be made unless the appropriate minister is satisfied that the establishment of a development council for the industry is desired by a substantial number of the persons engaged in that industry[5]. The order may assign to the development council any or all of specified functions[6] in order to increase efficiency or productivity in the industry, to improve or develop the service that it renders or could render to the community, or to enable it to render such service more economically[7].

1   Industrial Organisation and Development Act 1947 s 1(1). A development council order must designate, in such manner as appears to the Secretary of State or minister concerned (see note 2 infra) to be requisite for preventing uncertainty, the activities that are to be treated as constituting the industry for which the council is established, whether they are regarded for any other purposes as those of (1) a single industry, (2) a group of industries, or (3) a section or sections of an industry or industries: s 14(1). An order amending such an order may provide that further activities so designated are to be treated as included in the industry for which the council is established, or that designated activities so treated are no longer to be so treated: s 14(2). Such an order must not be made until a draft has been approved by a resolution of each House of Parliament: s 1(6). It may provide for any incidental or supplementary matters for which it appears to the Secretary of State or minister concerned necessary or expedient to provide: s 1(5). The expression 'the industry' where used in relation to a development council or to an order under s 9 (levies: see paras 888–890 post) is to be construed as referring to the industry that is for the time being that for which the council is established or in connection with which funds are to be made available, as the case may be: s 14(4).

2   The power to make such an order was originally conferred on the Board of Trade and several different ministers, collectively referred to as 'the board or minister concerned': ibid s 1(2) (as originally enacted). The power is now exercisable by the Board of Trade, the Secretary of State for Trade and Industry or the Secretary of State for the Environment, Food and Rural Affairs: s 1(2) (amended by the Transfer of Functions (Ministry of Food) Order 1955, SI 1955/554, art 3(3); and by the Ministry of Aviation Supply (Dissolution) Order 1971, SI 1971/719, art 3(2), Schedule). The functions of the Minister of Agriculture, Fisheries and Food were transferred in so far as they were exercisable (1) in relation to Wales, to the Secretary of State for Wales; (2) in relation to England and Wales, to that minister and that Secretary of State jointly; and (3) in relation to Great Britain, to that minister, the Secretary of State for Scotland and the Secretary of State for Wales jointly: Transfer of Functions (Wales) (No 1) Order 1978, SI 1978/272, art 9(1). Article 9(1) did not, however, apply to any function of the minister exercisable in relation to the Apple and Pear Development Council (now dissolved and replaced: see note 3 infra): art 9(2). The powers of the Board of Trade are in practice exercisable by the Secretary of State for Trade and Industry, who is President of the Board of Trade: see para 2 ante. The power to make a development council order relating to agriculture or fisheries and extending (but not applying solely) to Scotland was vested in the Minister of Agriculture, Fisheries and Food and the Secretary of State for Scotland jointly: Industrial Organisation and Development Act 1975 s 1(2) proviso (amended by the Transfer of Functions (Ministry of Food) Order 1955 art 3(3)). The functions previously exercised jointly by the Secretary of State, the Secretary of State for Wales and the Secretary of State were transferred to the Minister of Agriculture, Fisheries and Food: see the Transfer of Functions (Agriculture and Food) Order 1999, SI 1999/3141. For the meaning of 'agriculture' see AGRICULTURE vol 1(2) (Reissue) para 602 note 3. All functions of the Minister of Agriculture, Fisheries and Food are transferred to the Secretary of State for the Environment, Food and Rural Affairs: see para 123 note 11 ante.

       Since June 2001, the functions of that Minister are now exercisable as part of the remit of the Department of the Environment, Food and Rural Affairs: see *Delivering Effective Government* 10 Downing Street press release, 8 June 2001.

       In this paragraph, and in paras 881–894 post, the expression 'the appropriate minister' is used to denote the person or persons who may exercise the power to make development council orders.

       Administrative expenses incurred by any such authority in the execution of the Industrial Organisation and Development Act 1947 must be defrayed out of money provided by Parliament: s 12.

3   Ibid s 1(1), (2) (s 1(2) as amended: see note 2 supra). See the Horticultural Development Council Order 1986, SI 1986/1110 (amended by SI 1990/454; SI 1992/1836; and

SI 2000/1975), establishing the Horticultural Development Council. The order sets out the council's functions, provides for its membership and proceedings, makes provision for a register of growers, the collection of information and the imposition of a charge to meet the council's expenses, and creates a number of offences. Formerly there were development councils for the clothing industry, the jewellery and silverware industry, the textile industry and the furniture industry, but these have all been dissolved. The Apple and Pear Development Council was dissolved from 8 December 1989 by the Apple and Pear Development Council (Dissolution) Order 1989, SI 1989/2276, and a research council established: Apple and Pear Research Council Order 1989, SI 1989/2277. See also the Milk Development Council Order 1995, SI 1995/356 (amended by SI 2000/878), establishing the Milk Development Council; and the Potato Industry Development Council Order 1997, SI 1997/266 (amended by SI 1999/1413), establishing the British Potato Council. In addition to development councils, the Industrial Organisation and Development Act 1947 covers the raising of levies for certain development purposes (usually for scientific research) in industries without councils: see para 888 post. See also AGRICULTURE vol 1(2) (Reissue) para 851.

4　Ibid s 1(3).

5　Ibid s 1(4). The persons engaged in the industry are both employers and employees, and they are not to be considered separately when assessing the degree of support for a council: *Thorneloe and Clarkson Ltd v Board of Trade* [1950] 2 All ER 245, 66 (pt 1) TLR 1117.

6　The Industrial Organisation and Development Act 1947 s 1(1), Sch 1 sets out the following functions:
- (1)　promoting:
    - (a)　the production and marketing of standard products (Sch 1 para 5);
    - (b)　the better definition of trade descriptions and consistency in their use (Sch 1 para 6);
    - (c)　the training of persons engaged or proposing engagement in the industry, and their education in relevant technical or artistic subjects (Sch 1 para 8);
    - (d)　the adoption of measures for securing safer and better working conditions, and the provision and improvement of amenities for employees, and promoting or undertaking inquiry into such measures (Sch 1 para 9);
    - (e)　arrangements for co-operative organisations for supplying materials and equipment, for co-ordinating production, and for marketing and distributing products (Sch 1 para 14);
    - (f)　the development of export trade, including promoting or undertaking arrangements for publicity overseas (Sch 1 para 15);
    - (g)　the improvement of accounting and costing practice and uniformity therein, including in particular the formulation of standard castings (Sch 1 para 17);
- (2)　undertaking:
    - (a)　the certification of products, the registration of certification trade marks, and the functions of proprietors of such marks (Sch 1 para 7);
    - (b)　arrangements for making available information obtained, and for advising, on matters with which the council is concerned in the exercise of any of its functions (Sch 1 para 20);
- (3)　promoting or undertaking:
    - (a)　scientific research (Sch 1 para 1);
    - (b)　inquiry as to materials and equipment and as to methods of production, management and labour utilisation, including the discovery and development of new materials, equipment and methods and of improvements in those already in use, the assessment of the advantages of different alternatives, and the conduct of experimental establishments and of tests on a commercial scale (Sch 1 para 2);
    - (c)　research into matters affecting industrial psychology (Sch 1 para 3);
    - (d)　measures for the improvement of design, including promoting or undertaking the establishment and operation of design centres (Sch 1 para 4);
    - (e)　research into the incidence, prevention and cure of industrial diseases (Sch 1 para 10);
    - (f)　arrangements for encouraging entry into the industry (Sch 1 para 11);
    - (g)　research for improving arrangements for marketing and distributing products (Sch 1 para 12);
    - (h)　research into matters relating to the consumption or use of goods and services supplied by the industry (Sch 1 para 13);

(i)   arrangements for better acquainting the public in the United Kingdom with the goods and services supplied by the industry and methods of using them (Sch 1 para 16);

(j)   the collection and formulation of statistics (Sch 1 para 18);

(4)   advising on any matters relating to the industry (other than remuneration or conditions of employment) as to which the appropriate minister may request it to advise, and undertaking inquiry for the purpose of enabling it to do so (Sch 1 para 19).

7   Ibid s 1(1). For limitations under European Community law on a development council's functions, see Case 222/82 *Apple and Pear Development Council v K J Lewis Ltd* [1983] ECR 4083, [1983] 3 CMLR 733, ECJ.

881.   Constitution and membership of development councils. A development council is a body corporate, and is to be known by the name specified in the development council order[1]. Its members are appointed by the appropriate minister[2], and must be persons of the following categories: (1) persons capable of representing the interests of persons carrying on business in the industry[3]; (2) persons capable of representing the interests of persons employed in the industry[4]; (3) independent members[5]; and (4) where it appears to the appropriate minister to be expedient, persons having special knowledge of matters relating to the marketing or distribution of products of the industry[6].

The development council order must specify the number or a maximum or minimum number of persons in these respective categories, and ensure that the members under heads (1) and (2) above constitute a majority of members of the council[7]. Before appointing the members under heads (1) and (2) above, the appropriate minister must consult such organisations as are required to be consulted[8] before the establishment of a development council[9]. A development council must have a chairman, who must be one of the independent members and be appointed by the appropriate minister, who may also appoint another member as deputy chairman[10].

A development council order may specify requirements as to appointment, tenure and vacation of office and as to qualification or disqualification for membership[11]. It may also provide for the payment to members of such remuneration and allowances[12] as may be determined by the appropriate minister, and for the payment on the retirement or death of any member as to whom it may be so determined, of such pensions or gratuities[13] to them or others by reference to their service as may be so determined[14].

1   Industrial Organisation and Development Act 1947 s 2(1). A development council has a common seal: s 2(9), Sch 2 para 1. As to development council orders see para 880 ante.
2   Ibid s 2(2). As to the appropriate minister see para 880 note 2 ante.
3   Ibid s 2(3)(a).
4   Ibid s 2(3)(b).
5   Ibid s 2(3)(c). Independent members are persons as to whom the appropriate minister is satisfied that they have no such financial or industrial interest as is likely to affect them in the discharge of their functions: s 2(3)(c).
6   Ibid s 2(3).
7   Ibid s 2(4).
8   See para 880 text and note 4 ante.
9   Industrial Organisation and Development Act 1947 s 2(6).
10   Ibid s 2(7).
11   Ibid s 2(5). Members of a development council are disqualified for membership of the House of Commons: House of Commons Disqualification Act 1975 s 1(1)(f), Sch 1 Pt II; see PARLIAMENT vol 34 (Reissue) para 610.
12   The remuneration and allowances are to be paid out of the money of the council: Industrial Organisation and Development Act 1947 Sch 2 para 5.

13 The pensions or gratuities are to be paid by the appropriate minister: Sch 2 para 6(a).
14 Ibid s 2(8).

882. Acts and proceedings, contracts and staff. A development council order[1] may make provision with respect to: (1) the quorum, proceedings, meetings and determinations of the council; (2) council accounts and audits of the accounts; and (3) the execution of instruments and the mode of entering into contracts by and on behalf of the council and the proof of documents purporting to be executed, issued or signed by the council or a member, officer or servant of the council[2]. Subject to the provisions of the order establishing it, a development council may regulate its own proceedings[3]. It may appoint such officers, agents and servants on such terms as to remuneration[4] and other matters as it may determine, and there may be paid, on the death or retirement of any of them as to whom the council may so determine, such pensions or gratuities[5] to them or others by reference to their service as the council may determine[6].

1 As to the making of development council orders see para 880 ante.
2 Industrial Organisation and Development Act 1947 s 2(9), Sch 2 para 2.
3 Ibid Sch 2 para 3.
4 The remuneration is to be paid out of the money of the council: ibid Sch 2 para 5.
5 These pensions and gratuities are to be paid either wholly by the council or partly by the council and partly by means of contributions: ibid Sch 2 para 6.
6 Ibid Sch 2 para 4.

883. Registration, returns and information. A development council order[1] may secure that persons carrying on business in the industry are to be registered by the development council in a register in which any person claiming to be a person so carrying on business is to be entitled as of right to be or remain registered, subject to any provisions of the order as to notification to the council of such claims[2]. Further, the order may enable the council to require persons carrying on business in the industry to furnish such returns and other information[3] as appears to the council to be required for the exercise of any of its functions[4]. In order to exercise these powers generally as regards the industry or any section of it, the council must have the previous consent of the appropriate minister[5] and his approval of the form in which the returns or other information are required to be furnished[6].

1 As to the making of development council orders see para 880 ante.
2 Industrial Organisation and Development Act 1947 s 3(1). The register must be kept by the development council and must be open to public inspection at all convenient hours on payment of such reasonable fee, if any, and subject to such conditions, if any, as may be specified in the order: s 3(1). As to the meaning of 'the industry' see para 880 note 1 ante.
3 This includes information with respect to the productive capacity, capital assets, staff, output, orders, sales, deliveries, stocks and costs of any business: ibid s 3(2).
4 Ibid s 3(2).
5 As to the appropriate minister see para 880 note 2 ante.
6 Industrial Organisation and Development Act 1947 s 3(2) proviso.

884. Reports and accounts. A development council must prepare and transmit to the appropriate minister[1] annually a report setting out what has been done in the discharge of its functions during the financial year last completed[2], including a statement of the council's accounts for that year, together with any report made by the auditors on those accounts[3]. The statement of accounts must be in the form directed by the appropriate minister, being a form conforming with the best commercial standards, and must show the total remuneration and allowances paid during the year to members of the council[4]. A copy of each such report must be laid before Parliament by the appropriate minister[5].

1   As to the appropriate minister see para 880 note 2 ante.
2   Industrial Organisation and Development Act 1947 s 7(1). 'Financial year' means the 12 months ending with 31 March: Interpretation Act 1978 s 5, Sch 1.
3   Industrial Organisation and Development Act 1947 s 7(2). The report must be transmitted as soon as the accounts for that financial year have been audited: s 7(2). A person must not be appointed to audit a council's accounts unless he is eligible for appointment as a company auditor under the Companies Act 1989 s 25: Industrial Organisation and Development Act 1947 s 7(2A) (added by the Companies Act 1989 (Eligibility for Appointment as Company Auditor) (Consequential Amendments) Regulations 1991, SI 1991/1997, reg 2, Schedule para 3).
4   Industrial Organisation and Development Act 1947 s 7(3).
5   Ibid s 7(4).

885. Continuance and dissolution of development councils; amendment of development council orders.

At a date not later than the expiration of three years from the coming into effect of a development council order[1] and at five-yearly intervals while the council continues in being after that date, the appropriate minister[2] must consult the council and such organisations as must be consulted in the setting up of the council[3] on the question whether the council should continue in being, and if so whether the development council order should be amended in any respect[4].

An order for the amendment of a development council order (whether as originally made or as previously so amended), or for the dissolution of a development council, may be made by the appropriate minister after consultation with the council and subject to the like provisions as to consultation[5] and approval by Parliament[6] as apply to the making of a development council order[7]. At the request of the council, an amending order may assign to the council functions[8] which it appears to the appropriate minister expedient for the council to exercise for any of its purposes[9].

1   As to the making of development council orders see para 880 ante.
2   As to the appropriate minister see para 880 note 2 ante.
3   As to the obligation to consult certain organisations before setting up a council see para 880 text and note 4 ante.
4   Industrial Organisation and Development Act 1947 s 8(3). As to the power of amendment see s 8(1)(a), (2). For amending orders under this section see para 880 note 3 ante.
5   See para 880 ante.
6   See para 880 note 1 ante.
7   Industrial Organisation and Development Act 1947 s 8(1). An order for the dissolution of a development council must make provision (1) for the winding up of the council, the imposition and recovery of charges under s 4 (see para 886 post) if necessary to meet the liabilities and the cost of the winding up, and the application of any excess assets for specified purposes connected with the industry; and (2) for the revocation of the development council order either with or without savings: s 8(4). See eg the Apple and Pear Development Council (Dissolution) Order 1989, SI 1989/2276.
8   Ie functions of a kind similar to those specified in the Industrial Organisation and Development Act 1947 s 1(1), Sch 1 (see para 880 note 6 ante), or such as appear to the appropriate minister to be capable of being conveniently exercised in association with functions of such a kind which have been, or are to be, assigned to the council: s 8(2). However, functions assigned under s 8(2) may not include functions relating to remuneration or conditions of employment: s 8(2) proviso.
9   Ibid s 8(2). As to the purposes referred to see s 1(1); and para 880 text and note 7 ante.

(ii) Levies

A. LEVIES UNDER DEVELOPMENT COUNCIL ORDERS

886. Charges imposed by development council orders. A development council order[1] may provide for the imposition by the development council, with the approval of the appropriate minister[2], and for the recovery by the council (in such manner and through such channels, if any, as may be specified in the order), of limited charges[3] for enabling the council to meet its expenses, to be made on and recovered from persons carrying on business in the industry or on persons carrying on any business consisting wholly or partly in the production of, or dealing in, any materials of the industry[4].

1   As to the power to make development council orders see para 880 ante.

2   As to the appropriate minister see para 880 note 2 ante.

3   The order must either provide that the charges be computed so as not to yield more than a specified amount during a specified period, or provide that they are not to be levied at more than specified maximum rates: Industrial Organisation and Development Act 1947 s 4(2).

    An order relating to agriculture providing for such charges may contain provision (1) authorising such of the persons on whom the charges are imposed as may be specified in the order to recover all or part of the charges imposed on them from such other persons carrying on business in the industry as may be so specified; and (2) authorising the deduction from the charges payable by the persons with such a right of recovery, or the repayment to them, of (a) such amounts as may be determined by or under the order in respect of expenses incurred by them in exercising that right, and (b) any sums which are, in accordance with provision made by or under that order, to be treated as irrecoverable: s 4(2A) (added for this purpose by the Agriculture Act 1993 s 60(1), (3)). 'Agriculture' has the same meaning as in the Agriculture Act 1947 (see AGRICULTURE vol 1(2) (Reissue) para 602 note 3), and 'agricultural' is to be construed accordingly: Agriculture Act 1993 s 60(6). A development council order is to be taken to relate to agriculture if any of the activities that are to be treated as constituting the industry to which the order relates is an agricultural activity: s 60(5). As to the meaning of 'the industry' see para 880 note 1 ante.

    Before making the order, the appropriate minister must satisfy himself that the incidence of charges (taking into account, in the case of an order relating to agriculture, any provision made under the Industrial Organisation and Development Act 1947 s 4(2A) (as added: see supra)) as between different classes of undertakings in the industry will be in accordance with a fair principle: s 4(3) (modified in relation to orders relating to agriculture by the Agriculture Act 1993 s 60(4)). However, there is no elaboration in the statute on the phrase 'fair principle'.

4   Industrial Organisation and Development Act 1947 s 4(1) (modified in relation to orders relating to agriculture by the Agriculture Act 1993 s 60(2)).

887. Returns and information. So far as it may appear to the appropriate minister[1] reasonably requisite for the purposes of the imposition or recovery of the charges imposed by a development council order[2], the order may empower the council to require persons carrying on business in the industry, or any business consisting wholly or partly in the production of or dealing in any materials of the industry, to furnish returns and other information, to keep records and to produce for examination on behalf of the council such records as well as books and other documents in the custody or under the control of such persons[3].

1   As to the appropriate minister see para 880 note 2 ante.

2   As to the making of development council orders see para 880 ante. As to the imposition and recovery of charges see para 886 ante.

3   Industrial Organisation and Development Act 1947 s 4(4).

B. INDUSTRIES WITHOUT DEVELOPMENT COUNCILS

888.   Charges where there is no development council. If it appears to any of the authorities having power to set up a development council[1] to be expedient that funds should be made available for the purposes of (1) scientific research; (2) promotion of export trade; or (3) improvement of design in connection with an industry for which there is no development council, and that a body capable of carrying out that purpose satisfactorily either exists or is to be brought into being, the authority may, after such consultation as would be required prior to the making of a development council order for the industry[2], make an order providing for the imposition of charges on, and recovery from, categories of persons in relation to the industry corresponding to those who under a development council order may be liable to pay charges in connection with an industry which has a development council[3]. The order may empower the authority to require persons to furnish returns and information, to keep records and produce documents to the appropriate minister[4] in the same manner as a council may be empowered so to do under a development council order[5]. Any order imposing those charges may be amended or revoked by a further order of the authority making the original order[6].

1   See para 880 note 2 ante.
2   Industrial Organisation and Development Act 1947 s 9(8). As to the organisations to be consulted see para 880 text and note 4 ante. As to the meaning of 'the industry' see para 880 note 1 ante.
3   Ibid s 9(1). As to the categories of persons referred to see para 886 ante. Before making an order, the appropriate minister must be satisfied that the incidence of the charges as between different classes of undertakings in the industry will be in accordance with a fair principle: s 9(2). An order under s 9 must specify a public fund or account into which sums recovered in respect of such charges must be paid, and sums so recovered are issued from that fund or account to the body in question to meet its expenses: s 9(3). An order may not be made unless a draft has been approved by resolution of each House of Parliament: s 9(9). At the date at which this volume states the law an order was in force for the promotion of export trade by the National Wool Textile Export Corporation: see the Wool Textile Industry (Export Promotion Levy) Order 1970, SI 1970/348 (amended by SI 1971/880; and SI 1982/485). The Industrial Organisation and Development Act 1947 s 14(1), (2) (see para 880 note 1 ante) applies to orders under s 9: s 14(3).
4   As to the appropriate minister see para 880 note 2 ante. The functions under the Industrial Organisation and Development Act 1947 s 9 are to be exercisable by a minister of the Crown and the Scottish ministers: Scotland Act 1998 ss 44(2), 56(1)(c).
5   Industrial Organisation and Development Act 1947 s 9(6), applying s 4(4) and s 6 in relation to s 4(4); see paras 887 ante, 894 post.
6   Ibid s 9(7).

889.   Reports and accounts. A body to which sums for the purposes of scientific research, promotion of export trade or improvement of design are issued[1] must prepare annually a statement[2] of its accounts for its financial year last completed and transmit it to the authority making the order[3] together with a copy of any report made by auditors on the accounts[4]. The authority must lay before Parliament a copy of each such statement and of any such report[5]. As respects each financial year, the authority making the order must prepare an account[6] of sums recovered under the order and of their disposal by the authority, and the account must be transmitted, on or before 30 November after the end of the financial year in question, to the Comptroller and Auditor General[7] who, after examining and certifying the account, must lay copies of it, together with his report on it, before Parliament[8].

1 Ie an industrial body (having no development council) which is in receipt of sums under the Industrial Organisation and Development Act 1947 s 9: see para 888 ante.
2 The statement must be in such form as the authority making the order (as to which see para 888 ante) may direct: ibid s 9(5).
3 Ie the order under ibid s 9.
4 Ibid s 9(5). For the meaning of 'financial year' see para 884 note 2 ante.
5 Ibid s 9(5).
6 The account must be prepared in such form and manner as the Treasury may direct: ibid s 9(4).
7 As to the office of Comptroller and Auditor General see CONSTITUTIONAL LAW AND HUMAN RIGHTS vol 8(2) (Reissue) paras 724–726.
8 Industrial Organisation and Development Act 1947 s 9(4).

890. Excess in funds after revocation of orders. Where, after the revocation of an order applying to an industry for which there is no development council[1], there exists an excess of sums recovered under the order over the amount issued, sums not exceeding in aggregate the amount of that excess may be paid, out of the public fund or account into which the sums recovered were paid, to:

(1) any development council there may be in being for an industry comprising the whole or a substantial part of the industry in relation to which the order was made[2]; or

(2) if there is no such council, but the authority[3] is satisfied that there exists or is to be brought into being a body which is capable of carrying out satisfactorily purposes in connection with the industry in relation to which the order was made for which the authority considers it expedient that funds should be made available, to that body but subject to such provision for securing the disposal of the sums for such purposes as it appears to the authority to be practicable and expedient to make[4].

1 See para 888 ante.
2 Industrial Organisation and Development Act 1947 s 9(10)(a). This is now unlikely to be the case: see para 880 note 3 ante.
3 Ie the authority making the levy order under ibid s 9: see para 888 ante.
4 Ibid s 9(10)(b).

(iii) Restriction and Enforcement

891. Information to be given to independent members. If a development council order[1] imposes any requirement to furnish returns or other information relating to an individual business or to produce for examination books or other documents or records[2], it must provide that the returns or information are to be furnished to, or the examination done by, independent members of the council[3], or to or by officers of the council specially authorised in that behalf[4].

1 As to the power to make development council orders see para 880 ante.
2 For the power to impose such requirements see paras 883, 887 ante.
3 As to the independent members of a development council see para 881 note 5 ante. The order may designate certain independent members only: Industrial Organisation and Development Act 1947 s 5(1).
4 Ibid s 5(1).

892. Information regarding secret processes. A development council order[1] must make provision for ensuring that if a person required to furnish returns or information or to produce documents[2] claims to use a secret process in his business that ought not to be disclosed on the ground of risk or prejudice to his business, that person will not be subject to any liability for withholding disclosure of any particulars relating to the process unless, after considering the claim, the appropriate minister[3] has approved the form of the requirement and the making of it in that form[4].

1 As to the power to make development council orders see para 880 ante.
2 As to the power to make such requirements see paras 883, 887 ante.
3 As to the appropriate minister see para 880 note 2 ante.
4 Industrial Organisation and Development Act 1947 s 5(4).

893. Restriction on disclosure of information. Returns or information duly furnished or information duly obtained[1] on an examination must not, without the consent of the person carrying on the business to which the returns, information, books, or other documents or records relate, be disclosed except to specified persons[2], or in the form of a summary of similar returns or information furnished by or obtained from a number of persons and so framed as not to enable particulars relating to any individual business to be ascertained from it[3], unless such disclosure is made for the purpose of any legal proceedings[4] pursuant to the Industrial Organisation and Development Act 1947 or of any report of such proceedings[5]. Disclosure of information in contravention of this provision is an offence[6].

1 Ie subject to provision in the development council order under the Industrial Organisation and Development Act 1947 s 5(1): see para 891 ante. As to the power to require information etc see paras 883, 887 ante.
2 Ie (1) independent members of the development council (as to whom see para 881 note 5 ante), or such of them as are designated under the order to carry out examinations or receive information (see para 891 ante), or authorised officers of the council (ibid s 5(2)(b)); (2) the appropriate minister (see para 880 note 2 ante) or one of his officers (s 5(2)(c)); (3) the appropriate minister or one of his officers in connection with the execution or for the purposes of the Statistics of Trade Act 1947 (see para 951 et seq post) (Industrial Organisation and Development Act 1947 s 5(2)(d)).
3 Ibid s 5(2)(a).
4 'Legal proceedings' includes civil or criminal proceedings and arbitrations: ibid s 5(2) proviso.
5 Ibid s 5(2) proviso.
6 Ibid s 5(3). An offender is liable, on summary conviction, to imprisonment for a term not exceeding three months or a fine not exceeding the prescribed sum or both, or, on conviction on indictment, to imprisonment for a term not exceeding two years or a fine or both: s 5(3) (amended by virtue of the Criminal Law Act 1977 s 32(1); and the Magistrates' Courts Act 1980 s 32(2)). For the meaning of 'the prescribed sum' see the Magistrates' Courts Act 1980 s 32 (as amended); and CRIMINAL LAW, EVIDENCE AND PROCEDURE vol 11(2) (Reissue) para 806; MAGISTRATES.

894. Enforcement. A development council order[1] may provide for the enforcement of its provisions[2] as to the registration of persons carrying on business in the industry, the furnishing of returns or other information, and the production or examination of books or other documents or records or the keeping of records[3]. An order providing for levies for an industry having no development council[4] may make similar provision for the enforcement of those provisions of the order which require records to be kept, returns to be furnished and books and records to be produced for examination in connection with the imposition or recovery of charges[5].

1 As to the power to make development council orders see para 880 ante.
2 As to provisions requiring persons to maintain a register and to furnish information and returns see paras 883, 887 ante.

3   Industrial Organisation and Development Act 1947 s 6. The order may provide for the imposition of time limits for the satisfaction of obligations, with or without power to the development council or other specified authority to extend limits imposed: s 6. No punishment provided may exceed those provided by s 5(3) (as amended) (see para 893 note 6 ante) or, in the case of a fine for a continuing offence, £5 per day: s 6 proviso.

4   As to the imposition of charges where there is no development council see para 888 ante.

5   Industrial Organisation and Development Act 1947 s 9(6), applying s 6. The same provisions as to maximum punishments apply: see note 3 supra.

(4) THE RURAL DEVELOPMENT COMMISSION

895.   The Rural Development Commission. The Rural Development Commission (established as 'the Development Commission')[1] was a body corporate[2] whose function was to keep under review and advise the Secretary of State[3] upon all matters relating to the economic and social development of rural areas in England and which could carry out or assist others to carry out measures likely to further such development[4]. The commission could do anything which was conducive or incidental to the discharge of its functions and could in particular:

(1)   make grants and loans and give guarantees and any other form of financial assistance[5],

(2)   acquire land and other property;

(3)   provide or facilitate the provision of premises for occupation by industrial or commercial undertakings;

(4)   form, and hold controlling or other interests in, bodies corporate;

(5)   act alone or with other persons, either in partnership or otherwise[6].

The Secretary of State could give the commission general directions as to the exercise of its functions, and it had to comply with any such directions[7].

The commission is dissolved with effect from 1 July 2000 and its functions, property, rights and liabilities were transferred to the Countryside Agency and the Secretary of State[8]. The property, rights and liabilities of the commission may now be transferred to regional development agencies established under the Regional Development Agencies Act 1998[9].

1   The Rural Development Commission was created on 18 April 1988 by the merger of the Development Commission (established by the Miscellaneous Financial Provisions Act 1983 s 1, Sch 1: see the text and notes infra) with the Council for Small Industries in Rural Areas (set up in 1968 by the Development Commissioners): see Rural Development Commission Press Release, 18 April 1988. As to the Development Commissioners see note 2 infra.

2   Miscellaneous Financial Provisions Act 1983 s 1(1). The first members of the commission were the persons who were previously the Development Commissioners under the Development and Road Improvement Funds Act 1909 Pt I (repealed): Miscellaneous Financial Provisions Act 1983 s 1(2) (repealed).

3   The Secretary of State here concerned was the Secretary of State for the Environment (see para 845 note 1 ante).

4   Miscellaneous Financial Provisions Act 1983 s 1(3). As to the economic and social development of rural areas in Wales and the functions of the Development Board for Rural Wales see the Development of Rural Wales Act 1976 ss 1–22 (as amended); and TOWN AND COUNTRY PLANNING vol 46 (Reissue) para 1185 et seq. Transitional provision was made in relation to staff formerly employed by the Council for Small Industries in Rural Areas (see note 1 supra) on work relating to that council's activities in Wales: see s 25, Sch 6 (Sch 6 amended by the Employment Protection (Consolidation) Act 1978 s 159(2), Sch 16 para 26). The Secretary of State for Wales may give financial assistance to any person engaged in an activity in Wales contributing to its social development (see the Development of Rural Wales Act 1976 s 26(1), (3)–(5)) but this does not include a power to give financial assistance to a person who carries on or intends to carry on a business

(see s 26(2) (amended by the Government of Wales Act 1998 s 128, Sch 14 para 15)). 'Business' has the same meaning as in the Welsh Development Agency Act 1975; see para 856 ante.

For other statutory encouragement of rural businesses see the Farm Land and Rural Development Act 1988 s 1; and AGRICULTURE vol 1(2) (Reissue) para 589; and see generally AGRICULTURE.

5   The commission could not give financial assistance to any person except in accordance with arrangements approved by the Secretary of State and the Treasury: Miscellaneous Financial Provisions Act 1983 s 1(7).

6   Ibid s 1(4).

7   Ibid s 1(8).

8   By the Development Commission (Dissolution) Order 2000, SI 2000/1505.

9   As to regional development agencies see paras 896–905 post.

(5) REGIONAL DEVELOPMENT AGENCIES

896.   Regional development agencies: general   The Regional Development Agencies Act 1998 establishes regional development agencies for each of nine regions in England[1]. Each regional development agency is a body corporate and is to be known by the name of the region for which it is established with the addition of the words 'Development Agency'[2]. Each agency must consist of not less than 8 nor more than 15 members appointed by the Secretary of State[3]. In appointing a person to be a member of an agency the Secretary of State must have regard to the desirability of appointing a person who has experience of, and has shown capacity in, some matter relevant to the functions of the agency[4]. Before appointing a person to be a member of an agency, the Secretary of State must consult (1) such persons as appear to him to represent local authorities whose areas fall to any extent within the agency's area; (2) such persons as appear to him to represent employers in the agency's area; (3) such persons as appear to him to represent employees in the agency's area; (4) such persons as appear to him to represent the interests of those who live, work or carry on business in rural parts of the agency's area; and (5) such other persons as he considers appropriate[5]. The Secretary of State must designate one of the members of an agency as the chairman, and may designate another member as the deputy chairman[6]. Further provision is made concerning the constitution of such an agency[7].

A regional development agency is not to be regarded as the servant or agent of the Crown or as enjoying any status, immunity or privilege of the Crown and its property is not to be regarded as the property of, or property held on behalf of, the Crown[8]. Such an agency is subject to investigation by the Parliamentary Commissioner for Administration[9]. Members of regional development agencies are disqualified absolutely from membership of the House of Commons[10]. The records of regional development agencies are public records[11].

1   Regional Development Agencies Act 1998 s 1(1). The nine regions are the East Midlands, Eastern, London, North East, North West, South East, South West, West Midlands and Yorkshire and the Humber: Sch 1, which also specifies all the counties, metropolitan and non-metropolitan districts comprised in each region. References in Sch 1 to a local government or administrative area are to that area as it is for the time being: s 1(3). Subject to conditions, and in accordance with the specified procedure, the Secretary of State may by order make alterations in the extent of the regions in Sch 1: see further s 25 (amended by the Greater London Authority Act 1999 s 309, Sch 25 para 14).

2   Regional Development Agencies Act 1998 s 1(2). Provision is made in relation to the change of agencies' names: see further s 26 (amended by the Greater London Authority Act 1999 Sch 25 para 15).

3   Regional Development Agencies Act 1998 s 2(1).
4   Ibid s 2(2). As to the functions of regional development agencies see para 897 post.
5   Ibid s 2(3). Head (4) in the text does not apply in relation to the London Development
    Agency: s 2(6) (added by the Greater London Authority Act 1999 s 304). 'The London
    Development Agency' means the regional development agency established for the London
    region: Regional Development Agencies Act 1998 s 41 (amended by the Greater London
    Authority Act 1999 Sch 25 para 19). As to local government areas generally see LOCAL
    GOVERNMENT vol 29(1) (Reissue) para 23 et seq.
6   Regional Development Agencies Act 1998 s 2(4).
        Section 2(1)–(4), apart from s 2(3)(d) (see text head (4)), has effect in relation to the
    London Development Agency (1) as if references to the Secretary of State were references
    to the Mayor of London; and (2) subject to s 2(8)–(11): s 2(7) (added by the Greater
    London Authority Act 1999 s 304). As to the Mayor of London see LONDON
    GOVERNMENT. The Mayor of London must also consult the London Assembly before
    making an appointment under the Regional Development Agencies Act 1998: s 2(8)
    (added by the Greater London Authority Act 1999 s 304). As to the London Assembly see
    LONDON GOVERNMENT. The Mayor of London may only make an appointment under the
    Regional Development Agencies Act 1998 s 2(1) if, after the appointment takes effect,
    there will be at least four members of the London Development Agency who are, or were
    at the time of their appointment, elected members of (a) the London Assembly; (b) a
    London borough council; or (c) the Common Council of the City of London: s 2(9) (added
    by the Greater London Authority Act 1999 s 304). The Mayor of London may only make
    an appointment under the Regional Development Agencies Act 1998 s 2(1) if, after the
    appointment takes effect, at least half of the members of the London Development Agency
    will be persons who appear to the Mayor to be persons who have experience of running a
    business: s 2(10) (as so added). The Mayor of London may only designate a person under
    s 2(4) to be the chairman of the London Development Agency if that person appears to the
    Mayor to be a person who has experience of running a business: s 2(11) (as so added). The
    Regional Development Agencies Act 1988 s 2 is subject to Sch 2A (which makes
    transitional provisions for the purposes of the London Development Agency): s 2(12)
    (added by the London Development Agency (Transitional Provisions) Order 2000,
    SI 2000/1174).
7   See the Regional Development Agencies Act 1998 Sch 2 (amended by the Greater London
    Authority Act 1999 s 309, Sch 25 para 20), which is concerned with such matters as
    membership of an agency, the chairman and deputy chairman, remuneration and pensions,
    officers and staff appointed by an agency, regulation by an agency of its own procedures
    (including quorum), delegation of functions, members' interests, vacancies and defective
    appointments, the keeping of minutes, the execution of instruments by an agency and the
    proving of such instruments.
8   Regional Development Agencies Act 1998 s 3.
9   Parliamentary Commissioner Act 1967 s 4(1), Sch 2 (amended by the Regional
    Development Agencies Act 1998 s 37, Sch 7 para 2).
10 House of Commons Disqualification Act 1975 s 1(1)(f), Sch 1 Pt II (amended by the
    Regional Development Agencies Act 1998 Sch 7 para 4).
11 Ie for the purposes of the Public Records Act 1958: see s 10, Sch 1 para 3 Table Pt II
    (amended by the Regional Development Agencies Act 1998 Sch 7 para 1). Furthermore,
    for the purpose of the Local Authorities (Goods and Services) Act 1970, except s 2(2), a
    regional development agency amounts to both a 'local authority' and a 'public body' (see
    further LOCAL GOVERNMENT vol 29(1) (Reissue) para 417): Regional Development
    Agencies Act 1998 Sch 7 para 3.

897.   Purposes and powers of regional development agencies   A regional
development agency has the following purposes: (1) to further the economic
development and the regeneration of its area; (2) to promote business
efficiency, investment and competitiveness in its area; (3) to promote
employment in its area; (4) to enhance the development and application of
skills relevant to employment in its area; and (5) to contribute to the
achievement of sustainable development in the United Kingdom where it is
relevant to its area to do so[1]. Moreover, such an agency's purposes apply as
much in relation to the rural parts of its area as in relation to the non-rural
parts of its area[2].

Subject to certain provisions[3], an agency may do anything which it considers expedient for its purposes, or for purposes incidental thereto[4]. However, it may only (a) give financial assistance; (b) dispose of land for less than the best consideration which can reasonably be obtained; or (c) form, or acquire an interest in, a body corporate, if the Secretary of State consents[5]. Furthermore, an agency may only provide housing by acquiring existing housing accommodation and making it available on a temporary basis for purposes incidental to its purposes[6].

A minister of the Crown[7] may, to such extent and subject to such conditions as he thinks fit, delegate any eligible function of his to a regional development agency[8]. A function is so eligible if it does not consist of a power to make regulations or other instruments of a legislative character or a power to fix fees or charges, and the Secretary of State considers that it can appropriately be exercised by the agency concerned[9]. No delegation may be made without the agreement of the agency concerned, unless a corresponding delegation is made at the same time to all the other regional development agencies[10]. No variation of a delegation may be made without the agreement of the agency concerned, unless the delegation did not require the agency's agreement, and a corresponding variation of every corresponding delegation to another agency is made at the same time[11]. Any delegation under these provisions may be revoked at any time[12]. Further provision is made concerning transfer schemes in connection with the delegation of a function, or the revocation of the delegation of a function[13].

A regional development agency must formulate, and keep under review, a strategy in relation to its purposes[14], and must have regard to the strategy in exercising its functions[15]. The Secretary of State may give an agency guidance and directions[16] in relation to the exercise of its functions pursuant to that requirement, in particular with respect to the matters to be covered by the strategy, the issues to be taken into account in formulating the strategy, the strategy to be adopted in relation to any matter and the updating of the strategy[17]. The issues referred to include issues relating to any one or more of the following: (i) the agency's area; (ii) the area of any other regional development agency; and (iii) any part of the United Kingdom outside England[18]. Provision is made with respect to the London Development Agency strategy[19].

If the Secretary of State is of the opinion that there is a body which is representative of those in a regional development agency's area with an interest in its work, and that the body is suitable to be given the role of regional chamber for the agency, he may by directions to the agency designate the body as the regional chamber for the agency[20]. The Secretary of State may by directions require an agency for which there is such a regional chamber to have regard, in the exercise of its functions[21] to any views expressed by the chamber, and to consult the chamber in relation to the exercise of such of its functions as may be specified in the directions[22]. The Secretary of State may give an agency for which there is no such regional chamber such guidance and directions as he thinks fit for the purpose of securing that it carries out appropriate consultation in relation to the exercise of its functions[23].

The London Development Agency has power to promote or oppose Bills in Parliament[24].

1   Regional Development Agencies Act 1998 s 4(1). As to the regions see para 896 note 1 ante.

2 Ibid s 4(2).

3 Ie the provisions of ibid ss 6–33 (as amended): see para 898 et seq post.

4 Ibid s 5(1). A person who enters into a transaction with a regional development agency is not concerned to see or inquire whether there has been any failure by the agency to observe its purposes, or whether the transaction would contravene any direction given by the Secretary of State: s 30(1). Furthermore, a transaction entered into by an agency is not invalid merely because the agency fails to observe its purposes or because it carries out the transaction in contravention of any direction given by the Secretary of State: s 30(2). Section 30 has effect in relation to the Mayor of London as it has effect in relation to the Secretary of State: s 30A (added by the Greater London Authority Act 1999 s 309, Sch 25 para 18). As to the Mayor of London see LONDON GOVERNMENT.

5 Regional Development Agencies Act 1998 s 5(2). As to the consent of the Secretary of State see para 905 post. Section 5(2) has effect in relation to the London Development Agency as if the reference to the Secretary of State were for the purposes of head (c) in the text a reference to the Mayor of London: s 5(4) (added by the Greater London Authority Act 1999 Sch 25 para 2). For the meaning of 'the London Development Agency' see para 896 note 5 ante.

6 Regional Development Agencies Act 1998 s 5(3).

7 'Minister of the Crown' has the same meaning as in the Ministers of the Crown Act 1975: Regional Development Agencies Act 1998 s 41.

8 Ibid s 6(1).

9 Ibid s 6(2).

10 Ibid s 6(3).

11 Ibid s 6(4).

12 Ibid s 6(5). The power of a minister of the Crown to delegate a function under s 6 to the London Development Agency has effect subject to s 6A: s 6(7) (added by the Greater London Authority Act 1999 s 305(1)).

The power of a minister of the Crown under the Regional Development Agencies Act 1998 s 6(1) to delegate a function (1) may be exercised to delegate the function to the Mayor of London instead of to the London Development Agency; and (2) may only be exercised to delegate the function to the London Development Agency with the consent of the Mayor of London: s 6A(1) (s 6A added by the Greater London Authority Act 1999 s 305(2)). Where a minister of the Crown delegates a function to the Mayor of London under the Regional Development Agencies Act 1998 s 6(1) by virtue of head (1) supra, then s 6(3), (4), Sch 3 have effect in relation to the delegation as if the Mayor of London were for this purpose a regional development agency: s 6A(2) (as so added). In any case where a function has been delegated to the Mayor of London under s 6(1) by virtue of head (1) supra, and the Mayor of London, by an authorisation given in accordance with the Greater London Authority Act 1999 s 38 (see LONDON GOVERNMENT), makes the function exercisable by the London Development Agency, the authorisation must be made subject to such conditions as are necessary to ensure that any conditions subject to which the function is delegated to him are also imposed on the London Development Agency: Regional Development Agencies Act 1998 s 6A(3) (as so added).

13 See further ibid Sch 3.

14 Ibid s 7(1)(a)

15 Ibid s 7(1)(b).

16 As to guidance and directions given by the Secretary of State see para 905 post.

17 Regional Development Agencies Act 1998 s 7(2). Section 7(1), (2) does not apply in relation to the London Development Agency: s 7(4) (added by the Greater London Authority Act 1999 s 306(1)).

18 Regional Development Agencies Act 1998 s 7(3).

19 See ibid s 7A (added by the Greater London Authority Act 1999 s 306(2)) (the London Development Agency strategy); and the Regional Development Agencies Act 1998 s 7B (added by the Greater London Authority Act 1999 s 307) (Secretary of State's functions in relation to the London Development Agency strategy).

20 Regional Development Agencies Act 1998 s 8(1).

21 Ie under ibid s 7(1)(a) (see text to note 14 supra).

22 Ibid s 8(2).

23 Ibid s 8(3). Section 8 does not apply in relation to the London Development Agency: s 8(4) (added by the Greater London Authority Act 1999 Sch 25 para 3).

24 See the Regional Development Agencies Act 1998 s 26A, Sch 6A (added by the Greater London Authority Act 1999 Sch 25 paras 16, 21).

898.   Financial matters relating to regional development agencies   The Secretary of State may, after consultation with a regional development agency, and with the approval of the Treasury, determine the financial duties of the agency; and different determinations may be made for different functions of the agency[1]. The Secretary of State must give an agency notice[2] of every such determination of its financial duties, and such a determination may (1) relate to a period beginning before, on, or after, the date on which it is made; (2) contain supplemental provisions; and (3) be varied by a subsequent determination[3]. The Secretary of State may, after consultation with the Treasury, give a direction[4] to an agency requiring it to pay to him an amount equal to the whole or such part as may be specified in the direction of any sum, or any sum of a description, so specified which is or has been received by the agency[5]. Where it appears to the Secretary of State that an agency has a surplus, whether on capital or revenue account, he may, after consultation with the Treasury, direct the agency to pay to him such amount not exceeding the amount of that surplus as may be specified in the direction[6].

The Secretary of State may, with the approval of the Treasury, make to an agency other than the London Development Agency grants of such amounts, and on such terms, as he thinks fit[7]. The Secretary of State may, with the approval of the Treasury, make to the Greater London Authority[8] grants of such amounts, and on such terms, as he thinks fit[9].

A regional development agency is entitled to borrow in accordance with the following provisions[10], but not otherwise[11]. Subject to one condition, an agency may (a) with the consent of the Secretary of State[12], borrow temporarily in sterling, by way of overdraft or otherwise, from persons other than the Secretary of State, such sums as it may require for meeting its obligations and carrying out its functions[13]; and (b) borrow from the Secretary of State, by way of temporary loan or otherwise, such sums in sterling as it may require for meeting its obligations and carrying out its functions[14]. The condition is that an agency may not borrow under these provisions if the effect would be to take the aggregate amount outstanding in respect of the principal of sums borrowed under these provisions by regional development agencies over the collective borrowing limit[15], or to increase the amount by which the aggregate amount so outstanding exceeds that limit[16].

The Secretary of State may, with the consent of the Treasury, guarantee, in such manner and on such conditions as he may think fit, the repayment of the principal of, the payment of interest on, and the discharge of any other financial obligation in connection with, any sum which a regional development agency borrows from any person[17]. The Secretary of State may also, with the approval of the Treasury, lend to a regional development agency any sums which it has power to borrow from the Secretary of State[18].

A regional development agency must keep proper accounts and proper accounting records[19], and prepare in respect of each accounting period[20] a statement of accounts giving a true and fair view of the state of affairs and the income and expenditure of the agency[21]. Every statement of accounts so prepared must comply with any requirement which the Secretary of State has, with the consent of the Treasury, notified in writing to the agency and which relates to any of the following matters, namely: (i) the information to be contained in the statement;(ii) the manner in which that information is to be presented; or (iii) the methods and principles according to which the statement is to be prepared[22].

The accounts[23] of a regional development agency for each accounting period must be audited by the Comptroller and Auditor General[24]. A copy of any accounts of an agency which are so audited and the report made on those accounts by the Comptroller and Auditor General must be sent to the Secretary of State as soon as reasonably practicable after the report is received by the agency[25]. The Secretary of State must lay before each House of Parliament a copy of those accounts and that report[26].

1　Regional Development Agencies Act 1998 s 9(1). As to the regions see para 896 note 1 ante.

2　Any notice required or authorised by ibid Pt I (ss 1–33) (as amended) to be given to or served on any person may be given to or served on that person either by delivering it to him, or by leaving it at his proper address, or by sending it by post to him at that address: s 31(1), (2). Any such notice may (1) in the case of a body corporate, be given to or served on the secretary or clerk of that body; and (2) in the case of a partnership, be given to or served on a partner or a person having the control or management of the partnership business: s 31(3). As to the proper address of a person, and the situation where the name or address or a person on whom notice is to be served is difficult to ascertain, see further s 31(4)–(6).

3　Ibid s 9(2).

4　As to directions given by the Secretary of State see para 905 post.

5　Regional Development Agencies Act 1998 s 9(3).

6　Ibid s 9(4). Section 9 does not have effect in relation to the London Development Agency: s 9(5) (added by the Greater London Authority Act 1999 s 309, Sch 25 para 4). For the meaning of 'the London Development Agency' see para 896 note 5 ante.

7　Regional Development Agencies Act 1998 s 10(1) (amended by the Greater London Authority Act 1999 Sch 25 para 5).

8　As to the Greater London Authority see LONDON GOVERNMENT.

9　Regional Development Agencies Act 1998 s 10(2) (added by the Greater London Authority Act 1999 Sch 25 para 5(4)). Any grant made under the Regional Development Agencies Act 1998 s 10(2) must be made for the purposes of the London Development Agency: s 10(3) (as added).

10　Ie the provisions of ibid s 11.

11　Ibid s 11(1).

12　The Secretary of State must not give such consent without the approval of the Treasury: ibid s 11(3). As to the consent of the Secretary of State generally see para 905 post.

13　Ibid s 11(2).

14　Ibid s 11(4).

15　The collective borrowing limit is £177.77m or such greater sum as the Secretary of State may, with the approval of the Treasury, specify by order made by statutory instrument: ibid s 11(6) (amended by the Greater London Authority Act 1999 Sch 25 para 6(2)). Such an order must not be made unless a draft of the order has been laid before, and approved by a resolution of, the House of Commons: Regional Development Agencies Act 1998 s 11(7).

16　Ibid s 11(5). Section 11 does not apply in relation to the London Development Agency: s 11(8) (added by the Greater London Authority Act 1999 Sch 25 para 6(3)).

17　Regional Development Agencies Act 1998 s 12(1). Further provision is made in relation to the repayment by the agency concerned of any sums paid by the Secretary of State in fulfilment of the guarantee (s 12(4)), and in relation to the laying of both a statement of any such guarantee and a statement of any sums paid thereunder before each House of Parliament (s 12(2), (3)). Section 12 does not apply in relation to the London Development Agency: s 12(5) (added by the Greater London Authority Act 1999 Sch 25 para 7).

18　Ie under the Regional Development Agencies Act 1998 s 11(4) (see text and note 14 supra): s 13(1). Further provision is made in relation to the repayment of any such loan by the agency concerned (s 13(2)), the preparation of an account of the sums so lent by the Secretary of State, in accordance with Treasury directions, and the sending of such an account to the Comptroller and Auditor General (s 13(3)), the examination, certification and compiling of a report of the account by the Comptroller and Auditor General and the placing of both the account and the report before each House of Parliament (s 13(4)), and the payment out of the National Loans Fund of sums to facilitate such loans and the repayment to that fund of any sums repaid by the agency concerned (s 13(5)). As to the National Loans Fund see generally CONSTITUTIONAL LAW AND HUMAN RIGHTS vol 8(2) (Reissue) paras 727–739. Section 13 does not apply in relation to the London Development Agency: s 13(6) (added by the Greater London Authority Act 1999 Sch 25 para 8).

19   'Accounting records', in relation to an agency, includes all books, papers and other records of the agency relating to, or to matters dealt with in, the accounts required to be kept by the Regional Development Agencies Act 1998 s 14: s 14(6).

20   'Accounting period', in relation to an agency, means a period beginning with 1 April and ending with the next 31 March: ibid s 14(3). However, the Secretary of State may, in relation to an accounting period of such an agency, direct that the period ends with such other date as may be specified in the direction: s 14(4). Where the Secretary of State has given such a direction, the following accounting period of the agency to which the direction was given begins with the day after the date specified in the direction and, subject to any further direction, ends with the next 31 March: s 14(5).

21   Ibid s 14(1).

22   Ibid s 14(2). Section 14 does not apply in relation to the London Development Agency: s 14(7) (added by the Greater London Authority Act 1999 Sch 25 para 9).

23   'Accounts', in relation to an agency, include any statement prepared by that agency under the Regional Development Agencies Act 1998 s 14: s 15(3).

24   Ibid s 15(1). As to the office of Comptroller and Auditor General see CONSTITUTIONAL LAW AND HUMAN RIGHTS vol 8(2) (Reissue) paras 724–726.

25   Ibid s 15(2).

26   Ibid s 15(2).
        Section 15(1)–(3) does not apply to the London Development Agency (whose accounts are, by virtue of the Audit Commission Act 1998 Sch 2 para 1(bc), to be audited in accordance with the Audit Commission Act 1998): Regional Development Agencies Act 1998 s 15(4) (added by the Greater London Authority Act 1999 s 308). The London Development Agency must send a copy of its audited accounts to the Mayor of London and the Chair of the London Assembly: Regional Development Agencies Act 1998 s 15(5) (added by the Greater London Authority Act 1999 s 308). As to the Mayor of London and the London Assembly see LONDON GOVERNMENT.

899.   Information, reports and accountability   A regional development agency other than the London Development Agency must provide the Secretary of State with such information, advice and assistance as he may require[1].

As soon as reasonably practicable after the end of each accounting period[2], a regional development agency must prepare a report on its activities during that period and must send a copy of that report to the Secretary of State[3]. Such a report must (1) be in such form and contain such information as the Secretary of State may specify by directions[4] to the agency; and (2) set out any other directions given to the agency under certain provisions[5] during the period to which the report relates[6]. Following receipt of the report, the Secretary of State must lay a copy of it before each House of Parliament and arrange for copies of it to be published in such manner as he considers appropriate[7].

The Secretary of State may by directions require a regional development agency for which there is a regional chamber[8] (a) to supply the chamber with information of such description as may be specified in the directions; (b) to answer questions put by the chamber about information supplied to it by the agency and to do so in such manner as may be so specified; and (c) to take such other steps for the purpose of accounting to the chamber for the exercise of its functions as may be so specified[9]. An agency must hold a public meeting within such period after the publication of its annual report as the Secretary of State may by directions specify[10]. A regional development agency must give such notice[11] of the meeting as the Secretary of State may by directions specify and publish it in such manner as he may so specify[12]. The Secretary of State may give a regional development agency guidance[13] and directions with respect to the conduct of any such meeting[14].

1   Regional Development Agencies Act 1998 s 16 (amended by the Greater London Authority Act 1999 s 309, Sch 25 para 10). As to the regions see para 986 note 1 ante. For the meaning of 'the London Development Agency' see para 896 note 5 ante.

2   'Accounting period' has the same meaning as in the Regional Development Agencies Act 1998 s 14 (see para 898 note 20 ante): s 17(8) (renumbered as s 17(8) by the Greater London Authority Act 1999 Sch 25 para 11).

3   Regional Development Agencies Act 1998 s 17(1).

4   As to directions given by the Secretary of State, see para 905 post.

5   Ie the provisions of the Regional Development Agencies Act 1998 Pt I (ss 1–33) (as amended).

6   Ibid s 17(2). Section 17(1), (2) has effect in relation to the London Development Agency as if the references to the Secretary of State were references to the Mayor of London: s 17(4) (added by the Greater London Authority Act 1999 Sch 25 para 11). As to the Mayor of London see LONDON GOVERNMENT.

7   Regional Development Agencies Act 1998 s 17(3). Section 17(3) does not apply to the London Development Agency: s 17(5) (added by the Greater London Authority Act 1999 Sch 25 para 11). The London Development Agency must send a copy of a report under the Regional Development Agencies Act 1998 s 17 to the London Assembly: s 17(6) (as so added). As to the London Assembly see LONDON GOVERNMENT. The Mayor of London must arrange for publication of any report sent to him under s 17: s 17(7) (as so added).

8   Ie under ibid s 8(1): see para 897 text and note 20 ante.

9   Ibid s 18(1).

10   Ibid s 18(2).

11   As to notices generally, see para 898 note 2 ante.

12   Regional Development Agencies Act 1998 s 18(3).

13   As to guidance given by the Secretary of State see para 905 post.

14   Regional Development Agencies Act 1998 s 18(4). Section 18(2)–(4) has effect in relation to the London Development Agency as if references to the Secretary of State were references to the Mayor of London: s 18(5) (added by the Greater London Authority Act 1999 Sch 25 para 12).

900.   Vesting of land in regional development agencies   The Secretary of State may, in relation to land in England, by order made by statutory instrument provide that land specified in the order which is vested in a local authority[1] or other public body or in a wholly-owned subsidiary[2] of a public body is to vest in a regional development agency[3]. However, such an order may not specify land vested in statutory undertakers[4] which is used for the purpose of carrying on their statutory undertakings or which is held for that purpose[5]. In the case of land vested in statutory undertakers, the power to make the order is exercisable by the Secretary of State and the appropriate minister[6]. In addition, no such order may be made in relation to a universal service provider within the meaning of the Postal Services Act 2000[7]. An order under the above provisions has the same effect as a declaration under the Compulsory Purchase (Vesting Declarations) Act 1981 except that, in relation to such an order, that Act and the Land Compensation Act 1961 apply, subject to modifications[8]. Compensation under the 1961 Act as so applied is to be assessed by reference to values current on the date the order comes into force[9]. No order vesting land in a regional development agency[10] may be made unless a draft of the order has been laid before and approved by resolution of each House of Parliament[11].

Additional provision is made in relation to various consequential matters which arise following the making of an order vesting land in a regional development agency[12].

1   'Local authority' means a county council, a district council, a London borough council, the Common Council of the City of London and the Council of the Isles of Scilly and, for the purposes of the Regional Development Agencies Act 1998 s 19, 'local authority' also includes a county borough council and a parish council: ss 19(10), 33. As to the regions see para 896 note 1 ante.

2   'Wholly-owned subsidiary' has the meaning given by the Companies Act 1985 s 736 (see COMPANIES vol 7(2) (1996 Reissue) para 827): Regional Development Agencies Act 1998 s 19(10).

3   Ibid s 19(1).

4   'Statutory undertakers', except where the context otherwise requires, means (1) persons authorised by any enactment to carry on any railway, light railway, tramway, road transport, water transport, canal, inland navigation, dock, harbour, pier or lighthouse undertaking, or any undertaking for the supply of hydraulic power; (2) a relevant airport operator (within the meaning of the Airports Act 1986); (3) British Shipbuilders and the Civil Aviation Authority; (4) a person who holds a licence under the Transport Act 2000 Pt I Ch I (air traffic services) to the extent that the person is carrying out activities authorised by the licence; (5) any other authority, body or undertakers specified in an order made by the Secretary of State by statutory instrument (such instrument to be subject to annulment in pursuance of a resolution of either House of Parliament); and (6) any wholly-owned subsidiary of any person, authority or body mentioned in heads (1)–(3) or of any authority, body or undertakers specified in an order under head (5), and 'statutory undertaking' is to be construed accordingly: Regional Development Agencies Act 1998 s 19(10), (11) (s 19(10) amended by the Transport Act 2000 s 37, Sch 5 para 18; and the Postal Services Act 2000 (Consequential Modifications No 1) Order 2001, SI 2001/1149, art 3(1), Sch 1 para 120(1), (3)).

5   Regional Development Agencies Act 1998s 19(2).

6   Ibid s 19(3). The reference in s 19(3) to the Secretary of State and the appropriate minister is (1) in relation to statutory undertakers who are or are deemed to be statutory undertakers for the purposes of any provision of the Town and Country Planning Act 1990 Pt XI (ss 262–283), to be construed as if contained in that Part; and (2) in relation to any other statutory undertakers, to be construed in accordance with an order made by the Secretary of State by statutory instrument, such instrument to be subject to annulment in pursuance of a resolution of either House of Parliament: Regional Development Agencies Act 1998 s 19(4), (11). If, for the purposes of s 19(3), any question arises as to which minister is the appropriate minister in relation to any statutory undertakers, that question must be determined by the Treasury: s 19(5).

7   Ibid s 19(8A) (added by the Postal Services Act 2000 (Consequential Modifications No 1) Order 2001, SI 2001/1149, Sch 1 para 120(2)).

8   Regional Development Agencies Act 1998 s 19(6). As to the modifications referred to see Sch 4. See also COMPULSORY ACQUISITION OF LAND.

9   Ibid s 19(7). However, no compensation is payable under the Land Compensation Act 1961 Pt IV (ss 23–29) by virtue of an order under the Regional Development Agencies Act 1998 s 19(1): s 19(8).

10   Ie under ibid s 19(1).

11   Ibid s 19(9).

12   See ibid s 23, Sch 6, which make detailed provision in relation to such matters as the extinguishment of certain rights over land and public rights of way, the power to override easements, consecrated land and burial grounds, open spaces, the displacements of persons in possession of land in certain circumstances, telegraphic lines and statutory undertakers.

901.   Acquisition of land by regional development agencies   A regional development agency may for its purposes[1], or for purposes incidental thereto, acquire land by agreement or, on being authorised to do so by the Secretary of State, compulsorily[2]. Such an agency may, for those purposes, be authorised by the Secretary of State, by means of a compulsory purchase order[3], to acquire compulsorily such new rights over land[4] as are specified in the order[5]. Where the land[6] forms part of a common, open space or fuel or field garden allotment, an agency may (by agreement or, on being authorised to do so by the Secretary of State, compulsorily) acquire land for giving in exchange for the land or, as the case may be, rights acquired[7]. The Acquisition of Land Act 1981 applies to the compulsory acquisition of land[8], subject to certain modifications[9]. The 1981 Act also applies in part to the compulsory acquisition of a right[10], subject to one modification[11]. The Compulsory Purchase Act 1965 applies to the acquisition of such rights, subject to modifications[12]. Certain provisions of the 1965 Act[13] also apply to the acquisition of land by a regional development agency by agreement[14].

Any person who is duly authorised in writing by a regional development agency may at any reasonable time enter any land for the purpose of surveying[15] it, or estimating its value, in connection with any proposal by the agency to acquire the land or any other land or any claim for compensation in respect of any such acquisition[16]. A person so authorised to enter any land must, if so required, produce evidence of his authority before entry[17]. A person may only exercise a right to enter any land if at least 28 days' notice[18] of the intended entry is given to every owner[19] or occupier of the land[20]. Where any land is damaged in the exercise of such a right of entry, or in the making of any survey for the purpose of which any such right of entry has been so conferred, compensation in respect of the damage may be recovered by any person interested in the land from the regional development agency which authorised the exercise of the powers conferred by these provisions[21].

Any person who intentionally obstructs a person acting in exercise of his powers under the above provisions[22] commits an offence and is liable on summary conviction to a fine not exceeding level 3 on the standard scale[23]. Any person who is admitted into a factory, workshop or workplace in compliance with such provisions commits an offence if he discloses to any person any information obtained by him in it as to any manufacturing process or trade secret[24]. A person who is guilty of an offence in the latter case is liable on summary conviction to a fine not exceeding the statutory maximum, and on conviction on indictment to imprisonment for a term not exceeding two years or to a fine or to both[25].

Additional provision is made in relation to various consequential matters which arise following the acquisition of land by a regional development agency[26].

1   As to the purposes of a regional development agency, see para 897 ante.
2   Regional Development Agencies Act 1998 s 20(1).
3   'Compulsory purchase order' has the same meaning as in the Acquisition of Land Act 1981 (see COMPULSORY ACQUISITION OF LAND vol 8(1) (Reissue) para 34): Regional Development Agencies Act 1998 s 20(8).
4   'New rights over land' means rights over land which are not in existence when the order specifying them is made: ibid s 20(8).
5   Ibid s 20(2).
6   Ie the land referred to in ibid s 20(1), (2).
7   Ibid s 20(3). The London Development Agency must not by virtue of s 20(1) or (3) submit to the Secretary of State a compulsory purchase order authorising the acquisition of any land in accordance with the Acquisition of Land Act 1981 s 2(2) (see COMPULSORY ACQUISITION OF LAND vol 8(1) (Reissue) para 34) unless the Mayor of London has given his consent: Regional Development Agencies Act 1998 s 20(3A) (added by the Greater London Authority Act 1999 s 309, Sch 25 para 13). For the meaning of 'the London Development Agency' see para 896 note 5 ante. As to the Mayor of London see LONDON GOVERNMENT.
8   Ie by virtue of the Regional Development Agencies Act 1998 s 20(1), (3).
9   Ibid s 20(4). As to the modifications referred to see Sch 5 Pt I.
10   Ie by virtue of ibid s 20(2).
11   See ibid s 20(5); Acquisition of Land Act 1981 Sch 3.
12   See the Regional Development Agencies Act 1998 s 20(6), Sch 5 Pt II.
13   Ie the provisions of the Compulsory Purchase Act 1965 ss 1–30, 32, so far as applicable.

14 Regional Development Agencies Act 1998 s 20(7). In the Compulsory Purchase Act 1965 ss 1–30, 32, as so applied, 'land' has the meaning given by the Interpretation Act 1978: Regional Development Agencies Act 1998 s 20(7).

15 The power under ibid s 21(1) to survey land includes power to search, bore and remove soil samples for the purpose of ascertaining the nature of the subsoil or the presence in it of minerals or pollutants: s 21(5). No person may carry out under s 21 any works authorised by virtue of s 21(5) unless notice of his intention to do so was included in the notice under s 21(3) (see text and notes 18–20 infra): s 21(6). The authority of the appropriate minister is required for the carrying out under s 21 of works authorised by virtue of s 21(5) if the land in question is held by statutory undertakers and they object to the proposed works on the ground that the execution of the works would be seriously detrimental to the carrying on of their undertaking: s 21(7). Expressions used in s 21(7) have the same meanings as they have in the Town and Country Planning Act 1990 s 325(9) (supplementary provisions as to rights of entry: see TOWN AND COUNTRY PLANNING vol 46 (Reissue) para 33): Regional Development Agencies Act 1998 s 21(11).

16 Ibid s 21(1).

17 Ibid s 21(2).

18 Such a notice must state the purpose for which entry is required and must inform the person to whom it is given of his rights under ibid s 21: s 21(4). As to notices generally, see para 898 note 2 ante.

19 'Owner', in this context, has the same meaning as in the Acquisition of Land Act 1981 (see COMPULSORY ACQUISITION OF LAND vol 8(1) Reissue para 37): Regional Development Agencies Act 1998 s 21(10).

20 Ibid s 21(3).

21 Ibid s 21(8). The Town and Country Planning Act 1990 s 118 (determination of claims for compensation: see TOWN AND COUNTRY PLANNING vol 46 (Reissue) para 706) applies in relation to compensation under the Regional Development Agencies Act 1998 s 21(8) as it applies in relation to compensation under the Town and Country Planning Act 1990 Pt IV (ss 107–118): Regional Development Agencies Act 1998 s 21(9).

22 Ie under ibid s 21.

23 Ibid s 22(1). As to the standard scale see para 16 note 21 ante.

24 Ibid s 22(2). Section 22(2) does not apply if the disclosure is made by a person in the course of performing his duty in connection with the purpose for which he was authorised to enter the premises: s 22(3).

25 Ibid s 22(4). As to the statutory maximum see para 16 note 21 ante.

26 See ibid s 23, Sch 6, which provide for the same matters as are provided for in relation to an order vesting land in a regional development agency (see para 900 note 11 ante), with the exception of the extinguishment of rights over land.

902.   Connection notices   For its purposes[1], or for purposes incidental thereto, a regional development agency may serve a notice, known as a 'connection notice', on the local highway authority[2] requiring the authority to connect a private street[3] to an existing highway[4]. A connection notice must specify (1) the private street and the existing highway; (2) the works which appear to the agency to be necessary to make the connection; and (3) the period within which those works ought to be carried out[5]. Before serving a connection notice an agency must consult the local highway authority about the proposed contents of the notice[6]. Within the period of two months beginning with the date on which the connection notice was served, the local highway authority may appeal against the notice to the Secretary of State[7]. After considering any representations made to him by the agency concerned and the local highway authority, the Secretary of State must determine such an appeal by setting aside or confirming the connection notice, with or without modifications[8]. A connection notice becomes effective (a) where no appeal is made within the two month period, upon the expiry of that period; (b) where an appeal is made within that period but withdrawn before it has been determined by the Secretary of State, on the date following the expiry of the period of 21 days beginning with the date on which the Secretary of State is notified of the withdrawal; (c) where an appeal is made and the connection notice is confirmed by a determination[9], on such date as the Secretary of State may specify in the determination[10]. Where a connection notice becomes effective, the local highway authority must carry out the works specified in the notice within such period as may be specified and may recover the expenses reasonably incurred by it in doing so from the regional development agency which served the notice[11]. If the local highway authority does not carry out the works specified in the notice within such period as may be so specified, the agency which served the notice may itself carry out or complete those works or arrange for another person to do so[12].

1   As to the purposes of a regional development agency see para 897 ante.
2   'Local highway authority' has the same meaning as in the Highways Act 1980 (see HIGHWAYS, STREETS AND BRIDGES vol 21 (Reissue) para 46): Regional Development Agencies Act 1998 s 24(9).
3   'Private street' has the same meaning as in the Highways Act 1980 Pt XI (ss 203–237) (see HIGHWAYS, STREETS AND BRIDGES vol 21 (Reissue) para 709): Regional Development Agencies Act 1998 s 24(9).
4   Ie whether or not it is a highway which for the purposes of the Highways Act 1980 is a highway maintainable at the public expense: Regional Development Agencies Act 1998 s 24(1). As to notices generally see para 898 note 2 ante.
5   Ibid s 24(2).
6   Ibid s 24(3).
7   Ibid s 24(4).
8   Ibid s 24(5).
9   Ie a determination under ibid s 24(5).
10   Ibid s 24(6).
11   Ibid s 24(7).
12   Ibid s 24(8).

903.   Transfer of property, rights and liabilities from the Development Commission   The Secretary of State may by directions[1] require the Development Commission[2] to make one or more schemes for the transfer to regional development agencies of such of the commission's property, rights and liabilities as appear to him appropriate to be transferred in consequence of the carrying out by regional development agencies of an activity of the commission3.

The Secretary of State may by order made by statutory instrument (1) make provision conferring on the commission functions with respect to the provision of services of any description to regional development agencies; (2) make provision for the transfer of any function of the commission to another public body; (3) make provision conferring on another public body a function corresponding to any extent to a function of the commission; (4) make provision terminating the exercise by the commission of any of its functions; (5) make provision extinguishing any liability of the commission in respect of money lent or advanced to it at any time by the Secretary of State[4]; (6) make provision for winding up the commission's affairs; and (7) make provision for the dissolution of the commission[5]. Such an order may contain such supplementary, incidental, consequential or transitional provisions as the Secretary of State thinks fit[6]. The provision which may be made by such an order for the transfer of property, rights or liabilities of the commission includes provision (a) requiring the commission to make one or more schemes for the transfer of such of the commission's property, rights and liabilities as appear to the Secretary of State appropriate to be transferred in consequence of the order; and (b) applying certain statutory provisions[7] in relation to a scheme under the order, with such modifications as the Secretary of State thinks fit[8]. The provision which may be made by such an order includes provision amending, repealing or otherwise modifying any enactment[9]. No such order may be made unless a draft of it has been laid before and approved by resolution of each House of Parliament[10]. Any sums arising out of the transfer of property, or out of property transferred, to a minister of the Crown[11] by such an order must be paid into the Consolidated Fund[12]. Provision is made in relation to the corporation tax and stamp duty implications of a transfer scheme under the above provisions[13].

1   As to directions given by the Secretary of State see para 905 post.

2   As to the Development Commission see para 895 ante.

3   Regional Development Agencies Act 1998 s 34(1). Further provision is made as to the making and approval of such a transfer scheme, the contents of a scheme, its effect (including its effect on contracts of employment), modification of a scheme and the provision of information to the Secretary of State: see s 34(2), Sch 8.

4   No provision may be made under head (5) in the text without the consent of the Treasury: ibid s 35(2). If an order under s 35 makes provision under head (5), the assets of the National Loans Fund are to be reduced by the aggregate amount by which the liabilities of the commission are thereby reduced: s 35(9). As to the National Loans Fund see generally CONSTITUTIONAL LAW AND HUMAN RIGHTS vol 8(2) (Reissue) paras 727–739.

5   Ibid s 35(1). See the Development Commission (Transfer of Functions and Miscellaneous Provisions) Order 1999, SI 1999/416, which (1) provides for the Development Commission to have functions with respect to the provision of certain services to regional development agencies; (2) transfers to the Countryside Commission (now renamed the 'Countryside Agency' by that Order) the Development Commission's functions and powers under the Miscellaneous Financial Provisions Act 1983 s 1(3), (4); (3) requires the Development Commission to make one or more schemes for the transfer to the Countryside Agency of such of the Development Commission's property, rights and liabilities as appear to the Secretary of State to be appropriate; and (4) specifies the limited residual functions of the Development Commission following such transfers. See also the Development Commission (Dissolution) Order 2000, SI 2000/1505, which dissolves the Development Commission with effect from 1 July 2000, and transfers some property to the Secretary of State and any remaining functions, property, rights and liabilities to the Countryside Agency (see para 895 ante). As to the Countryside Agency see OPEN SPACES AND ANCIENT MONUMENTS vol 34 (Reissue) para 120 et seq.

6   Regional Development Agencies Act 1998 s 35(3). The provision which may be made under s 35(3) includes (1) provision changing the name of a public body which acquires functions by virtue of provision made under heads (2) or (3) in the text; and (2) provision for the transfer to another public body of any of the commission's property, rights and liabilities, including rights and liabilities under the contracts of employment of its staff: s 35(4). See the Development Commission (Transfer of Functions and Miscellaneous Provisions) Order 1999, SI 1999/416.

7   Ie the provisions of the Regional Development Agencies Act 1998 Sch 8 (see note 3 supra).

8   Ibid s 35(5).

9   Ibid s 35(6). In this context, 'enactment' includes any instrument made under any enactment: s 35(10).

10   Ibid s 35(7).

11   For the meaning of 'minister of the Crown' see para 897 note 7 ante.

12   Regional Development Agencies Act 1998 s 35(8).

13   See ibid ss 38, 39 respectively.

904. Transfer of property, rights and liabilities from the Urban Regeneration Agency   The Secretary of State may by directions[1] require the Urban Regeneration Agency[2] ('the Agency') to make one or more schemes for the transfer to regional development agencies of such of the Agency's property, rights and liabilities as appear to him appropriate to be transferred in consequence of the carrying out by regional development agencies of an activity of the Agency3.

The Secretary of State may by order made by statutory instrument (1) make provision conferring on the Agency functions with respect to the provision of services of any description to regional development agencies; (2) make such provision in relation to the functions of the Agency as he thinks fit for the purpose of changing it into a body whose only purpose is to hold, manage and dispose of property; (3) make provision changing the name by which the Agency is to be known; (4) make provision terminating the exercise by the Agency of any of its functions; (5) make provision extinguishing any liability of the Agency in respect of money lent or advanced to it at any time by the Secretary of State[4]; (6) make provision for winding up the Agency's affairs; and (7) make provision for the dissolution of the Agency[5]. Such an order may contain such supplementary, incidental, consequential or transitional provisions as the Secretary of State thinks fit, including provision for the transfer to another public body of any of the Agency's property, rights and liabilities, including rights and liabilities under the contracts of employment of its staff[6]. Such an order may also, in connection with the transfer of property, rights or liabilities of the Agency, contain provision establishing a new body corporate, or enabling an existing body corporate established under any enactment[7], to receive property, rights or liabilities transferred[8]. The provision which may be made by such an order for the transfer of property, rights or liabilities of the Agency includes provision (a) requiring the Agency to make one or more schemes for the transfer of such of the Agency's property, rights and liabilities as appear to the Secretary of State appropriate to be transferred in consequence of the order; and (b) applying certain statutory provisions[9] in relation to a scheme under the order, with such modifications as the Secretary of State thinks fit[10]. The provision which may be made by such an order includes provision amending, repealing or otherwise modifying any enactment[11]. No such order must be made unless a draft of it has been laid before and approved by resolution of each House of Parliament[12]. Any sums arising out of the transfer of property, or out of property transferred, to a Minister of the Crown[13] by such an order must be paid into the Consolidated Fund[14]. Provision is made in relation to the corporation tax and stamp duty implications of a transfer scheme under the above provisions[15].

1   As to directions given by the Secretary of State see para 905 post.

2   As to the Urban Regeneration Agency see TOWN AND COUNTRY PLANNING.

3   Regional Development Agencies Act 1998 s 36(1). Further provision is made in relation to the making and approval of such a transfer scheme, the contents of a scheme, its effect (including its effect on contracts of employment), modification of a scheme and the provision of information to the Secretary of State: see s 36(2), Sch 9.

4   No provision may be made under head (5) in the text without the consent of the Treasury: ibid s 37(2). If an order under s 37 makes provision under head (5), the assets of the National Loans Fund are to be reduced by the aggregate amount by which the liabilities of the Agency are thereby reduced: s 37(9). As to the National Loans Fund see generally CONSTITUTIONAL LAW AND HUMAN RIGHTS vol 8(2) (Reissue) paras 727–739.

5   Ibid s 37(1). See the Development Commission (Transfer of Functions and Miscellaneous Provisions) Order 1999, SI 1999/416, which (1) provides for the Urban Regeneration Agency to have functions with respect to the provision of certain services to regional development agencies; and (2) requires the Development Commission to make one or more schemes for the transfer to the Urban Regeneration Agency of such of the Development Commission's property, rights and liabilities relating to its equivalent functions (see para 903 note 5 ante, head (1)) as appear to the Secretary of State to be appropriate.

6   Regional Development Agencies Act 1998 s 37(3).

7   In this context, 'enactment' includes any instrument made under any enactment: ibid
     s 37(10).
8   Ibid s 37(4).
9   Ie the provisions of ibid Sch 9 (see note 3 supra).
10   Ibid s 37(5).
11   Ibid s 37(6).
12   Ibid s 37(7).
13   For the meaning of 'minister of the Crown' see para 897 note 7 ante.
14   Regional Development Agencies Act 1998 s 37(8).
15   See ibid ss 38, 39 respectively.

905–950.   The role of the Secretary of State   The Secretary of State may
give a regional development agency guidance or directions in relation to the
exercise of its functions[1]. Such directions may restrict the agency in relation
to the exercise of its functions or require it to exercise its functions in any
manner specified in the directions[2], and may be of a general or particular
nature[3]. Any power to give guidance[4] is exercisable only after consultation
with the agency concerned[5]. In exercising its functions, an agency must have
regard to any such guidance[6]. Any power to give such guidance includes
power to vary or revoke the guidance[7]. The Secretary of State must arrange
for any guidance given to be published in such manner as he considers
appropriate[8].

A consent given[9] by the Secretary of State to a regional development
agency (1) may be given unconditionally or subject to conditions; (2) may be
given in relation to a particular case or in relation to such descriptions of
case as may be specified in the consent; and (3) except in relation to
anything already done or agreed to be done on the authority of the consent,
may be varied or revoked by a notice[10] given by the Secretary of State to the
agency[11].

Any power to give a direction[12] is exercisable only after consultation with
the body concerned[13]. Any such direction must be in writing[14]. It is the duty
of a body to which such a direction is given to comply with it[15]. Any power
to give such a direction includes power to vary or revoke it[16].

1   Regional Development Agencies Act 1998 s 27(1). As to the functions of regional
     development agencies see para 897 ante.
          Section 27(1) has effect in relation to the London Development Agency as if the
     reference to the Secretary of State were a reference to the Mayor of London: s 27(1A)
     (added by the Greater London Authority Act 1999 s 309, Sch 25 para 17). For the
     meaning of 'the London Development Agency' see para 896 note 5 ante. As to the Mayor
     of London see LONDON GOVERNMENT.
2   Regional Development Agencies Act 1998 s 27(2).
3   Ibid s 27(3). The generality of the power conferred by s 27 is not prejudiced by any other
     power conferred by Pt I (ss 1–33) (as amended): s 27(4).
4   Ie under ibid Pt I.
5   Ibid s 28(1).
6   Ibid s 28(2).
7   Ibid s 28(3).
8   Ibid s 28(4). Section 28 has effect in relation to the Mayor of London as it has effect in
     relation to the Secretary of State: s 30A (added by the Greater London Authority Act 1999
     Sch 25 para 18).
9   Ie under the Regional Development Agencies Act 1998 Pt I.
10   As to notices generally see para 898 note 2 ante.
11   Regional Development Agencies Act 1998 s 29. Section 29 has effect in relation to the
     Mayor of London as it has effect in relation to the Secretary of State: s 30A (as added: see
     note 8 supra).
12   Ie under the Regional Development Agencies Act 1998.
13   Ibid s 40(1).
14   Ibid s 40(2).

15 Ibid s 40(3).
16 Ibid s 40(4).

10. STATISTICS

(1) INFORMATION AND CENSUS

951. Returns and estimates. In order to obtain information necessary to appreciate economic trends, to provide a statistical service for industry and to provide for the discharge by government departments of their functions, a competent authority[1], by notice in writing served on any person[2] carrying on an undertaking[3], may require that person to furnish, in such form and manner and within such time as may be specified in the notice, periodical or other estimates or returns about certain matters[4]. Those matters are:

(1) the nature of the undertaking (including its association with other undertakings) and the date of its acquisition;

(2) the persons employed or normally employed (including working proprietors), the nature of their employment, their remuneration and the hours worked;

(3) the output, sales, deliveries and services provided;

(4) the articles acquired or used, orders, stocks and work in progress;

(5) the outgoings and costs (including work given out to contractors, depreciation, rent, rates and taxes, other than taxes on profits) and capital expenditure;

(6) the receipts of and debts owed to the undertaking;

(7) the power used or generated;

(8) the fixed capital assets, the plant, including the acquisition and disposal of those assets and that plant, and the premises occupied;

(9) assets (other than fixed capital assets) and liabilities of the undertaking, including the acquisition and disposal of those assets and the incurring and discharge of those liabilities;

(10) prices of articles and services;

(11) income (including rents, interest and investment income) received or receivable by the undertaking;

(12) dividends and interest paid or payable;

(13) profits and losses;

(14) taxes paid or chargeable on income or gains;

(15) services acquired or used[5].

The Secretary of State[6] may, by notice, require a trader[7] concerned with an essential commodity[8] to make periodical and other returns, at such times and containing such particulars as are specified in the notice, as to the stocks of the commodity held by him and as to the facilities available for storing and utilising stocks of the commodity[9]. If so required by the Secretary of State, any government department or body of persons having power by virtue of any Act to obtain information as to such matters must exercise that power for the purpose of assisting him to obtain information regarding essential commodities[10].

1   Each of the following ministers and authorities is a competent authority: the Treasury, the Chancellor of the Exchequer, a Secretary of State, and the Board of Trade: Statistics of Trade Act 1947 s 17(3) (substituted by the Ministry of Aviation Supply (Dissolution) Order 1971, SI 1971/719, art 3(2), Schedule; and amended by the Transfer of Functions (Economic Statistics) Order 1989, SI 1989/992, art 3(a)). All functions of the Minister of Agriculture, Fisheries and Food (mentioned in the Statistics of trade Act 1947 s 17(3) as a competent authority) are transferred to the Secretary of State for the Environment, Food and Rural Affairs: see para 123 note 11 ante. For the purposes of the Statistics of Trade

Act 1947, Scottish Enterprise and the Highlands and Islands Enterprise are each a competent authority: Enterprise and New Towns (Scotland) Act 1990 s 12(1).

2   The notice must state that it is served under the Statistics of Trade Act 1947 s 1 and generally the purpose for which the estimates or returns are required: s 1(2). Unless the contrary intention appears, 'person' includes a body of persons corporate or unincorporate: see the Interpretation Act 1978 s 5, Sch 1.

3   'Undertaking' means any undertaking by way of trade or business, whether or not the trade or business is carried on for profit; and the exercise and performance by a local or other public authority of the powers and duties of that authority must be treated as a trade or business of that authority: Statistics of Trade Act 1947 s 17(1). Where an undertaking is wholly or partly carried on by means of branches situated at several premises, the competent authority may agree with the persons carrying on the undertaking that for the purposes of the Statistics of Trade Act 1947 a separate undertaking is to be deemed to be carried on at all or any of those branches by the branch manager or a specified person; any such agreement (1) may contain such supplemental provisions as may be expedient for giving effect to it; (2) continues in force for a specified term; and (3) is subject to any provisions as to variation and revocation specified in the agreement: s 17(2).

4   Ibid s 1(1).

5   Statistics of Trade Act 1947 s 1, Schedule (amended by the Statistics of Trade Act 1947 (Amendment of Schedule) Order 1963, SI 1963/1329; the Statistics of Trade Act 1947 (Amendment of Schedule) Order 1987, SI 1987/669; and the Statistics of Trade Act 1947 (Amendment of Schedule) Order 1990, SI 1990/2597). The listed orders were made under the Statistics of Trade Act 1947 s 5, which gives a general power to amend the Schedule, subject to the approval of each House of Parliament. In a case where the undertaking is related to a body situated outside the United Kingdom the following information may also be required: (1) the nature and the extent of the relationship; (2) the nature and extent (and any changes therein) of the financial interest of the one body in the other; (3) the country in which the related body is situated; (4) particulars in respect of issued share capital, minority share-holders' interests, loans, reserves and provisions as recorded in the accounts of the undertaking or such particulars in respect of the related body where it is under the control of the undertaking; (5) net gains or losses of the undertaking attributable to changes in exchange rates, being gains or losses arising out of the relationship; (6) the profit or loss of the undertaking or related body attributable to the relationship and dividends declared by either body arising out of the relationship; (7) where the body is not a company incorporated in the United Kingdom, its net value to the related body, and where the related body is not a body corporate, its net value to the undertaking: Schedule (as so amended). For the meaning of 'United Kingdom' see para 37 note 1 ante.

6   For these purposes 'the Secretary of State' is the Secretary of State for Trade and Industry, to whom the functions of the Board of Trade were transferred: see para 3 note 2 ante.

7   For these purposes 'trader' in relation to any commodity means any person who for the purposes of any trade or business carried on by him, whether as a producer, merchant, broker, warehouseman or otherwise, holds from time to time a stock of that commodity: Essential Commodities Reserves Act 1938 s 6.

8   'Essential commodity' means any commodity which may be declared by order of the Secretary of State to be a commodity which, in his opinion, would be essential for the vital needs of the community in the event of war: ibid s 6. Any commodity which, in the opinion of the Secretary of State, may be required as food for man, forage for animals or fertiliser for land, any raw material from which any such commodity can be produced, and petroleum and any product of petroleum, may be declared to be such a commodity; s 6, Schedule. See the Essential Commodities Reserves (Declaration) Order 1938, SR & O 1938/1110.

9   Essential Commodities Reserves Act 1938 s 1(1).

10 See ibid s 1(2). Any such information obtained by any government department or by any such body of persons, whether upon the requisition of the Secretary of State or otherwise, may, notwithstanding anything in any enactment, be furnished to him: s 1(2). The Secretary of State is given the power to make payments to traders for the purpose of augmenting or maintaining stocks of essential commodities, or the improvement of storage facilities: see s 2(1). Additionally, the Secretary of State may acquire and store such stocks and take various steps in relation to them: see s 2(2), (3).

952.   Census of production and distribution. For the purpose of providing, at intervals, general surveys of the state of trade and business, the Secretary of State[1] must in each year take a census of production, and may in any year[2] prescribed by order take a census of distribution and other services[3]. Any person[4] carrying on an undertaking may be required to furnish returns[5] for the purpose of any census[6]. A census must require returns to be furnished with respect to the calendar year next preceding the date of the census[7], unless the Secretary of State permits a person for whom it would be inconvenient to furnish returns with respect to that calendar year to furnish returns with respect to some other period of 12 months[8].

1 The functions of the Secretary of State under the Statistics of Trade Act 1947 ss 2, 3, 6, 7, 8, 9(2), (3), 10, 11 and 17(2) (see the text to notes 2–8 infra and para 953 et seq post) and the functions of the Secretary of State as a competent authority within the meaning of that Act (see para 951 note 1 ante) are transferred to the Chancellor of the Exchequer, so as to be exercisable concurrently with him, by the Transfer of Functions (Economic Statistics) Order 1989, SI 1989/992, art 2(1), (2).

2 Ie a calendar year beginning not less than 12 months after the date of the order: see the Statistics of Trade Act 1947 s 2(1). As to the making of orders see para 964 post.

3 Ibid s 2(1). Individual orders made under s 2(1) prescribed certain years for each census: see eg the Census of Production Order 1993, SI 1993/3037, relating to the census of production to be taken in 1994 and in subsequent years and prescribing the undertaking to which the census is confined and the matters to which returns relate and providing for the exemption of certain persons. The census may either (1) be taken to cover all undertakings in the field of production, distribution or other services, as the case may be; or (2) be confined to such classes or descriptions of those undertakings respectively as may be prescribed: Statistics of Trade Act 1947 s 2(2). The Secretary of State may by order provide for exempting from the obligation to furnish returns for the purpose of a census, either wholly or to the prescribed extent, and either unconditionally or subject to prescribed conditions, any persons or any prescribed class or description of persons: 2(2). See eg the Census of Production Order 1993 exempting persons carrying on certain activities relating to the extraction of crude petroleum and natural gas: see arts 4, 5. For the meaning of 'undertaking' see para 951 note 3 ante.

4 As to the meaning of 'person' see para 951 note 2 ante.

5 The matters about which a person may be required to furnish returns for the purposes of a census are such of the matters set out in the Statistics of Trade Act 1947 s 2, Schedule (as amended) (see para 951 note 5 ante), as may be prescribed: s 2(3).

6 Ibid s 2(2).

7 Ibid s 2(4).

8 Ibid s 2(4) proviso.

953. Census forms and instructions. The Secretary of State[1] must prepare and issue such forms and instructions as he deems necessary for the taking of a census of production or of distribution and other services[2]. A person[3] is not required to furnish returns for these purposes except in pursuance of a notice in writing from the Secretary of State requiring him to do so; and the Secretary of State must issue, with the notice, the forms required to be filled up by that person[4]. The Secretary of State may delegate any of these functions to any other competent authority[5]. A person required to furnish returns must comply with the notice, in such manner as may be specified in the notice, on or before a day so specified being not less than two months after the service of the notice[6].

1 As to the Secretary of State see para 3 note 2 ante. As to the transfer of functions to the Chancellor of the Exchequer see para 952 note 1 ante.

2 Statistics of Trade Act 1947 s 3(1).

3 As to the meaning of 'person' see para 951 note 2 ante

4 Statistics of Trade Act 1947 s 3(2).

5 Ibid s 3(3). For the meaning of 'competent authority' see para 951 note 1 ante. On delegation, references to the Secretary of State include references to any other authority to whom the functions have been delegated and a notice issued by a competent authority in pursuance of powers delegated to that authority must state that it is so issued: s 3(3).

6 Ibid s 3(4). In their application to a person who has been allowed to furnish returns with respect to a period ending not later than 31 October in the calendar year preceding the date on which the notice is served on him, the provisions of s 3(4) have effect as if for the reference to two months there is substituted a reference to one month: s 3(4) proviso. As to the service of notices see para 966 post.

954.   Lists of undertakings subject to census. The Secretary of State[1] or any competent authority[2] to which he has delegated the function[3] may by advertisement in the Gazette[4] and in such newspapers as appear to him to be sufficient for notifying the persons[5] concerned, publish a list of any classes or descriptions of undertakings[6] in relation to which returns will be required for the purposes of a particular census of production or distribution and other services[7]. Upon such publication it is the duty of every person carrying on an undertaking of any specified class or description who has not received a notice requiring him to furnish returns[8], both to inform a person specified in the advertisement within a specified period (being not less than at days after the publication) that he is carrying on such an undertaking, and to give to that person such prescribed particulars of the undertaking as are so specified[9].

1 As to the Secretary of State see para 3 note 2 ante. As to the transfer of functions to the Chancellor of the Exchequer see para 952 note 1 ante.
2 For the meaning of 'competent authority' see para 951 note 1 ante.
3 The Secretary of State may delegate any of his functions under the Statistics of Trade Act 1947 s 6(1) to any other competent authority, and references in s 6(1) to the Secretary of State include references to any competent authority to whom those functions have been so delegated: s 6(2).
4 'The Gazette' means (1) in relation to an advertisement concerning undertakings in England and Wales only, the London gazette; (2) in relation to an advertisement concerning undertakings in Scotland only, the Edinburgh Gazette; and (3) in relation to any other advertisement, the London Gazette and the Edinburgh Gazette: ibid s 6(5)(a)–(c).
5 As to the meaning of 'person' see para 951 note 1 ante.
6 For the meaning of 'undertaking' see para 951 note 3 ante.
7 Statistics of Trade Act 1947 s 6(1).
8 Ie a notice under ibid s 3(2): see para 953 ante.
9 Ibid s 6(1). As to offences of failing to give such information or particulars or giving false information or particulars see s 6(3), (4) (as amended); and para 957 post.

955.   Information from air travellers. The Secretary of State[1] may by order make provision whereby any person entering or leaving the United Kingdom[2] by air may be required to give[3] particulars of his age, sex and marriage, of the nature of his occupation and of the country in which he last permanently resided and that in which he intends next permanently to reside[4]. If it is not reasonably practicable to require any such person to give the particulars, any other person in whose company and under whose care he is travelling may be required to give the particulars on his behalf[5].

1 As to the Secretary of State see para 3 note 2 ante. As to the transfer of functions to the Chancellor of the Exchequer see para 952 note 1 ante.
2 For the meaning of 'the United Kingdom' see para 37 note 1 ante.
3 Ie to give to such persons and in such form and manner as may be prescribed by order at the Secretary of State: Statistics of Trade Act 1947 ss 10(1), 11.
4 Ibid s 10(1). At the date at which this volume states the law no such order had been made.
5 Ibid s 10(2). As to offences of failing to give such information or particulars or giving false information or particulars see s 10(3), (4) (as amended); and para 957 post.

956.   Trading of goods between member states. Provision is made for the collection of statistics relating to the trading of goods between member states of the European Community. Such statistics are compiled by means of a statistical collection system known as 'Intrastat' from VAT returns and supplementary declarations made by VAT registered traders who are engaged in the trading of goods between member states[1].

1 See the Statistics of Trade (Customs and Excise) Regulations 1992, SI 1992/2790 (amended by SI 1993/541, SI 1993/3015, SI 1997/2864, SI 1999/3269, and SI 2000/3227).

(2) OFFENCES AND DISCLOSURE

957. Failure to give information, and giving false information. It is an offence for any person[1] to make a default in making any return or furnishing any information which he is duly required to make or furnish under the Essential Commodities Reserves Act 1938[2]. It is also an offence for any person knowingly or recklessly to make a false return or furnish false information or, for the purpose of obtaining any payment under that Act, knowingly or recklessly to make an untrue statement or untrue representation[3].

It is an offence for any person required to furnish estimates or returns under the Statistics of Trade Act 1947 to fail to furnish such estimates or returns unless he proves that he has reasonable excuse for the failure[4]. It is also an offence (1) knowingly or recklessly to make a statement in estimates or returns which is false in a material particular[5]; (2) for any person to fail to give any information or particulars required by the Secretary of State when he has advertised his requirements, unless the person can prove that he did not know and had reasonable cause for not knowing that he was required to give that information or those particulars[6]; and (3) knowingly or recklessly to make a statement in any such particulars which is false in a material particular[7]. Where any person is required to give information on entering or leaving the United Kingdom[8], it is an offence to fail to comply with that requirement unless he proves that he had reasonable excuse for the failure[9].

1 As to the meaning of 'person' see para 951 note 2 ante.
2 Essential Commodities Reserves Act 1938 s 4(1). A person guilty of such an offence is liable on summary conviction to a fine not exceeding level 3 on the standard scale: s 4(1) (amended by virtue of the Criminal Justice Act 1982 ss 38, 46). If after being so convicted a person continues to make the like default, he is guilty of a further offence and is liable on summary conviction to a fine not exceeding £50 for each day on which the default continues: Essential Commodities Reserves Act 1938 s 4(1). As to the standard scale see para 16 note 21 ante. As to the liability of officers of bodies corporate convicted of such offences see para 958 post.
3 Ibid s 4(2). It is irrelevant whether the purpose of the person making the statement or representation is to obtain payment for himself or any other person: see s 4(2). A person guilty of such an offence is, in respect of each offence, liable on summary conviction to a fine not exceeding level 3 on the standard scale or to imprisonment for a term not exceeding three months, or to both: see s 4(2) (amended by virtue of the Criminal Justice Act 1982 ss 38, 46).
4 Statistics of Trade Act 1947 s 4(1). A person guilty of such an offence under s 4(1) is liable on summary conviction to a fine not exceeding level 4 on the standard scale: s 4(1) (amended by virtue of the Criminal Justice Act 1982 ss 38, 46). If after being so convicted a person continues to fail to furnish estimates or returns he is guilty of a further offence and will on summary conviction be punished accordingly: Statistics of Trade Act 1947 s 4(2).
5 Ibid s 4(3). If a person is guilty of such an offence he is liable on summary conviction to imprisonment for a term not exceeding three months or to a fine not exceeding the prescribed sum, or on conviction on indictment to imprisonment for a term not exceeding

two years or to a fine, or in either case, to both: Statistics of Trade Act 1947 s 4(3) (amended by virtue of the Magistrates' Court Act 1980 s 32(2)). For the meaning of 'the prescribed sum' see the Magistrates' Courts Act 1980 s 32 (as amended); and CRIMINAL LAW, EVIDENCE AND PROCEDURE vol 11(2) (Reissue) para 806; MAGISTRATES.

6 Statistics of Trade Act 1947 s 6(3). If a person is guilty of such an offence he is liable on summary conviction to a fine not exceeding level 1 on the standard scale: s 6(3) (amended by virtue of the Criminal Justice Act 1982 s 46).

7 Statistics of Trade Act 1947 s 6(4). If a person is guilty of such an offence he is liable on summary conviction to imprisonment for a term not exceeding three months or to a fine not exceeding the prescribed sum, or on conviction on indictment to imprisonment for a term not exceeding two years or a to fine, or, in either case, to both: s 6(4) (amended by virtue of the Magistrates' Courts Act 1980 s 32(2)).

8 Ie by virtue of the Statistics of Trade Act 1947 s 10(1); see para 955 ante. For the meaning of 'United Kingdom' see para 37 note 1 ante.

9 Ibid s 10(3). If a person is guilty of such an offence he is liable on summary conviction to a fine not exceeding level 2 on the standard scale: s 10(3) (amended by virtue of the Criminal Justice Act 1982 s 46).

958. Offences committed by a body corporate. Where an offence under the Statistics of Trade Act 1947[1] has been committed by a body corporate, every person who at the time of the commission of the offence was a director, general manager, secretary or other similar officer of that body, or was purporting to act in any such capacity, is deemed to be guilty of the offence unless he proves that it was committed without his consent or connivance and that he exercised all such diligence to prevent its commission as he ought to have exercised having regard to the nature of his functions in that capacity and to all the circumstances[2]. Where an offence under the Essential Commodities Reserves Act 1938[3] has been committed by a body corporate and it is proved to have been committed with the consent or approval of, or to have been facilitated by any negligence on the part of any director, manager, secretary or other officer of that body, he, as well as the body corporate, is deemed to be guilty of the offence and is liable to be proceeded against and punished accordingly[4].

1 Ie offences committed under the Statistics of Trade Act 1947 ss 4, 6(3), 9(6), 10(3), (4): see paras 954–955, 957 ante, 959 post. An offence committed under s 10 (see paras 955, 957 ante) is inapplicable to a body corporate. Where a person convicted is a body corporate, such of the above provisions as limit the amount of the fine which may be imposed do not apply, and the body corporate is liable to a fine of such amount as the court thinks just: s 13(1); cf the Criminal Law Act 1977 s 32(1); and CRIMINAL LAW, EVIDENCE AND PROCEDURE vol 11(2) (Reissue) para 1232 note 5.

2 Statistics of Trade Act 1947 s 13(2).

3 As to these offences see para 957 ante.

4 Essential Commodities Reserves Act 1938 s 4(3).

959. Unlawful disclosure of information. It is an offence to disclose information with respect to any particular undertaking obtained under or by virtue of the Essential Commodities Reserves Act 1938 without the consent of the person carrying on that undertaking otherwise than in pursuance of the performance by the Secretary of State[1] of his functions under that Act, unless such disclosure is made for the purposes of any legal proceedings which may be taken under, by virtue of or in consequence of that Act[2].

It is an offence to disclose any individual estimates, returns or any information relating to an individual undertaking[3] obtained under the Statistics of Trade Act 1947 without the previous consent in writing of the person carrying on the undertaking which is the subject of the estimates, returns or information, except either in accordance with directions given by the minister in charge of the government department in possession of the estimates, returns or information to a government department for the purposes of the exercise of its functions, or for the purposes of any proceedings for an offence under that Act or any report of those proceedings[4].

1 As to the Secretary of State and the transfer to him of the functions of the Board of Trade see para 2 note 1 ante. As to the transfer of functions to the Chancellor of the Exchequer see para 952 note 1 ante.

2 Essential Commodities Reserves Act 1938 s 1(3). If a person is guilty of such an offence under s 1(3), he is liable on summary conviction to imprisonment for a term not exceeding three months or to a fine not exceeding the prescribed sum, or on conviction on indictment to imprisonment for a term not exceeding two years or to a fine, or in either case, to both: see s 1(3) (amended by virtue of the Criminal Law Act 1977 s 32(1); and the Magistrates' Courts Act 1980 s 32(2), (9)). For the meaning of 'the prescribed sum' see the Magistrates' Courts Act 1980 s 32 (as amended); and CRIMINAL LAW, EVIDENCE AND PROCEDURE vol 11(2) (Reissue) para 806; MAGISTRATES.

3 For the meaning of 'undertaking' see para 951 note 3 ante.

4 Statistics of Trade Act 1947 s 9(1), (6) (amended by the Import Duties Act 1958 s 16(4), Sch 7 (repealed)). If a person is guilty of such an offence he is liable on summary conviction to imprisonment for a term not exceeding three months or to a fine not exceeding the prescribed sum, or on conviction on indictment to imprisonment for a term not exceeding two years or to a fine or, in either case, to both: Statistics of Trade Act 1947 s 9(6) (amended by virtue of the Magistrates' Courts Act 1980 s 32(2); and the Criminal Law Act 1977 s 32(1)). Detailed exemptions from the duty not to disclose are enacted in respect of (1) European Community institutions (see the European Communities Act 1972 s 12; and EUROPEAN COMMUNITIES); (2) certain bodies performing functions under the Employment and Training Act 1973 s 4(3)–(5) (as amended) (see EMPLOYMENT vol 16 (2000 Reissue) para 600); (3) the Health and Safety Commission and the Health and Safety Executive (see the Health and Safety at Work etc Act 1974 s 27 (as amended); and HEALTH AND SAFETY AT WORK vol 20 (Reissue) para 464); (4) the Welsh Development Agency (see the Welsh Development Agency Act 1975 s 24(6) (as amended)); (5) the Advisory, Conciliation and Arbitration Service (see the Trade Union and Labour Relations (Consolidation) Act 1992 s 247(5); and para 1436 post); and (6) the Environment Agency (see the Statistics of Trade Act 1947 s 9A (added by the Environment Act 1995 s 120(1), Sch 22 para 2)). As to the Welsh Development Agency see para 856 et seq ante; as to ACAS see paras 1436–1446 post; and as to the Environment Agency see PROTECTION OF ENVIRONMENT AND PUBLIC HEALTH vol 38 (Reissue) para 51 et seq; WATER vol 49(2) (Reissue) para 159 et seq. As to unauthorised disclosure of information provided by member states to the Statistical Office of the European Communities see para 960 post.

960. Disclosure of information provided to the Statistical Office of the European Community. It is an offence for an officer or employee of the Statistical Office of the European Community ('the SOEC') or any individual who, under a contract for services with the SOEC, is required to carry out duties on its premises, knowingly or recklessly to disclose within Great Britain[1] confidential statistical information without the authority of the member state who provided that information. If a person is guilty of such an offence he is liable on summary conviction to imprisonment for a term not exceeding three months or a fine not exceeding the statutory maximum, or on conviction on indictment to imprisonment for a term not exceeding two years or a fine, or in either case, to both[2].

1 For the meaning of 'Great Britain' see para 31 note 2 ante.

2 Provision of Confidential Statistical Information to the Statistical Office of the European Communities (Restriction on Disclosure) Regulations 1991, SI 1991/2779, reg 3. 'Confidential statistical information' means statistical information which has been declared or classified as confidential in accordance with its law or national practice by the member state providing it, and provided to the SOEC by a member state in accordance with EURATOM: EC Council Regulation 1588/90 art 3. As to the statutory maximum see para 16 note 21 ante.

961. Additional restrictions on disclosure of information. If any information to be obtained for the purposes of a census under the Statistics of Trade Act 1947[1] is also obtainable under any other enactment which restricts the disclosure of information obtained thereunder, and the Secretary of State[2] is of opinion that similar restrictions should be applied to any information to be obtained for the purposes of the census, he may provide by order[3] for those restrictions to apply, without modifications or with such adaptations or modifications as he thinks fit, to the information to be so obtained[4]. Moreover, if it appears to him that the nature of the information to be obtained for the purposes of a census, or the nature of the undertakings[5] to be covered by the census, would make it desirable to impose any other restrictions, he may by order prohibit the disclosure of information relating to particular undertakings obtained by means of the census, or any part of that information, except to specified persons or for specified purposes[6].

1   As to such a census see paras 952–954 ante.
2   As to the Secretary of State see para 3 note 2 ante. As to the transfer of functions to the Chancellor of the Exchequer see para 952 note 1 ante.
3   No order may be made under the Statistics of Trade Act 1947 s 9 (as amended) unless a draft is laid before Parliament and is approved by resolution of each House of Parliament: s 9(4). As to the making of orders see para 965 post.
4   Ibid s 9(2). If a person is guilty of such an offence he is liable on summary conviction to imprisonment for a term not exceeding three months or to a fine not exceeding the prescribed sum, or on conviction on indictment to imprisonment for a term not exceeding two years or to a fine or, in either case, to both: s 9(6) (amended by virtue of the Criminal Law Act 1977 s 32(1); and of the Magistrates' Courts Act 1980 s 32(2)). For the meaning of 'the prescribed sum' see the Magistrates' Courts Act 1980 s 32 (as amended); and CRIMINAL LAW, EVIDENCE AND PROCEDURE vol 11(2) (Reissue) para 806; MAGISTRATES. ·
5   For the meaning of 'undertaking' see para 951 note 3 ante.
6   Statistics of Trade Act 1947 s 9(3). See the Census of Distribution (1962) (Restriction on Disclosure) Order 1960, SI 1960/2364, and the Census of Distribution (1967) (Restriction on Disclosure) Order 1965, SI 1965/2061. As to the penalties for contravention of such an order see note 4 supra.

962. Disclosure in public reports. No report, summary or other communication to the public of information obtained under the Statistics of Trade Act 1947 may disclose the number of returns received with respect to the production of any article[1] if that number is less than five[2]. In compiling any such report, summary or communication the competent authority[3] must prevent any particulars published in it from being identified as particularly relating to any individual person or undertaking[4], except with the previous consent in writing of that person or the person carrying on that undertaking; but the total quantity or value of any articles produced, sold or delivered may be stated, provided that prior to disclosure of such a total the competent authority has regard to any representations made to it by any person who alleges that the disclosure would enable particulars relating to him or to an undertaking carried on by him to be deduced from the total disclosed[5].

1   'Article' includes substances, plant, vehicles, vessels, animals, water, gas and electricity, and 'plant' includes any machinery, equipment or appliance: Statistics of Trade Act 1947 s 17(4).
2   Ibid s 9(5)(a).
3   For the meaning of 'competent authority' see para 951 note 1 ante.
4   For the meaning of 'undertaking' see para 951 note 3 ante.
5   Statistics of Trade Act 1947 s 9(5)(b). For the penalties for offences under s 9 (as amended) see para 960 note 4 ante. The information protected by s 9 is not obtainable as a public

record at the Public Record Office: see the Public Records Act 1958 s 5(3), Sch 2 (as amended); and CONSTITUTIONAL LAW AND HUMAN RIGHTS vol 8(2) (Reissue) para 840.

(3) ADMINISTRATION AND NOTICES

963. Advisory committees. The Secretary of State[1] must arrange for the appointment of one or more committees to advise him, or any other competent authority[2] to whom functions have been delegated[3], with regard to the preparation of forms and instructions necessary for the taking of a census, the making of orders by him and to such other matters as may be referred to such a committee[4]. Committees may be appointed to advise specially about any special forms, instructions or orders, or generally about any class or description of forms, instructions or orders that may be assigned to them[5]. Every committee must include persons engaged in, or otherwise conversant with the conditions of, various trades and businesses[6].

1   As to the Secretary of State see para 3 note 2 ante. As to the transfer of functions to the Chancellor of the Exchequer see para 952 note 1 ante.
2   For the meaning of 'competent authority' see para 951 note 1 ante.
3   Ie under the Statistics of Trade Act 1947 s 3: see para 953 ante.
4   Ibid s 8(1).
5   Ibid s 8(3).
6   Ibid s 8(1). With the consent of the Treasury, the Secretary of State may determine any travelling or other allowances to be paid to the members of the committee: s 8(2). With Treasury approval any expenses incurred by the Secretary of State or other competent authority are defrayed out of moneys provided by Parliament: s 15.

964. Census report by the Secretary of State. As soon as practicable after any census under the Statistics of Trade Act 1947[1] is complete, the Secretary of State[2] must present to Parliament a report of his proceedings in connection with the taking of the census and a summary of the statistics obtained[3].

1   As to such a census see paras 952–954 ante.
2   As to the Secretary of State see para 3 note 2 ante. As to the transfer of functions to the Chancellor of the Exchequer see para 952 note 1 ante.
3   Statistics of Trade Act 1947 s 7. If the Secretary of State thinks fit, he may include in the summary of statistics any statistics obtained by him or a competent authority otherwise than by means of a census, or statistics obtained by a Northern Ireland department and communicated to him for the purposes of inclusion in the report; and the summary must contain separate statements relating to Scotland and Wales: see s 7. For the meaning of 'competent authority' see para 951 note 1 ante.

965. Making of orders. The Secretary of State[1] may by order[2] make provision for prescribing, either generally or with respect to any class or description of persons or undertakings[3], anything which under the Statistics of Trade Act 1947 is to be prescribed, and generally for the purposes of carrying that Act into effect[4]. He may also make orders declaring commodities to be essential commodities[5] for the purposes of the Essential Commodities Reserves Act 1938[6].

1   As to the Secretary of State see para 3 note 2 ante. As to the transfer of functions to the Chancellor of the Exchequer see para 952 note 1 ante.
2   All orders made under the Statistics of Trade Act 1947, other than orders made under s 9 (as amended) must be laid before Parliament immediately after they are made, and if either House of Parliament, within 40 days, resolves that the order be annulled, the order ceases to have effect, but without prejudice to anything done under it or to the making of a new order: s 11(2); and see PARLIAMENT vol 34 (Reissue) para 945. Orders under s 9 (as

amended) must not be made unless a draft has been laid before Parliament and approved by a resolution of each House: see s 9(4); para 960 note 3 ante; and PARLIAMENT vol 34 (Reissue) para 944.

3 · For the meaning of 'undertaking' see para 951 note 3 ante.

4 Statistics of Trade Act 1947 s 11(1). Any such order may be revoked or varied by a subsequent order made in like manner and subject to the like conditions as the original order: s 11(3).

5 For the meaning of 'essential commodity' see para 951 note 8 ante.

6 See the Essential Commodities Reserves Act 1938 s 6, Schedule; and para 951 note 8 ante. All such orders must be laid before Parliament (s 5(2)) and may be varied or revoked by an order made in like manner (s 5(1)); see PARLIAMENT vol 34 (Reissue) para 943.

966–1000.   Service of notices.

Any notice required or authorised by or under the Statistics of Trade Act 1947 to be served on any person may be served by delivering it to that person, by leaving it at his proper address[1] or by post[2]. Any notice required or authorised to be served on a body corporate is duly served if served on its secretary or clerk[3].

Where a notice is served by post otherwise than in a registered letter or by the recorded delivery service, service is not deemed to have been effected if it is proved that the notice was not received by the person to whom it was addressed[4].

1 The proper address of any person on whom a notice under the Statistics of Trade Act 1947 is to be served is the last known address of the person to be served: s 12(3); Interpretation Act 1978 ss 7, 17(2)(a), Sch 2 para 3; and cf COMPANIES vol 7(1) (1996 Reissue) para 151. Where the name of a person carrying on an undertaking at any premises is not known, then, if any such notice is sent by post in a registered letter or by the recorded delivery service so addressed as to show the name in which and the premises at which the undertaking is carried on, the letter is deemed for the purposes of s 7 to be properly addressed: s 17(2)(a); Statistics of Trade Act 1947 s 12(4); Recorded Delivery Service Act 1962 s 1(1), (2), Schedule para 1. For the meaning of 'undertaking' see para 951 note 3 ante.

2 Statistics of Trade Act 1947 s 12(1).

3 Ibid s 12(2). In the case of a secretary or clerk of an incorporated company or body, the proper address for service of such a notice is that of the registered or principal office of the company or body: see s 12(3); the Interpretation Act 1978 ss 7, 17(2)(a), Sch 2 para 3; and cf COMPANIES vol 7(1) (1996 Reissue) para 151.

· 4 Statistics of Trade Act 1947 s 12(1); Recorded Delivery Service Act 1962 s 1(1), (2), Schedule para 1. This has the effect of disapplying the Interpretation Act 1978 s 7 (which provides that a properly addressed, prepaid and posted letter is deemed to constitute proper service of a document contained in it) other than to a registered letter or a letter sent by recorded delivery.

11–15. TRADE UNIONS ... EMPLOYMENT TRIBUNALS AND OTHER LEGAL PROCEEDINGS

1001–1616.   **Meanings of 'trade union' and 'federated trade union' ...**
Procedure before the certification officer.
Material relating to these parts has been revised and published under the title EMPLOYMENT vols 39–41 (2009)

INDEX

Trade, Industry and Industrial Relations

Vol 47

ACCOUNTS
British Shipbuilders, 644
development council, 882, 884
Hairdressing Council, 668
industrial body, 889
regional development agency, 898
tourist board, 817
Urban Regeneration Agency, 850
Welsh Development Agency, 870

AGENT
commercial. *See* COMMERCIAL AGENT

AGRICULTURE
EC competition law, 328, 436

AIRCRAFT
meaning, 611n9
export control—
dual-use item, 617
generally, 611n9
manufacture, privatisation, 656
scheduled journey: meaning, 617n23

**AIRCRAFT AND SHIPBUILDING
INDUSTRIES ARBITRATION
TRIBUNAL**
appeal to Court of Appeal, 649n4
conduct of proceedings, 648
constitution, 647
establishment, 647
members, 647
order of, enforcement, 648
president, 647
referral of question for report, 648
special case, statement of, 649
staff, 647

AMMUNITION
export control, 611n11

ARBITRATION
aircraft industry. *See* AIRCRAFT AND
SHIPBUILDING INDUSTRIES
ARBITRATION TRIBUNAL

ARBITRATION—*continued*
shipbuilding industry. *See* AIRCRAFT
AND SHIPBUILDING INDUSTRIES
ARBITRATION TRIBUNAL

BARBER. *See* HAIRDRESSERS AND
BARBERS; HAIRDRESSING COUNCIL

BOARD OF TRADE
jurisdiction, 2
President, 2n1

BRITISH AEROSPACE LTD
creation and statutory provisions,
656

BRITISH SHIPBUILDERS
accounts and audit, 644
activities, 638
annual report, 641, 644
arbitration. *See* AIRCRAFT AND
SHIPBUILDING INDUSTRIES
ARBITRATION TRIBUNAL
assets, vesting. *See* vesting of assets
below
borrowing by, 642
chairman, 637
commencing capital, 643
company formation by, 638
constitution, 637
corporate plan, 638n20
directions to—
generally, 638
matters affecting national interest,
as to, 639
disclosure of information, 638
excluded loan: meaning, 642n8
financial duties, 641
loan to, 642
loss of employment etc, compensation
for, 652
members, 637
overseas development, 639

References are to paragraph numbers; superior figures refer to notes

References are to paragraph numbers; superior figures refer to notes